I Am Who I Am

I Am Who I Am

TRIALS AND TRIBULATIONS
OF A
RESOLUTE RECRUIT

Sir E. J. Drury II

RIVENDELL BOOKS

ST. LOUIS

I Am Who I Am

Published in the United States of America
By Rivendell Books
PO Box 29348
St. Louis, MO 63126-0348

All rights reserved. First Edition.
Copyright © 2022 by E. J. Drury II

Cover art by Sir John Tenniel
and Dante Gabriel Rossetti

No part of this book may be reproduced or transmitted in any form
or by any means, electronic or mechanical, including photocopying,
recording, or by any information storage and retrieval system, without
permission in writing from the author.

Library of Congress Control Number: 2020939346

ISBN: 978-0-9797023-6-5

To Brook Hart,
For planting the idea
In my head
To write the book,
I Am Who I Am
Would pen
With a hand from me.

Contents

Preface viii

PART I: AN EVOLVING IMAGE OF WHO I AM

1. The Evolution Revolution 1
2. The Real Information Superhighway 37
3. Intrusions into Dark Matters 72

PART II: THE UNION OF I AM WITH WHO I AM

4. The Gauntlet 95
5. Shadow of the White Kind 122
6. Trial of a Special Kind 143
7. A Testament to Who I Am 208
8. Unshackled 238

Index 266
One Final Note 299

Preface

Had Sir E. J. Drury II not internalized the war he had been fighting as an irresolute recruit who had been condemned to the bowels of a man–o'–war for what he knew not, Sir E. J. may well have written a different kind of sequel to "A Different Kind of Sentinel".

"No man of war nor destroyer's escort am I," had he declared to the ship's Captain, a pronouncement that would usher in another year of active imagination on the wings of the transcendent function by which he is guided, through dialogue with his unconscious, toward the person he is meant to become.

"How much longer do you think you can keep me from the true intent of these encounters?" Questions he the master of deceit.

"As long as there are images that can keep their secrets to themselves," replies the snake, *"I shall prevail."*

Stonewalled at every turn, is he led by the transcendent to seek help from an unlikely trio—a professor, an attorney and the First Lady of the Resistance—all of whom work no harder than the attorney to rescue him from the jaws of the beast, intent on sucking any semblance of a real life from him as it has from his fathers and countless other poor souls who have been forced to kill on command, or be killed, in opposition to every moral fiber of their bodies, the carnage of which cries out unceasingly, "but thou shalt not taketh another man's life, lest ye loseth thine as recompense".

"Dammit! Give me liberty or give me death," captures he the sentiment of a generation so hell–bent on serving the ego, they kill for it. *"And that,"* says he, *"is the crux of the matter: how to give up the false sense of liberty onto which we cling when, in reality, it's our own death we seek in that of our neighbor's, for you can't have one without the other—liberty without death to the ego or all that we are not."*

A beacon is he who beckons the few to inflame the rest of us with the fervor of Paul Revere as the Spirit of a revolution in values rides roughshod over the Wraiths of State to warn us of our impending doom if we do nothing to deter business-as-usual from plundering Her physique, a body that hangs on a cross awaiting the death it must endure to give birth to a new world where the ego is no longer commander in chief.

"'Tis impossible," contends the author, *"to be conscious in real time and dreamtime at the same time. If I'm awake in one, I'm asleep to the other and risk loosing consciousness, living dreamtime in real time."*

"Is not our goal to express dreamtime in realtime?" Asks his soul.

With that, does he find his self running scared because he doesn't know if he is fleeing her world or his as he can no longer tell them apart—a dream come true, he is told, to alleviate his fear of having lost touch with reality.

"When Mr. Drury describes his experiences," attests the professor, *"he does so with an exuberance and a joy which, in terms of what has happened to him, is to me deeply impressive. I don't want to exaggerate his character, but I think of people like Thomas More and Franz Jägerstätter, who exuded a similar kind of joy that comes out of any person who is expressing something which they believe in, and of any person who is fulfilling himself in terms of standing up for what he believes in a nonviolent, loving and truthful way."*

So imbued is he with the Spirit, he can do no wrong as long as he lives in Her as She lives in him—a daunting task for one who has lost touch with the feminine side of the Trinity as he had when he joined forces to fight against Her rather than with Her at the helm as Queen of all that reflects what She embodies.

Like Her Son, had he been asked to sweat blood rather than shed it with a vengeance as doth the Beast and Knight Tempter of all who find it far easier to attack and kill the evil we see in our neighbor but not in ourselves, a rift we have perpetuated by not giving our neighbor what is theirs, saddling them, instead, with debt to increase our net worth, for without debt

x

there would be no money to spill blood over, nor ideology to sweat when they come after us with pitchforks demanding we turn everything over to them that is rightfully theirs.

"Have you adopted an evangelical approach to your personal views?" Is he asked at one point.

"Having found Who I Am has filled me with so much joy that it is hard not to share that joy with others who may not know where they belong. Sir, you don't know how wonderful that is, until you have gone astray for as long as I have, and like a lost sheep, have been found again. For I Am Who I Am and no other god before thee, and must therefore act accordingly, more like Jonah, if you wish, than St. Paul the Evangelist, and for that reason alone, must be about the business of getting the beast to cough me up," gives he flesh to the words he writes.

October 21, 2021   Sir E. J. Drury II

Acknowledgments

To one of the holiest spirits I know, my wife, Lady Valerie, do I owe the greatest gratitude, first, for giving said knight the room to write this book, and second, for providing him with such a marvelous image of the mediatrix between that mad-hatted ego of his and his imagination. To Marty, Harold, Greg and Red, wherever they may be, am I forever indebted for their friendship when I needed it most. And I thank Jim Douglass for having introduced me to Walter and First Lady of the Resistance Betty Johnson, my lawyer Brook Hart—the party most responsible for planting the idea in my head to write this book—and all the other knights and ladies of the Hawaii Resistance, who helped me through those trying times with their love and support, both in body and in spirit. My hat goes off to those, too, who had to endure the vagaries of the melancholy mood that'd descend upon said knight as he wrestled with the creative spirit within, over the contents of the book. My heart goes out, as well, to my parents for the story of my life. And last but not least, I would like to thank the Father, Son, and Holy Spirit—the Trio most responsible for the book—for the experiences of a lifetime and the willingness to share them with you, the reader of this madcap escapade through the mind of one crazy knight in his quest for the Grail and the courage to drink from it.

PART I

An Evolving Image of Who I Am

1

The Evolution Revolution

As I jetted onto the runway in the stream of consciousness which flowed forth from me, I fell from one flight of fantasy into another, a HUAC hearing of sorts to determine what type of HUman being I was, whether I was AntiCommunist or Un–American, and therefore, undesirable for further service in the military. On the way, I found a paperback on my knee which, I presumed, had been responsible for the dreadful flight I'd had the night before—that is, for having kept me awake all night testifying before the Un–American Activities Committee of my own House.

With that, did not I find the better part of myself back behind bars again where I belonged.

Why I'd been away so long, I hardly remembered the place. Greeted by my own lofty thoughts, the guardian of my soul, Sir Michael the Archangel, as I walked through the pearly gates of the Naval Station Brig at Pearl Harbor, only this time to the beat of my heart, I had to admit, it felt good to be back home.

Having fallen back into the habit of putting off till tomorrow the unfurling of my case against the Navy, had I unwittingly lost touch with my soul. And in spite of the great demand I placed upon her to be ever at my side in the struggle to bring this wayward individuality of mine back into harmony with the other members of my body, I knew that her showing me round the great obstacle which lay before me, by taking me back down to the hinterlands of my being to give form to what still plagued me, would be music to my ears.

Looking around at the incentive of my old mentor, Hewhay, I caught sight of her true beauty, the ability to govern and discipline oneself through reason alone.

"Such prudence comes at a high price," had her father, my old mentor, informed me as my soul stepped out of the shadows of my mind to stand before me in all her beauty, in spite of how dreadful the truth can sometimes be.

"To pluck this fruit from the Tree of Life," interjected my soul from her vantage point within the image in which she stood, "you must strip me of all pretense."

"Look into the mirror through which you see," proffered Michael, who did, on such occasions as these, give space to the place in my life where, contrary to conventional wisdom, everything is just as real as the sorry life it reflects.

"I told you about the wolf," piped up my mentor. "But what I failed to show you was its mirror image, which has only recently come to the surface in the guise of Paul the Apostle."

On that note, was I sent crashing back down to the ground of my being, like a shooting star, to reconcile the primitive man within me with Milady Madonna.

"I hope you-all will bear with me," had Paul begged of those of us foolish enough to give this one-time persecutor of the very men and women, who had come out to hear him speak, the consideration he sought.

"Untrained in speech, though I am," he went on to say, *"I sometimes find it necessary to boast about my limited knowledge of the spiritual realm. And while nothing may be gained by it, I will go on speaking, like a fool, about those visions and revelations the Lord has bestowed upon him. For I know a person in Christ who fourteen years ago was caught up to the third heaven—whether in the body or out of the body I do not know, for only God knows—was caught up to Paradise and heard things that are not to be told, that no mortal is permitted to repeat... considering the extraordinary nature of these revelations. To keep me from getting too elated, a thorn was given me in the flesh, a messenger of Satan to torment me. Three times I appealed to the Lord about this, that it would leave me, but He said to me, 'My grace is sufficient for you, for power is made perfect in weakness;' whenever I am weak, then am I strong."* 2 Cor 12:1-10.

"Look into the beam within your own eye!" Suggested my shadow, Michael, as his voice came crashing back into my awareness, like the sudden peel of church bells at the hour of the Angelus.

"Within the world of the looking glass," reiterated my soul.

With that, did I fall prey to the fire that burned within. Down I fell as the flames shot higher. And as my body burned with the desire to express what I knew not, I fell prisoner to the beast within. Filled with an insatiable desire for union with soul, was I driven to penetrate ever more deeply the womb of my imagination in my never-ending search for what would unite us forever.

In having been pulled up from my animal existence by the indomitable forces of an evolving image of God—to stand tall like St. Paul as a beacon to all who have succumbed to the falsetto call of a wrong way of life—had I finally deciphered the holographic prescription that'd been etched into the stony altar of my heart late last fall? Or had I given my self over to fantasizing too much?

"Look into Who You Really Are," proclaimed my mentor from somewhere across the great void that did still separate me from nirvana, or at least from seeing things the way he saw them. "Look into the Pearl of Great Price."

Why, I had gotten so wrapped up in my fantasies that I had lost touch with my soul. Having had my experiences overseas last year limited by my command to the virtual realities of my mind, much like those pot-smoking, acid-head friends whom I had chastised for the same crime, I awoke, one morning, with the realization that I'd even lost contact with the other members of the crew. When I realized how close I was to becoming an island unto itself, I panicked at the thought of succumbing to the schizophrenia that waited for me around the bend.

Confronted again, by my worst fear, was I forced to swim round the bend in my stream of consciousness, so as to avoid falling through a crack or split in my personality. Pulled from the raging water of this stream, as my nature rose up against me in the only way she knew how, through those contents of the imagination of which I still remained unaware, I found my self sitting in a row boat with that ever faithful old coot and mentor of mine, Hewhay, and guardian extraordinaire, the White Knight himself, Sir Michael the Archangel.

"Why were you so afraid of the truth of your being as she rose up in anger at how poorly you've been treating her lately?" Asked my mentor.

"What d'ya mean?" I asked.

"Other than what she demands from you when her Mother nature forces you to go off and play with the truth of your being, which still remains hidden from you within the masculine and feminine poles of your animal nature," responded Michael instead, "you give her little body."

"I still don't understand what you're trying to tell me," grappled I with a mere glimmer of the truth.

"Don't you see, my son," chimed in my mentor. "When a man asks a woman for her hand in marriage, he is really asking her to take his soul's place until he becomes aware of the part in life, his soul must play to free him from his lust for her. Thus does the natural man bind himself to what would one day make him a eunuch or whole man—his own muse—in the ultimate act of love in which she sings to him, in words that are music to his ears, as long as he shall live, the inspiration he seeks to embody. Only the natural man must know who he is before he can join hands with his soul to become a eunuch. Otherwise, he just takes her place, and is then driven to seek union with his yet hidden male identity in every Tom, Dick, and Harry who strikes his fancy, for he must bring to the relationship between him and his soul the skill that will unite him with his imagination."

Left holding onto my inordinate desires for union with soul, I screamed out in anguish over my condition, that sinking feeling whereby one gets sucked down to the level of an unconscious animal after having failed to find the god, or god-like behavior which would satisfy the cravings of the beast within oneself on a more humane level—that mythological place, the more adventuresome folk among us call Middle Earth, the end result of the long tug of war twixt god and beast to create a more homogeneous will, in which the image is finally reunited with its true intent. Sucked down through the swirling hot, desert sands of my mind, like some poor hapless grain of sand in an hour glass, which has run out of time in its never-ending search for another way out of having to slog through this hell, over and over, I found my self racing through the narrow winding streets of a small city in Spain, out in front of a thousand other guys with a bull at our heels. To the incessant drumbeat of my heart and the cymbals that clanged around in my head, did not I race against the rhythms of my body and its bullheaded tendency to gravitate down to the level of a beast to satisfy this great need of mine to give body to soul.

"O baby!" Screamed out my shadow from somewhere across the great void that still separated me from my soul, who seemed to be asking something more of me than being in the brig with her again, as I gallivanted off, in the guise of a wolf, to sniff out the one female who could excite my imagination to greater heights.

Confronted instead, by one bullheaded, all-American son of the Great Sea Bitch Herself, a chaplain whose name eludes my memory, was not I transformed into the very pussy I sought—the moment I expressed the desire to be processed as a conscientious objector. By the time it dawned on me why I'd been unable to find my soul in any of her usual haunts, in my hour of greatest need, was I shot down by the unholy side of this bungling billy for having switched roles with her.

When I asked via that little cherub within me, my own nascent conscientious objectorship, if to kill was not a sin, why the old billy looked at me with such surprise at the surfacing of the truth, that if looks could kill, he would have kilt me.

"Hey! Look at what you've done now, ya bungling old fool," rang out the voices in my head as I left my first interview ever with a chaplain of the sixth fleet, dressed in a kilt instead of the usual twill.

Having recognized, in his voice, that same all-American, bullheaded son of the Great Sea Bitch, who had invoked the War Prayer of Lady Madonna's invert, that Medusa, the Great Gray Whore herself, back over in Nam late last summer, how could I have told the bungling billy, without having prejudiced him against me, that he prayed to the gorgon who turned men's hearts to stone whene'er they gazed into her eyes or the moral equivalent of their lust to take life into their own hands? How could I have ever convinced this stubborn old salt to sever the head of this gorgon from its host, the very body he had given it?

Having given the salty old dog a brief history of my entry into the Navy, had I responded to his serpentine line of questioning as best I could. When asked upon what I did base my conscientious objection to military service, I replied, "Why upon the very tenant that one shall not kill, if one understands the true meaning of military service."

"And what do you understand the true meaning of military service to be?" Had he inquired with a smile behind which hid the devil waiting to ambush me.

"Why to kill," I had stated with the steel of Perseus, "which then obligates me, as a nonviolent, to refuse military service if I understand this to be its true purpose."

Having lopped off the head of this gorgon, much to the surprise of my interlocutor, I still refused to look into her eyes in spite of repeated attempts on his part to ensnare me or get me to turn from the reflection that so shielded me from falling prey to such rigid thinking.

"Do you believe in self-defense or the just war theory?" Had he struck back in a supreme effort to gain ascendancy over the moral superiority that did permeate my body with the scent of frankincense and myrrh.

"The truth needs no defending," had I put forth in my struggle to bag the head of this gorgon before its lies overcame me, "for the truth is its own defense against the illusions that spring forth from the head, like so many snakes. Have you not heard it said that he who saves his life will lose it, while he who loses his life for Christ's sake or the sake of His message will save it? As far as a just theory of war, why I've never heard of such an animal. Or if indeed, such a beast does exist, I have yet to lay eyes upon this gorgon of which you have spoken, in such a way as to keep its lies from turning my heart to stone—as they have yours, ya old fool," I concluded within the confines of my being.

Moved by the tears of my soul to have pity upon those still living out of the Old Testament, had I seen the beauty of this chaplain's soul lying there asleep within the hinterlands of his being, waiting for the old prince to awaken her from the Big Sleep. As I looked down upon those who'd fallen by the wayside, fighting real people instead, I watched them get swept away like dead leaves in a whirlwind, while my soul wept over the way, Nature rid herself of such rigid thinkers.

"I don't know why," cried out the more philosophically inclined side of my nature, that little band of resisters hidden away somewhere deep within my psyche, "nobody ever showed you how to free your soul from the terrible fate of being bought and sold into slavery to another."

As I looked at life from their perspective, I was not too surprised, when I stumbled upon my soul again, to find her weeping over our stubborn refusal to let go of the rigid thought patterns that set us so at odds with each other.

"How easily you-all are diverted from the truth by your own stray thoughts," my soul reminded me. "The more you entertain such negative projections, the more rigid does your thinking become, and perverse, your behavior, as you give body to these dark intimations of the truth. Thus do you allow the beast in you to ascend to the throne, in spite of our best efforts to alert you to this mishap. And so are you driven to expand your genitals instead of your minds, to orgasm rather than to realize, while I weep over the fate of yet another hapless generation."

With that, did I take off on yet another flight of fantasy, no longer afraid of the catatonia into which I feared falling if I continued to pursue these notes from the underground. Grounded, at an early age, by the crash of my real father from the flight of fantasy we call reality, I was instilled with a fear of flying that bordered on the unholy. Little did I know I would suffer the same fate, a complete breakdown of my mental makeup to rid it of those attitudes deemed detrimental to the well-being of the God struggling to give birth to Himself from somewhere deep within my being. Only I'd been led astray, taught by my stepfather to beat off the advances of this loving God, when all this creative potential wanted from me was a body willing to do its bidding. Having been thwarted by my tunnel vision—that dark night of the soul through which we must all pass to see the light at the other end—I fell into the hands of that evil magician, Instinct, whose actions had once reflected the thoughts of my mentor. O how I longed to see Who I Am, to be free from the spell of the Evil Magician to act instinctively when all else failed to satiate the constant need of mine to give body to soul. For now, I had to content my self with the task of trying to catch the wind, or spirit of such lofty thoughts, in some concrete way if I wished to capture the moment and immortalize my soul.

She didn't miss much—my soul, that is. Untainted by the Midas touch or need to objectify that which we do not possess, she could easily see through all the hocus-pocus of that master of deceit, the Evil Magician, Instinct himself, for it was Wisdom who had taught him everything he knew. In Her great wisdom, had She the foresight to hold back on sharing with this Satan anymore of Herself than Her images, when he began to show signs of an unwillingness to face the other side of himself, or truth of his being.

In his lust for Her, did this primitive will of ours rebel against the Creator's plan to reveal the true identity of the Original Being to those who accepted the challenge to evolve into both the image and likeness of God. Ignorant of the consequences of pursuing one over the other, did he embark upon one of the most ambitious campaigns ever devised by this obtuse will of ours to bring about the annihilation of the imaginable by the unimaginable—the mass extinction of the last species of humans on the planet. Having filled our heads with the need to destroy this obtuse image of our selves, before it destroyed us, had he succeeded in getting us to accept his destiny as our own. So did the shadow of the will of God lock horns with its own fully evolved potential in mortal combat for the Soul of mankind, She Who Must Be Obeyed, if ever we are to inherit the face of the earth.

In my hour of greatest need, did I slip and fall into the very abyss I thought I had left behind when I stepped back from its edge, late last spring.

Pulled back down into the Pit of Despair by that reprehensible, obsessive–compulsive alter ego of mine, I found my self sitting in a fox hole, back in Nam, with a gun in my hand and my sights set on shooting off another round of bullets. To ease the pain of separation from whom I had yet to become, I took aim at the first thing that moved, only to be surprised by some vague facsimile of myself, claiming to be the Author of my being. Before disappearing, I learned, through osmosis, that I'd one day become a servant of His versus the state, but only after a long backbreaking bout with Him to convince me of the efficacy of doing things His way. Forced by the nature of my being to act upon the impulse to fill this gap in my life with the seeds of consciousness, had I opened fire in my inability to give expression, in any other way, to that which I still did not know about myself.

In choosing to live out this fantasy on such a low level, had I acted too hastily? Or had I simply responded to Nature's call to jump the gun again?

Or was I in need of a little prodding, to keep me from getting too caught up in my fantasies? Had I simply soared too high, that I needed some thorn in the flesh to prick the bubble I so often used to insulate my self from the real world?

Had I acted upon this fantasy because it was so much more compelling than the truth yet hidden within it? Or had I acted like a caged animal that'd been deprived of the means for expressing itself in any other form than the instinctive?

"Happiness is a warm gun. Bang! Bang!" Fired Instinct into the night.

"True happiness," interjected my mentor, "comes only to those who learn to disseminate the seeds of consciousness without spilling the body's fluids, whether sanguineous or seminal, upon the ground. For those who attempt to save their life, through wanton dissipation of their own or someone else's, will surely lose it, while those who lose it for the sake of this message or that of its Author will save it."

"When you get hold of Nature," shot back Instinct from the hip, "and put your finger to her trigger, no one can stop you from taking life into your own hands."

"In other words, my son," interjected my mentor, "when a man has been deprived of a life as long as you have, he can only be driven, like your stepfather, to take life into his own hands. If along the way, he should acquire a wife, he may find, as he puts his finger to her trigger, that he really has nothing to fear but the mind–expanding aspects of his imagination. If on the other hand, he fails to face the beastly fear of the truth of his being, he will be driven to take the life of another, as he literally takes on a life that is not his own. Thus does the rich man, like the killer, force the rest of you to seek happiness in your own gun."

"Ah, but no greater joy is there, than to take Life into your hands," shot back Instinct, "and pump her full of bullets."

"Where do the conflicts and disputes amongst you originate?" Asked my mentor in response to modern man's murderous mesmerization with the gun. *"Is it not your own inner cravings that make war within your members? What you desire you do not obtain, and so you resort to murder. You envy and cannot acquire, so you quarrel and fight. You do not obtain because you do not ask. You ask and you do not receive because you ask wrongly, with a view to squandering what you receive on your own pleasures."* Jas 4:1-3.

Rent in two by my craving for the truth, did I find my self standing in front of the mirror that never lies—she who hid the identity of her beloved behind the many skirts of her mother, the Mistress of All Imagery, Nature. As I stood there in the image of a wealthy young man, so proud and so full of my self, I took time to gaze upon this marvelous creation of mine before I went to work. Only, I was horrified to see, standing within the mirror, the image of a thief and a murderer instead.

"I thought..." Blurted out the one to the other.

"...'Twas you," injected the unrepentant thief, standing outside the mirror.

"...When, all the time, it was you," rebutted the repentant thief from Paradise.

"Liar!" Screamed the rich young man who had kept all the commandments.

"...Who took my life from me," added the younger, more able-bodied son of Adam from whom everything had been taken to line the pockets of his older, more instinctive brother, that wealthy Citizen standing outside the mirror in the ever increasingly popular image of Kane.

At these words, the young man's face fell, for he had accumulated much at the expense of his brother, from whom he had taken all but his soul or what is eternal.

"It is easier for a camel to pass through the eye of a needle than for a rich man to enter the kingdom of God," (Lk 18:25) proclaimed the crucified criminal that hung between the two, like a seamless gown.

"Then how can a man, like me, find salvation?" Begged the rich young man for the first time in his life.

"Take up your cross," replied the seamless gown, "instead of inflicting it upon others. Give back to them what you have accumulated at their expense—the opportunity to enter the kingdom of God as a whole person."

Turning from the mirror, the young man went away sad, for he couldn't let go of the cross from which he hung—that constant need to crucify others for his sin.

Just then, a shot rang out as the rich young man slumped to the floor, mortally wounded by his own shadowy creation, the Frankenstein in the mirror that did haunt him still.

"Had he taken his own life?" I wondered as the life which he had taken from his counterpart slipped through his fingers as it had through those of the beastly side of his nature.

"Jesus, remember me when you enter upon your reign," (Jn 23:44) cried out the franker of the two thieves, in a last ditch effort to grab hold of the life which had escaped this poor beggar.

"I assure you," replied the seamless garment, *"that today, you will be with Me in Paradise."* Jn 23:43.

From the abode of the dead where the rich man now lay in torment, longing for an end to his hell, did he see Abraham afar off. And upon seeing the beggar whom the Just One had freed from his bondage to the earth, he called out, "Father Abraham, have pity on me. Let the thief, who stole my life, dip the tip of his finger in what would refresh my tongue and free me from my desire for more."

"My child," replied Abraham, "remember how well–off you were in your lifetime while poor Lazarus suffered an agonizing death outside your door, the very gates to heaven itself. Where he has found consolation, you have found torment. And that is not all, for between us has been fixed a great abyss, so that we cannot take away your pain, and you cannot steal your way into heaven."

"I ask you then," replied the rich man, "to send someone back to the land of the living to warn my brothers that they may not end up in this place of torment."

"They have the prophets," answered Abraham, "to warn them of the dangers of squandering their lives away. Let them heed the words of their prophets."

"No, Father Abraham," replied the rich young man, "if only someone could go to them from the dead, surely they would change their ways."

"If they do not listen to their own prophets," retorted Abraham, *"they will not be convinced even if one should rise from the dead."* Lk 16:19-31.

With that I woke up to the evil of pursuing anymore in life than what would satisfy my soul. Anything else, I realized, was a sham to be shot down as soon as it rose from the dead to take on any other form than Who I Am.

"Don't you see, my son," explained my mentor from somewhere across the great gap in my understanding of all this mumbo jumbo, "you must free Who You Really Are from the image that keeps you from grasping the truth, whene'er you shoot for it."

"Or," offered Michael, "you can sit on your duff until you are driven, like your ol' man, to take the low road and fill some poor bloke's ass with lead when you've reached the end of the rope that tethers you to the Great Gray Whore."

"Or," added my soul, "you can get up off your ass, go for the gold and sell me to the highest bidder, taking the high road until your past catches up with you and pulls you down to the level of the devil to whom you belong."

"Or," concluded the voice of that sensuous part of me, I had tried so hard to keep locked up behind bars, "you can take the middle road, the one less traveled, to free the frog from the prince and the prince from the frog."

"What nonsense is this?" Bemoaned the two thieves in unison, the one from his vantage point in paradise, the other from his disadvantage in the netherworld.

"Because your will," responded my mentor, "or more princely side of your nature has risen so far above the instinctive responses of the primitive side of you, it has lost touch with its true purpose in life, to serve the poor pauper croaking at your gate. In its inability to reunite itself with the essence of your obsessive–compulsive alter ego, has it condemned the more creative aspect of you to a hellish existence. Left with no other choice but to go after you like a flaming faggot, does he shoot down every effort of this recalcitrant will of yours to pursue any other love than his. For whatever it shall hold bound to the earth shall likewise be held bound to the heavens. Whereas, whatever it shall loose from the body shall be loosed from the imagination. And the two shall become as one again."

"How do you propose that I accomplish this feat?" I begged to know, in spite of the fear I felt in letting go of what I'd held onto, so long, for dear life.

"You must first die to your self," he replied, "before descending into hell, to rise above it, should you succeed in freeing Who You Are from its grip."

"You mean to tell me," reared up the ugly side of my nature, in its natural aversion to any more pain and suffering than it'd normally be asked to endure in the course of a lifetime, "after all I've been through, over the past year, that I'm to be subjected to yet more of the same—for some half-crazed notion that I might gain control of my self. Well fuck this shit! I'm so sick and tired of hurtin', I could scream. You hear me? I've had it with all this highfalutin, pain–in–the–ass shit of yours.

"I just want you to leave me alone and let me live in peace," I ranted on. "Life couldn't be any worse than what you–all are trying to ram down my throat.

"So get the fuck outta my life. Go on, get outta here," I yelled at the old coot, as he hightailed his scrawny little ass off center stage, much to my satisfaction.

O how the Evil One did rejoice, for it was he who had sown the seeds of enmity between me and my mentor.

"I have the power to make you into whomever you wish," did the black robed rogue tempt me. With that did he point to the images of those whom, like the posters of the Ten Most Wanted, he had helped to frame and hang from the walls of this vile den to which I had descended in my rejection of Who I Am.

"Get behind me, Satan," I yelled out, as he laughed in my face at how easily I had slipped back down to the level of an animal.

"I'm sorry!" I shouted out over the raucous laughter of my detractor, only to find that my words seemed to have fallen upon deaf ears.

"Jinny, my dear," rang out that side of me, so desperate for companionship, I'd gladly have spent my days in the brig, in conversation with my soul, if only she hadn't abandoned me, as so it seemed she had.

The Evolution Revolution

Because I hadn't heard from Mary since I returned from leave, I had written her a Dear John letter before leaving the brig, in my inability to cope any longer with her lack of response to my letters. Before returning to the ship, however, I received the following explanation from her:

Dear Butch,
This letter will be short and to the point. Today, I received the last three letters you had sent me. Having failed to first look at the postmarks on them, I ripped into the one on top—the last one you'd written. Boy, was I sorry for having done so, as I began to feel as you must've felt when you wrote it. And now that I must explain to you why I haven't written for so long, I only pray that you'll understand.

I went into what the doctors call a "thyroid storm", I imagine, just as you were getting on the plane to leave. I lost all concept of time until I came out of surgery last Thursday. I topped the old record at the hospital with the biggest, most toxic goiter ever removed from a patient. Anyway, now I'm on the road, hopefully, to a speedy recovery.

I thought you should hear the other side of the story. I hope you understand that I didn't mean to break my promise to write more often. I think this is the first time I've cried in years.

One more thing before I sign off, you're not selfish.
Love,
Mary

Boy did I feel like a heel as I sat down to write her another letter.

With that, I realized how much I needed to get out and wander through the wilder side of nature, to reconnect with the ground of my being. Having found such excursions to be an inspiration, I knew it'd do me good to get out of myself for awhile, as my soul kissed me good-bye upon my departure from the brig.

"Boy, that sure was some storm I pitched back there—a result, I presume, of having been confined to my mind, with little or no human contact, for nigh on a month. How can I avoid getting so toxic in the future?" I asked my soul in earnest.

"Instead of writing me off," chided this greater will of mine, "whenever things don't go your way, you must learn to give into me as I have you for so many years. That way, I can show you how to live more fully in the present than does this male dominated ego of yours in its struggle to become independent of its dependence upon others for sustenance—a grave mistake indeed. For you need them, as much as they need you. You were made for each other. Go now, to them that would have you, for they call you. Deny them not yourself, for it is only in giving of yourself that you will find true happiness."

Feeling a bit overwhelmed, I exclaimed, "But how can I give to others what I, myself, do not yet possess?"

"For you it is impossible," she replied, *"but not for God. With God all things are possible."* Mk 10:27.

"Then show me Who I Am," I begged of her, "that I might come and go, as you do, through the Gates of Eden."

With that, was I left standing in the presence of Marty who was all excited to see me. Instead of wallowing, as usual, in my disappointment over having been deposited back onboard the ship, I went out of my way, at the prodding of my soul, to embrace what little happiness, or heaven on earth, there was to be found in this encounter of him. So did I go gallivanting off with him, to ease the pain of having been forgotten on my twenty-first birthday, of all days, by the two most important women in my life, Mary and my own mother, of all people.

"Mary/Jinn," had I written my estranged soul mate, "you have always been an inspiration to me. Please, Marijin, my dear, do not forget me. Do not forget your knight in shining armor, Margin."

So did the White Knight head off for parts unknown, with the only inspiration he'd had in weeks, that old nag, Martin the talking horse. Having been marginalized by life back home, had the White Knight done the same to his self, for he had a way of isolating me from others, whenever the need arose, which I took to the extreme. Deprived of virtually any contact with my soul as she went out ahead of us and hid herself, like one of Pan's nymphs, in the hope of drawing out the best in me, would this vagabond lead me ever more deeply into the wildest reaches of my being. Dressed like a hermit monk, did he stalk this instinct to play with my self. With his left hand on the reins of that white steed of mine as we slogged through the thick tangle of old growth impeding my progression to full human stature, did he lead me, ever on, towards that goal where lie the truth of my being.

Having escorted me to the water's edge, had he left me standing in the guise of my soul, down on Waikiki Beach with the talking horse rather than the old nag. So did he meet the need of the beastly side of my nature for a little enjoyment for its own sake—something I rarely allowed my self to indulge in, except when forced to by that obsessive-compulsive alter ego of mine. For on the seventh day had he decided to step back from the work of creation, simply to enjoy it.

I never had so much fun as I did that afternoon. Exhausted, at one point, I laid down on my beach towel and fell fast asleep where, in a dream, I continued to enjoy the rarity of the company of my soul.

"Ya know," I concluded as I sat there laughing at my self, "new life can be very demanding—so much so, that one needs to get away from it, on occasion, for the sake of his sanity."

"Yes," she agreed, "one does need to step back from the new life he has fostered, to let it be, lest he lose sight of these little reincarnations of himself."

"Why, I hardly know anything about our new life together!" I exclaimed.

"Nor do I," proclaimed my soul, "for I've been learning from you as we go along, just as you've been learning from me. The more attached I get to this joint venture of ours, the more I realize how much I have yet to learn from it."

"Well, I sure am glad you are here with me," I declared, "for I was beginning to think that we might not see each other again."

"So was I," reaffirmed my soul, "until I realized you were going through another much-needed growth spurt."

"Only this time," I added, "I felt as if I had to climb out of a straight jacket."

"Such cocoons, or straight jackets as you call them, consist of former selves," she proclaimed, "which can be very confining, as they restrict one's perception of himself until he is able to shed them and embrace those aspects of himself which have pushed their way into his life."

"Well, at any rate, I sure missed you while you were gone," I admitted to her.

"I missed you too," she replied.

"I love you," I added.

"I love you too," she concurred.

At that moment, I felt at one with her as she went running off down the beach, tickled pink by how seriously I was again taking her. And as I got up to chase after her, I woke up just in time to catch a glimpse of this fiery red ball as it disappeared over the horizon.

"What a glorious sunset!" Declared I to Marty ere losing sight of my soul.

"Indeed!" Exclaimed the talking horse, as it plopped itself down in the sand beside me, with a sigh.

"I don't know about you, Dury," complained the talking horse, "but I'm starvin'!"

"Me too," concurred the missing link.

So did the White Knight and the white horse go gallivanting off after that food which only their pockets could afford in this land of plenty.

Having satisfied the appetites of their lower natures, were the two driven by their high-spiritedness, to venture forth where neither had dared to go before—to skirt the perimeter of this lovely isle, or breast of Nature, in search of soul. Instead of running off to the horizon where she had disappeared—an impossible feat for those with clay feet—they disappeared into the misty shrouded lands of the east where had risen, just above that sleepy ol' crater known as Diamond Head, a full moon to guide them on their way. Hindered by their obstinacy to pursue such rough terrain under poorly lit conditions, the two quickly changed course. Opting to take the high road that led up to the summit of this ancient cauldron, they hoped to catch a glimpse into the not too distant past, by geological reckoning, when it still oozed with the potential for reshaping the earth. Peeking up over the rim of this inverted nipple, did they find, much to their chagrin, a military installation within.

As the old nag flew into a rage, condemning those who had used Nature's pot to concoct such rot, the missing link peered into the opening which had availed itself to him, only to find himself standing on the boundary between two epochs. Before he could step off into the more futuristic one, he witnessed the unparalleled mass extinction of over half the known species of plants and animals in existence. Turning to the future lest he get caught up in this maelstrom, he found himself standing on a holy mountain where nigh a creature, that'd survived this cataclysm, was capable of hurting or destroying another, as in the past. For he realized they had all been satiated with the knowledge of Who They Really Are.

"Come on, Dury," groaned the old nag as it pulled the missing link back into that Cretaceous period of its life, in which the dinosaurs of this age did still reign supreme, "let's get the fuck outta this hellhole."

Taking one last look into the twat of the whore that mad—hatted ego of ours, Uncle Sam, had made out of Mother Nature, the day he left her for some Adonis named Mars, I turned in disgust to follow my horse's ass down the leeward side of her body. Sickened by the unholy alliance between the old business tycoon and his military attaché, at the expense of his own mother and those of her children who have been forced to suckle at her barren breasts for naught, did I hurry down the side of this fossilized tit, in a race to reach the opening in the boundary between this epoch and the next before it closed itself off and left me to fend for myself in the insanity of the present age. But I never made it, as the hole disappeared into the tiny tide pool over which I found my self standing.

As I stood there staring at the image of the full moon that writhed and wriggled around on the surface of the pool, like some naked woman in a mirror, there at my side, appeared the talking horse.

"Ya know, Dury," he finally interjected into the long silence that had engulfed us in wonder, "it almost looks as if she were taunting us to plunge our selves into her for the encounter of a lifetime. Doesn't it?" He inquired of me as he nudged my arm in his usual manner, to make sure I'd heard what he had said.

I remained silent, hoping he'd take his fantasy further, but he never did. Instead, he led me down this beautiful, moonlit beach—an extension of some grassy little cove situated between two legs of the mountain that jutted its jungled self up from the floor of the island, like an old skyscraper which had long been abandoned to the wiles of Nature that she might hide these bony protuberances from her detractors. Wandering back in between the legs of her body, did he yell for me to come quickly if I didn't want to miss out on the encounter of a lifetime.

"Look!" he shouted as I came running up to his side.

All around us, in that grassy moonlit meadow, could be seen hopping about, and heard croaking, what seemed like a zillion frogs.

"Why I've never seen so many in one place, in my whole life!" I exclaimed.

"Nor I," mused a bewildered Martin as he wondered aloud at what'd brought them here for this big of an occasion.

"Need you ask?" I inquired of him with a chuckle. "It's a full moon."

"What d'ya mean?" He snapped back.

"They're croakin' at the moon," I blared out, amidst the laughter I could no longer contain.

Just then he started kicking them up into the air, like little footballs, while he rambled on about "how dumb the motherfuckers were".

"Marty, what're ya doin'?" I shouted out of my astonishment with such a cruel response. "Your're hurting them!"

Like the grim reaper, he kept plowing his way through them, as if he'd heard nigh a word I'd said.

"Stop it!" I yelled into his face as I grabbed hold of him by the arm. "What the hell's the matter with you?"

"Aw, I ain't hurtin' the motherfuckers," retorted Marty.

"The hell you aren't!" I screamed in his face. "How the hell d'ya think you'd feel after I drop-kicked your ass halfway across this field? I daresay like that sailor ya coldcocked back in Subic Bay."

"Come on, Dury," he replied, "I was only havin' a little fun with 'em."

"Yeah," I retorted, "only at their expense."

With that, we both broke out laughing—the whole scene was so darn funny. But the funniest thing was that we found nigh a frog when we returned, the following morning, to see if they were still there. Having gathered no hard evidence, the night before, to prove what we had seen, were we left with nothing but another cock-and-bull story to tell.

That night, I dreamt that a bunch of horny toads had come out to pay homage to the sacredness of Life as She shined forth in the night sky under the guise of a full moon. Having been transformed into a wolfman, was I left standing there, howling at the moon, out of my ignorance yet of how best to serve She Who Must Be Obeyed as I drew closer to some of the queerest feelings I'd ever experienced.

Catching sight of someone beating up on another creature, I sensed that I was no longer standing on God's holy mountain. Seeing this creature as my own obsessive-compulsive alter ego, I was horrified to find his attacker to be none other than a facsimile of me, dressed as Uncle Sam. Having scared off that mad-hatted ego of mine, I came face to face with the most vile-looking creature I'd ever seen.

For the first time in my life, did I feel moved to embrace the damned thing. Fearful of the sexual feelings this unknown aspect of myself had stirred up, I cringed, whereupon it hissed ere disappearing into the darker recesses of my mind.

As I slipped from this dream, I was left with the disconcerting feeling that I had desired union with a male member of my body. Horrified at first, by the appearance of the desire for such a liaison, I quickly realized that I had just blown another opportunity for union with my creative daimon.

"Dammit!" I hissed as I woke up to a new day. "Why does it have to be so hideous? Couldn't You (meaning God) have made it easier for me to grasp?"

But there was no response from across the great void in my life, which did still separate me from Who I Am.

"How can I ever accept this obsession of mine?" I wondered to no avail.

Upon awaking, Marty and I made our way back down to Waikiki to satisfy the ache inside our stomachs. Having each spent the night wrestling with his own demons, we had worked up quite an appetite.

Having satisfied the one ache, we went off in search of what might satisfy the other until She returned to see how far we'd come since last She laid eye upon us. So did we exhaust every avenue that had availed itself by midday's sun.

With no choice left, did we enter a theater to observe the unfurling of an old myth in new clothes. Absconded from our seats through the magic of modern-day cinematography, did our portrayers find themselves scrounging around in the most desolate place on earth—the human mind—for the tiniest morsel that might enable them to evolve beyond the instinctive responses of our savage animal past. Having stumbled upon the key to the future, did they force from the ground of their beings, the archetype they had yet to accept. So did they turn to worshipping this black monolith as a god instead of embracing it as a part of their natures.

In their failure to subdue Nature through the sheer efforts of that Herculean will of ours, were they driven, in time, to explore further their own inner space. Having landed on the moon, they were astounded when they again stumbled upon that black archetypal stone, which the builders of this Great Society had rejected in their hurry to appease that satanic will which thinks it can damn well do whatever it pleases. For in their failure to grasp hold of the true meaning of the actions of our more alchemically minded ancestors, had they fallen into the trap of taking the myths of their imaginations literally rather than figuratively. Duped, like Jupiter, by the myth of Medusa, were they thus driven to give body to some edification in stone of one aspect of the Original Being over the other.

So did we venture forth with our portrayers on the screen into the new millennium. In their struggle with that Jovian will of mankind, the god of all gods, and its propensity to act upon its thoughts without feeling, like some omnipotent technological wizard, only one of them would outwit the twit and see his self reborn. Having silenced that satanic will of ours, did he free his self from its bondage to a purely materialistic view of life. In the process, had he opened himself up to encountering the greater will of mankind as it presented itself to him in the form of that much coveted prize of the philosophers of old, that stony altar within his heart upon which had been written, long ago, in symbolic language, those words which could transform the baser aspects of his nature into what is truly human, should he decipher their true meaning. Stepping inside himself, once he had pierced his tunnel-visionedness, did he cross the threshold between this world and the next, to observe his own metamorphosis, or shedding of the outer man for that of the inner one. Having brought to naught modern man's first odyssey into the far reaches of inner space, like the eggman, did he give birth to what few men on earth have ever given berth, his own worth or Who He Really Werth.

"That was the stupidest goddamn movie I've ever seen," claimed the talking horse as we emerged from the theater.

"It was a great movie," replied the hermit monk in me as he looked back upon the most befuddling symbol of all, the black monolith. "Evolution is the stone the builders of this doomed society have rejected in their blind pursuit of the Great Gray Whore, Ms. Matte Progress, and that mad-hatted militarist, Uncle Sam."

"Where the hell d'ya dig that up?" Inquired that faithless sidekick of mine.

"I tell you," interjected the One Voice as it leapt free of the constraints of the frog in my throat that normally tempered my ability to speak so fluently, *"no one can see the kingdom of God without being born from above."* Jn 3:3.

"How can anyone," posed that pharisaical phantom hidden deep within this bosom buddy of mine, *"be born after having grown old?"* Jn 3:4.

"Truly, I tell you," proclaimed the One Voice in its infinite wisdom, *"no one can enter the kingdom of God without being born of both water and the Spirit."* Jn 3:5.

"So how the hell are you supposed to get there?" Inquired the phantom that was inhibiting Marty from seeing what remained hidden in plain sight.

"Like the astronaut in the movie," replied the I That Can See, "must you penetrate the womb of your imagination, ever deeper to give berth to consciousness."

"The wind blows where it chooses," interjected the One Voice again, *"and you hear the sound of it but do not know where it comes from or where it goes. So it is with everyone who is born of the Spirit."* Jn 3:6-8.

"How can that be?" Inquired that incredulous interlocutor whose black form overshadowed my bosom buddy, the balking horse.

"In your dreams," added the I That Can See, "have you not had conversations, like the one we're having now, with your own spirits? And did not the images for these spirits come from your impressions of the world around you that day? From whence came the wind that gave them their voices? Did it not come from deep within your being? Why then do you fail to heed these messages from above, that is, from your imagination? Is it because you do not understand them? Or is it because you are afraid of giving form to the Spirit Who Is You?"

"If, in having told you about earthly things," exhorted the One Voice, *"you do not believe, how can you believe if I tell you about heavenly things?"* Jn 3:11-12.

"Have you never encountered the triune nature of your being?" Inquired the god who could barely see beyond the beastly side of his nature. "If, after having shared with you my struggle to integrate my wants and needs with those of the larger community of mankind, you cannot yet distinguish your will from that of your parents, how will you ever resolve the rift between them? And yet you, who speak with a forked tongue, at times so thoughtlessly, and at others, so heartlessly, still refuse to open yourself up to the mind—expanding thoughts hidden deep within your heart. For just as Moses lifted up the serpent in the desert to sacrifice our tendency to run our lives as we see fit to that greater will of mankind, so must you. Otherwise you will never heal yourself of the split between body and mind—the result of choosing to live contrary to the dictates of either one.

"For the Creator so loved the world, He came down to her the moment she had evolved into the image of His own likeness. Within the womb of this Holy Spirit did He deposit the essence of Himself, that She might bear Him a Son born of both water and the spirit.

"Indeed, Consciousness did not come into the world to condemn her, but to save her from blind instinct. While those, who have not yet emotionally evolved into human beings, are condemned by their own actions to living like animals, those who have overcome the split between body and soul are free to move onto the next level from which the snake has been banished forever. But Consciousness was not well received when He came into the world, as most of us preferred to live like our ancestors, in ignorance of the truth of those actions which run contrary to the true nature of our beings. For this vast segment of our species, whose emotional growth remained stuck down around the bottom of the tree of evolution at the level of some beast, so hated the light of Consciousness that they refused to come under its scrutiny lest their deeds be exposed. At the same time," concluded the I That Can See, "there arose from amongst these ungrateful dead a few stalwarts to champion the cause of evolution. Stepping into the light, they lived out the truth hidden deep within the darker side of their natures, that generations to come could clearly see their deeds had been done in God."

So was this New Age Jonah led back to ship instead of jail by that constant companion of his, the fear of associating anything else but whales with the tails that always turned up whenever he flipped that imaginary coin in his head.

Thrown off by my self-will, I wondered if I was not my own worst enemy as this black rider took off, later that night in a dream, with the libidinal energy I had liberated from the instinctive layers of my psyche, earlier that day.

How was I to ever mediate its mother's world with that of its father, if this will of mine continued to see the world as revolving around itself, as had its mother's, rather than around that only-begotten son, my own conscientious objectorship? Why had it not seen, in the reflection of its mother's life, the truth at the very core of its being, that its life must revolve around another's?

Left with only the brilliance of a black hole to look into, I woke up feeling so tired, I could hardly move. And as I lay there, wondering whether I should even get up to imbibe anymore of the watered-down life I'd been forced to lead, I wandered off in search of what would truly satisfy my Self.

Had I not set my mind on getting out of the Navy as a conscientious objector, I would not have been so disappointed when nothing happened. As I struggled to connect my latest brainchild to the real world, I wondered what its mother would do if I abandoned it as another one of her hopeless causes.

"Ya know, I'm so tired of nothing happening," proclaimed that I who like HAL, the technological wizard in the movie, *2001: A Space Odyssey*, had tried to take over the whole show, to his demise.

In my exasperation with the limitations which had been placed upon me, by both God and the Navy, I fell to huffing and puffing, like some mangy ol' gray wolf, pacing back and forth within the confines of its own thickheaded cage.

With that I fell to wondering how much I'd hurt my soul when I joined the Navy. If it was anyting like the pain I generally felt, then I must have hurt her deeply. How deeply, though, I never realized until I went into labor to give birth to this newest brainchild of ours, my conscientious objection to military service.

"I came to bring fire to the earth," proclaimed that Promethean Voice from somewhere deep within my being. *"How I wish it were already kindled!"* Lk 12:49.

"Until you come to a better understanding of the life into which you must immerse yourself," added my mentor, "you will continue to experience the mental and physical anguish of the One Who so desires to see you baptized."

"I'd give anything, to bring an end to the division between you and that drummer-upper of instinctive responses hidden within you, long ago, to provide the antagonsim needed to reproduce the Trinity in the flesh. Anything," reiterated Michael, to the chagrin of that puny will of mine which had yet to see what little, other than its self-image, it had to give up to find peace of mind.

For I had yet to learn the hard truth, that one doesn't always get his way, especially in the military. But for the life of me, I couldn't figure out where my soul was hiding. Little did I know that she had gone out ahead of me, as usual, to prepare the way, like the calm before a storm. Because this fuckup had yet to prove himself with actions that spoke louder than words, I knew only that the day was fast approaching when the world would see how much greater than the Navy's was this newly acquired will of mine.

When it was announced from the bridge, later that morning, that all hands, not involved in maneuvering the ship over to the munitions depot, were to report to the quarterdeck to help reload her magazines, I went below to pass out laundry. Having let the Navy know, on several occasions, of my desire to be processed as a conscientious objector, I had assumed I would no longer be required to perform those tasks which, like the handling of ammunition, offended my sensibilities. So was I left alone to attend to the needs of this only–begotten son of mine, like a father in heaven, after the master–at–arms had brushed aside this task, in his sweep of the compartment space for stragglers, as unworthy of such a venerable god.

Nor was I asked to participate in any of the war games that filled up the rest of the crew's week out at sea. When general quarters was called, I simply got battened down in our sleeping quarters, to contemplate my next move in this one–man stand of mine against the Navy. For I wasn't too sure how much longer this pawn could protect its young king, that newly acquired will of mine, from being checkmated, without some assistance from its mother and queen of my soul.

"Check!" Hollered the White Knight as he ran the Black Knight through with his lance, driving fear forever from such a central position in my life.

"What is that black king, the Captain, going to do now that he's lost his first line of defense, fear itself," I wondered. "With the demise of his blackest knight, and some of the other projections that surrounded it, how will he protect his queen, the Great Gray Whore, from the onslaughts of the keener intellect of the white knight? How will he rook me out of a victory over his black will? Will he castle or throw me back in the brig for having moved against his kingship? Or will he simply wait for this impetuous young ward to make a stupid move?"

As I approached the fire that burned within, the very source of life itself, later that week, I found little to console me. Where was I to find soul when I needed her most, or food for thought and insight into my life without Michael and my mentor? Where indeed would I find a way to control the fire that consumed my flesh at such an alarming rate? Would I end up becoming an old man, like the astronaut in *2001: A Space Odyssey*, before my time? Or was I simply trying to give birth to an idea before its time?

Having peered ever more deeply into the fire that burned within, I caught sight of an image of my mother, I had never seen before—the inability to accept my own sexual feelings. No wonder I couldn't find soul, for I had damned her to hell with my own unsavory thoughts. With what timidity, did I first approach this

Black Madonna in the guise of a lone and rejected wolf! Like a long lost pet, was I accepted back into her arms.

"Why do you persist in refusing to accept Me as the Holy Spirit?" Inquired this image of the Virgin Mary, which did now stand before me in all Her glory.

Having been transformed back into my old self, was I left sitting there, staring into the red-hot coals of the fire which had just flickered out in a flash of bluish-white light. As I succumbed to the ground swell of thoughts and feelings this insight into the Trinity had stirred up, I found myself back in full possession of my faculties.

"Where have you guys been?" I affectionately inquired of them, for it seemed as if a long time had passed since last we had all gathered around the fire which burned inside my heart, to discuss anything of such import.

"We've been waiting for the beast within," chimed in my mentor, "to accept its rightful inheritance as the fourth member of the council."

"For you are the only link we have to She Who Must Be Obeyed," concluded my soul.

With that, they all got up to shower their affection on the wolf into whose form I had, once again, been unwittingly transformed.

"What's going on here?" Yelped the wolf in me, only this time, in a tongue that could be understood by both man and beast.

"You've acquired the form," replied my mentor, "with which you may descend to the depths of your animal nature without having to act like one in real life."

"For what purpose?" Inquired this dual aspect of myself.

"To free your humanity," answered my mentor, "from the clutches of Instinct."

"You see, my son," continued my mentor, "you need the beast, as much as it needs you, to give form to the formless."

"For is not the aim of the very act of sex, to fill that great void in one's life with the essence of Who He Really Is?" Inquired that greater intellect of mine, in whose shadow I stood.

"Blessed is he who enters the womb, a second time, with such noble intentions," declared my soul, "for he shall be born again as a eunuch."

"What is the formless?" Inquired I out of the beast's sense of something greater here, than a Jonah.

"Why it is the Original Being, She Who Must Be Obeyed and He Who Really Is rolled into one, of whom Jesus Christ is the prototype," replied my mentor.

"It is the image of the Trinity," added that guardian of the truth, hidden deep within the shadows of my nascent intellectual capabilities, "which has filled your body to overflowing with the desire to bring itself into existence."

"It is not enough," complained my soul, "that this image of the Virgin Mary has been freed from its bonds to that Black Madonna, Mother Earth, to flit about the void in heavenly bliss. No! For now She seeks to break through that glass ceiling, hidden deep within the mind of modern man, which has barred Her from entering that all–male bastion, the boardroom of the Holy Trinity. To unseat from the throne of God the flaming, masculine queen which mankind has placed there beside the Father and the Son, She needs a church mouse like you. She knows, though, that without Her blessing, no one in his right mind would dare to take on that bastion of men who have stood guard over Her womb since Her death. Thus has She chosen you, because of your openness to the truth, to champion Her cause."

Through the wolf did I finally succeed in focusing the compound eye of that fruit fly, which has hampered my sight since puberty, upon the true object of its lust, Wisdom in all her glory. For it appears I'd been summoned to that tiny islet in the South Pacific, known as Kahoolawe, to free this image of the Goddess from the once sacred grounds of the fertile minds of men over which now stood guard the big guns of our species, like ogres, in their readiness to shoot down any loose cannons like me. How could I persist in refusing to accept this holiest of spirits, the Virgin Mary Herself, as the embodiment of the Third Person of the Holy Trinity?

"Blasphemy! Blasphemy!" Screamed the big guns as they projected their irreverence for the sacred onto the tiny islet that served as a firing range instead.

Tossed up onto the jagged shores of Hawaii's biggest island, like a hermit monk did I stumble into the town of Hilo with my sidekick, Martin the talking horse, where I rented an old Datsun sedan to explore this cauldron of possibilities. For I sought a few days reprieve from the belly of the behemoth that now sat tethered to its anchor at a more respectable distance from the shores of the KT (Cretaceous-Tertiary) boundary in my life. And as I looked up at the mountain of new life slowly taking shape, I caught sight of that ever–elusive hole in the boundary between this epoch and the next, up along the east side of this sleeping giant. Filled with the desire to catch another glimpse of the Promised Land, I jumped into the car and sped off, barely cognizant of my chitchatting companion.

Captivated by the ever–changing face of the island, I could've sworn I passed through that time warp between this world and the next as I entered some of the most sacred ground on earth, those of Hawaii's Volcanoes National Park, where I observed, for the first time, the very act of creation in process. Having penetrated the womb of Mother Nature, I was excited, to no end, by the possibilities for expression that began to stir, like hot magma, from somewhere deep in the pit of my being. Overcome by the sudden rise of seminal ideas, I watched as the essence of Who I Am spewed itself out all over the ground of my being, in one of the most ecstatic eruptions of consciousness I'd ever experienced. Screeching to a halt, I jumped out of the car to get a closer look at the white coral–like fungus that covered, as far as the eye could see, the lava flow onto which we had stumbled.

"So that's how He does it!" Remarked the I That Can See.

"How who does what?" Muttered a mystified Marty.

"How God creates new life," I replied. "Through such concrete images, does He encourage us to play with our imaginations whene'er the tension in our bodies, between what is and what is not, rises to such a level that our bodies can no longer contain it. Whether we choose the more imaginative route or not, this essence of Who We Really Are is spewed out onto the ground of our beings, like the hoarfrost you see here, in a monumental effort to break the deadlock between what is and what isn't yet. Until the concrete images of the horrid reality we have created for ourselves are broken down by the fungus among us—individuals like you and me—the seeds of Consciousness will have no place to take root. For He is in great need of fertile minds in which to implant Himself and grow, if we are to survive the evolutionary changes being wrought upon us by our incorrigibility."

Only, I was being forced to live out the masturbatory fantasies of an unholy alliance between me, my self-image, and the I that cannot see—the bait the masters of this age used to attain their brand of immortality. To gain noteriety as a Master Baiter, or fisher of men, I would have to get these suckers hooked on another paradigm than the American Dream.

Wondering if I had stumbled upon the Gates of Eden, I climbed back into the car with my buddy, to continue our journey up God's holy mountain. Catching a glimpse, through the fluff that clouded my mind, of the paradise with which man had lost touch when he stepped from the womb to choose his fate, I stumbled upon a real-life facsimile of the back door through which this great evil had entered our lives. Jumping out of the car to get a closer look at the crack in Mother Nature's physique, from which arose this odor like the breath of some foul sulphurous fiend, I experienced some of the queerest feelings I'd ever encountered. In response to the urge to penetrate this crack, I stepped back for a moment to ascertain the true significance of this variation on the image I'd tried to fill back in Sasebo, Japan, last year. In my aversion, for such an unnatural act on the physical plane, I lost the opportunity to connect with something greater than a Jonah here. For unbeknownst to me, I could not have entered the Gates of Eden unpaired.

Nauseated by the stench of my thoughts, I hopped back into the car with that constant companion or facsimile of my body, Martin, the talking horse, to search for that way of life which could end this separation of wills between me, my self, and "I". Driven by my lust for the truth, I raced up the other side of this androgynous body of ours to embrace that breast of Mauna Loa, known in these parts as the Kilauea Krater. Ignoring the signs posted, to pass not beyond the bounds of behavior befitting a reasonable human being, like a horse's ass did I bolt for the rim of this great cauldron. Standing in awe of the sheer size of the gaping hole to which I'd been drawn, I searched in vain for the miracle that, like the one at Cana, could transform me into something a little more spectacular than a horned toad.

As I stood there, for a moment or two, the time it took for my buddy to catch up with me, I looked out over the two-mile wide orifice in her body to the seemingly bottomless secondary pit or back door to the interior world. There did I catch a glimpse of the marriage feast at Cana, a union of body and mind with this self of mine, the likes of which I had never encountered. The instant my body caught up with me, I was swept off my feet and transplanted onto the back of that gallant white steed of mine as the White Knight. Grabbing hold of my soul with one hand and the mane of the horse with the other, I flew across the heavens towards the Gates of Eden, lest they close before I got there. Upon passing through her gates, did I orgasm without ejaculating, at the same time that I felt someone else, oddly enough, orgasm as well.

"What the hell are you doin', Dury?" Shouted out that horse's ass who had come to a screeching halt just outside the Gates of Eden.

"Why I'm climbing down into the main pit to see how it is connected to the secondary one," I responded as I stepped off onto the first black boulder to greet my feet.

"You're nuts!" He shouted as I slid from one boulder to the next in my haste to get to the bottom of the great wall which had been erected, long ago, in the minds of men, to keep young acolytes, like me, from entering the sanctuary of God.

"Wait for me," yelled out my buddy ere I slipped from this world into the next, oblivious of the sights and sounds of the former.

For I'd found, that it is impossible for the self to remain fully present in both worlds at the same time and remember what has transpired. Since I couldn't be in two places at the same time to observe any single event, I generally opted to view it from the imaginal realm to get a better handle on what I was feeling in that instant. So would I temporarily lose touch with the material world, until she pulled me back, as she always did, from these paired experiences of the truth.

Thus did I get a closer look at the inner workings of the Trinity. With the fading of consciousness, was not I forced to return to the womb of she who rose up in the night sky to greet her beloved son, the sole disseminator of the truth of the event about to take place simultaneously on two different levels of reality.

Where else was I to find the hand to guide me through all of this, but within the confines of my imagination whose spirit knew not the separation from my body that I did? Had I indeed stumbled upon the very place where body and mind came together in the pursuit of that single-minded organism which might best reflect the intentions of these two seemingly irreconcilable opposites to overthrow Instinct, once and for all, as ruler of this precocious body of ours?

"Dammit, Dury, it's hotter than hell down here," bemoaned that nagging buddy of mine as he caught up with me.

Brought back to my senses, I turned around to capture on film the great barrier which, like the walls of Jericho, had collapsed in the face of the God Who dwelled hereabout. Having had the heat turned up on me, to either get with the program or crack, I spun around, despite the admonition not to—lest I be transformed into a pillar of society—to confront the destructive side of Sodom and Gomorrah. Like a knight in shining armor, did I leap from this body of mine and race after the desire to penetrate the secret of my dual nature. With a single thrust of my sword into the belly of this bisexual beast, I opened myself up to an encounter of my own conception. Filled with Sodom's desire for Gomorrah, did I get sucked into that eternal triangle, where I was subjected to the unkindest cut of all when Sodom tried to stab me in the back. Forced to the brink of this bottomless pit by his superior swordsmanship, I screamed out in unison with my body. In the hue and cry that went forth from our mouth, I watched as this image of him came tumbling down, till there was naught left but a huge black hole in the ground of my being.

Stepping back from the edge of this bottomless pit of hot gases and liquid shit, lest I jump in, I stood there, for God knows how long, frozen in time beside my body. While the earth whispered sweet nothings to me through the cracks and the fissures in this newly formed skin of hers, I found security in her love for me. As I turned to leave these sacred grounds before they burned the shoes of an old way of life off my feet, I ran into the realization that the Creator loved me too, only in a way, I was yet barely cognizant.

"Come on, Dury," cried out that riderless companion of mine, Martin the talking horse, "let's get the hell out of here while there's still enough light."

"Yeah," concurred the hermit monk in me whose feet were burning to get out of this black hole before their souls stumbled upon anymore of the ghostly images that seemed to erupt at the slightest nudge of Nature's breast for more milk. Nor did I have much else to say as we left Sodom and Gomorrah ere the sun set and shut us up in this tomb for having failed to leave this black hole in the time allotted.

Having put some distance between my self and this experience, I turned around, at the wolf's behest, to take another look, through his eyes, at what I had missed. Consumed by the red glow that emanated from the remains of this image of Sodom and Gomorrah, I found my self looking into the possibility of expressing these intangible views in a more tangible way. As the wolf then, was I being driven to reunite my self with my desire to give form to the formless.

On the way back to the car, was I inundated by those thoughts that'd been struggling to take shape in my mind, around that objection of mine to military service. For I wanted so badly to jot them all down ere losing their sound to the jabberwocky of my own body, I could've screamed "woe is me". Instead, I tried to remain focused on all this hocus-pocus, until I could compose it in lead.

"Well done!" Exclaimed my mentor as he drew near.

"And where have you been?" I inquired of him.

"Why I've been out getting a little exercise," he replied with great satisfaction. "How about your self?" He asked.

"You know damn well where I've been," groaned that pitiless self of mine.

With that did I break the spell that had held me bound to this rich black ground—a victim of my own bod's hell—till I should free from this pell-mell, the thoughts that did abound deep within the vast mound of Sodom and Gomorrah's swell or that which surrounds the one orgasm found with the scent of Wisdom's sweet smell. Like Sodom, would I have to slip through the back door to the mind, to free the creator within me from Nature's view of things. Having spent all the energy available to me for creating consciousness, I would have to wait until the next eruption of such codified material, to find out where to go from here.

Having not quite gotten to the bottom of the myth onto which I clung, I sank back down into the driver's seat of that hallmark of twentieth century space travel, ere I passed out from sheer exhaustion. Rent in two, did I sit there, next to this tired body of mine, wondering how long I'd been out of it—lost in the interstitial spaces of its own labyrinthine mind. Not until early the following morning, as I struggled to wake up from this dream, did I encounter the truth of the matter.

"I know a young man," proclaimed the wolf in me, "who fourteen hours ago was caught up to the third heaven, neither in the body nor out of the body, but with it. And I know that this same young man—again neither in the body nor out of the body, but with it, as God is my witness—was caught up to Paradise and heard things difficult to understand, much less to explain."

"Let me interrupt you here," interjected my mentor, "lest you slip from that twilit zone twixt wakefulness and sleep without some awareness of the importance of getting to the bottom of the desire for union with your body, before it gets to you."

"So that's it," I thought to my self as the devil at the bottom of this desire for union with my body lashed out at me.

"What're you gonna do now?" Inquired the deceitful snake as this mirage of a dick incognito gave way to the image of the private eye, I had taken on, late last summer, to unravel this mystery for me.

Left standing in front of a urinal holding onto an image of my mentor, I had never seen before, I slipped this newfound ability of mine, to penetrate the darker recesses of my being, back into its proper place in my life. For I had finally assumed the role of my mentor, the driving force behind this urge to get to the bottom of this desire for union with my body.

"You must write these experiences down ere you forget them," whispered my mentor from someplace so unusually close, I almost mistook his voice for my own.

"Write?" I muttered as I bent over a basin to splash some water on my face.

"That's right," echoed he this paired experience from somewhere across that great expanse of time which had elapsed since last this hermit monk had uttered these very words to his self.

"How much longer do you think you can keep me from the true intent of these encounters?" Asked the I That Can See of the one that cannot.

"As long as there are images that can keep their secrets to themselves," replied the snake, "I shall prevail."

"Then let the game begin," commanded that Private Eye who could see through all the hocus-pocus of this one-eyed jack and master of deceit, his twin brother and greatest adversary, Instinct.

"You see, my son," continued my mentor, with the disappearance of Instinct, "my brother and I represent the same force, only from two different points of view. With man's fall from grace, were we separated from each other for the first time, for up until then we had enjoyed a union of spirits no two entities have ever experienced, neither before nor since our break-up. Joined at the hips like two Siamese twins, were we pulled apart, in the ensuing divorce of man from his nature, and prevented by our parents from ever seeing each other again.

"As a result, neither of us see what the other sees in himself. For without insight, he cannot see me, or I, him, without sight. To each, the other is but a mere reflection of his self. Thus do we appear to be identical when, in reality, we are as different as the light and dark sides of your being, where only you can see first with the one eye that was born before me, then with the other. While I see only the truth in him, he sees me as a mirage, which leaves him with the advantage of having a picture worth a thousand of my words. And yet he possesses no more of that body of knowledge, to which he has laid claim, than I do.

"That is why," concluded my mentor, "he is trying to pigeonhole you before you find the way out of our dilemma."

"What d'ya mean?" I inquired.

"He means this," interjected my shadow, "be wary of Greeks bearing gifts."

What this enigmatic prattle had to do with me, I knew not. For I simply put off making any further inquiries into the matter until a later date, when the fear of what only my shadow knew had subsided enough to lay to rest the unsettled feelings this mirror image of them had stirred up. Thus, did I come to the realization that my thoughts were but mere reflections of my feelings, that Michael and Jinny were but two sides of the same coin like my mentor and Instinct. But whatever it was my faculties were trying so hard to hone in on had escaped me for now.

"Here you stand," neighed that nagging buddy of mine, Martin the talking horse, "up in the head, staring at Lord knows what, while we wait for your lordship to come down out of the clouds before you piss away another day dreaming."

Pulling myself together, I bid my mentor adieu, leaving behind this reflection on the greatest faculty I possessed for attaining direct knowledge of a matter without having to think about it or deduce it from the facts at hand.

"I'm coming," replied that hermit monk in me whose patience with the unreal life, he was being forced to lead, had worn thin. "Give me a minute."

"All right!" Neighed the old nag in Marty, with the same impatience.

Having freed the wolf within me from the lower strata of my being, I was a bit surprised when he rose to the surface to take possession of my body before I left the head. Boy did I feel bright-eyed and bushy-tailed. For I had finally slipped into the mode with which I was to greet this day.

"Blessed are the meek," declared Harold the hare to Red the fox as the two sat down opposite each other at the same table Marty and I had likewise plunked our selves down for breakfast, "for they shall inherit the one body."

"Nay," neighed the talking horse, "'tis a dark horse that wins the grand prix."

Now Red the fox said to Martin the talking horse, "rather, blessed be the most cunning 'n' lingual, for it is they who shall override the body's code."

"Nay," said the wolf in me, "it is the love of the soul that tames the beast."

"I think," said the fox to the wolf, "that it's the peacemaker, thy soul shall wed."

"What's going on here?" Wondered the wolf to my self.

"Does not the red fox fill a void in our life?" Asked my self.

"Yes!" Exclaimed the wolf. "For where there were three, there're now four."

"Is he the missing link?" Questioned that self of mine the wolf again.

"Nay," said he.

"Why do we all seem to represent the same person?" Inquired my self.

"That's the motto of the council," replied the wolf, "all for one, and one for all."

"What does that mean?" Snapped back that snide self of mine.

"It means," he assured me, "that you must walk in their shoes to become one."

"I take shit from no one," staunchly stipulated the stalking horse.

"That's you," cried out the wolf as he caught sight of my self in the horse's ass.

"You're goddamn right," asserted the horse's ass.

"And that is why you are persecuted," I replied, "for righteousness' sake."

"You mean fucked with," rebutted the horse that did stalk me.

"Lord have mercy!" Yelped the red fox as he choked on all of these feelings.

"Rather, have mercy on those of us whose lot in life is to be hunted down and devoured by the likes of you," demanded the Old Buck, "that you may have food for thought."

"You poor unpretentious thing," sneered the fox. "Why you'd be nothing but a bundle of nerves without my ability to assimilate you."

"And without my ability to tell you which, if any, of your pompous thoughts are real," asserted the White Rabbit, "you'd have nothing to chew on."

"O who will comfort me!" Muttered the White Wolf to my self after that lame-brained Martin had trampled my poetry with the vulgarity of a horse's ass.

"Blessed are those who hunger and thirst for the truth," proclaimed the White Rabbit, "for they shall indeed find it."

Thus did I come to the realization that intuitions alone are pretty lame until we give thought to the feelings stirred up by the senses that arouse intuitions from their slumber.

O how the wolf in me did long to return to the heights of God's holy mountain to free my faculties from their imprisonment in nature.

So did I come to a better understanding of that cryptic saying of Christ in which He tells us that we do not live on bread alone, but rather on every word that comes forth from the mouth of God. Only I never realized how much the form in which this manna came down from the heavens, depended upon those with whom one associated.

"Let's go you guys," proffered the wolf in me a way out of this stalemate.

So did I take off for God's holy mountain, only this time, with all of my faculties. Filled with the expectation of seeing the Creator, I was disappointed when we reached the peak of this experience, to find it blanketed in a thick cloud cover. Coming to a halt, ere I drove off the deep end, I got out of the car only to find my self standing there with my head literally in the clouds.

Disappointed, I turned around in time to see the talking horse transfigured into my mentor. And as his clothes grew dazzlingly white, I saw the one orgasm within the other. For in place of Harold the hare and Red the fox were left standing on either side of my mentor, in all their glory, my soul and Michael the Archangel, the archetype behind the White Knight. With that, I experienced a certain distaste in my mouth when it was mentioned that my mentor would soon be departing, as his work here neared completion.

Seeing how they were getting ready to leave, I said to my mentor, "Master, let us dwell here a little longer as I sense more lurking about this dark cloud."

As the terror of what I did not know, consumed my flesh at an alarming rate, there came from this dark cloud a voice. "Listen, my son, for you have been chosen to be a spokesperson for the Holiest of Virgins," it said, to allay my fears.

On the heels of the words of this singularity, did I find my self standing in the mist of a light shower from which the others had already sought refuge. As I too gathered my wits about myself, I was told to utter nigh a word to anyone concerning this encounter, until I understood it more fully. To this day, have I remained silent on the subject of the development of my faculties to their fullest extent.

Having cultivated a closer relationship with the talking horse than any of the others, I'd been left hanging from a cross with little support from the horizontal beam. In other words, I had given so little thought to the feelings which welled up from deep within my body that I suffered greatly at their hands. Had not I been used by the officials of this country to commit the most capricious acts of violence against a supposed lesser breed of man, I would never have been driven to seek out the red fox. For I had never learned to relate to my fellow man in any other way than the picturesque manner in which these feelings came to me on the vertical beam of this cross. And yet, I was being asked to not relay these feelings to my contemporaries in the manner in which they had appeared to me, thus forcing me to develop my own thoughts and feelings. Because I'd relied upon the white horse to do my talking for me, I had little else to share with my shipmates but what I'd dreamed up, until the red fox taught me to think for myself.

"How does one learn to think for himself?" Had I asked the fox back in the earlier stages of the development of a closer relationship between these bodily sensations of mine and the conjectures of a guilty bystander.

"One must first gather his wits about himself and whatever evidence he gleans from them, like the pieces of an unsolved mystery," had my cohort in crime replied. "And for that one must become a good listener, lest he stumble over a clue without recognizing it as such, and fall for something irrelevant to the matter at hand."

"Thus had I fallen from grace when I joined the Navy," I recalled thinking to myself that day as I sank back down into the fox's lair to listen to my thoughts.

So had I cut my self off from the life–giving waters of the steady stream of consciousness that had flowed so freely from the Gates of Eden in my youth, when I took on my mother's habit of worrying unduly. As a worrywart, had I lost touch, over time, with the objective truth of my dreams. Like Pan, had I gone off in search of the one nymph who could satisfy my desire for union with the truth of my being.

"Now you know how we feel," complained the White Rabbit.

"When emotions run high," captured the red fox my sentiments exactly.

"And seek expression," added the White Rabbit as it scurried on past me on the crest of an undulating wave of emotion.

"In one form or the other," concluded the red fox, "mine or the rabbit's."

With the disappearance of the white rabbit, I fell into a black hole as I tumbled from one side of my brain to the other. Having taken the rabbit up on its suggestion to exit stage left, did I scoot on over to the car. For had not I stumbled upon this place and seen, with my own eyes, the transformation of my faculties, I would never have come to believe in the evolution of the body.

"Blessed are those who have not seen and yet have come to believe," (Jn 20:29) commented the One Voice from somewhere across the great void which did still separate me from Who I Am.

"On behalf of such a one alone would I boast," addressed the Wolf this self of mine with all of its weaknesses—the cross from which did hang, like the crucified Christ, the truth of my being. "If I were you, I'd keep the extraordinary nature of these revelations to your self, so that no one may think better of you than what is seen or heard coming from you."

"My God!" Blurted out the red fox as it looked into the eyes of its soul, the white rabbit, and saw, for the first time, its own reflections. "Is that really you?"

"In the beginning was the Word, and the Word was God," (Jn 1:1) had the passage of the white rabbit from this world concluded.

To close the gap between my thoughts and feelings then, I had only to find a picture of my feelings worth a thousand words to the more thoughtful side of me.

For the more reactive side of my nature seemed to favor going back to a time when man, because he lacked the wherewithal to think for himself, had only to react to his projections as he saw fit.

In our failure to bring to the surface those parts of ourselves which remain far from consciousness, are we driven to turn on with whomever or whatever fills the bill, the price we pay for our projections. Thus do we fall for the quick fix, the picture worth a thousand words, rather than its true intent. For we find it hard to think when the senses can be satiated on such a low level at someone else's expense.

It's hard to see life for the zoo it is," concluded the more thoughtful side of me.

"Where the hell have you been?" Snarled the talking horse.

"At the zoo," I muttered much to Marty's bewilderment.

Only Red knew where I'd been, as he smiled at me from the back seat.

Why it was raining so hard by the time I got the car started, that I had to open the door and follow the white line down the middle of the road to get us out of there—the visibility was so poor. Never had I been inundated by so many thoughts as I followed the trail the white rabbit had left. Greeted by the sun as we descended from the peak of this experience, I could've sworn I'd seen the mating of the masculine and feminine sides of my nature, the one orgasm within the other—whether in the body or out of the body, only God knew for certain.

"Boy, is it steamy in here," declared the wolf as he rolled down the window to let a little fresh air into the car.

For I wasn't sure where I was being led till we hit bottom, one of the few black sand beaches in the world. Fearful of venturing out into the rough waters, which lashed out at us like an angry god from somewhere beneath the threshold of consciousness, I slipped from my shoes, at the behest of my soul. Using my hands and toes, I climbed up a nearby palm tree on the ridges left behind by succeeding generations of growth, to fetch her a coconut. Like my arboreal ancestors, did I use my head to satisfy that incredible hunger for the forbidden fruit of the gods or union with my body in thought and in deed—that orgasm within another I so sought.

Despite my lineage, I didn't know how I was going to open the coconut until I hit the ground. There, as Marty took the coconut and bashed it against a sharp volcanic rock with his thick powerful hands, did I rediscover the tool with which our arboreal ancestors had first gained access to their noggins. As I watched him rip through the hairy hide of the coconut, like the ape-man in *2001: A Space Odyssey* was I stirred from the deep slumber which has had us in its grip since the inception of life. Driven by the passion of the primitive man within to penetrate ever more deeply this thick skull of ours, I was so excited when Marty broke through the hymen-like membrane that has separated man from the womb of his imagination since the fall. Before he spilled the seminal contents of this nut onto the ground, I grabbed it and gulped down, with great relish, what not a single one of them dared to imbibe—the gall to resist the Navy in body as well as spirit.

"Why must I alone drink from this bittersweet cup?" Had I asked as the others milled about this dreamscape unaware of anything but the material realities that surrounded them, like a buffer zone to the truth.

"Was it not you," inquired that genie, I AM, "who summoned Me forth from the lamp of your imagination, in the brashness of your youth, to grant you your one wish in life, to be filled with the wisdom of Solomon?"

"At whose urging but your own," added that image of my self which had yet to define itself in terms of the Other.

Thus did I come to see that orgasm within another as an encounter of the third kind, or third heaven, depending upon whether it was experienced on the physical or the metaphysical plane. Whether in the body or out of the body, I saw this experience as key to freeing the truth of my being from its imprisonment in nature. Only I never knew whether I'd stumbled upon the truth, until I experienced that sudden release of energy or orgasm which almost always accompanied it across the threshold of consciousness, like a groom his new bride.

As the news of Martin Luther King's assassination spilled out over the airways, like the blood of some giant Christ-like figure, I turned to my shipmates to discuss the paradoxical nature of this orgasm within another, or annihilation of the imaginable by the unimaginable.

"I'm tellin' ya, Dury, this country's like a tinderbox, waitin' to explode," interjected Martin, the talking horse and self-proclaimed proponent of the violent overthrow of this country's plutarchy—that one-half of one percent of its population which now controls forty percent of its real wealth.

"A storm is indeed a-brewing," had that Moses, who failed to reach the Promised Land, forewarned what nigh a soul on earth shall be spared when the seas of the Permian kind rise up to vindicate She whom we disobey at our own peril.

For we are fighting on the wrong side of an evolving revolution to free ourselves from the masters of our slavery, the materialism and militarism that weaponize friend and foe alike to protect their transmutation of everything into gold as they continue to misuse and abuse the least to fill their coffers.

As card-carrying members of Uncle Sam's brand of service, we must recuse ourselves from a civil war that napalms the women and children of one house but leaves them widowed and orphaned back home, or returns the once humane, now mangled and deranged, to cope with the loss of the humanity he left lying at the foot of the cross from which he now hangs.

"Only we don't have much time," had he concluded, four months shy of his murder in Memphis, Tennessee, "to channel the anger of a world so out of kilter with the dictates of its own soul."

At that point, I fell prey to the unimaginable forces of nature and the despair that generally accompanied such falls from grace.

"Now that he is dead," inquired the missing link, "who'll lead us out of Egypt?"

"Do you really think King could've led us to the Promised Land?" Asked that other Martin in my life.

"I did," snapped the wolf in me ere Marty could bite back.

"Did you not see Moses in him?" Inquired the I That Can See beyond a stained looking glass.

"Now I guess you're gonna tell me that you saw Elijah in him, too," sniped the snide snip in Marty.

"No," I fired back, "because I see Elijah in you."

"I can't make myself as transparent as you, Dury," complained this pain in my ass, after having obviously been touched by what I'd said.

"If only you could step outside of yourself, and into my shoes," insisted the Elijah in me, "you'd see what I'm trying to say."

"If I could see what you are saying," replied the talking horse, "do you think I'd be standing here, begging you to help me see it?"

"Then close your eyes," reverberated the One Voice within me.

"What good'll that do?" Beseeched the blind beggar in my buddy.

"You'll never know until you try," rebuked the One Voice.

"I see trees," besmirched my blind buddy his field of vision.

"Take a closer look," encouraged the One Voice in me.

"Why I see..." stopped short he of the one Martin within the other.

"Jesus Christ, Marty! What the hell's the matter with you now?" I scolded him.

"I got somethin' in my eye," flicked he free the fleck of dirt that'd blinded him.

Whatever Marty saw that day earned his respect, for he never used the King's name in vain again. Often, thereafter, could he be heard putting in a good word for King, Martin Luther that is, and when the going got rough, even standing up for the dead man. Again, whatever it was that'd been resurrected from the dead, that day, sure transfigured Marty's outlook on life from thereon.

How easy it is, and yet so hard, to see things from another's perspective until we stumble upon an image shared by both. Facilitating such encounters, without sinking to the level of an animal, requires an openness to the truth that pushes us to the limits of our imaginations where we are forced to leave behind the concrete points of view which cause this normally placid sea of untamed feeling to rise up against us to rid ourselves of the rigid thinking that leads to war.

"The world can ill afford to lose men like King," reiterated the missing link.

"But neither could we afford to lose Christ when we did," echoed the lone monk who did bind the highest and lowest of the masculine pole into one person.

As the only link between my mentor and the wolf, did he begin to assume more authority in my life. For he'd apparently been conjured up by that blacksmith in the sky, to pound some sense into my head of where to go from here.

"Had not Christ died so that we might become more like him in his absence?" Had the fox asked of that unintelligible mass of flesh which doth surround us. "For does not absence make the heart grow fonder?" Had he pushed on.

"What are we to do?" Cried out the very soul of this massive mountain of flesh, as it pushed its way up from the south, to condemn this generation.

"Prepare for the Great Disruption!" Proclaimed the dead man's spirit to those of us who'd lead the survivors of the next mass extinction into the new millennium.

"How revolting!" Exclaimed the White Rabbit, in its natural aversion to death.

"Yes, how to revolt," rejoined the missing link, "without killing ourselves off first, that's the question to which there is but one answer, death to this recalcitrant self of ours which has set itself up as lord and master of the human race."

"For a mere pittance, do we sell our souls to the devil," interjected the red fox. "We would sooner stake our lives on Daniel Webster's hand than on Martin Luther King's. Such is the fate of this lot of reluctant revolutionaries."

"Until the dinosaurs die off," added the hare, in its earthy wisdom, "so must we like our ancestors, the mammals who survived the Cretaceous Period, bide our time, for we shall inherit the earth as they did."

"Having evolved as far as you have," concluded that insightful old steed, Martin the talking horse, in his finest performance as a supporting actor, "you obviously have a larger role to play in the evolution of the revolution to overthrow the dinosaurs. For it is you who has been cast in a leading role in this farce."

"It's not a farce," insisted the Creator of this modern-day Don Quixote.

"Yeah, right!" Snapped back the old nag in Marty.

"Just because you don't see things the way I do," insisted the I That Can See, "does not diminish the way I see reality."

"Well I'll tell you one damn thing, Dury," argued that snag in my ass, "I'd hate to have to rely on your story if I was standin' before the hangin' judge, cause I'd be a dead man."

"They refused Jesus too!" Fired back the young revolutionary in me.

"You're not Jesus," retorted this pain in my ass.

"Neither are you," sniped the guerrilla warrior in me.

"At least I don't try to act like Him," shot back the horse's ass.

"Isn't that what life is all about, the imitation of His?" I inquired.

"You're impossible," neighed the talking horse.

"Not so," I insisted, "for do I not stand before you, wounds and all, in the flesh? Persist no longer in your disbelief. Examine my wounds, and you will see they're as real as I AM."

So did end another round in the ongoing debate between the young god, whom my shipmates saw as their savior, and those reluctant revolutionaries upon whom I had foisted the burden of bearing the likenesses of my faculties. Was it asking too much of them, to bear some of the burden I carried as I made my way back up to Golgotha? Or was I asking them to do no more than what'd been asked of me, to take that next great step in the evolution of mankind while the opportunity did still dwell among them in a tangible way?

"O where the truth doth lie," quoth the poet in me, "I surely will not see, though time may reveal thee, till I hear thy sweet sigh."

Having deposited the once and future king back on board that vessel of destruction onto which this recalcitrant self of mine did cling, I fell fast asleep. As my mind drifted across the void, which separated me from this king, little did I know the death this kingship did entail. But how could I have known what awaited the king who had once presided over this body of mine, when Love did still reign supreme. Until She Who Must Be Obeyed departed from my body with Who I Am, and left behind my self, to live out a fate worse than hell, an eternity without soul, I longed for the return of the King and the death it implied.

When it came time for the Old King to rescue this body of ours from its mother's sin, the same attachment to Instinct that'd almost brought His reign to ruin before He'd had the chance to show us what a snake His alter ego had become, He molted. Rejected by the very monster He'd created out of His love for the instinctive, He now stood the chance of losing everything to this Frankenstein if He didn't step down from His throne and confront the ego like a man. Not until soul had freed herself from His side, could He consider taking on the task of recreating Himself in her image and His likeness. For had He not allowed Himself to be killed off by His own creation, He would never have moved beyond the cycle of life and death, the old way of life had engendered. Thus did He give berth to the Original Being, that existed before It split Itself into heaven and earth—the masculine and the feminine.

So, too, did the Old King throw off the instinct to recreate one's self in its own image and likeness rather than that of the Original Being.

As an observer of the divine drama unfolding before my eyes, did I come to see the breadth and depth of the evolution revolution that has been coming, like a slow train around that bend in the space–time continuum we inhabit.

2

The Real Information Superhighway

"May I have a seat?" Inquired the wild boar of its unwary quarry, that Adonis in me who did sit there, like a monument to the dead, on a park bench back down on Waikiki, pining away for his Aphrodite.

"We feel so much," proffered the White Rabbit in me as this Adonis looked up into the eyes of his predator to catch a glimpse of the Adonai or that aspect of God, which did still elude his grasp. "And yet we know so little about ourselves. Wouldn't you agree?" Had the White Rabbit asked of its bane to no avail.

What this namesake of mine saw in me remained a mystery until he decided to invade my space in such an obtuse manner. Having chased Aphrodite off, did he like Pan appear in all his glory to name my demon, of all things. Only he exposed his own, for Pan was and still is his image of god, not mine.

"I work for that mad-hatted ego of ours, known in these quarters as Uncle Sam," had I responded to the next question to pop out of the mouth of this predaceous bore once he'd determined that I shared his name, however remotely.

"And you?" I finally got around to asking him. "Whata you do for a living?"

"Why I'm a drama student at the University of Hawaii," had he responded forthrightly.

"Another James Dean," the thought occurred to me.

"Well I'm a rebel too," I went on to say, in a manner of speaking, like the dead actor, "but not without just cause."

"I wanna be an actor," interjected this James Dean wanna-be.

"Why I'm already an actor," replied the rebel, "in a divine tragedy."

"How so?" Inquired the would-be actor.

"As a sentinel for the House of Uncle Sam," responded this New Age Jonah, "am I being crucified for my stance against the war in Vietnam."

"How noble of you!" Declared the wanna-be in his lust for real life without having to walk that extra mile in the image of anyone else but his own puffed-up ego, for he wanted badly what was not yet his nor mine—a life of our own, no matter how mismatched.

"And O how my soul does pine away for union with its Creator!" Exclaimed the I that could still not see what did yet prey upon my mind.

"Only you lack the balls to stand up to these assholes," had that aspect of the Adonai, with which he identified, so prophetically proclaimed.

"Maybe so," muttered the Adonis in me who seemed to have lost his way in the face of this real-life facsimile of my own obsessive-compulsive alter ego.

Just then did the heavens rain down upon our heads a shower of such magnitude that we were forced to seek shelter.

"Come with me!" Commanded he who had not the balls to act out his fantasies on any other stage of life than the beastly side of nature.

"Enter ye instead, through the narrow gate," commandeered the One Voice as I raced off after he who sought to penetrate the back door to the mind of this god, *"for wide is the gate and easy the road that leads to destruction, and many are they who take it. How narrow is the gate and hard the road that leads to life, and how few are they who ever find it."* Mt 7:13-14.

Once inside his beach-front lair, did this other butch disappear into his den to don dry duds—a short pair of hot pants overridden by a tight-fitting tank top—before plunking himself down on the couch beside his next intended victim, an unwary white rabbit, and placing his hand upon the thigh of this Adonis, much to its surprise. Sensing the uneasiness of his quarry as it leapt free of his grasp and bounded down to the other end of the couch to keep from getting gored by this boar, did the foul fiend spring forth from this fen of iniquity, only to come bouncing back from his boudoir with a full-length photo of the pud puller of the month, a real-life facsimile of Pan himself in all his glory.

"My god—what do you think of him?" Inquired one hell of a sexually aroused boar of his Adonis.

"Beware of Greeks bearing gifts," came back the words of my shadow from somewhere out across the great void in my life which did still separate me from the truth of this matter.

Wounding the boar with a verbal thrust that sent it reeling to its boudoir, did this avid admirer of Aphrodite make a mad dash for the very door, which alone could free him from having to live out this fantasy on the physical plane. Leaping free of the physical restraints that held his friend, now turned foe, bound to the male member of his body, did not this Adonis find himself the object of a manhunt by the angry boar, as it chased him through the backyards of reality and over her fences in a last-ditch effort to bring him down to its level, for it knew not how to meet the demands of its masculine pole in any other form than the rapaciousness of a mad rapist. Hopping out onto the main drag where lay hidden yet, in the safety of numbers, the road less traveled, that narrow byway between body and mind which doth unite both image and likeness, without force or farce, back into one harmonious whole, did thus the rabbit escape this hellhole or warp in the face of this man's soul which doth impose the flaming queen's role upon those of us who bear the toll of carrying for him his own pole.

And so did I get a closer look at this desire for union that my creative daimon had for me. Having yet failed to meet this challenge on the metaphysical plane, was I forced, much to my chagrin, to confront it on the physical side of reality, for SHE must be obeyed one way or the other. To meet the demands of my masculine pole, I had to forgo the animal aspect of whatever its polar opposite was asking of me. In denying my host communion with me on such a low level, did not I give the male member of my body access to its self, for the first time ever, with all the force and the farce of a bard instead.

"Bravo! Bravo! Bravo!" Yelled out that triumvirate of faculties, which did enter my awareness as I stepped forth from this real-life fantasy to examine it, as usual, from a more objective point of view.

"Damn, that was close!" Exclaimed the White Knight in me who had just defeated the Fat Man, only this time in the guise of my soul.

"Had not you taken Jinny's place," insisted my mentor, "you would never have freed your imagination from the grasp of this goaty god of rape."

"And had not you been seen, by the Adversary, as a molly or flaming queen," interjected my shadow, "you would never have gotten involved in the affairs of that other man in your life, the male member of your body. Nor would you have ever freed him from his tendency to go poking around in the affairs of other men's lives via the holes in everyone elses but his own."

"For the beast doth speak with a forked tongue," proclaimed my mentor.

"In other words," piped up my soul, who'd been sitting quietly by, until now, "doth he speak in double entendre, the language of both the body and the mind."

"Only he doesn't know that," added my mentor, "for he never sees any other side of the story but his own."

"What my father's trying to tell you in a roundabout way," exclaimed my soul, "is that the beast interprets everything in terms of its own bodily functions."

"Had not the Creator hidden Truth in Nature," insisted my mentor, "this amalgam of the two would never have been born."

"True," exclaimed my shadow, "but then neither would we, for we'd have no body upon which to reflect."

"So must you," concluded my mentor, "learn to speak from both sides of the brain, for mankind faces no greater danger than sincere ignorance whether it comes from the right or from the left."

Thus had I, in a moment of weakness, almost allowed a male member of the body to venture forth where no man has ever dared to go, to wreak havoc upon my soul. Only I'd failed to find anyone in real life with whom I could satisfy that ever-growing need of mine to unburden myself of soul with impunity. So did I saunter off, wrapped in feeling, like the man in the mood, that paired experience from which I seemed so unable to free my self, for now.

Having made, without bail, the ship instead of jail, I collapsed in a heap to make the quantum leap from here to a tourney with him whom I journey that male member of mine who'd yet to rise 'n' shine in serendipity for all eternity.

Like a queen who'd lost her king, or so she thought, to the hinterlands of the mind, did I drag my ass out of bed the following morning to saddle up for the next available search party to leave the here and now for parts unknown. Accompanied by my thoughts, as I set off in the guise of the feminine member of my body, did I pick up on the idea to approach the base chaplain, a kindly old soul surrounded by an aura of truth which did ooze from his being with the smell of Wisdom's sweet scent. Having been attracted to him through his homilies, did not I stop by his office roundabout noon, only to find that the integrated old fool had gone on vacation, according to his secretary, for two weeks.

Alas! How was I to deal with the constant barrage of conscientious objections that my body, which prodded me on to union with itself, threw up in my face at every turn. Whether in the body or out of the body, I knew not until I'd dragged its feet long enough to force it to prey upon my self in the only manner left him who refuses to enter the narrow gate, that back door to the mind of this god, to put to rest this god-awful thing, Pan at his best. Like Jesus, the key master of old, would I need a hand from someone beside my self, a gatekeeper as it were, to the road less traveled. How else was I to free this son of mine, or newest-born aspect of myself, from the myth of the eternal return, from being conceived over and over in the minds of men with no shot at real life because no one dared to take his place other than by stealth, disguised as that member of the body known in these parts as the Old Fisher King.

With that, did I slip a little further into the Pit of Despair, only because I hadn't sunk low enough to come to the bottom of the matter at hand, the true nature of that orgasm within another bottom, that is. With nowhere to turn, did not I wallow around in the midst of this paired experience with little hope of finding anyone to fit the bill. Like an ass, had I slipped off, into the asinine hole I'd dug for myself in my despair over ever finding a way out of having to live out this myth on any other level than that of an animal.

Looking a bit like some Looney Tune caricature, did I rise up, before the threshold of Consciousness, to confront he who had been masquerading as the master of my household for some time now. Shot down, not once but twice, by this image of Pan for my insubordination, had I slunk from the confessional a broken man. Having failed to grab hold of any other image for the Creator, was not I compelled to take Pan's place, instead.

As I fell further into this fit of despair, I plopped my self down on a pew nearby, in an attempt to gather my wits about its ever-vanishing form before I took what remained of its life into my own hands.

Grabbing hold of the New Testament from the pew to which I'd been drawn, did I open my self up instead to a visitation from the dead, that I might end this fight to catch sight, in one frightfully bright flash of light, the St. Paul in ol' Saul with the gall to stand tall before all ere he fall into the hands of ol' Saul's demon, the pandemonium of Pan.

Through his writings, did I first learn of Paul's problem with Pan, one much like my own in every respect but this: he never gave into Pan after he'd been knocked from his high horse by that bolt from the blue, to grovel about the ground of his being on all four until he stumbled upon the real power of the male member of his body or that which is made perfect in weakness. For my own regeneration did not I seek such unmerited divine assistance, as I would otherwise have remained blind to the true nature of the male member of my body. In other words, had not I been allowed to explore this third heaven of Paul's, or head of mine, a little further, that is, from my own perspective rather than someone else's, I would never have learned to think for myself, a prerequisite for freeing the creator within oneself from the power of Pan.

Having heard things that are not to be told, that no mortal is permitted to repeat, had I, like Paul, wandered off in my blindness to those regions of the mind where lay hidden, in the queerest of synchronistic events, The Way—Catholic viewpoints of men who shared my sentiments with regard to war, from the perspective of a magazine of the same name, loaded with the kind of ammunition I would need to defend myself against the Navy. Like Eve did I pluck this fruit from the magazine rack at the back of church to arouse the natural man in me from his slumber, that he might turn to reason instead of treason for guidance. And as I slipped through the back door to the mind of God via the cover of the magazine, I finally got to the bottom of the matter at hand, for indeed had not I found someone with whom I could correspond or at least have intercourse with impunity.

"No more war! War, never again!" Repeated the magazine the words of Pope Paul VI, which did cut a great swath or abyss between himself and the massive military machine from which the bigger piggies of this country gross billions while the little piggies at the bottom, for whom life is only getting worse, exact no more from their piggie masters than their share of the nightmare.

"The oligarchy in America acts as if it doesn't exist," interjected my shadow, "a slight of hand that depends entirely upon the little piggies' unwillingness to face reality. Any piggie, big or little, who can't see the oligarchist for the trees, need only walk down the main drag of any large city, choked with its monuments to commercialism, like an overcrowded cemetery..."

As I stepped from church, armed with the only weapon that could save mankind from himself, the truth of the male member of his body, did not I stumble upon those monuments or erections of Pan to which my attention had been drawn.

"Well do you love me?" Inquired the Male Member of my body."

"You know that I do," replied the saintly Peter who stood in my stead.

"Then feed my body," commanded the head of this Peter.

"Well do you love me?" Persisted the only member of the body to have given life His best shot.

"I do," did the cock crow, not once but twice.

"Do you love me?" Asked the Male Member of my body, a third time.

"Jesus, you know I do," exclaimed this Peter of mine ere he collapsed in a heap trying to get to the bottom of this matter with impunity.

"Then tend to my body, only from the bottom up," commanded He Who did stand out from this mountain of flesh as a beacon to all, "and I will raise you up, on the last day."

And so did the Male Member of my body indicate the sort of death by which this self of mine was to give glory to God.

"So voracious is the appetite of this bigger breed of pig," said my shadow, "that it sends two–thirds of its own flesh, runts like you, to bed hungry if not starving for a life of your own, while they spend billions to avoid reaching critical mass or that weight at which these hogs are rounded up and butchered by the rest of you, in a mad frenzy of the survival of the fittest, for having tipped their scale of consumption beyond the current threshold of three–quarters of the world's resources."

"The closer you get to the heart of the oligarchy," added my shadow, "the more alike the bigger piggies begin to look. In fact, the bigger piggies that run big business start looking a lot like the bigger piggies that run big labor and the bigger piggies in charge of the big media chains and big universities. They don the same piggie appparel. They use the same piggie lingo and mannerisms, and walk with the same piggie swagger. They devour the same vittles and imbibe the same libations. They dabble in the same sports and drool over the same pabulem..."

"Many moons ago," interjected my mentor, "when Love was still Lord of all, did the body of man reject me as its seer, as it had, many times over, the Lord as its ruler, desiring instead to be governed by a king, like other nations. And so was it warned, as I had been instructed by the Lord, of the pitfalls of appointing a male member of the body to such a prominent position.

"These will be the ways of the king who will reign over you," had I told them. *"He will take your sons and appoint them to his chariots and to be his horsemen, and to run before his chariots, and he will appoint for himself commanders of thousands and commanders of fifties, and some to plow his ground and to reap his harvest, and to make his implements of war and the equipment of his chariots. He will take your daughters to be perfumers and cooks and bakers. He will take the best of your fields and vineyards and olive orchards and give them to his courtiers. He will take one-tenth of your grain and of your vineyards and give it to his officers and his courtiers. He will take the best of your cattle and donkeys, and put them to his work. He will take one-tenth of your flocks, and you shall be his slaves. And in that day you will cry out because of your king, whom you have chosen for yourselves; but the Lord will not answer you."* 1 Sm 8:11-18.

"Now the body was so desirous of union with the divinity of its male member," concluded my mentor, "that the Lord set a king over it, thus giving rise to that military-industrial complex hidden deep within the psyche of modern man."

I returned to the ship to fire off a letter of distress to the editor of the magazine I'd found there for less. Ere falling asleep at this fork in the road, was I consumed by my zeal to get the rogue who had taken off with my heart, earlier, on my steed for the wilder side of nature. On crossing the threshold tween wakefulness and sleep, in my haste to recapture the dastardly thief, I let my bod smolder and fume beyond belief. With nobody to turn to but a rascally baboon, did I go traipsing off to the exchange roundabout noon, to trade in the fur under which I did broil, for the shell of an incubating egg's toil. Checking into that room with a view, my head, to escape the encounter that lie ahead, did I stumble upon the Bible instead. And as this cock emerged from its shell, did not I find strength in my own hell. Half-cocked, like some silver-haired baboon, did I go off to shoot down the goon, my rival in human form, who'd demand me to conform, very shortly, to the norm.

Thus did I, at the mere mention of my name, fall from grace that day.

"Drury, why haven't you saluted me?" Demanded this Dapper Dan of his unwary quarry as I fell from my tree, wounded by this shot in the dark.

"I didn't see you," took I to task this petty tyrant.

"You do now," admitted this mirror image of my self.

"I do?" Questioned a somewhat befuddled baboon, what he actually saw.

"Then salute me," commanded that fastidious fob, First Division's junior officer.

"There is but one Lord to Whom I pay homage, and that's not you by any stretch of the imagination. For you fall so far short of the mark that you don't even deserve a simple salute," lashed out that fiery tongue of mine as I marched off to mail my manifesto to the editor of Way.

"Come back here, Drury, and pay homage to me," lorded his lordship over this lordling no more.

Having unseated my self from the throne, did I make way for the return of the King, who was closer to me now, than I imagined. As I sat up topside, listening to my heart beat to the pitter-patter of soul's feet coming up this drive for wholeness, I wandered off into that timeless realm where ticked my body's clock in anticipation of tomorrow's summary court-martial for the subordination of this instinctive will of mine to that of the only other member of my household, besides His Mother, to have survived His death. Like Christ, did I sweat the night away, for had not I been smitten with such passion for union with the Male Member of my body, I would never have found the courage to face the death of "me". With the impalement of this snake upon life's turnpike, had I awakened from a restless night's sleep, looking a bit more like the risen Christ than a condemned man.

With the arrival of the Judas priest, the Captain had appointed to preside over this facade of justice, did my soul burst upon the scene in an unprecedented move to grab my attention. Looking a bit like the risen Mary, she left me standing there dumbfounded by this outward appearance of her in his stateroom, of all places.

Breathing a sigh too deep for words, did I, in my own dyslexic way, beseech the holy spirit who had just availed herself to me as the Holy Ghost.

"Nolo contendere," pled he who, at the prodding of the XO to enter a plea without counsel, had so readily dissociated himself from his feelings.

"You don't trust me," contended this ghostly counterpart of mine, who had so often in the past come to my aid at such times as these.

"I'm sorry," stammered the self-styled sociopath that'd surfaced.

With that, did the embodiment of the most sacred of these feelings come crashing back into my awareness, the modus vivendi I reluctantly shared with her, to renew our wedding vows, of all things.

So did the resister in me vow to resist her no longer in his testimony before the high priest presiding over this matter. In his stubborn refusal to pay homage to the false fatherly figure of the Great Gray Whore who had demanded it of him, the day before, had he embraced a whole new way of life, She Who Must Be Obeyed if he was to make peace with the little bit of flesh that stood between them as a constant reminder of their indissolubility. Having been docked one month's pay and sentenced to thirty days of confinement at hard labor, did this cock stand up, at her enticement, to inform the Captain's cronies to expect more of the same until the son, who had risen up in him, had been put into a noncombatant status ere being discharged from the Navy as a conscientious objector.

In the guise of a lone jailbird, was this thorn in their side hauled off to the brig to pay for its awful crime as an accomplice to the reunion of its seemingly disparate members, that dynamic duo of body and soul responsible for the birth of this bright idea to disparage an icon of the Great Gray Whore with such acridity.

Confined to medium security, a densely populated barracoon of bunk beds bordered by bars of steel on all sides but the head to the south, I spent the rest of the day listening to my cellmates unburden themselves of soul as she struggled in vain, on the threshold of consciousness, to push open the door that stood between them and the real source of their discontent. I was the only one who could see her hand in their unsuccessful elopements down the darker avenues of life, those long drug induced stupors and absences without leave or meldings of self with a new identity incapble of fooling forever the vultures over in CID, the Criminal Investigations Division of the Navy, with nothing better to do than to prey upon those serving time for an offense they had not committed. Unable to contain myself any longer, like the cryptographer I had met earlier, who'd been turned on by the little shit disturber LSD—the code name by which he knew her—did I reveal the conscientious objector hidden behind the behavior responsible for the capture of the lover at the bottom of this matter, that orgasm within a significant other.

Having sensed, as I lay there, later on that evening, struggling to close the door on the day long after the others had stumbled across its tiny threshold, that I was being watched, looking up I caught sight of my soul standing at the foot of my bunk, determined to debunk the myth that had me in its grip.

"What d'ya want?" Asked the need for instant gratification of its reflection.

"Take me," reflected she who stood to take my place if only I'd let her.

"Here, in the middle of the brig?" Let loose the lazy lout lying on his bunk.

"Why not?" Teased the temptress trying to get him to stand up for himself, as she clawed away at the gap that'd grown up between them but now seemed to be narrowing itself down to a mere slit in the fabric of life.

As a compassionate man did I rise above the ways of the world to meet the need of mine to penetrate the imagination in such a compelling manner. Thus did I learn how one's conscience is pricked. And to think, I had only to rub the lazy lout the wrong way in the privacy of my own womb. Via guilt by association did I find my way back to Paradise, that peak experience which doth take us beyond our selves—whether in the body or out of the body, only God knows.

"Look!" Exclaimed that part of me which'd just leapt free of my body in ectasy.

"'Tis the yellow brick road," rejoined my soul, "that doth wind its way betwixt your domain and mine, the right and left lobes of the brain."

"The road to heaven," cried out its creator in conjunction with my voice.

"Or orgasm within another," persisted this imponderable projection of the implausible onto the superficially pleasing.

"Or need to ejaculate," wondered the womb in whose shadow I now stood.

"In words," called out that concern of mine with the conception of the inconceivable ere the poor pauper petered out on the impeccable.

"Rather than deeds," whetted she my curiosity for what I knew not.

Consumed by a great gray notion to protest any attempt on the part of the Navy to assimilate me, I found my self in the belly of a whale of an idea that wouldn't let me shrink, as customary after such encounters, from my responsibility to this newly conceived brainchild of mine no matter how nascent the concept.

"Do it as I duet," created the creator of this creation.

"That's it!" Exclaimed Michael and Jinny in unison with each other.

"Do it as we duet," alluded she to that orgasm within another, the little bit of flesh I had to give them before I could take their place.

"Don't you see," surmised that shadowy sidekick of mine, "the true significance of the bisexual beast which has taunted you—both in the body and out of the body as only God knows—to defrock it of its main attraction, that oral/anal stage in the development of an individual whereby one gets sucked into a passive dependency upon the very aggressor who continues to fuck with him and his soul until he learns to speak up on their behalf?"

"So have we come as close as we can," concluded my mentor, "to getting you back in touch with your thoughts and your feelings. It's up to you now, my son, to act upon them one way or the other, as man or beast."

Having grasped the essence of soul, I embraced the role imposed upon me by my own pole and stepping across the threshold did, as I'd been told, act very bold ere my feet got cold. Aback pants and shirt of dungaree and shirt down under, my last you see, did I with a peace symbol's cross wrought words o'er which men fought without much thought, nonviolence taught the Christ I sought.

"What the fuck's this shit?" Growled the guard who'd been barred, before now, from the bard in his ward.

"Why it's a peace symbol, sir," sported the cat in the pokey, "encircled by the words 'Christ taught nonviolence'."

"I can read, Dury," sneered the sentry who wondered why I had mired the uniform down with the sign of the cross.

"Why for the same reason you admire the uniform," maintained the marked man in me, "its opposition to change."

The Real Information Superhighway

"Gimme the goddamn shirt, Dury," demanded that Darwinian throwback to the dictatorial days of yesteryear, when the uniformity of natural selection prevailed over the forces of evolution.

Responding to the dictates of my soul, I let 'm have it right between the I(s), that is, betwixt his self and mine, the "not I" and I. Caught off guard by the appearance of yet another sign from God to evolve, did "not I" request my self to relinquish control of the shirt from down under as well. With great disdain did "not I" receive what was not I. And had not I exposed the real culprit here, the dove riding my ass, I would never have stripped my soul of all pretense, the pants that set me at odds with the man upstairs. Having thus bared my soul of what was truly not I, was I left standing there alone in my skivvies, but not for long.

Turning around, I found my self standing neath the trees of Eden. At one with my own nature again, I stood back to take in the fullness of this experience before it disappeared. "I Am Who I Am," thought I ere being pulled back by the sound of keys slamming up against the locked box that normally held such intrusions at bay.

"Dury, get your ass over here," barked that badgerer of bards, the red-haired rednecked marine sergeant who'd blasted my butt once before with brigandage, the language of this new age of Neanderthals.

Like Adam and Eve after the fall, did I respond to his lordship's call.

"Wipe that smile off yer face," bellowed the Cro-Magnon man's bane.

Overjoyed by my union with soul at this level, did I seek out the David in old Saul's devil.

"What the fuck's this shit, Dury?" Let rip the red devil, as David's foe flung his face up into mine with the uniformity of natural selection—a stepfather's glare.

Nonplussed by his emotional bluster, like a full moon did I beam with love's luster.

"I think yer yella, Dury, one of those pussy-assed peace protesters," pecked away the petty tyrant at my chest, with his finger, in a feeble attempt to open up Pandora's box to his aggression.

I had naught to say as I held 'm at bay, for I was okay as long as I held sway.

"They shoulda shipped yer yella ass over to Nam," proclaimed the polecat who'd stripped me of the lie they had thrown up into my face with such uniformity.

"To hell and back I've been," slung the slayer of Goliath the words of his Bathsheba at this bright shining lieth.

"You ain't seen nothin' yet, Dury, till you find yer ass back in solitary, starin' at four white walls," reared back the red devil. "And that's where yer gonna find yer fuckin' ass if I see anymore of this goddamn shit on yer clothes. Ya got that mister."

"Peace I leave with you; my peace I give you," exorcised my pole this poor devil's soul, to escape death's throe to no avail though.

"As far as I'm concerned, you can take yer God and His peace and shove it up yer fuckin' ass, Dury," maligned this maniac marine the only member of my body to have risen above such cockamamie.

From the two rose the one passive-aggressive son, child of both moon and sun, a light overcome by none.

"And ya better get some clothes on that scrawny ass of yers," warned the wasp who had tried to sting me, "if you don't wanna find it sittin' on a cold slab back in solitary."

Having come out of the closet, as a poet did I posit in boxer shorts ere my cohorts, a new folk hero of sorts, whom they so graciously redressed lest he be pressed, as had been stressed by the red guard with no regard for the feelings of this young bard, to penetrate that hellish hole within his soul where lie his role, the inherent predicament of solitary confinement.

To set this poetry in motion, I had only to put my trust in my soul as she set off with my hand in hers, down that byway betwixt her domain and mine, the right and left lobes of the brain wherein dwelt the purest of thoughts and the holiest of feelings in perfect harmony. However, until I walked that extra mile in her shoes or took her place, I found not the words to express what I was feeling, for she gave naught to him who gave not his all to her. For I had only to give my feelings a little thought, to gain access to the womb of my imagination.

As sleep overtook my body that night, I rose from this near death experience to roam about its dreary landscape—whether in the body or out of the body, only God knows—in search of dreamtime's secret, the reunification of what had been torn asunder that day to create consciousness, for I had yet to embrace the more aggressive side of my nature without being devoured by it like the sacrificial lamb. Consumed by the lion's share of this desire, I coughed up the half-digested body of a red and white knight, one well dressed in the aggressivity and passivity of his nature. As the lion and the lamb on his shield embraced each other in a manner unheard of in nature, I saw a knight of incredible stature rise up from the remains of the day to become one with me. So did I rise from the dead, the following morning, like that passive-aggressive son of mine, to show my contemporaries how the opposites are reconciled both within oneself as well as without.

With this shift to the red end of the spectrum, was I brought before the Brig Warden to explain myself. Having gravitated to my feelings, did I blush at my loss for words as this truth radiated from my face on an inaudible wavelength.

"I want to see a priest," unfurled the red and white knight the truth that had surfaced.

"The only thing yer gonna see," belied the Keeper of the Keep, "are yer own goddamn clothes."

The Real Information Superhighway

"Take 'm down to the yard," instructed he the guard I'd let down, "and have 'm scrub these marks off his clothes with a brush, soap and water."

"But Sir," protested the prisoner of their minds, "the marks are indelible."

"That's yer problem," sneered the lieutenant, "not mine."

But it was his. And I wasn't about to let him forget it, either.

Given a can of scouring powder, a bucket of water, and a small stiff-haired brush, I scrubbed my shirt till I'd rubbed a hole in it, into which hopped the white rabbit with the disappearance or letting down of my guard, the one who'd been watching me, to see that I didn't cross the line between his world and mine. With the collision of that mad-hatted ego of mine with my old friends the red fox and white rabbit, that is my own yet unrevealed thoughts and feelings, I picked myself up off the ground of my being, dressed as a red and white knight. Armed with a can of scouring powder, did I scour a huge peace symbol in the blacktop.

"Come here, Dury," commanded the guard whose job it was to keep such incursions at bay.

"Yes, sir," responded this recalcitrant self of mine.

"Take this box of soap and long-handled brush," demanded not my god, "and clean up the fuckin' mess you've made."

"Yes, sir," replied the dreamer in me eager to earn his wings.

Carried aloft by my imagination, I found my self adrift in a sea of white foam from which there seemed to be no escape until the guard, I'd let down, decided that rubbing him the wrong way wasn't what he had in mind when he took the God in me to task for playing with my self.

"Dury, come here," ordered he who still could not see God's handiwork in me. "Take this bucket and pick up every pebble on the blacktop."

RECORDER: *Objection. I object to this line of testimony as being totally irrelevant to the proceedings here.*

SENIOR MEMBER: *The objection is noted. But due to the fact that this is his statement, he will be allowed to continue on until he has finished.*

"Yes, sir," asserted the young God in me as he reached out to grasp hold of my hand while holding tightly onto his mother's with his other hand.

So did we play together as a family for the first time since the birth of this "little objection" of mine to military service as we arranged the pebbles in the bottom of the bucket, in the form of a peace symbol, the sign of my having finally reconciled this will of mine with the true intent of the inclinations of my body.

"Dury," groaned the guard I had let down, a third time, "I want you to take this push broom, and sweep up all the dust from the blacktop."

To seal the pact I'd made with my soul, I swept a huge peace symbol in the dust that'd gathered due to prolonged disuse of this region of my brain. With that, I reached the limit of what patience the guard had left as he pulled me back into his world by the collar of my shirt. Like Christ was I hauled before the procurator of the facade behind which I did reside as a prisoner of their minds.

"You yella–bellied, motherfuckin', goddamn–communist peace creep," snarled the Brig Warden as he got up into my face with a fist full of wet clothes and sour puss to demand the meaning of all this. Having caught sight, as he circled round me, of an unconscious aspect of himself with which he could not deal, he grabbed hold of me, by the scruff of the neck and the back of my pants, spinning me about before I realized what was happening, and threw me out the door.

For all of my efforts to bring to the surface the young whippersnapper within, who doth so oppose the makers of war, I was taken aback, after I picked myself up off the floor, to seg, segregated confinement, that is, where I was confined to a cell of my own after having been charged with the disruption of daily routine.

O how wondrous was this union with my cell, as it swallowed me up like an egg, a single spermatozoon. What remained of this immensely pleasurable albeit evanescent experience, as I recall, had shattered with the big bang that'd sent this miniscule facsimile of my self hurling through space while the bulk of my being collapsed in upon itself, creating a black hole of such magnitude, only the undaunted could escape the pull of its gravitational field with the information contained therein. With the appearance of the hand of the God who'd been responsible for this inversion of the nipple to which I seemed so attracted, did the remains of the day pull together quite nicely as I dozed off to sleep, that evening.

Like Humpty Dumpty, had I taken a great fall when I latched onto a piece of the puzzle of my life, that'd begun to take shape before its time. Letting go of it, out of the real fear of losing sight of the truth, should I stray too far, I found my self freelancing again in the vicinity of the Creator's hand. Grabbing hold of the piece He had just hurled my way, did I learn what to hold onto and what not to, as it left a trail of images in its wake, that sent me scrambling, like all the king's men, to put them back together in a manner of speaking instead.

Upon reentering the erogenous zone, or black hole into which I had fallen, did I wind up in the arms of Jesus.

"You did it!" Proclaimed the King of Hearts as He broke my fall from grace.

Like an incubating egg, did I lie there basking in the warm hold of His love and mine, that one burning desire for union with the Creator, hell's only light.

"Go to him now. You can't refuse," exclaimed the only other Person, besides His Mother, to have risen from the dead after He had descended into hell to free those parts of the body, Instinct still held captive.

Having made it to the bottom in one piece, was I left standing there alone with no other light to guide me, than the lamp of my soul, that aura of good will which doth radiate from one's being at such times, to facilitate one in capturing the essence of one's feelings in words.

In my haste to give berth to the Creator, did I stumble upon that obsessive-compulsive alter ego of mine as it slunk to the floor of my mind locked into an image that, like the eggman, had just taken a great fall, splattering itself about the ground of my being as food for thought. In my inability to let go of this image of my self, as Jesus had, I grabbed hold of what I could, only to be sent reeling from this scene, with a hand from God, to recreate the events that then took place.

"Hold on," yelled out my mentor from somewhere across that great crack in the physique of Mother Nature from which sprang Adam's bane—a pillar of a man of no less stature than Goliath's—to prick my conscience.

"Hold onto what?" I screamed back.

"Hold onto what you have grasped," mentored he who saw things as they are, "for anything else is a wanton lie."

Into the cavernous depths of my being, like a bolt from the blue, shot Michael, with sword in hand, to push back into the abyss the lie which had convinced me for so long, I couldn't find union with the male member of my body on any other level than that of an animal.

At sword point, was this demon-lie swallowed up by the crack which had been preparing itself to give form to this serendipitous conception. With the collapse of this colossal lie in upon its self, did this piece of the puzzle fall into place.

Having sunk to the bottom of my being, I rose up to give God my glory. As I struggled to hold onto the unconscious content that did cling to me for dear life, with one big push from Nature equivalent to the explosive force of a volcano, did I bring to the surface the whole sordid affair. Finding my self awash in a sea of white-hot lava as I came to, I jumped up out of my bunk to confront no grander an allusion to Who I Am than that which did avail itself to me, that morning.

"Hiya, froggy," pricked he my conscience with some crazy notion of himself.

"Who're you?" Asked I of him who was, is, and always will be.

"Earnest Hemmingway's the name," shot back this quid pro quo.

"Ernest Hemingway, the writer?" Fired I a salvo of my own at this image of God which had just resurrected itself from the dead.

"Nay," said he who'd been hemming way in earnest to reveal the writer in me.

"Then who are you?" Demanded I of this ghostly specter.

"I am what you despise most yet desire more than anything else in the world," declared the author of my being in a manner that did soothe these frayed nerves of mine while, at the same time, keeping alive the thread of hope, which did run through this story, of reuniting me both mentally and emotionally with this member of my body.

"I don't get it," belched back the stupid get in me, this half–digested tidbit.

"There's nothing to get but these words alone," remonstrated he who did stand out from my body as a monument to the capabilities hidden within it.

"Now sit down and shut up," put down he my feelings into words that would bolster the story of how I'd come into my manhood, the second of three great truths to be resurrected ere the last one rose up to give me a hand.

"I object," directed he my hand in a style that did suit me fine, "to the destruction, under the pretense of God and country, of any life–form made in the image and likeness of the Author of my being, bound by the same law of Nature to end the self–abuse that perpetuates the fantasy that we can have it all at the expense of another if we but shoot for it from the hip. And I object to being coerced into participating in the masturbatory acts of a whole generation of Piltdown men so bent on their own self–destruction, they don't even see it coming."

Having learned, the hard way, how to love my neighbor to the south as my self, did I embrace the male member of my body in a way unheard of in Nature. No longer did I see him as the enemy, for I'd finally destroyed the image that had beaten me down over the years, damn near killing the writer in me before he'd had the chance to speak out on the horror of projecting one's hell out onto the world to engage those aspects of ourselves that demand we give them liberty or give them death. Only I couldn't see killing myself as Hemingway had, or anyone else for that matter, to satisfy this need to write, until I realized I had no other choice. I had to give it all I had to meet his demand for union with me on the physical plane, that I might live in him and he in me in one orgiastic encounter after another. To this end, or until death did us part, did I disavow myself from that god of the underworld behind the draft, military service, and the war in Vietnam.

MR. HART: *Now, when was that?*
RESPONDENT: *About the 18th of April, as I recall, while I sat in earnest, hemming way at the intricacies of the webbed sight with which I'd been endowed to help me make sense of this inner net or highway of information that did weave its way through my mind, like a spider in search of food for thought or the one truth that would free her from having to spin all these tales to ensnare it.*

Alas, would I go hungry for several days, until those in charge of this ward of the state let the young wart in me see a real priest, the Merlin who'd help me draw forth what had been written in stone, long ago, the blade of truth that could set the king in me free from his imprisonment in Nature.

The Real Information Superhighway

"O where art thou, Merlin?" Cried out the young author in me.

Having been summoned forth by the guard I'd let down earlier, did I arise from this medieval slumber to greet my old mentor in whatever form he might appear for the first time in real life.

"Hi," greeted he the I that could not believe what I saw in the eyes of this humble magician as I plunked myself down at the other end of the monolith at which he sat. "I'm Chaplain Carroll," closed he the gap between him and his projection, that Alice in Wonderland who did skirt my imagination in the guise of his soul.

Via the white rabbit did he proceed to pull forth from that mad-hatted ego of mine the truth which lay buried neath the trees of Eden, that Pearl of Great Price upon which I had staked my life as a conscientious objector. Seeing how feelings mask the truth though never lie, how quick had he been to accept the image of soul I projected, thus narrowing the great gap that'd gutted my life with innuendos of insanity, that lust for what is real in a world so unreal as our own. So too had he, in having allowed me to take Jinny's place—that orgasm within another I so sought—granted me the wish that had filled my life with emptiness.

"Upon my return," quoted he the great magician in heaven, "I shall bring back to thee the scrip for what ails thee, that portion of the secret scrolls of the Great Gray Whore, known in these quarters as the BUPERS Manual, which doth apply to thine own situation as a conscientious objector." With that did this mirage of Merlin give way, to the young author in me, something a little more tangible than an Alice in Wonderland ere disappearing from my purview.

MR. HART: *Now is that the first time, the latter part of April, 1968, you had ever heard of the existence of provisions within the Navy's own personnel manual pertaining to the processing of a claimant's request to be discharged as a conscientious objector?*

RESPONDENT: *That's correct.*

MR. HART: *All right, you may continue.*

Filled with the hope of his return, did I spend the days ahead in the company of my soul as I traversed the real information superhighway, that inner network of neurotransmissions sparked by the engine that doth drive one's brain, in its desire to reunite the Creator of these webbed sights with its own reflections, those pictures worth a thousand words to the bard in me. As I sat in earnest, hemming way at the image that'd cropped up from the floor of my mind, did I set that mad-hatted ego of mine down on paper with the Alice-in-Wonderland image I had of my soul, the White Rabbit, to differentiate her from all the emotional fluff with which we Homo sapiens do so often identify our feelings as we tear into each other with those pictures, worth a thousand words to him alone who can reunite both sides of the brain in heavenly bliss—that infusion of the impossible into the possible whereby flesh is given to the truth contained therein.

"D'you remember," asked my soul, "when you were too busy to give me the time of day?"

"I do," renewed that mad-hatted ego of mine its promise to the white rabbit, long ago, to give my feelings the consideration they deserved.

"'Twas before I'd been introduced to you by my father at the tea party he'd thrown for you and the white rabbit. Remember?" Nudged she ever closer to my fondness for the old buck ere she'd come along and stolen my heart.

Having been caught, so to speak, with my pants down, I had nothing to say.

"O how in love were you with your feelings," rubbed she her bosom into mine. "For you seemed so unable to let go of the magic of your lamp until you had summoned forth the genie therein, my father, to fulfill your wish to see yourself as you are—three persons in one. Having learned to walk on water, did you proceed, as the Creator had, eons ago, to fashion from this mass of confusing feelings the woman of your dreams, who had risen from your side, at His behest, to deflate that mad-hatted ego of yours whene'er it got carried away with itself."

"As I recall," lashed back that mad-hatted ego of mine, "I had gone up topside, that evening, to turn on to *"Sergeant Pepper's Lonely Hearts Club Band"* when, lo and behold, who should beam themselves aboard but you and your father, Hewhay, to addle my brain with your perceptions of reality."

"I'm sorry I hurt your feelings," nailed down she the truth to the wood of my cross, the only attachment I'd had, back then, to my feelings.

"And yet, to this day," pulled I from that mad cap of mine the white rabbit, "am I consumed by my desires for you to pull forth from my being these same feelings."

"That is the beauty of the beast," reflected she my lust for the truth.

And so, did I find my self lying there, like Adam, on the eve of my destruction.

"No one can deflate a man's ego faster than I," stole she the very words from my mouth, ere I could spit them out and lay claim to their fame.

"'Tis your image, not mine, that doth need to be pricked," fired I another round into the womb I dared to poke my head.

"Nay, 'tis Death's," dropped she this bomb upon the whole affair, blowing to smithereens any image I might have had to the contrary, as I came to the same conclusion she had, that one must give one's self up completely to the other to find out who he is.

Having died in each other's arms, had we come together to recreate ourself, as the masculine aspect of the Deity had done eons ago when He fostered, on the Eve of the Adam He had split asunder, this new way to conceive ourselves.

The Real Information Superhighway

"I love you," inspired she this new Adam to write down ere letting go of the grip she had on his pen.

"I love you too," quoted he who sat in earnest, hemming way at the hole in his life he no longer feared penetrating with his pen.

"Come away with me," begged she who saw no end to the intercourse we were having.

And O how great was the delight she took in seeing me spill my guts out onto page after page of the real information superhighway to which my pen had fallen prey as it came and went with each new deposition of what I saw in her.

"What's goin' on here?" Wondered that mad-hatted ego of mine as it chased after the dish who had just run away with the spoon that'd fed my head this image of my muse and her author, the one she seemed to love more than me.

Having lost my way to the lance a lot sharper than my own, did the author in me teach me a lesson in humility—that I must give my self up to him whom she did love. So did this molly step forth to take his place as a writer of the poetry of their prose, as they made love to each other under the cover of these pages.

"Very good," proclaimed she who did find fulfillment in my newfound love as I sat in earnest, hemming way at the triangle in which I had entangled my self.

Like this author of mine did I wrestle with the *Old Man in the Sea* over what to say, since he adamantly opposed expressing my feelings in any other form than the poetry of his flings with soul as the two flitted about this arcane world in search of the Third Person of the Trinity that did still elude my grasp.

"Take off yer hat," suggested the elfish person in me, the selfish one did seek.

"If I do, the white rabbit will escape," admitted he his feelings into the picture.

"Fear not," rubbed she the magic lamp that'd just released them from my cap in the guise of the white rabbit.

"For does not the white rabbit," surmounted she the obstacle that stood between us, "correspond with you via the little bit of flesh you share with us, to capture what still eludes your grasp?"

In my pursuit of the white rabbit down the hole, was I tricked into having intercourse with her, only this time, in the poetry of our prose. For the deeper I plunged, the closer I came to accepting my lot in life, the rigidity of having to sit, day after day, in earnest hemming way at the contents of my imagination.

Over and over did my soul bring back to me, as if she were on a mission from God, that myth of the eternal return to which all this coming and going did allude, the never-ending tale upon which I did feast, now that I knew it was he my sweet Guenevere did love. Only I had yet to take on this white phantom, for that is what her name means, in any other guise than that of an adulterous white knight, the bane of the author in that pitiless self of mine which, like Mordred, still refused to give up its claim to the throne of the prince of this poor pauper. Having drawn the queen of hearts from the deck, did not I put down on paper, my resistance to the author in me ere taking off for parts unknown with her hand in mine.

"Why, I could've gotten killed back there," protested he who did still oppose the author in me.

"'Twas nigh the time or place," lamented the creator of his own adversary.

"The more dread you draw from me with your lance, the further you drive this molly from your side," played I the devil's advocate with this author of mine, "for 'tis obvious that you need me as much as I do you to win her freedom."

"Then let that be the cause which draws us together," extended he, in whom no treachery did lie, an olive branch ere I could toot my horn in harmony with his.

O how wondrous was this union as we came together in a way unheard of in nature, that phantom behind which hid our love for each other in a single image, she who had finally made it to third. With him on first and me on second, did the inner course taken prove the most difficult to describe in any other form than the poetry of our prose as she and the author of my being raced to see that the batter in the box got the balls he needed to get us all back home in one piece. Having implanted in my brain, a whole new way of looking at myself, had not the dish run away with the spoon, in one of the most daring attempts ever undertaken by my imagination to reconnect me with its Creator, I would never have experienced that explosion of mind or orgasm within another which tells one, in the language of the body, whether he has succeeded in communicating the true intent of his feelings.

"'Tis interesting how our life together has evolved, is it not?" Inquired my soul as I stepped forth from this fantasy uncertain of the new role I'd assumed.

"Am I not just a pawn," brokered I a question of my own from this fantasy, "to be used as this dear sweet author of yours sees fit?"

"Nay," said she, "for you are not what you think you are."

"So that's how attitudes are changed," quoted I her father instead.

"I am but a mere glimpse of the truth," reflected he upon that image of himself as a father who had turned to writing, to save his soul.

"As am I," mirrored she that image of herself which had yet to stumble upon Adam's snake, for I had yet to lose my virginity.

"I'm lost," put down I this snake ere it bit me.

"In him," shot back that dick incognito, or private eye, my old mentor, Hewhay.

"Only the shadow knows," whispered the author of these loose associations with the other members of my body with any clue as to what was going on here.

"Where have you been?" Barked the wolf in me at the sight of its shadow.

"All over the place," raised he the specter of my inability to write without divine intervention.

Having latched onto the right association, did I emerge from this latest attitude adjustment a changed man, for I'd finally taken on the writer that'd hidden himself away, years ago, in the images of the darker side of my nature. And as I sat in earnest hemming way at these images, I saw their faces come together in my own ere the author in me took off again, with this new face of mine.

"Give you a penny for your thoughts," laid claim he to my shadow at such little expense to his self.

Via the magic of this lamp of mine, did I find comfort in the privacy of my own womb, for I enjoyed exchanging ideas with him as much as I did her. And since I wanted her no more than he did, I accepted this new persona without reservation.

"Let it be done according to thy will," reflected he upon his own immaculate conception, for 'twas in the making of such loose associations that I learned to write, to connect the impossible with the possible as I traded one compulsion for another, the anal for the oral in the language of Freud.

For in my reckless pursuit of that ever-elusive fox who could cool my desires for union with the true intent of my feelings, had not I followed the lead of that author of mine down the hole, soul had disappeared with the white rabbit, I would never have stumbled upon the inner course taken every time this heavenly body of mine gravitated towards some weak attraction with the force of a highly charged particle of the true nature of the strong bond that did fuse instinct to soul, the worm to its own black hole, with the fission of the first Adam that resulted in the expulsion of these ideas from the womb in whose image they had mushroomed to unify the forces of nature around this single thread of truth.

"O how my father and I have labored to bring you to this realization," exclaimed the queen of my evolution, for I had never allowed him to express himself in any other form than that of an old Indian who had passed the prime of his life.

In the darkness of my shadow had this light lived like a hermit monk ever in search of the author of my being. With that in mind did this insight pull forth from the shadowy depths of the father instinct that great need I had to recreate my self in the poetry of my own prose. And as I sat in earnest, hemming way at this flashback, it left me standing inside the Gates of Eden in the guise of my old mentor, Hewhay, whose real image had yet to surface.

"Go out and stand before the Lord," dropped soul this bomb, "for the Lord is about to pass by."

There rose a great wind, a feeling so strong it split mountains and broke rocks into pieces before the Lord, but the Lord was not intimating his whereabouts; and after this big letdown, a panic attack of such magnitude it shook the foundations of my being, but the Lord was not into shaking me up either; and after this earth-shattering event, a burning feeling of orgasmic proportions, but the Lord was not in the mood for pleasing feelings, and after they'd burnt themselves out on each other, the sound of sheer silence, for in no other image was the Word to be found.

"You don't know what it's like," proclaimed he in whose image I now stood, "to have no voice."

"You don't know what it's like," reflected I, his image, "to have no dreams."

"It's terrible!" Ejaculated he and I in sync with that image of the body in which we had just come together, for it seemed to take all three of us, working in conjunction with each other, to produce these little vignettes.

Via oral intercourse with both aspects of my personality, the masculine and the feminine, did I find my way back to that image of God which stood out from me like a sore thumb, for this novice in the ways of Nature knew not where he was being led in his naïveté.

"Mother Inferior shot you down," flung my soul, this image at me of my eighth grade teacher.

"She sure did!" Shot back I a salvo of my own into this black robed rogue, the nun who had wrongly accused me of lifting the contents of my first literary piece from another source, driving the author in me underground to live like a dick incognito till he cleared his name of the years of shame under which he'd strive to free himself from the oppression of this obsession of Mother Nature's to put down creatures who reason in rhyme rather than mime. "In a way she was right, for 'twas his hand that'd set this whole thing in motion. Only she made sure, from thereon out, it was mine that pulled the trigger after I refused to let him have a hand in my affairs. And to think, the old biddy'd had the nerve to give the Author of my being a failing mark for having shown His hand in my work."

"Only you didn't take it that way," came she to the same conclusion I had, for we'd all come together to recreate the events backstage of this scene from my life.

With that, did we three sit down around the fire of my heart's desire to see the wonders of nature in their own light as they went up in smoke before our eyes in one billowing image after another ere Mother Superior could shoot me down as she had back in the garden of my youth, from which I'd been cast to play the parts of Adam and Eve, that ever elusive image of God its self had just unfurled.

In my search for the key to Eve's gate—that expulsion of prose from my being which captured in poetry the emotion of their coming together ere being cast from paradise to fend for themselves—did I stumble upon the love of my life, the sex this Adam couldn't let go of in his haste to retake what had been taken from him. In the image of Eve, did I find what I'd been looking for—life everlasting, even if it was by proxy or, in my case, a son or two.

"For had not the one killed the other with kindness," concluded the author of my being, "Adam would never have found salvation in the arms of Eve, as that is the only way to overcome Instinct—by bringing love and understanding to one's relationship with him.

"And that is why Mother Superior shot you down," exposed she, my own Eve, the true nature of her mother's response, "for 'twas Instinct who showed her the real author of the piece you, as Adam, had given your best shot."

"Bang! Bang! You shot me down," grabbed he, the author of my being, the little bit of flesh that stood between us ere Nature could squeeze off another round in the big tussle over this gun of ours.

"Having wounded the Old Fisher King," inserted she, my soul, her own image back into the picture, "were the two of you sent packing, along with Instinct, down the road that leads to the womb, she who doth take back, in bits and pieces, the flesh you have been given to complete this journey ere the old order dies out."

"As beautiful as she is," collected I this image of Nature about my self before penetrating it, "I never realized how cruel she can be."

"'Tis the Old Fisher King's wound," thrust she, my soul, this image my way.

"The longer you hold onto the pleasure of this pain," ejaculated the author of my being, "the harder it will get to let go of this paradox."

"For he is the father whose skin you must shed," came she, my soul, to the same conclusion as her creator, only in a different form.

"Your wish is my command," slid in the little bit of flesh that stood between us.

"You are more beautiful than I ever imagined," proclaimed that archetype of me who did write so much better than I could ever have dreamed.

"As are you," reflected she, my soul, upon the true nature of her pen pal.

Having held on, far too long, did I finally stumble upon that need of mine to have intercourse with someone other than the members of my own body. Only I had nowhere to go with these feelings—seeing how I was locked up in a cell all by myself—but down that long lonesome highway which led back to the womb or grail from which Percival had drunk to heal the Old Fisher King of the wound he'd incurred with the separation of Eve from his side.

"Aaah!" I screamed across the void. "Look at what you've created—a being so incapable of speaking in any other language than that of its own body."

"Listen to what is not being said in your conversations with others," responded She, the Great Comforter of men, "and you will have plenty to say, for I will fill in for you whatever is lacking, as I am now and always have in the past."

Having isolated my self from everyone in the brig but my own ignorance, did I trudge off down the real information superhighway to the sounds of silence.

"O where art thou, Merlin?" Cried out the Old Fisher King in me as he passed from this world to the next in search of the soul which had abandoned him for that lance a lot sharper than his own.

"Away on leave," came back the response of the Chaplain whose Alice in real life had just had a baby, with the passing of my mentor from here to eternity, never to be seen or heard from again in the guise of Old Hewhay.

As Jinny and I lay to rest this image of her father, I wept over the loss of the only real mentor I'd ever had. Having sustained such a sore buffet to the head, did I fall into a swoon, a vortex of feeling so vast it threatened to take my life if I didn't give it my soul, for Instinct seemed to always get what he wanted, come hell or high water. So did I, upon having had the soul of my being ripped from my side by this instinct of mine to reproduce itself over and over in ever varying forms, find my self drifting about—in the boat in which I'd first met her—a sea so calm the surface could do little else but reflect the heavens above in their entirety. Left with no other choice but to die to that instinctive will of mine, did I rise up, on the third day, from this catatonic state or sarcophagus in which I'd been laid to rest, to greet the only mentor I had now, that archetype of me which had resurrected its self from the father instinct to reproduce this passage from hell in its entirety.

"Get hold of yourself!" Reprimanded he alone who could capture in words what I was feeling.

"'Tis a ghost!" Did my self cry out instead.

"'Tis but a mere reflection of the truth," explained he the image that did haunt me still.

"If it's really *you,"* shot back his quid pro quo, "then let me *come to you* across *the water."*

"Come!" Roused he this penchant I had for playing with my self.

Leaving me with no other alternative, but to reach out and touch the image that I had created, did this pitiless self of mine start sinking instead.

"How *little faith* you have!" Exclaimed he in whom my self had failed, once again, to put its trust. "*Why did you* falter?" Mt 14:27-31.

"I never realized," admitted I the truth back into my life, "how bent you were on getting me to look at these projections from that instinct par excellence which allows one to see things as they really are—as mere reflections of the truth."

To master the art of walking on water without giving into the emotions that accompany the truth across the threshold of consciousness, did I pluck from the black hole in my eye the pupil I'd become. Left standing beside my self on the surface of my eye, I looked out across the sea that covered this tiny globe without stirring up a single emotion. Having lost interest in them, did I see the real objective of this encounter as the subjugation of my will to something greater here than a Jonah.

"Come!" Ejaculated that projection of me ere plunging itself into this latest fantasy, the nymph I had just captured on film—that thin layer of water which doth coat the eye, as far as one can see, with the images of Pan.

The Real Information Superhighway

With my eyes closed did I descend to the depths of the looking-glass world, only this time in conjunction with that greater will of mine.

"For heaven's sake, open your eyes," lashed back he at my impotence—for having succumbed to him with my eyes closed.

"I thought the water was deeper," regurgitated that self of mine which has always had difficulty getting a handle on its feelings until it has spewed them out onto the ground of its being, like a sower of seed his next harvest of images.

"Your feelings know only the depths to which you, yourself, have sunk," dove he to the heart of this latest projection, to give this fantasy the reality it so desired.

With that, did I run into my soul again who wanted nothing more than to fulfill his desire for union with this unholy body of ours—meaning I would eventually have to give them flesh, one way or the other, either in the body or out of the body, or on paper, that is, to meet such a tall order, for my fantasies seemed to always get what they wanted, come hell or high water. Until they typecast me in a role that no longer suited me, or held me spellbound, I was doomed to play the same part over and over in varying forms until I grasped the meaning of such behavior on an emotional level.

"So that's how you walk on water!" Exclaimed he who had overcome his attachment to his emotions.

"To stay on top of them," wrote he who walked these waters regardless of the weather, "takes real fortitude, the kind that demands you give your soul to the devil, so to speak, for the devil's in the details not the emotions. Only when you have let go of your attachment to them, are you free to grasp the details they embody. Otherwise, you remain tied to them as they pull you back down to the level of an animal to retrieve that part of you which still eludes your grasp."

"What part?" Rode I this emotional roller coaster to its logical conclusion.

"The will of God," rode he, like Pecos Bill, this sudden twist of words about the more cerebral regions of my brain before disappearing from my purview.

Until I gravitated towards yet another warp in the space-time continuum or curved surface of my eyeball, I wandered about as if I were treading on thin ice, never quite knowing when or where the rods behind these projections might pick up on a glimmer of light emanating from the black hole or cone of emotion so central to the production and release of the next image in Technicolor with which I was to match wits ere petering out, at the peak of such experiences, like a writer who has given it his best shot. I either sank or swam as I emoted or felt my way through these dark nights of the soul aided only by a sense of wonder at what was waiting for me up around the bend, if anything.

On one such occasion, while struggling to keep up with my soul as she cut through these waters like a mermaid, I darted off after some poor hapless little fish basking in the bent rays of the sun near the surface or threshold of consciousness, totally oblivious of the threat I posed to its well–being. Devouring this unconscious tidbit before it escaped me, I quickly rejoined my soul who, like Clark Kent, seemed to disappear, at such times as these, with the regularity of a singularity or that point at which one's purview of things is infinitely distorted by the gravitational forces of one's body resulting in what is widely held to be the final state of a matter falling into a black hole, the revelation, that is, of its real significance, for there was a far superior man hidden within me yet, than met the eye.

As the mourning over the death of my old mentor subsided, with the return of evening to this corner of the looking–glass world, I fell into that burning ring of fire from which there seemed to be no escape. As the flames of this emotion shot higher, I poked my head around the corner into that hole in my life for which my body, in its insufferable poverty, did burn with such passion—a purgatory so black it took me by surprise, scattering the contents of my mind about the farthest reaches of space for further scrutiny. Thus did I come to see these spurts of energy as a ploy to get me back in touch with the workings of my mind.

There, at the forges of hell, did I find the hand of God hardest at work, hammering away at this iron will of mine, day after day, to make it more malleable or amenable to the changes taking place in my body as He turned up the heat on me to get with the program or true intent of my feelings ere I collapsed in upon myself like some bright shining lie, never to be seen nor heard from again, by the likes of men, in any other guise than the black hole I'd dug for my self in my search for immortality. Doomed to the womb of my imagination, I rose to the occasion only to find my self freelancing in the vicinity of that great hand which seemed to have attached itself to the right side of my body. And as the invisible hand to the left of my field of vision kept it preoccupied with images, I was amazed by its command of the language of the body, for there wasn't anything, upon which it focused my attention, that I couldn't see through. Otherwise I fell under the spell of the other, more invisible hand of Nature which doth still rule over the mind of man with such an iron will, that inflexible image of our selves which can't see through a damned thing on its own or sees only what it wants to see, what pleases it, or satisfies its hunger for the truth on an emotional and totally unconscious level. Having latched onto an emotion, would I be sent reeling through space towards some black hole or distortion of the true object of its thrust, to mingle with it until I got it, one way or the other, either mentally or emotionally. Whether in the body or out of the body, God knows I worked like hell, with love and understanding, to forge ahead despite the many pitfalls I encountered along the way.

"O where art thou, Merlin?" Cried out the young author in me as I passed from here to eternity, without guile or guise, to gain further insight into my plight.

"You are he," drowned out this passage from hell my own voice.

Having taken the place of my old mentor, I needed his image no longer. Thus did I become a seer in my own right. And as Nature bared her soul to me, I wrote down what I saw.

Only I couldn't figure out where my shadow'd disappeared to, until he showed up in my dreams, one night, unannounced. And as he emerged from the tunnel of my shortsightedness, that passage from hell, which enticed me to penetrate further than I had ever gone before, I backed off from this phantasm fearful of the feelings it'd stirred up. Orgasming without ejaculating as the essence of this emotion swept over me, leaving me to burn yet not be consumed, I found my self standing there in the guise of a sage who yearned to speak but couldn't because his tongue was tied to his pen instead of his head.

"Where does one go with this desire to service one's fellow man?" Inquired I of the author of my being.

"Into serving the Creator with his whole mind, his whole heart, and eventually his whole body," authorized he this deposition, "for there is no other antidote.

"To quench the insatiable fires of hell, such a man must meld with the Creator, lest he fall for every Tom, Dick, and Harry who strikes his fancy," had he concluded at my expense, for he needed me as much as I did him to complete these passages from hell.

To find my way, I had to let go of mine to hear what he had to say. Otherwise, I missed the boat, the image to get me from here to eternity, that is, She Who Must Be Obeyed, one way or the other, as Nature or the Third Person of the Holy Trinity, the essence of all emotion of which these images were but a brief glimpse or snapshot of Her yet invisible form. Hidden deeper still within the shadows of my emotions, did I find the words to express them lying there, like a babe in swaddling clothes, waiting to be picked up and held or put in proper perspective by the Father of all insight. Only I had to start at the bottom of the chain of command with the mother of all insight, my own sultry emotions, before I could rise above them, like the Son of Man, and sit at the right hand of the Father.

"For it's the details that kill ya," commented He Who had died at the hands of His own splintery cross, that I might live in His image and He in mine in a way unheard of in nature before now, as three persons in one.

Having gotten to the bottom of this emotion, did I slip from the womb of my imagination, only to be confronted by the real information superhighway. Whether in the body or out of the body, God knows I struggled with the nature of my relationship to Mary. And as I pored over the last bit of remorse I'd received from her, I wondered if I hadn't fallen in love with that part of me she never was, is not now, nor ever shall be.

"I don't have the slightest idea of what's going on," she wrote, *"other than feeling a need to write to you. I've been so mixed up since I last heard from you; I hope you don't get mad at me for writing. And even though you probably don't ever want to hear from me again, I just had to write. Don't ask me why.*

"It seems I've changed since the operation, so much so, that I'm not even the same person I was before. Only I don't know if I'm all straightened out now or more confused. But I guess I'll find out, in time. It's just that I miss hearing from you and finding out how you are doing. By now you probably even hate the mere mention of my name. I'm sorry if that's the case, because I do really miss you. Even now I don't know what happened between us. All of a sudden I got this letter saying so long. Oh well, I guess there's no sense in bringing up water under the bridge. But I would at least like to know what happened. I keep thinking I must have missed some of your letters while I was in the hospital. At any rate, I hope you don't feel you have to answer this letter, because you don't. And above all, I pray you are well and happy. Take care of yourself, Butch; for you have a lot to offer this old world. Don't ever forget that. And always do the very best you can."

Signed,

Mary

She missed my letters all right, but only because I hadn't been sending her any, unintentionally, that is. Now she knew what it felt like to not hear a word from her bitter half, the real information superhighway in this relationship. Like water under a bridge, had she exhausted the one natural resource she never realized she had until it quit flowing—that steady stream of consciousness, which did pour forth from me no more for her benefit. And because she had shared so little of herself over the past year and a half, she had left me with no more lasting an image of herself than a one way street going nowhere fast, the direction in which my life seemed to be headed, these days. In other words, she no longer captured my imagination in the way she had in the past, for I wanted more out of life now than she could have given me at the time. Nonetheless, she would hear from me again, but not until I had completed my dissertation for the Navy, substantiating my beliefs as a conscientious objector in a more acceptable format. Having grown old before her time, did she lay claim to my soul no more.

For I loved floating around in the vicinity of that dark black emotion which did reunite me with the hand of the Creator in an effort to put into proper perspective the more puzzling aspects of my life. And to think, I didn't even need a space suit or a straitjacket to protect me whenever I flew off the deep end, lost my head, or got caught up in my fantasies, that descent into hell, which preceded the resurrection of all truth from the emotional and intellectual incongruities of the body.

The Real Information Superhighway

Having latched onto some preconceived notion, like a falling star would I be sent reeling from this scene to embrace the shadows of my emotions in whatever form, these depictions of the truth might appear. Not until I had fallen silent, would I grasp the true meaning or master of the emotion in a handshake that was out of this world or at least reached beyond the old attitude that'd clung to me, like a demon or pattern of thought which no longer held sway over me.

In reality, I had nothing to fear but my own beastly thoughts or attempts to live life as I saw fit. For the life of me, I couldn't figure out why these unruly thoughts would want to take it from me until I realized that I too was nothing but a figment of the imagination which had yet to die, that the author of my being might live in me and I in him in a way unheard of in Nature. Or I could give my thoughts the life they sought that they might live on in me and I in them and my progeny until we drove our selves extinct, for that is what eventually happens to all bad ideas or at least those to which Nature remains forever emotionally unattached.

Like some egoless animal on the endangered species list, did I look on, that day, as the old guard locked up another prisoner of the mind, a young black man who'd fallen off the deep end in his struggle to hold onto the nothingness of his ego, that pack of lies the Marine Corps had fed him in the hopes of turning out one of the most efficient killing machines to have ever stalked the face of the earth.

"Man, I's cool!" Ranted on the poor idiot in his identification with the god of the underworld, that ego of all egos which doth suck the blood from other life forms, be they men, women, or children, as he had done over in Nam, destroying the thought processes of millions of years of evolution to keep its self alive.

Possessed by the demon lies of a whole generation of men, did he turn, with no hope in sight of ever regaining consciousness, to the instinct that'd gotten him here, the will to survive come hell or high water.

"Man, I's cool!" Praised he the god of the underworld, as he trudged down the banks of the River Styx, knee deep in the slurry of the carnage he had left behind in Nam.

Like a caged animal, did he pace the floor of the stygian split to which he had fallen prey in his struggle to evade the truth of his emotions, that narrow band of consciousness along the real information superhighway which applied to him alone if ever he should stumble upon such a pearl in his wanderings about the depths of his emotional hell. As cut off as he was from his feelings, he had not the slightest clue that he had lost touch with reality, much less why. Nor would he ever understand the need to return to his hell so that he might live in them and their reality as they have lived in his, are now, and ever shall until he recognized them, whether in the body or out of the body, only God knew for certain. Having worked like a dog to save himself from these feelings, would he be forced to find it within himself to walk that extra mile in their shoes if he didn't want to spend his life running from them. In other words, he'd have to surrender himself to the enemy he had killed in Nam, to overcome the body/mind split that'd swallowed him up in the process of his accepting someone else's interpretation of his feelings, as so many of the members of our generation had, continue to do, and probably always will, to the benefit of themselves though detriment of others, the poor hapless souls who fall for such schlock, the rot concocted by that mad-hatted ego of ours which leads to the madness of war on one front or the other, depending upon whether one has internalized the conflict or gone out of his mind to solve it on the physical plane, an impossibility without help from one's feelings.

Haunted by the memories of the past as well as the present, did not he strike back in the only way he knew how, with psychotic force. Having been tormented for days, by an obnoxious white guard from the Old South who had failed to lock him down after a head call, did he leap free of the constraints of his cage to deal his tormentor an immortal blow. Like Tarzan, had he flung himself through the air via the bars over the open gate, kicking his opponent in the nuts, so hard, he knocked the yahoo out. Thus did he prevail, that day, over the white lie which had gotten him into this fix, for had he not been fighting on the wrong side of a truly revolutionary war to free the peoples of the South from their enslavement to the last bastions of colonial rule holed up in the former capital of French Indochina, known in those days as Sài Gòn in Vietnamese.

"Man I's cool!" Yelled out the brute that'd gone out of his mind, both literally and figuratively speaking, to liberate himself, for one brief moment or orgiastic fling in time, from his own hell, that separation from soul which doth still vex this generation of men with such fantasies about its self.

"Man, I's Cool Hand Luke," reiterated the shadow in which the white guard did find himself lying.

"Fool," said I, "you do not know how this silence grows. Listen that you might learn from it. Take stock in what you find there that you be spared a worse fate."

But my words like dead leaves fell to their silent grave.

Having been put back in his place by the other guards on the block, did he stand poised to deal decisively with the paleface lying there on the floor as the blood rushed back into its deadly pallor with a vengeance.

"Let me at 'm," cried out the beast that hovered down at the other end of the spectrum, like some red giant sitting on the edge of the universe, waiting to explode on a moment's notice from the ego whose lily-white image had been besmirched by its own seething shadow.

Restrained by my presence, did they corral their companion ere the enraged bull could gore the matador who had so skewered his ass as to make him see red.

"Man, look what I's done," conquered he his fear of identifying with the ego that'd done him so much harm in the past. "Why I's Cool Hand Luke."

Having raised hell to ever new heights, as he'd done in Nam, was not he captured by an insane desire to play the devil's advocate, that god of all shadows, the ego he had hated in the other but revered now that it belonged to him.

"I'll kill the motherfucker," blasted back the angry bull that cast this shadow of its self out onto the blacker of the two for lack of a better hook on which to hang its filthy Hyde.

"What we have here," had the shadow informed its ego, "is a failure to communicate."

"Ain't no motherfucker gonna fuck with me and get away with it," bemoaned that aspect of our selves—ere they hauled his ass off—which downright refuses to embrace the truth even when it's standing right in front of our eyes, as clear as day, in black and white.

"I's Cool Hand Luke," orgasmed he, over and over in the image of me, the ego's soul love in life, till they'd hauled his ass off too, to God knows where.

Until the ego starts fuckin' around with its own shadow, whether in the body or out of the body, as only God knows, they both appear to lead totally separate lies. In reality, they are as inseparable as two peas in a pod, for the ego can't live without its shadow anymore than Adam could, without his evil, and she, without her Satan, as a means of explaining away that constant need of theirs "to fuck with somebody," in the words of ol' Rulli, to maintain this symbiotic ofttimes chaotic relationship between the upper and lower echelons of our beings. Only in drinking from the grail, as Christ had, or in becoming Who We Truly Are, and that alone, do ego and shadow, like Father and Son, come together in a way unheard of in Nature before now, to heal the Old Fisher King of his wound.

And so did heaven rejoice as earth proclaimed solidarity with the King, that orgasm within another in which those aspects of the personality, so opposed to unity on any other level but the physical, come together on the metaphysical plane, in such a way that one becomes all things to everyone else but himself.

Like a single spermatozoon, was I transformed by this experience to bring yet another resemblance of soul to the surface, to mingle with the more unsullied features of my face, to rid it of the last vestiges of an ego. No longer did I stand out from the body of man as an entity entirely unto its self, since I now stood for something far greater than all of mankind, the very head of this estate and heart of all matter, that Original Being, the real missing link, I Am Who I Am in Whom exists no evil simply because there is no ego to cast a shadow, or that part of itself it has projected onto another to make itself look better than it is. Thus was I driven to seek out she who could deflate my ego and make me feel whole whenever she blew my mind out on life's main drag, the real information superhighway or only avenue she'd had to get me to think about someone else besides my self, that one-way street which leads back to the womb or snake pit from which there is no escape. At last, I understood why I was so attracted to her, wherein lie her true beauty, for she had put her whole life into me, never once thinking of herself, hoping against hope that I would rise up with her as a single entity, to suffer no more the agonizing fate of Adam and Eve, that terrible separation of one aspect of God from the other which so plagued me with misappropriated desires, that I almost forgot about my soul and her need to be loved, not as I loved my self but as she loved me, for it was my love, not hers, that was incomplete.

Finding my self knee deep in a sea of grass, that same unified force field upon which I'd stumbled, in one of my first trips through the mind early last summer while at Yankee Station off the coast of Vietnam, did not I ask of this experience its name, that I might share with others, or at least those interested in such encounters, the true nature of this singularity.

"I Am Who I Am, She Who Must Be Obeyed, and you all in one," replied the driving force behind this string of theories regarding the true nature of man.

Having stumbled upon the narrow gate through which we must all pass to enter this world, did not I set off down the path that'd been laid out for me, like a new outfit, by the mother of my nature and its father, her one true love in life, the Old Fisher King himself, whose wound could only be healed if I granted him his one wish, the freedom to use my body as he saw fit. For the further I went, the more I realized how impotent I was without him at the helm steering the boat in which we do find ourselves sailing through life. Thus did I come to see the ego as a necessary evil to be left behind, where it belonged in never-never land, that two dimensional realm through which I did roam, ever in search of the shadow that could free it from its own tyranny, the insanity of holding onto half the truth as if it were the whole truth and nothing but the truth so help me God.

"So don't worry about your self," scared the author of great expectations, the dickens out of me. "Let go that someone else might give you a hand."

But how could I, after having lost faith in my fellow man, trust those who, like all the chaplains I'd ever seen—and even my old girlfriend—had failed to produce anything more tangible than a bag of empty promises. And yet, I was being asked to do no more than He demanded of Himself, to rely upon the same individuals He had in the past—no matter how poorly they had served His purposes—to help me stay the course, a rather frightening thought if you asked me.

"So the devil's nothing more," reached out I for satori, "than what we make of him in our shortsightedness, a will that thinks it can do damn well what it pleases. That, my friends," addressed I this line of thinking, "is man's greatest evil, brought

The Real Information Superhighway

on by a house divided against itself which, like the Old Fisher King, has lost sight of the true intent of its desires, the wisdom that'd been plucked from its side to create the illusion of consciousness, or at least something a little more tangible than a mere fantasy. For the prick needs 'some body to fuck with,' in the words of ol' Rulli, to keep the truth from coming out in any other form than Nature's."

"Therein lies the true beauty of natural selection," foisted he the terrible burden of my cross or shadow upon my shoulders, the strongest desire known to mankind, the urge to mate or match wits with one's soul in whatever form she might appear for the express purpose of forcing one to evolve into a more complete human being, a body no longer wracked with the desire for what the other has got, that part of me which still eluded my grasp, the way to go, that is, whenever I found my self chasing other women—whether in the body or out of the body only God knew—to capture in one form or another the spirit of giving.

"For you have so much potential within you, Butch, that can't be kept inside but must be given to others as God intended," had Mary once captured, so eloquently, the essence of my soul. *"And it's up to you to find a way to give it to them."*

"Until then, *I was given a thorn in the flesh, a messenger of Satan to torment me,*" quoted I the Paul who stood behind this devil, in the shadow of my own ego. *"Three times had I appealed to the Lord about this, that it would leave me."*

"My grace is sufficient for you," had the Lord responded, *"for power is made perfect in weakness."* 2 Cor 12:7-9.

Enhanced by the magnitude of my own weakness, from thereon did I rise with the sun, to greet the face of God, no matter how steamy got the mirror into which I longed to look with the spirit of giving—my pen in hand, that is—that I might free the Saul in me from his passion to give flesh to this spirit in any other form than the written word. Otherwise, I'd have been out there, like any other unfocused young buck in those days, scrounging around for my next meal, that piece of ass, which could satisfy the lion's share of my appetite for giving when, in reality, I was being asked to do no more than what had been demanded of Abraham, to sacrifice, on the altar of life, the very ego I'd fostered, the old king on the hill my soul had yet to topple once and for all. And yet like God, I couldn't allow my self to extinguish this lamp, to take what did not truly belong to me, the very flame that'd set my heart on fire with the desire that He might live in me and I in Him as He lived in her, in perfect harmony.

"To take another's life," commented he with whom I did sit in earnest hemming way at the truth of this matter, "that's the real irony of suicide, the ego in a nut shell, for it can't live without taking life into its own hands, the very thing it must do, on the one hand, but absolutely refuses to do, on the other, until it is left with no other choice but to take its own life.

"So, my young friend," cajoled the *Old Man in the Sea*, "don't go chasing after other lives when the one you seek is lying here, right in front of you, under the cover of these pages, like the apple of your eye, the forbidden fruit of paradise."

Having overcome the urge to take life into my own hands, did I sit back to reflect on the true nature of this thorn in my side to evolve—whether in the body or out of the body, only God knew—into a more complete human being. At that point, was I brought back down out of the clouds by one of the temple guards to confront yet another high priest of the Great Gray Whore concerning the resurrection of my body from the Navy as a conscientious objector. With one eye on the sword in the stone, did I draw forth from the high priest the article that could set the author in me free from his long imprisonment in nature.

"When you get back to the ship," instructed he the young wart in me, "look up Article C–5210 in the BUPERS Manual. There you should find everything you'll need to establish your claim..."

...To the very throne of God did I ascend with a sword at my side where the thorn had been.

"My grace is sufficient for you," proclaimed the Lord in His infinite wisdom as I bowed down to receive His blessing, "for real power is made perfect in weakness," had He concluded at my expense.

"And may God be with you," had the high priest bestowed upon me, in a rather ominous tone of voice, this blessing instead. "Lord knows, you're gonna need 'M again," muttered he under his breath as he departed with a view of the crucifixion I had yet to undergo to bring the reign of God back into my life.

In my hunger for any news of the outside world, did I grab hold of the newspaper lying there on the table to which this Abraham had been drawn for the express purpose of sacrificing his only–begotten son—the conscientious objector in me to which my ego owed its existence—ere that angel of the Lord, the temple guard, returned to save me from the self and its suicidal tendencies, the attention getting device it used, whenever it didn't get its way, to maintain its hold on life, the last temptation I'd experience as I stepped forth from this dream to embrace Who I Am, the professor featured in the article that now stood out from all the others in the Honolulu Star–Bulletin, like the star of Bethlehem.

"It is Professor Douglass' conviction," devoured I, with the rapaciousness of a mad rapist, the gist of this article, over and over, as if I couldn't get enough of it, "that in times like these, it is the Christian theologian's primary task to show the way toward a nonviolent transformation of man.

"Our world is on the verge of suicide," had he stated before being so rudely interrupted by the temple guard who stood between us now, like a thorn in my side, to take me back down to the insanity of my own hell.

"You like traditional husband," complained my soul on the way down, "whose life is locked up in the womb with no more hope of getting out of this morass than the man in the mood."

Alarmed, I asked her how I could change the condition my condition was in.

"Die!" Lambasted she the ego that stood in her way.

Down came Abraham's knife to remove this thorn from my side with the skill of a twentieth–century surgeon.

What exactly had to go, I did not know until Abraham pulled himself forth from the side of his son, unscathed by the sudden thrust of my pelvis into the dark night that did surround me in the stifling heat of my stepfather's lust for real life.

"Is he dead?" Inquired the right hand of the other.

"Did you die?" Asked I of the Old Fisher King.

"Rescue me," rang out the voice of the dead man from somewhere across the great void that did now separate me from Abraham.

"Let go," cried out my old mentor from on high, "that, like the rich man, this image of your stepfather might die, never to rob you of life again, my son.

"Remember Douglass' proposal," did my mentor remind me of the Professor instead, "'to remake' oneself 'through nonviolence and the patient acceptance of suffering, that is, through the nonviolent cross,' the very title of his new book. In this way alone may you take life into your own hands, to have and to hold until death do you part," had he concluded at my expense.

"O how much more than a mere fantasy am I," did my soul remind me, at that point, of real life.

"For is not the ultimate goal of sex," cried out she from un'neath her oppressor, "to unite one's self with his own path whene'er he has strayed too far."

"And are we not all together now in your resolve to convey this collective endeavor of ours to the rest of the world?" Asked the Lord of me as He tweaked this last screw into place with a little bit of a different twist to it than a mere thorn in my side, that I might accept this ability of mine to create life on one level and apply it to the other.

Thus did I find someone with whom I could finally share my feelings in a very real way, that information superhighway I longed to travel but had yet to experience on any other level than that of my imagination. With my release from the brig, in the days ahead, did not I steal my way back down to the beach to reunite my self, in body as well as in spirit, with this image of my old mentor.

3

Intrusions into Dark Matters

"Professor Douglass, I presume," had I done a double take on Stanley's line when I saw this living stone rise up from behind his desk to shake my hand, only this time in the flesh.

"What can I do for you?" Had this angel asked of the Lord and me as we plunked ourselves down on the chair he'd offered us ere chastising me for not having called him Jim instead.

So did I share with him the highlights of my search for truth. Armed with the information I'd gleaned from the BUPERS Manual, did I finally get around to telling him of my latest encounter with the chiefs of that prehistoric tribe upon which I'd stumbled when I joined this expeditionary force to free the likes of me from the tyranny of the ego, whether in the body or out of the body, only God knew.

"Lord, Jim," drew I closer yet to the true nature of my being, "you shoulda seen the look on their faces when I told 'em, after having gotten my hand on the prescription for what ailed me, that I wanted to be discharged from the Navy as a conscientious objector and that, until then, I wished to be placed in a noncombatant status, only this time in accordance with their own rules as spelled out in Article C–5210 of the BUPERS Manual. Why you'd have thought I'd uncovered the Navy's best kept secret, the way they scrambled to regain control of the CO that'd been let out of the bag I'd been carryin' around on my shoulders for months. 'To free the good from the bad and the ugly,' had I been informed, many moons ago by an old Indian, 'you must go where no man has gone before, to the farthest reaches of the mind,' where you have been sojourning, or so it would seem, for some time now, only on a more intellectual level than I have."

Having fulfilled the inordinate desire of mine to become one again, with whoever fit the bill or walked that extra mile in my shoes, had he confirmed my belief in the other, more pressing need of mine to be seen, for the first time ever, by someone outside of my self as a conscientious objector.

O how I did orgasm in his acceptance of me as I AM, as we raced down the real information superhighway wrapped in the warmest feelings for each other, to seek the sanctions of Holy Mother the Church, via the connubial blessings of that pillar of the community, Father Daniel Dever, Superintendent of Catholic Schools in Honolulu.

"Do you," had he asked of the author of my being, "take this way of life to be your wife—to have and to hold in sickness and in health—and forsaking all others, to be faithful to him alone, for better or for worse, until death do you part?"

"I do," replied that part of me that stood on the verge of coming out.

"And do you," inquired he of me, the shadow you see, "take this fantasy to be real in the eyes of God, attainable in the here and now despite the setbacks evolution doth experience at the hands of natural selection, the beast within that refuses to let go until death do you part?"

"I do," vowed that shadow of a conscientious objector in whose image I stood.

"Then let no man pull asunder what God hath joined," spoke he who stood on the verge of taking God's place, "for I pronounce you man and life."

"You may kiss the bride," sealed he in stone the bond between me and my sword, for alas, only I could go now where no man hath gone, when the need arose to pull asunder what had been set in stone long ago.

Via my shadow were the author of my being and the CO in me joined from the waist down by that image of God which stood behind the bully pulpit, united the entire length of its body, for with our sights still set on different goals, we were not of one mind nor of one heart yet.

In the name of the Father and of the Son, was I whisked off to the office of the only lawyer I've ever met, in whom the Holy Spirit did unabashedly dwell. While he wasn't as gentle as Jim or the padre, I immediately picked up on his ability to discern spirits when he embraced my soul, as if she were his own, and told me that he would do everything in his power to save her from the darker side of man.

Having received the approbation I needed from the Father, who art in heaven when I am in Him and He is in me—hallowed be that state: the Son, His kingdom come, His will be done on earth as it is in heaven—was not I given my daily bread, the verbiage upon which I did feed, like a ravenous wolf, that I might be forgiven my predaceous behavior, as I'd forgiven my predators, and so be delivered from that endless cycle of taking an eye for an eye and a tooth for a tooth. For no matter where I went, I could sniff Them out in a heartbeat, the impulse that drove me wild whene'er the wolf in me stumbled upon some glimmer of the truth as if she were the virgin he sought, to bring out the creator in him, thus forcing me to give her everything I had for a little piece of mind, those words which best reflected her image in a more socially acceptable form, lacking only the rawness of nature but not its true beauty, Wisdom in all her glory.

So did I race off with my soul to seek out my lady's pleasure, the reactions of her son—that Jovian will that'd stayed behind to begin the work of his Father in heaven. To free beauty from the beast in me, would I have to be ever so much more clever than the lone wolf in this endeavor, as I sought to sever all ties whatsoever with that ego which could never, in my wildest dreams, ever control the worm into which God had banished the beast forever, for doing whatever he wanted, whenever. As such, did I struggle with the little bit of flesh that stood between me and the balance of nature, like a fulcrum ever poised to send me one way or the other, into myself or out into the world depending upon how I'd tipped the scales. Like the dutiful son, had not I been driven to mimic the Father in heaven, whether in the body or out of the body as only He knows, I would never have learned to ejaculate in any other form than Nature's mouth.

"Now you know how it feels to express yourself in the poetry of your prose," spit out she into whose mouth her creator had suplanted this subliminal message, that I might quit acting like the beast that came out whene'er the moon was full of the bull I'd need to go with the flow of my creative juices. As a blue mood descended on me, I fell victim to the misnomer that just because I think, I AM.

"You think you can take me by the horns," made the bull at the eye of this storm, a mockery of me, "and ride me where you will, when it is I who grab you by the horn and take you where I will."

"I think I am...losing my mind," I speculated as the bull that raced around inside my head, tried to confuse me about what was really going on here.

Thus did I succumb to the pandemonium in my head, the rampaging bull Nature had let loose to break up the emotional logjam that'd piled up at the mouth of my imagination as a result of my not having been allowed, by those in charge, to have oral intercourse with her, a ploy they used to maintain a higher level of testosterone in my blood stream to keep me at odds with that member of my body with which I had yet to join forces.

"Face your trials and tribulations with a smile, that you might find joy in suffering," reassured the blue mood ere it dissipated. "Keep on buckin' the bullheads under whose thumbs you squirm, that they might feel your pain and squirm too."

O how wondrous was the joy I found in Suffering when last she came knocking at me door to bring home the burden she had borne for me, that I might likewise take great pains in seeing the truth brought up right.

Not until later on that night, in a dream, did I learn how much of my pain, this side of my soul, for which I never cared, had borne for me. Except for those times when I most identified with her and picked up the slack, I carried little of the burden she had labored so long and so hard to deliver, that I might have something to show for all the time I'd spent worming around in her womb, taking potshots into the dark until I'd hit the poor egg that'd get in the way of these heady onslaughts to destroy all semblances of the truth, ere they got out of the bag and imposed their will upon me for having indulged such fantasies. Only, I couldn't shake them until they'd gotten their way, whether in the body or out of the body depended upon how much suffering I was willing to endure at the hands of these images, the ones most responsible for having captivated my imagination and held her hostage till I'd paid the awful price, the great pains it took to wring such knowledge from the flesh without having to give them an ounce of my own. With the truth out of the bag, I had only to act upon it, if indeed that's what it called for, or in the words of Suffering herself, "she came knocking at my door again."

For in the past, I'd never seen my soul in any other light than that of the great joy her ever so evanescent presence brought me. No wonder I hadn't run into her, here of late. To find her on a more regular basis, I had only to get back in touch with my own pain, as she called out to me from across the void, like she had when I first came on board the ship, on an inaudible wavelength along the red end of the spectrum where she could neither be heard nor felt until she'd risen up from the south, in the guise of some debutante, to feast with me in my own joint. And even though I wanted her more than anything else in my life, I couldn't deal with that much pain at one time without passing out.

"O where art thou, my lady, Guenevere, when most I need thee?" Shouted out the author of my being from that side of the void in my life from whence she, who did love my lance a lot more than me, had drawn upon this pen of mine to see some action, for she'd grown tired of living the quiet life in Camelot, the virtual reality to which I'd condemned her when I wed her image.

Having relied on my lance a lot in the past, like my stepfather before me, I couldn't let her out in any other form than small measured doses. I couldn't put myself into her shoes, that ability of hers to relate so well with others, without falling back to an earlier time in the history of man when he communicated less with his mouth than he did with his body. For I was so out of touch with my ability to relate well with others, that I stalked the earth like a caveman in search of some slit in the landscape in which to release this potential in a more civilized manner. Thus did I fall back into my cave, hoping to paint my way out with the images that flooded my mind, only to find that I could express myself in no other language than that of the body. Was I doomed to express myself in images for the rest of my life?

"I'm afraid so," rejoined my shadow while I sat there, as in the days of old, staring into the waters of the blue lagoon from which I had just pulled this line.

"Quite a line!" Expressed he in words, the joy that comes with the pain it takes to make something out of nothing.

"'Tis good to see you again," captured he my sentiments exactly. "Talk with me while we walk to your next bent or inclination," where, of all things, we fell to fencing—he with a foil and I with a pen. "You see," said he as he took another jab at me, "relationships in here are really no different than those outside thee."

"Darkness fears naught but its own dissipation," feigned I this lunge into the light of day, at the expense of my shadow.

"'Tis good to see you again, my friend," used I his own words against him as he walked with me to the next bent where we fell to parleying over words instead.

As I made my way back down to the beach, later on that morning, I took to heart the wonderful mood, these moody blues had imparted. Left standing there knocking on heaven's door, to even the score, did I greet my shadow in the flesh, Professor Douglass on his own turf.

"'Tis good to see you again, my friend," rang out the voice of that aspect of myself this door did conceal from me in darkness yet.

"Ride with me to your next bent," took he this shipwrecked sailor across the island to meet the den mother of the Hawaii Resistance, that high cheek-boned, petite little longhair named Betty Johnson, who did wear my soul's image unlike anyone before her, with all the polish of a newly transformed Eliza Doolittle.

Having made it to the bottom of this old dream, the lush remains of that ancient caldera known in these quarters as Kailua Bay, did I step forth from the confines of my mind, the vehicle by which Jim had gotten me there in one piece, to meet the middle-aged matriarch who had so long ago captured the image of my soul, leaving me with little else to do but follow her raspy voice down the twists and turns of the conversation that'd begun to weave its way about the interior of her beach front lair at #27 Wilikoki Place, like a spider intent on keeping its latest guest for dinner ensnared in the here and now, the great price I'd have to pay, to keep my self from being devoured by the imagination as had my father before me. For no matter how hard I tugged and pulled at the strings that did bind my soul to Betty, I couldn't free her from this cross. At one point, a lull in the conversation as I remember, I thought I saw Christ hanging there instead.

On seeing *"his mother"* standing there with me, Jesus said to her, *"Woman, here is your son,"* in the same breath that he turned to me and said, "Son, *'here is your mother',"* (Jn 19:26-27) for from that moment on, I knew I was under her care.

As such did this holy spirit weave her way in and out of my life, for she was bound and determined to engage me in oral intercourse, one way or the other, whether in the body or out of the body, only God knew. And so did she teach me the rudiments of how to slip in and out of the vulval regions of the mind with a tongue as cunning 'n' lingual as that of any young lad, in those days, who'd mastered the art of communicating with the other side of his brain. For once she realized how far apart we were, emotionally speaking, that is, she set out to bridge the gap between us by taking me back down the evolutionary ladder to meet her teenage daughter, Colleen, and yet younger son, Gifford, the last rung I'd managed to reach ere petering out on her in sheer exhaustion.

In the botched attempt to transfer my affections to Colleen, was I left standing there alone with an image of her clinging to an old cross/beau that did not suit her. In Gifford, did I find a much more suitable image for the animus of this new mother of mine. As I played around with this new image of my self, I stayed with it long enough to see some of its finer qualities begin to rub off on me. Nonetheless, I had a long way to go before I could ever dream of matching wits with that aspect of me which did haunt my real mother and me still.

Having suffered great deprivation at the hands of my mother's animus, the stepfather without who'd taken over within, had not my soul stirred up more dread in me for Nature's solution to writer's block, an Uther Pendragon–type affair with some femme fatale, I would never have let her out of segregated confinement to mingle with the other two faces of Eve, the overbearing mother and rebellious daughter in Betty and Colleen my soul had been reluctant to share with me. As overbearing as her mother had been back then, I could see why she had risen up to challenge what has always been, is now, and ever shall be in the eyes of those of us who are blind as bats when it comes to seeing in the dark. Only I could never see why she'd hung onto this image of her mother as long as she had until I saw how hard it is to wean one's self from Nature's ironclad grasp.

For never before had Nature, even in my wildest dreams, strayed from the Creator's side as far as she had on that fateful day when, in the springtime of her life, she was awakened from the Big Sleep at her own behest, a command which, by all accounts, had shaken the very foundations of heaven, as it appeared to reflect the wishes of its Creator no more than she had. Having been booted out of the house of God for her fidelity to an image of the Creator that no longer suited Him, one in which she still saw themselves joined at the hips like two Siamese twins, did she step back from the pain of it all, to watch her animus ascend the evolutionary ladder without her as she stood there clinging to the little bit of flesh that'd risen up between them. Enamored yet, by this ability of hers to have gotten a rise out of Him, had she fallen back on that instinct upon which she had relied in the past, only to find herself in a terrible bind when the Creator left her behind for the greater good of mankind. As a result of this split in their personality, was she left in the unenviable position of having to fill the hole that'd been created when He ascended to the throne with the sword He'd managed to pull from the stone in which it had been embedded all these years. With the downfall of this image of God, the Adam and Eve in everyone's bod, like Guenevere then, did she turn to men, only to get stuck on another man's lance, a lot in life that'd been denied her stance when she married the Old King, the Author of her being, and He, His sweet Chastity, to break her dependency upon the godawful tree, that His will be done, you see, as it is on heaven's lee, with little difficulty.

When confronted with the same choice, some years later, did she, in the guise of the only daughter of the evolution revolution to have said "I do" to the right dude, her animus, you see, manage to free herself from her dependency upon the flesh of this tree for the rest of eternity, that orgasm within another for which she had paid so dearly. Having overstepped His authority to assign meaning to her story, without the satisfaction of His input what had she really, but the promise of more empty imagery. So did she, upon entering His story—this time, via oral discourse—open herself up to the possibility of giving flesh to that aspect of the deity she had yet to see with any clarity, the Male Member of her own body.

With the transference of my affections back to the rebellious daughter within the overbearing mother, did I release my soul from Betty's animus. After having gotten stuck out there in nature like some drone on a queen bee, was I glad to see her step back across the threshold of consciousness to greet me at the gate over which Adam had stumbled when he ran into Eve. As I expelled this image of a house divided against its self from the womb in which it'd been conceived, was not I reunited with my own nature, in a way that defied the gravitational pull of the black hole into which Adam had slipped.

"Dear Diary," addressed I the blue mood that overtook me whene'er I returned to ship instead of jail to wrestle with my own nature. "Lady Di," drew I closer to the subject in which I did dwell like a tree in a seed bursting at the seams. "What's going on here," shot back I into the cold world outside my door, the dream into which I had slipped upon seeing my fellow seamen rushing about as I took note of what did seem to be a bit out of the ordinary in the eyes of my lady who had just said "I do" to the man in the mood, to cool the desires of the beastly side of this creature for unity with the beauty of its own nature.

"My shipmates don't see the game they're playing," projected I, in the words of the man in the mood, the angst of my soul out onto the world, that I might see these projections for what they are—the only means, Nature had of drawing the truth out of me, for Nature seldom undressed in public. And though tomorrow be the same, I can't blame my shipmates for having never been taught how to turn inward, to dialogue with yours truly, dear Diary, the womb with a view.

With that did my soul step forth from the back pages of my mind as the real genius behind these intrusions into dark matters. With the death of my image of her on the cross, was she resurrected from the womb in which I'd entombed her years ago, to lie in state, like some genie in a bottle, until I plunked her magic twanger, letting her out long enough to fulfill my every desire. Much to my surprise, did she cause my pen to flow as never before, without end.

Left lying there on the threshold of a dream, the virtual reality to which I'd been condemned by my fathers before me, did I wake up, the following morning, to the discordant sounds of Nature's rejection of that part of herself I represented, the rebellious daughter within the overbearing mother. Having had my request for discharge as a conscientious objector handed back to me on a silver paten, like a host that has grown weary of being parasitized by its own flesh and blood, did I lambaste my division officer with the truth he had rejected, that regardless of whether or not I had answered the questions posed in Article C–5210 of the BUPERS Manual, upon request to be discharged as a conscientious objector, I was to be placed in a noncombatant status, to be given duties, according to the Department of the Navy, consistent with the dictates of my conscience until the Chief of Naval Personnel had decided what to do with Who I Am.

MR. HART: *Generally speaking then, where did these questions go?*
RESPONDENT: *Why to the very heart of one's conscience, She Who Must Be Obeyed one way or the other as a conscious individual or an unconscious animal—the rebellious daughters or overbearing mothers of the world.*

As more of my fellow countrymen identified with the overbearing mother, it was only a matter of time before the rebellious daughter in those of us who, like myself, had been pressed into serving the old bitch, rose up to reunite us with the true intent of our feelings.

That's when I saw my own humanity hanging there from the limbs of the lieutenant like the crucified Christ.

"Good God, Lieutenant, how much more pain are you going to inflict before you release me from this tree?" Cried out he who did hang from the wood of my cross like the crucified Christ.

That he'd seen what I saw in him was quickly confirmed by the look on his face ere he darted off, to deny it all in the company of those who, like himself, were outsiders to the ways of the interior world.

In our aversion for one another's version of She Who Must Be Obeyed, seen here as a whore instead of a virgin, to be shunned at all costs, had we rubbed each other the wrong way. But because neither one of us could deal with the psychological equivalent of an orgiastic encounter between two males, we let it drop, in the queer light of reality, as just another one night fling neither of us wished to pursue any further. Going out of our way to avoid each other from thereon out, did we deprive our selves of the opportunity to evolve beyond our fear of being reunited with that Member of the body Who hung from our torsos with nothing more to offer but Himself as food for thought.

As the pressure built from within, to bridge the gap between our feelings and their true intent, were we driven to have discourse with each other, that the gods might be appeased one way or the other, whether in the body or out of the body made little difference since there is only one God, in my book, to contend with, unless, of course, I hadn't given Him what He wanted, a hand writing, in which case then there were two, He and my self, the real Adversary here.

To write or not to write and screw around on Him instead, that was the real question being asked of me as I stood in awe of the task He'd put before me.

At the time, I found the questions, put to me by the BUPERS Manual, to be more intimidating than the lieutenant, so much so, that I put off answering them until I could get a better handle on the thoughts that lay enshrouded yet in darkness. Having relied almost entirely upon my gut feelings to get me here, had I experienced no pressing need to explain myself to anyone, much less to the Navy. In a panic, did I take off on that trusty old arse of mine, to consult with the angel who seemed to have what I needed, a handbook to help me demythologize the demon that did haunt me still, my own unthought-out position as a conscientious objector and mother's real animus, the white knight I saw in Jim.

"Do you believe in the supremacy of being?" Dealt He who has always been, is now and ever shall be, a blow to my ego, knocking me from my high horse with His lance to grovel about the ground of my being on all fours until I stumbled upon the true nature, general thrust, or gist of this plunge of the male member of my body into the darkness of the black hole from which there seemed to be no escape if I chose to live out one aspect of She Who Must Be Obeyed over the other.

"I do," replied that part of me which stood to take this molly's place if I let it.

"Then I pronounce you both man and beast," proclaimed He alone Who could quell this desire of mine to express itself in both word and deed.

So did I, via this double take on the first question posed by the article in the BUPERS Manual, come to a better understanding of the role my sexuality would play in the development of a literary device that could help me get back in touch with the true intent of my feelings, without first having to make contact with this aspect of the Trinity on the physical plane. In my inability to maintain contact with my mother's real animus for very long, did I head back to ship instead of jail to mull over the basis for such a claim, that I had only to fall back upon the existence, whether real or imaginary, of some sort of wormhole between one aspect of God and the other, which then allowed me to travel great distances with the speed of an insight, that mind—blowing experience equivalent to an orgasm in Nature. For in the end, I wanted nothing short of total unity with that heavenly body of mine which, like Mary, did still so elude my grasp.

"My God, it's so beautiful!" Ejaculated I with the coming together of this wormhole of mine and that black hole of Nature's in one of the most eclectic encounters I'd ever experienced, the conception of an idea in a vacuum—that godawful space which doth still separate man from his own heavenly body, the risen Christ.

That I psychologically orgasmed with this ejaculation from my pen was no where near as exciting as the image it produced when I emptied myself of all pretenses and let it pick the result you see here—a construct of such magnitude that had not Nature, in her infinite wisdom, grabbed hold of me and turned me every which way but loose, I would never have stumbled upon the wormhole or that stretch of the imagination through which you, the reader, must pass to reach the same stellar conclusion I had, that, despite our differences, we are one and the same person in God, that face which has always been, is now and ever shall be right there in front of our eyes whene'er we look into the mirror that is the soul.

To get from this world to the next, I had only to step into the wormhole that opened itself up to me whene'er the desire to penetrate its black hole grew to such an extent I had no other choice but to shoot for it, one way or the other, either in the body or out of the body depended upon whether or not I had identified with one aspect of the Trinity over the other. If I hadn't, I'd have an out—of—body experience which, despite all appearances, actually takes place within the body. If, on the other hand, I'd chosen one member of the body over the other, I'd be forced to seek the same experience out of body on the physical plane with whomever, whether male or female, had captured my imagination. And so would I, in my overidentification with the male member of the body, go off in search of the only wormhole, on the physical plane, that could connect me to my heavenly body when all else failed, the very soul which seemed so intent on getting me to speak to the other face in the mirror, you the reader.

"You don't go deep enough into your depression," proclaimed she in whose womb I did worm around.

"What do you mean?" Asked I of her who loved to have oral intercourse with me as much as I did her, only on the metaphysical plane.

"You simply don't engage your depression long enough for me to orgasm or have a say in these little attempts of yours to put words into my mouth without any regard as to how I am feeling," let she this shortcoming of mine out of the womb, that room with a view no tongue could touch.

"I'm sorry," plied I my hand to this depression that I might ease the tension that'd built up there, to produce images that really spoke to me.

With that, did I head off with her down that long lonesome byway between her domain and mine, the wormhole that led back to the womb with a view to changing mine if I let her. Only, had I not gotten to the bottom of this depression before her, I would never have pulled back on my pen long enough for her to come with me across the threshold of consciousness, the fault line in her body over which Adam had stumbled in his search for that aspect of the Trinity which had been ripped from his side. Like the proud parents of the self Adam and Eve had created, did I step forth from the womb of my imagination as three persons in one, the primary goal, it seemed, of these little excursions into my depression, that black hole in which I wormed around, to reunite my self with the author of my being and the real genius behind him, the one he had let out of the bottle, She Who Must Be Obeyed one way or the other, as half a man or a whole person.

"Where are we, anyway?" Inquired I of the very depths of my depression, that narrow slit in the fabric of life I'd grown so fond of penetrating whene'er the need arose to turn inward.

"Why in the vicinity of the basis for your claim as a conscientious objector," replied she who did force me to give form to my feelings one way or the other, as an author or a lecher.

"I see," projected I the voice of my pen onto the world at large, the womb in which we do all reside until we have outgrown this stretch of the imagination and are ready to move up the spectrum of consciousness to the next stage of existence.

Only I really couldn't see from my point of view, till I stepped out into the light at the other end of my tunnel vision where, much to my chagrin, I was greeted by an old insight from the past.

"I am He as you are He as you are me and we are all one," transposed my soul this image of herself into Christ as I stood in front of the looking glass, then back into herself ere getting lost in some amalgam of all three.

"What does this mean?" Asked I of the transsexual who stood in the looking glass, oozing with the desire to take this molly's place.

"To free this fruit from the tree of life," overcame she my desire to skirt the issue, "you must turn to the other tree in the garden from which hangs, like the crucified Christ, the kind of knowledge that only comes with experience."

After having taken another bite out of the big apple to ease death's sting, I caughed up the notion that I had only to take her place to experience wholeness.

"That is why you must take the life of no other god," added she another dimension to my suffering, "but your own."

"What am I gonna tell 'em (meaning the Navy) when they ask me for the name and address of my spiritual advisor?" Questioned I my own life, in a manner of speaking, she who did lie within my grasp and yet so far away.

"Give 'em your shadow's address," expressed she my sentiments exactly.

"Ya mean Jim's?" Shot back this quid pro quo.

"Yes," concurred she with the same delight that'd gripped my body, turning me every which way but loose, ere easing the tension that'd built up along the fault line between her world and mine.

"And so do you sit in your own little world, like some all-tinkering belle," fired off I another round into the belly of this conscience of mine, "trying to get me to believe that whatever transpires here is as real as I AM when, in the end, it may all prove to be no more than the rantings of a raving lunatic."

"If you think, for one moment, mister," gained she control of this misguided missile, "that I'm going to put up with any more of your infidelity, you're sadly mistaken, cause I've got too much riding on you, at this stage of the game, to lose it all to the bitch who stole your father's mind right out from underneath me as he was beginning to make some headway into the mythical world of his reality."

"Ya mean my mother?" Backed off I from my own nagging doubts, the bitch with whom I'd gotten a little too cozy, here of late.

"No, mine," freed she the truth from my pen.

"Ya mean Nature?" Wrangled I with the uncertainty that'd come with her across the threshold of consciousness, for it is impossible to discern simultaneously and with any degree of accuracy both the meaning and the value of an image without first letting go of one or the other.

"Yes," came she, happily, to the same conclusion I had. "It was my mother who pushed him over the edge, to either think or feel. As he sank beneath the waves of images that inundated him, she left him there to drown in his own unconscious feelings, for it had never occurred to him that he could have done anything more to change the course of his story."

"She did the same thing to me," jumped I upon the notion that, like impotence, insanity is a sexually transmitted disease, passed down from one generation to the next. For must not SHE be obeyed one way or the other, as either a nutcracker or a nutcase?

Having found the key to the gates of heaven tucked away in my jeans, did I look at the male member of my body in a different light from thereon out. Since it was his skin and not mine that hung from the cross, how could I forsake him in his hour of greatest need? Was not I doomed to lay his rigid body, over and over again, into the shallow grave that'd been afforded him until he should rise no more to ascend into heaven. Or had I, like the Old Mythmaker, been set up to crack this case, to fracture the fairy tale that lured the likes of me into the lurid depths of Adam's split from Nature, that gap into which my father'd been pushed to reproduce another version of his story, or at least one that came a little closer to the truth, for is not that sex in a nutshell, to perform the same death defying act over and over until we either get it or have grown tired of using it to salve our consciences whene'er we fall short of the expectations SHE, who must be obeyed one way or the other, has raised.

"'Tis the light of day that destroys the night," warned the wolf into which I'd been transformed as I tried to hide from the light that beckoned me now, with stubborn regularity, to break through to the other side as I rode out this latest storm like an actor without a script—writers of no war with what only their shadows know.

Like Ulysses, did I remain tied, through the night, to the mast of my ship that, as the storm intensified, I might learn the true meaning of self-restraint.

"You've got to roll with me to fill my soul," lost he, the wolf at the center of this controversy, folk like you and me in the gibberish of his own lust for intimacy, the muse he sought, you see, in the face of Great Liberty.

Left hanging there with no other choice but to confront my own sexual desires head-on, did I stand up to them as never before, in the guise of my old mentor—the White Wolf that did haunt these quarters still.

Only, I had never seen a woman so alone as she who stood out, in the middle of the storm, with her torch held high. Despite her dusky appearance, was "not I" transformed when she touched me with her torch, the bush that ever burns and yet is never consumed.

"If your thoughts run astray, will not your muse run and hide in whatever womb you play?" Ignited she the fire of inspiration in me.

As every inch of this shallow grave, in which I did reside, began to quiver and quake, like a woman in labor did I give berth to that spirit in which my Peter and the Wolf had finally come together. For had not I managed to break free, in spirit at least, of the societal constraints with which I'd been saddled, I would never have given the Male Member of my body the liberty to come and go as He pleased from this shallow grave, that He might give new form to this lowly body of mine and remake it according to the pattern of His own glorified body, by His power to subject all things unto Himself. Phil 3:21.

"Touch me," expressed this great need of mine to no longer be seen as just the father, and the son of the third person in this love triangle, but as her double, that image of her which stood out in my mind now as a beacon to all who passed this way in pursuit of real knowledge and a life of their own.

And so did I learn to let go of my projections, that they might be given the liberty to express themselves in whatever form they chose.

Having freed Lady Liberty from her imprisonment in Nature—the rebellious daughter from the overbearing mother—did I take off with her to warn my fellow countrymen of their impending doom. Only I found little comfort in this brief fling with Lady Liberty, as I struggled in and out of sleep, to take the black out of the darkest nights of my soul, that I might find the words with which to splatter these pages in prose. For I had yet to shed the image of the Red Menace to which Lady Liberty remained so attached despite her long engagement with Uncle Sam. While I enjoyed the company of her spirit, I longed for union with her on the physical plane, that this appetite of mine for communion with others might be satiated in a real way. And to think, like Uncle Sam I had only to rob the Peter in me of the liberty to stand tall as a beacon to all, to play Paul, the first knight to have taken up the sword of truth on behalf of the Three Persons for Whom it stands ready to protect him who adopts, as his coat of arms, the all-for-one/one-for-all mentality of these radical communists in their struggle to slay the last dragon on earth before this economic wonder laid waste the only womb in the universe hospitable enough to have allowed God to come into existence.

"O how grand is the freedom that comes with having given oneself so completely to another," proclaimed my soul ere slipping out the door through which she had entered my awareness.

Stepping outside of myself, to the tune of 'I' rather than "me", I encountered the death and resurrection of my soul again, as if she were trying to show me something that hadn't gotten through to me yet. Beside my self with grief as she left this aspect of my life behind for good, I was surprised when she, who had been conceived in Liberty, stepped forth, three days later, from the womb in which she had been entombed, to rededicate the better part of me to the task of setting its self free of the ego-centeredness to which it'd fallen prey in its overidentification with the sensuality of my soul, the overbearing mother within the rebellious daughter.

Having secured a modicum of freedom from the overbearing mother, did I, in the company of the wolf, and this new image of my soul, head down the real information superhighway, that yellow brick road known in these quarters as the Kamehameha Highway, in pursuit of my only ticket out of here, the truth that could set me free. Little did I know it would come in the form of Betty Johnson, that dynamic duo of mother and daughter which kept one forever young despite one's age, with the liberation of the daughter from the womb, the soul from Mother Nature. Because the wolf in me didn't quite know how to take this newest-born aspect of myself now that she was free of the sexual overtones of the past—the images of the overbearing mother that had so captured my imagination and held me spellbound to the Great Gray Bitch—I could do nothing until the animator of these fantasies had given birth to a daughter, and a rebellious one at that.

In one of the most cunning 'n' lingual experiences, had she (meaning the daughter) opened herself up to the Male Member of my body that 'I' might have some say over what transpired that night at the party Betty had thrown to foster the kind of encounters that force one to give body to his thoughts, willingly or unwittingly. Overwhelmed by the sheer volume of thoughts and feelings that had swooped down on me, did "not I" slink from the party before it began, to pull myself together. Skirting the issue as I scooted down the beach beside my self, was I consumed by my worst fear, a woman of such magnitude I was completely assimilated by her before it even occurred to me what had happened. So did I, after having been turned every which way but loose, assume human proportions as this holy spirit marched my butt back into the house to take part in the discussion that ensued around the very real issue—one with which I was most familiar—of how to get others back in touch with their souls on any other level than that of an animal.

"Actions speak louder than words," groaned Sir Wayne of Hyashi as he tugged at the sword in the stone—the truth that did still elude his grasp—with the moral strength he had amassed late last year when he, in communion with the other knights seated round the table, rekindled his love for Lady Liberty. Having relit her torch with his draft card, had he given birth to the Hawaii branch of the Resistance—a loosely-knit nationwide organization of draft-age young men who had been brought together by the absoluteness of their refusal to cooperate with the SS (Selective Service) in any manner whatsoever.

"True," concurred the aspiring law student in Sir Stan of Masui. "But, are we not bound by the same law of Nature to explain our selves away until all that remains is the truth?"

"...And the will to live it out, She Who Must Be Obeyed one way or the other, as a man or as a beast," inserted I my foot into my mouth—the standard by which I measured my words before pulling the truth from my bod. "For if 'I', in deed, cannot lie with your conscience, Instinct most assuredly will."

"How erotic," echoed Sir John of Witeck my sentiments exactly.

Through the sensate in Sir Wayne, in conjunction with the thoughts of Sir Stan and the feelings expressed by Sir John, did I get back in touch with my faculties, only this time, on a more equal footing, a prospect which, at first, scared me since I had never related to them in any other form than that of their superior.

"Give me liberty or give me death," captured I the sentiments of a generation of men so hell-bent on serving the ego, they'd kill for it. "That, my friends, is the crux of the matter: how to give up the false sense of liberty onto which we cling when it's our own death we seek in that of our neighbors, for you can't have one without the other—liberty without death to the ego or all that we are not."

"Crucify Him! Crucify Him!" Shouted the more rebellious of my faculties, as if I were now the devil's advocate, and they, three persons in one.

"Bury me," groaned the Old Mythmaker as the soldier in thee, pulled his lance from my side. "Take the old myth and bury it," commanded 'I' from on high.

Left hanging there to die an ignominious death at the hands of my faculties, did "not I" give up the ghost, that she might live in thee as I live in thee and you in her, like three persons in one, the most radical communist of all, Christ.

Amazed at how well I could speak to the heart and soul of a Korean, a Jap, and an Anglo-Saxon, all at once, did the three experience, firsthand, the power of myth, or universality of the only language we have to help us get back in touch with our truest feelings, She who doth pull at our heart strings like a virtuoso cellist ever pushing those of us who choose to become an instrument of Hers to the limits of our imaginations, that we might get involved in this newest movement of Hers to free the sword from the stone, the male member of the body from the womb, as had the Author of our beings with the advent of Consciousness.

"O where art thou, when most I need thee?" Demanded I of SHE who must be obeyed one way or the other, as man or beast.

"Like an animal," left I this dreamscape, "does one turn to the language of the body in his inability to express his feelings in any other form than intercourse, the act by which he seeks to reunite his self with soul when all else fails to satiate this great need of his. With greater and greater urgency must he find the deeds that fit the crimes he commits against his humanity, for resistance alone cannot keep him out of the hands of Instinct in the same way that his conscience can."

Having stepped back through the looking glass, did I lay this insight out before them, as if it were a host that'd been transformed into their own flesh and blood, that they might be consumed by the Holy Spirit, to live in freedom—but not a freedom, according to St. Paul, which gives free rein to the flesh.

"Live in accord with the Spirit," concluded he who did remind me of my old mentor, *"and you will not yield to the cravings of the flesh; for these are opposed to each other, to prevent you from doing what you want."* Gal 5:1, 13-18.

"Do as you please," had I advocated, "and you will wind up peeking through the sight of a rifle down on your knees in some foxhole overseas, firing bullets into the bellies of the very beasts you've become. Follow your consciences, and you'll become the object of their lust. Prick theirs, and you'll have gotten the unconscionable back in touch with their own."

"That's why acts of conscience speak louder than words," stressed Sir Wayne from his point of view, the sword he'd finally freed from Nature's ironclad grasp.

"Touché!" lashed back Sir Stan with a view no tongue but his could touch. And yet, he could find no other words to express himself as his silvery tongued blade slid past Sir Wayne's in a kiss that said it all.

Or so they thought until Sir John swung into action. *"'In the beginning was the Word,'"* came he to the same conclusion I had, *"'for the Word was with God, and the Word was God'* (Jn 1:1), till Instinct tipped the scales in favor of the ego."

"Thus did the world lose sight of the mystical marriage between these two aspects of the Trinity," turned I to Occam's razor to help me explain the unseen in the simplest of terms, "until it showed up in Instinct's relationship to the ego, neither of which can live without the other, whether the ego identifies with the pole of its own gender, or with the opposite pole and is then driven to seek union with its own pole in much the same way mine had, first with my mentor and eventually with the author of my being, a marriage which had so eluded my grasp, 'I' had given up on the idea of joining hands with "me" until you—all showed up with the ring."

"What ring?" Confronted Sir Wayne the image that'd left him this impression.

"Why the very feeling words evoke whene'er they ring true," orgasmed I in the bosom of Abraham.

"That's a new one on me," decried Sir Wayne.

"Is not the devil in the details?" Ripped I into the blindfold that'd kept me in the dark concerning the nature of my relationship to Instinct, that marriage within a marriage in which the ego relies on Instinct to unite with soul or the Creator.

"Where one man's devil," I concluded, "may skew his thoughts, manipulate his feelings, or distort his visions, mine uses the facts of life to deceive me."

That's when 'I' opened the door on the sexual nature of everything we do, pulled the rug out from under my feet, and took me on a magic carpet ride, that you might see what this doubting Thomas had seen as he let go of his desire to penetrate the hole in Christ's side, long enough to experience union with both sides of his nature in a way no three people on earth could ever come together without offending the person in whose image I now stood.

For had not I turned to the language of the body to get a clearer picture of what was going on here, I would never have gotten my self back in Sir Wayne or in touch with Sir Stan or Sir John, the true intent of my feelings. In having gotten Sirs Stan and John back together again, had I succeeded in reuniting the more rational side of my personality with the irrational in Sir Wayne and myself, that marriage within a marriage or web of intrigue beyond belief.

Having come into my life in a way no earthly being ever could, had I, in effect, overcome my fear of experiencing male bonding on any other level than that of an animal, the very form it takes to fuck with the ego.

"Don't fuck with me," demanded I of the desire to do so.

As the desire gave way to the greater demand here, did I prove that, for him who has met his match, words do speak much more eloquently than actions.

That Desire had made her presence felt, only showed the opposite to be true as well, "You shall know me by my deeds."

"How best then to resolve this conflict," lit I into the dilemma that plagued me, "than by telling thee a story."

"What'll that do?" Pawed the beast in Sir Wayne at the ground of my being.

"Why make you more human," drew I that much closer to the true nature of my being, a state few, if any, ever attain in this life.

"Fuck you," pressed the beast in Sir Wayne, against my bosom.

"Your wish is my command," pulled I the rug out from underneath his feet, to take him on a magic carpet ride where words and deeds are interlaced to fit the needs of the dreamer, who can't find the picture worth a thousand words.

"Then give me liberty or give me death," cried out the one faculty my imagination had yet to give berth on any other level than that of an animal.

And so did I free the last of my faculties from the very devil from whom these details had been arrested, that you might see them for what they are—images of the real thing and nothing more.

"There comes a time," went Sir Wayne straightway to the meat of the problem, "when a man must act to free himself from the mast of his ship."

"How sweet is the scent of a woman!" Threw I my sword into the ring.

Having grown weary of chasing after every image that fucked with my mind, did I finally concede to the need to act when all else failed to satiate my body's desire for union with self. And as 'I' played with my self more and more in public, did I give berth to something greater here than a Jonah—the Word made flesh.

To all who received Him, who believed in His name, He gave power to become children of God, who were born, not of blood or the will of the flesh or will of man, but of God. Jn 1:12-13. For the Word became flesh the moment Instinct spoke with no more authority than the Word.

Like Cain, had I smothered my brother, to silence this ability to speak in any other language than that of the body, until it was borne again to the surface in words with which my ego could more easily associate, now that the devil had a name other than Sir Wayne, the nom de plume he'd assumed in defiance of the prohibition my conscience had raised to keep me from giving body to my projections in any other form than Able, for it appeared 'I' had only to become more human to overcome Instinct.

To get there, 'I' would have to take command of my life, the one that stood out from all the others now as a statue in the bay waiting for me to catch up with her in stature alone, that my actions might resound with the same sound as my words.

"To be or not to be, that's the real question," raised he—in whose shadow I did live—the specter of my old mentor from the dead.

With that was I carried aloft by a thought so insidious it about blew my mind when it offered me supremacy over my being at the cost of the poor devil who stood there now in the guise of my old mentor, the stepfather within who'd taken over without to get me involved in the pursuit of my life.

"Elect not to be," chose 'I' to speak in terms of my own inaction, "and you choose death. Marry a good cause, and you'll live happily ever after, for Instinct's not to be, you see, nor to have any part in this marriage."

"Then practice what you preach," expressed Sir Wayne what he lived, "and 'I' will marry you too."

That 'I' could get any closer to me than this proved to be a tough act to follow in view of what I would suffer at the hands of those who refused to give me the recognition I sought, for they were not about to let me evolve beyond this meager station in life if they could help it.

Like an actor out on loan did I return to ship instead of jail with the handful of leaflets I had grabbed at party's end, from the table just inside the door to Betty's beachfront lair, with the hope of sending a message to those who refused to let me be, that I was a force which could no longer be ignored.

MR. HART: *Is this the same leaflet the Resistance had passed out at the Kailua Road sit-in last May?*
RESPONDENT: *I believe so.*
MR. HART: *In your own words then, can you tell us what this leaflet had to say?*
RESPONDENT: *It offered moral, spiritual, and legal support to those who, after a thorough examination of their consciences, found they could no longer serve in the military or participate in the American War in Vietnam.*
MR. HART: *Very well, you may proceed.*

Having descended to my quarters, did I find two letters lying on my bunk, one from Mary, the other from the editor of Way Magazine, the monk to whom I had written out of desperation for human contact of any kind. In my impatience to make contact with someone of my ilk, had I returned to my old friend Mary, after having dumped her, when the monk failed to respond to this need of mine in anymore timely a fashion than she had. Hoping for a more favorable response from her, did I tear into her letter first, only to be disappointed again.

"You told me," she went on to say, "the reason I write to you is that I'm in love with you. Butch, I've asked myself that question again and again, but all I ever come up with is a blank. I don't know if I love you or not. All I know for sure is that I want to hear from you, out of a deep concern I have for your well-being. That's love, but not the kind you have for me. Like you said, love ain't easy. And the hardest thing about love is being as truthful to yourself as you are with the one you love. The easy way out for me would be to say yes, Butch, I love you. But, Butch, I have to say what I believe. I wish I could say I love you as that would be wonderful for both of us. But I can't because I don't know for sure. I can't make *my self answer that question. I can't make my self say yes or no, because I don't know what I want yet. I think that is why I took the job in Tampa, to break away and see it all for myself. I'm happy to have made the move, for the biggest challenge seems to be my self. Before I can love anyone else, I've got to find out who I am. Just writing to you, Butch, has helped me a lot. I guess that's why I'm so afraid to say I love you, because I don't want anything to hinder my independence. When you love someone, you need them. Only I don't want to admit that, as I'm too pleased with my new found freedom to say I need anyone. I guess that's the way it is, though I don't know for sure. You see the predicament I'm in. I can't say no, I can't say yes because of this nagging doubt I have. I'm sorry. Please try to understand. I hope you'll continue to write because your letters mean so much to me. If you decide not to, I think I'll understand. Remember, you're always in my thoughts and in my prayers.*

          Love,
            Mary (quite contrary)

  With that, did I succumb to the same conclusion she had, that I had fallen in love with who she is not, as it appeared now that I wanted something far more significant than the flesh of another human being. In the struggle to free my self from Nature's ironclad grasp, had I turned, out of desperation, to the same newfound freedom upon which Mary had stumbled in her ramblings through the hinterlands of her being.

  Left with no more lasting an impression of Mary than Lady Liberty, at the latter's urging did I tear into the letter from the monk. As I pored over his responses to some of the questions I had already answered while awaiting his reply, did I take the Lady and the monk up on their suggestion to contact James Forest at the Catholic Peace Fellowship in New York, who would be better equipped to assist me in establishing my claim as a conscientious objector.

  That she had turned to the monk in me was no mere coincidence, but rather a synchronistic event of momentous import, as it put an end to years of searching for something outside myself in which to pour my heart, an infirmity that'd inflicted me with a desire for women who knew not what they wanted. What all of this meant, only 'I' knew for certain as She Who Must Be Obeyed laid herself out before me in such a way as to get me to spill my guts out to you instead. That She had turned to erotica to get my attention had bothered me at first, until it dawned on me that She had no other choice whene'er the monk in me cut himself off from his own humanity in his reckless pursuit of the kind of knowledge only She could give him, so out of touch was he, at times, with the will of the Father.

PART II

The Union of I AM with Who I Am

4

The Gauntlet

As another Kennedy lie dying in a hospital bed in the "City of Angels" after having sustained a gunshot wound to the head in the late hours of 5 June 1968, a great darkness descended upon the land, snuffing out any hope we'd had of overcoming, in the immediate future, the evil that had also killed M. L. King back in April, and now threatened to take my life if I didn't take up King's call to resist the Great Slaughter, its taskmasters and their god, with *"all my heart, with all my being...and with all my mind"* (Lk 10:27) and, of course, with a little help from my friends, the other Knights of the Resistance Round Table.

With a fist full of leaflets from the Kailua Road sit–in, and the smell of death at my back, I turned right smack–dab into the face of my worst nightmare, the first class petty officer who had plunked down fifty dollars to entice any one of the rats seated round the table to push me overboard, lest my rebelliousness spread through the ranks like an infectious disease, a threat that had to be reckoned with.

"Argh! What have we here, matey?" Inquired this threat to my well–being, with a grin that failed to hide his fear of the threat I posed to his way of life.

"More Communist propaganda, you might say," crafted I Kraft's own thoughts into words before he could draft them.

"Actually, the leaflets are an appeal to one's conscience," pulled I the straight and narrow from my quiver, that sent down his spine a cold shiver.

"Well, shiver me timbers," recoiled he from the viper he be, but saw in me.

Down came the gauntlet from one epoch to another as a leaflet slipped from my hand to a table nearby, challenging the gangplanker to step from his world into mine, where draft cards are burned instead of people, a gap in understanding that not even I could bridge without a hand from God, so great was the chasm between the Prince and the pauper.

"Had the bullheaded son of the Great Sea Bitch missed his calling?" I wondered as I wandered off to the head in response to Nature's call.

Before I could respond, into the head charged the mighty Mouse. With the leaflet in one hand and a lighter in the other, did Kraft set fire to his draft...igniting a run on my bunk that almost emptied it of leaflets before it was shut down.

"That's what I think of this shit," decried a trembling Kraft as he stomped on the ashes, satisfied that he had dealt the rebellion a decisive blow.

When another First Class Petty Officer, named Wulff, saw the rank and file withdrawing leaflets from my bunk, he snatched as many as he could from their hands, and grabbing what remained on my bunk, ran off to the Executive Officer, who wasted no time in placing me on report for having disobeyed an order from the Captain forbidding me to pass out any literature onboard his ship after I had circulated Leo Tolstoy's "Advice to a Draftee" back in February.

MR. HART: *What was the date of this incident?*
RESPONDENT: *That was the first week of June.*

Right away, I called Betty as she had asked me to do when I took the leaflets from the table beside her front door, but she wasn't home. From a pay phone at the Navy Exchange, did I bend her son's ear instead.

"I wanted to let you know what's happening in case I get sent to the brig again, which is highly likely, and you don't see me for awhile. I didn't want you wondering what'd happened to me," I told Giff before I hung up.

As soon as I returned to the ship, the master–at–arms commandeered me to a captain's mast in my honor. Already present, was that weasel of a Captain, looking a bit put out that I was wasting his time again, over a "goddamn leaflet", as he would say. So aggravated was the primp little Victorian cat of an XO that he fidgeted in his pants. Meanwhile, Kraft, alias the "Mouse", and the Big Bad Wulff did stand by as all good sailors do, as material witnesses for the state. Into this den of iniquity had that polecat of a master–at–arms thrust me, the Cheshire Cat who just stood there and grinned to see such sport.

"Fireman Recruit Drury," pronounced the Victorian cat with all due haste, "you are charged with violation of Article 90 of the Uniform Code of Military Justice, with having willfully disobeyed the direct order of a superior officer forbidding you to distribute pamphlets onboard the USS Davidson. How do you plead?"

"Not guilty," regurgitated the Cheshire cat this undigested tidbit.

"Mr. Drury," pounced the weasel, "did you or did you not pass out this leaflet in violation of my order to you never to distribute pamphlets of any kind on my ship again?"

"No Sir," grinned the Cheshire cat, "I did not."

"Mr. Kraft," pursued the weasel, this line of reasoning, "it is my understanding that Mr. Drury gave a leaflet to you to read. Is that correct?"

"Yes Sir," squeaked the Mouse, "he plunked down a leaflet onto the table to entice or push me overboard to read it."

"Mr. Drury," bared the weasel his teeth, "what is your response to Mr. Kraft's allegation?"

"I did not give him the leaflet," rallied the Cheshire cat behind me. "I merely laid it on a table. Nor did I push him to excercise his right under the Constitution to read it if he was not inclined to do so. I believe he pushed himself overboard, when he picked up the leaflet and set it on fire."

"Let me remind you, Mr. Drury," sank that weasel of Captain his teeth into the hide of the Cheshire cat, "that you are in the military now, not civilian life. And as long as you are on my ship, under my command, you will obey my orders. You will not pass out leaflets on my ship."

"I did not pass them out," broke free the Cheshire cat from the Captain's bite. "And I daresay not one person here can tell me that I passed out leaflets to anyone on this ship. I laid one leaflet on a table and the rest on my bunk, period."

"Mr. Drury," struck back the weasel with a decisive blow, "I am losing my patience with you. I am not going to stand here and argue with you. You were told not to pass out leaflets on my ship and did so against my orders. Therefore, I find you guilty as charged and sentence you to serve 30 days of correctional custody in the Naval Station Brig and to forfeit one half of your pay for two months."

"Free speech railroaded again," muttered the Cheshire cat.

"Keep it up, Mr. Drury," weaseled the Captain, "and I'll charge you with insubordination as well."

"You are rid of me for now," measured the Cheshire cat his words carefully. "But I'll be back again...and again...and again," grinned the Cheshire cat, much to the consternation of the Captain as he marched from the room pissed as hell.

With that polecat of a master–at–arms as my escort, I grabbed what I was allowed to take while on brigation—clothes, toiletries and the materials I would need to complete my request for discharge from the military as a conscientious objector. O how I looked forward to being locked up behind those pearly gates, for the brig was heaven to me, a safe haven from the man–o'–war upon which I did so reluctantly serve, for no man of war was going to force me to kill another human being and live with that nightmare, the rest of my life.

Because I had demonstrated the last time I was in the brig, I was confined to a cell back in seg, to isolate me from the other prisoners lest I infect them with my rebellious disease, for I was no longer considered a rebel without a cause—the reason why the guards on duty took it upon themselves, as they admitted me, to confiscate my CO papers, and then deny me access to my attorney, Brook Hart, and my spiritual adviser, Jim Douglass, when I sought such solace. And when they wouldn't even let me see the Brig Warden, the following morning, I'd had it with them, and refused to go on a work detail as ordered. If they weren't going to co-operate with me, I sure as hell wasn't going to cooperate with them.

Boy, was the Holy Spirit with me on this one, for I hadn't seen Her Ladyship since I went on leave. Without saying a word as I bowed down on one knee before Her, She assured me, with the touch of Her hand to my cheek, that I need not worry, that all would end well, at which point I simply melted into Her hand as She melded with me, leaving behind two persons in one.

So filled with the Holy Spirit was I, that even the guards said I glowed as they led us up to the brig warden's office to shed light on my noncooperation for having cooperated with My Lady instead.

Left standing in the front entry to the brig while one guard locked the Main Gate, and the other stood between me and the only way out, I turned right smack–dab into the face of the only knight who could help me now, that godsend Sir Brook of Hart.

"Boy, am I glad to see you," exclaimed the brig's only outlier to the status quo as I proceeded to pummel him with the particulars of the pickle I was in.

"All right! Calm down!" Consoled Sir Brook the knight who'd been stripped of sword and shield.

"If you'll calm down," extended Sir Brook an olive branch to the impassioned young knight, "we'll go up together to settle the matter with the Brig Officer."

"Hold up, Sir," commanded the guard to whom I was shackled in my quest for life, liberty and the pursuit of happiness. "Who art thou, and what right dost thou hath to be here?"

Off came the shackles of a bygone era when Brook replied, "Well son, I happen to be Mr. Drury's attorney. With regard to 'what right do I have to be here', Mr. Drury has the right under the laws of this land, which you are supposed to be upholding in your defense of this country, to consult with his attorney. And I have the right to consult with him as my client. Does that answer your question?"

"Dost thou hath an ID, Sir?" Inquired the old guard, caught off guard by the new guard.

An attorney admitted to joust before the Bar of New York and Hawaii, Sir Brook had been retained by the Hawaii Resistance to defend a growing number of knights who, like me, refused to cooperate with either the military or the draft.

"Now, shall we all proceed upstairs to see the wizard," quipped Sir Brook in an attempt to ease the tension that had us all in its grip.

"It is my understanding," swung Sir Brook into action after exchanging introductions with the Keeper of the Keep, "that the guards who supervise Mr. Drury's detention here have confiscated the materials he needs to comply with the requirements of the Director of Naval Personnel that he answer a number of questions concerning his beliefs as a conscientious objector. Is that correct?"

"When a sailor is confined to the Naval Station Brig," defied the Keeper of the Keep in keeping with that kept, "his belongings are taken from him until they can be inspected for illegal contraband such as drugs. Then, only those items permitted a prisoner in the brig are returned to him. The others are held in safekeeping until the prisoner is released from the brig.

"If the brig were an oasis where one had all the creature comforts of home, there would be no desire to change, would there, Mr. Hart?" Stonewalled the Keeper of the Keep.

"While I understand the purpose of the rigors of brig life," fired back Brook, "I hardly believe pens and paper, a bible, and a handbook for conscientious objectors fall into that category. Mr. Drury is here because the Navy has repeatedly denied him access to the information he needs to file a claim for discharge as a conscientious objector. I see the actions of the guards in this case as an overzealous recrimination of my client, an extension of this continuing pattern of denial by the Navy. If you will show me in the brig regulations where a prisoner cannot have in his cell, pens and paper, a bible, and a handbook for COs, I'll wish you good day and go about my business. But if you cannot, then I want to see these materials, that belong to Mr. Drury, returned to him before I leave the brig."

Hobbled, yet not defeated, did the Bullier of Prisoners order an underling to retrieve the materials that undermined his authority over me, sending a cold shiver down his spine.

"You are aware, Mr. Hart, that Drury has committed a serious offense, refusing a direct order to go on a work detail this morning," lashed back the Big Bully.

"Again," delved Sir Brook of Hart into matters of the heart, "I believe we have to understand the context of his actions. On the surface, it looks as if he has simply refused to do what has been asked of him. Underneath is the desire to be brought before you to inform you that he is not being treated fairly when the materials he requests are being denied him. With access to you also being denied him, how else can he see the brig warden but by breaking the law. So Mr. Drury refuses an order and is being brought before you when I run into him."

"Nevertheless," bludgeoned Sir Bully the helm of my attorney with the letter of the law, "Mr. Drury has refused a direct order, and must pay the consequences."

"I agree," expounded Sir Brook on the letter of the law, "that Mr. Drury has broken the law as did his overseers to a lesser degree, who, I daresay, will never be reprimanded for infringing upon his rights as a prisoner. In this case, I believe Mr. Drury acted reasonably, as you or I would have under such circumstances. So I ask you to put yourself in his shoes."

Sir Bully could never fill my shoes and he knew it. "Mr. Drury has broken the law and must be punished," insisted he with an iron fist instead.

"If my client is to be punished for standing up for his rights," dodged Sir Brook his fist of steel, "then mete out a punishment commensurate with what you'd impose upon the guards for their infraction of Mr. Drury's rights as a prisoner."

As Sir Bully stared down the double-edged sword of Justice, I swear she lifted her blindfold long enough to wink at me before resuming her statuesque pose.

"In view of the circumstances surrounding his offense, I sentence Mr. Drury to seven days of extra duty," pronounced the beleaguered Keeper of the Keep in keeping with that kept. "I don't want to send the wrong message that it's okay for a prisoner to refuse a direct order to make a point. I believe Mr. Drury was wrong and that my guards acted responsibly. However, from hereon, I will see to it that Mr. Drury has access to me and the materials he needs to establish his claim."

"Thank you," replied Sir Brook from the heart.

"Do you think you can live with seven days of extra duty?" Inquired Sir Brook of Sir Eodor, Knight Exemplar. "I really believe that's the best we can do. I feel the Brig Warden is attempting, as best he can, to ameliorate a situation that had gotten out of hand. Correct me if I am wrong," begged Sir Brook for the affirmation he received from the Brig Warden's nod.

"I guess," grumbled the White Knight in me who felt I should not have been punished for having cooperated with the Holy Spirit.

With all eyes now focused on the disputed materials as the returning guard handed them to the Warden, the Keeper of the Keep was quick to judge them in keeping with that kept. "I see nothing contraband or un-American here," he said as he handed them over to Brook who then proceeded to pass them on to me, proving once again that the pen is indeed mightier than the sword.

"Mr. Drury, you and your attorney can wait outside my office while I have a word with my guards," proffered a somewhat more conciliatory Brig Warden.

As the door closed behind us, Brook spoke up first. "I don't believe you'll have any trouble with them from hereon. So please do me a favor and don't stir up any. Get to work on your claim. Make that your top priority. You have 30 days to work on it. Don't blow this opportunity. Okay?"

"Okay," I acquiesced. "And thanks for helpin' me out. I still can't believe you showed up when you did—it was uncanny!"

"Well, I get this call from Betty who tells me she's worried that the Navy has locked you up and thrown away the key—would I check on you—to which I offer her my assurances. After learning from your command what they've done with you, I turn to leave the ship when something smacks me upside the head, stopping me dead in my tracks, and tells me to check on you, that you're in trouble. So I hurry over to the brig, where I run right smack–dab into you, as if I'd been sent there by God—unbelievable!"

With that, did the guards emerge from the Brig Warden's office to escort me back down to my cell.

"Remember what I told you, now," admonished Sir Brook, his young charge.

"How can I forget," I chortled as he rode off with my libido on that gallant white steed of mine.

And as I took joy in the external friendships unfolding between my self and den mother of the Resistance, Lady Betty, their attorney, Sir Brook and humble professor, Lord Jim, I wondered what had happened to my old internal friends, my soul, Jinny, guardian extraordinaire, Sir Michael, and author of my being, Old Hemmingway, for I hadn't seen them in quite a while.

"O where art thou, my sweet Jinny, when most I have need of thee?" Cried out her one and lonely as I tripped over the threshold of consciousness.

On I staggered as an angry surf pounded the endless stretch of beach that'd lured me into that twilit zone tween wakefulness and sleep, only to besiege me with a hurricane of sexual feelings so strong, it was hard not to indulge them. But indulge the I of the Storm I did, asking the 'I' at the center of my turmoil, to take these feelings from me lest I be led astray. Instead, I was informed that as a writer I'd been tasked with giving form to these feelings, and assured divine assistance sufficient to overcome these urges as long as I held up my end of the bargain.

To write or not to write and fall from grace was the choice that faced me as I approached the fire within that yearned to create, whether in the body or out of the body, only God knew for certain. And as I sat down in front of the fire to ponder my next line, I longed for the company of my old mentor and the discussions we used to have while seated round this very fire. Looking up in response to an inner urge to do so, I spied someone seated opposite me on the ground in front of the fire. Believing that my mind was playing tricks on me, I rubbed my eyes and looked again, only to see my old mentor sitting there with a smile on his face.

"I must be seeing a ghost," I thought to my self.

"Do you not believe in the Resurrection of the Dead?" Inquired he who had indeed risen from the dead.

"You know that I do," replied the Peter in me.

With incredualty, I lept to my feet, as did he, and ran laughing and crying at the same time to embrace this holy ghost with all my heart, for I did love the Old Indian even though he had abandoned me when most I had needed him.

"By dying, I abandoned an old image you had of me," responded the Old Indian, "and took on the form of two persons in one, that of a young man as an aging author. For I Am Who I Am as you know I AM, the father you never had in the flesh but always carried within you. I am He as you are He as you are me and we are all one and the same person of the Trinity, I AM."

"I am...?" Wondered I about the once and future father of two fine sons.

"O," exclaimed my mentor, "and so much more, my son, for you are the Author of your being as well."

"You mean Old Hemmingway?" I begged to know. "Is that why I haven't seen the old gaffer here of late?"

"As you flip through the pages of the book you see before you, whose handiwork do you see?" Asked the Old Indian while I grappled with this mirage.

"Why, the Author of my being, I Am Who I Am," I replied.

"Look closer," cajoled my mentor from afar. "Tell me what you see now."

"I see a knight who's lost his way, chasing an impossible dream," I conceded.

"How could I have lost my soul?" Beseeched I the only real father I ever had.

"When you rejected Mary," proffered the Old Indian with a heavy heart and a sigh too deep for words, "you also closed the door on your soul, banishing her to a life of chasing after a monk always on the run."

"Do you see a monk anywhere in this fire?" Asked my mentor.

"No, I see only a shadow of what might have been," I confessed, "clinging to me for dear life, one, alas, that is not his to have nor mine to entertain."

"Rescue her," implored my mentor, "from this neverending nightmare."

"Where can I find her?" Inquired my sorry ass.

"She often walks this stretch of beach," answered the Old Indian, "hoping against hope to catch you in the twilight zone."

What more could I say as I rose up to the occasion, with the Old Indian's blessing, and started down the beach hoping against hope that I might run into her as I vaguely recall lumping her with Mary when I rejected the latter and went over to the monk's side. But I saw no sign of her. Nor did I come any closer to understanding why I had rejected an aspect of myself, so intrinsic to my being as my soul, as I searched this stretch of endless explanations for the one meant for me.

"O where art thou, my sweet Jinny?" I yelled out into the void in my life, she had once filled.

As I picked up the pace, hoping to catch up with her ere the sun set, I ran into a delirium in which I see my self running from her instead. In my struggle to keep up the mad pace as she drew closer to dispelling the myth of the monk, I stumbled and fell, hitting my head on a rock that knocked out the monk and left me lying there until I felt a hand gently running its fingers through my hair.

"Do you understand what happened to you?" Asked the queen of hearts and ground of my being—image of the once and future mother of two fine sons.

"Not exactly," responded the once and future father of the same duo.

"Quit dissociating your self from your sexual feelings and those who love you, not as you love your self but as God loves you," exhorted the queen of hearts. "You are not the monk you pretend to be, never were nor ever shall be, for you are to wed as fine an incarnation of me as ever lived, and father two fine sons. When you become a monk, my dear Dr. Jekyll, you reject me and condemn your self to a life of unfulfilling, willy–nilly sex, looking for me in all the wrong faces. Cling to the author of your being, Mr. Hyde, and you fulfill your destiny as the cocreator of two fine sons and a duology. So accept the male member of your body for who he is, a conscientious objector who will father an author, but no monk, to tackle climate change and theoretical physics in his later years."

"Tackle what?" Shot back her quid pro quo.

"Don't worry about tomorrow," chastised my soul, *"tomorrow will take care of itself. Sufficient for a day, is its own evil."* Mt 6:34.

"And don't let that impostor steal your identity from me again," she asserted.

"When you rejected us, you stirred up quite a storm," insisted Old Hemmingway from afar.

"When did I reject you?" Questioned I this accusation.

"Have you been writing as Brook instructed you to do?" Shot back the I of the Storm who did tempt me sorely with primal urges to give form, as either a beast or a writer, to the storm I'd stirred up.

"No, because I've been waiting for you guys to give me a hand," lashed back that insolent tongue of mine.

"Ya know it takes two to tangle," admitted my soul, "one to inspire, the other to conspire, for it is I who give you images worthy of the words he gives you. What more could you ask for, my love? In giving form to the formless, you give us what only you can, a hand writing.

"Should you accept this task, you will be required to write every day for the rest of your life," delved she to the heart of the matter. "It's the only way, my love, if you do not want to live like an animal, always on the run.

"Run from us, on the other hand, and you run right smack–dab into the arms of the very beast you are fleeing, who, knowing where you are most vulnerable, grabs you by the testes, turning you every which way but loose with every salacious image that pops into your head urging you to give form to him instead.

"Think about it. If this thorn had not been given you *'in the flesh, a messenger of Satan to torment'* (2 Cor 12:7) you, what would have provoked you, or St. Paul, for that matter, to write?" Rattled she my cage with the parting shot of a saint.

"That is why I think it is high time we cultivate the conscientious objector that lies fallow within you," came she to the same conclusion her father had as we approached the fire—that yearned to speak—filled with a renewed sense of purpose, that is, with her hand in mine.

How long we sat engrossed in flame only God knows for certain, for it was His hand, not mine, that did part the lips of my mentor with a burning ember from the fire that yearned to speak.

"We died to you, that we might live on in you, and you, in us, as three persons in one," proffered the Old Indian through whose eyes I could now see as if they were my own. "No longer are you a seer in your own sight, but in ours as well.

"Love thyself as thy soul doth love thee, for greater love hath no man than this, that he lay down his life for his soul," pierced he my heart with true love.

"With us out of the picture, working behind the scenes, were you forced to find a new mentor in Lord Jim, legal counsel in Sir Brook, and new mother in Lady Betty, all soulmates of the highest order drawn to you as you were, to them, in your need for the kind of help we could not provide you without form. To resurrect us, you had only to embody the way we had laid out before you. In that alone, did you find us, *'for hard is the way that leads to life, and few are they who find it'*," (Mt 7:14) concluded my mentor as the last flame fled from our scrutiny, leaving behind a crystal that spoke to me in the first person.

"When the Chief of Naval Personnel asks you to substantiate your claim, tell him that you are a conscientious objector because 'I' made you that way," vibrated the crystal with words that spoke to me.

"Should he ask," played I the devil's advocate, "who made me that way?"

"I Am Who I Am," revealed the source of these subliminal messages. "For it was 'I' Who called you, and mentored you in the ways of a conscientious objector. Through every step of the way, have 'I' been with you, watching over you as you grew in spirit, nudging you from time to time, even chastising you when 'I' deemed it necessary, only to be left in the end, wondering who you might say you are, should 'I' ask."

"I Am Who I Am," replied the I That Can See who gave me a hand writing.

"That is why you may never take the life of another human being. Never. Do you understand?" 'I' asked my self.

"I do," renewed I my vows to the King in waiting.

"No greater force may you use than the laying down of your life as My Son, the King of Hearts, has done for you," 'I' told that pitiless self of mine.

"Nor may you crucify anyone other than the self within, who crucified the Son without, or harm a single soul, including your own, as it is to Him alone that she owes her allegiance.

The Gauntlet

"*'For no one can serve two masters. He will either hate one and love the other, or be devoted to one and despise the other. You cannot serve God and'* (Mt 6:24) the military, as they are as diametrically opposed as Able and Cain.

"In no way, are you to aid and abet your Uncle Sam in killing Able, Vietnamese upon whom the old fool has cast his shadow, Cain. Your mission, should you accept it, is to persuade the fool to release you from the Navy, and to withdraw his forces from the whore he created when he attacked Miss Vietnam.

"If the Chief of Naval Personnel has any problems with that, you tell him to get back in touch with God," had 'I' instructed me.

And as the crystal fell silent, I was left with a burning ember to which, I was told, I could return, should the need arise.

"What is the significance of the crystal?" I asked my mentor.

"It is an interface between you and I AM," he replied, "Who, knowing full well that you could not answer the questions in the BUPERS Manual without a hand from God, gave you exactly what you needed, a gem of a response that no one can refute."

"Duty–bound to tell our story, you fear the Chief of Naval Personnel and others of his ilk will see you as delusional if you tell it like it is, and will not take your conscientious objection seriously. Change the story to suit your self, on the other hand, and you alter our relationship with you forever," forewarned my mentor.

"Does that mean I will never see you again?" I asked my soul.

"No, my love," she replied. "My love for you is too great to ever part from you. Without you, I'd be another disembodied spirit with '*nowhere to rest*' its '*head*'. (Mt 8:20) For giving body to me is how I know you love me. Sharing the way with you is how I love you. But I refuse to be a distraction from your responsibilities to the outer world. And if you should choose to live contrary to Who I Am, I will bother the hell out of you until you give your body back to me, for your body is just as much mine as it is yours."

"Do not be afraid, my son," interjected the Old Indian," to tell the Chief of Naval Personnel how profoundly your life has been affected, how much you have suffered at the hands of an insane father and alcoholic stepfather, both of whom came back from the South Pacific after WWII, psychologically and spiritually damaged almost beyond repair as they struggled to cope with the immensity and cruelty of the death and destruction that'd filled their heads with images that wouldn't go away. Tell the Chief how your paranoid schizophrenic father chased after you with a butcher knife, and tried to kill you before he was arrested and subsequently committed to an asylum for eight years; and how your gun–toting stepfather will later shoot a man, supposedly in self-defense, and then empty his revolver into the body of this father of three, to make sure he has killed the demon that haunts him and will result in his serving time for manslaughter. Having experienced, first hand, the effects of war on the human psyche, be sure you tell the Chief that you do not wish to kill anyone, to commit the very acts that robbed you of your fathers, outright killed your sonship and hijacked your soul, stripping you of your humanity—the Father, Son and Holy Ghost—and leaving behind but a shadow of what was once you, a beast without a conscience, 'Mr. Edward Hyde,' the perfect killing machine in the eyes of the military."

"So lost were you at that point," empathized my soul, "you had nowhere else to go but the Navy, where you hoped, against all hope, that you might find your way. Boy, were you disappointed when the Navy stuck you on a ship bound for Vietnam. Little did you know that we were setting the stage for our initial contact with you. And you played right into our hands just as we had hoped you would."

"Well, you sure picked a hell of a way to contact me," barked the wolf in me, "if that's all you had in mind."

"What we really needed was an antagonist," conceded the Old Indian, "to bring out the conscientious objector in you, so oblivious were you, at the time, of anything going on outside yourself, much less a war of attrition. But we had to do it in a way that preserved your sanity, and at the same time, pricked your conscience enough to goad you into rejecting war as a tool for resolving the political differences between two nations. We saw the Navy as the only way we could protect you from harm while we exposed you to the dark side of war that plays hell with the minds of men like you and your fathers.

"You see, my son, it is evil to live contrary to who you are, to lead a way of life that is forcing you, by its very nature, to live contrary to who you are."

"That is why you love me, for I am Who I Am, a conscientious objector," captured she—my soul, that is—the essence of who I am.

"Give us form or give the beast body," maintained the Old Indian, "that is the choice you face."

"That is, give me liberty or give me death," projected my soul as she stepped forth from the fire that burned between us, "for I am the true intent of the beast."

"Then, let it be done to me as you will," deferred I, on bended knee, to the queen of hearts.

"And as I knelt there before the Queen of Heaven and Earth instead, with my head bowed low, I received a blessing from Her as She lay Her hand upon my head, that did heal the schism between me and my body.

With that, did the form of the Queen of Heaven and Earth give way to that of my soul as I rose up at her behest to embrace the queen of my heart, and she, her knight in shining armor, for we were one again in mind and body, a single form that only gave way to me and my soul for consciousness' sake.

"When the Chief of Naval Personnel asks for the name and address of the person upon whom I rely most for guidance, what shall I tell him?" Asked the beleaguered knight of his mentor.

"Just tell him to get in touch with God," chortled the only mentor I ever had.

"Remember, my son, the greatest commandment of them all is this, that *'you love'* Who You Are *'with all your heart, with all your soul, with all your mind,'* and with all your body, and that *'you love your neighbor as'* (Mt 22:37, 39) Who You Are, for you are Who I Am as your neighbor is Who I Am as you are your neighbor and you are all one and the same person of the Trinity, I AM."

"How does this command of God apply to one's enemies?" Tested I the mettle of my mentor.

"If you see your neighbor as Mr. Hyde and yourself as the good Dr. Jekyll when your neighbor sees himself as Jekyll and you as Hyde, are you not your own worst enemy? Why kill your neighbor if you are the enemy? Does not the law command you to love your neighbor as yourself? Then love your enemy as yourself, and make not an enemy out of your neighbor."

"How does one love the enemy within?" Questioned I his authority over the enemies of this estate.

"Must not he suffer the death of the serpent on the cross? For greater love hath no man than this, that he suffer the death of what is not him to allow what is him to rise from the dead," insisted he at my expense.

"As long as the law of the land of Uncle Sam doesn't contradict God's laws," flew off he on another tangent, "you must obey the law of the land. The moment, however, the law of the land contradicts God's commands, you must disobey the law of the land, and *'obey God rather than men'*. Acts 5:29. That is why you must remove yourself from the Navy of the land of Uncle Sam, whose sole purpose is to kill those human beings, Uncle Sam has deemed to be enemies of the land, before they kill you or expose the real enemy here, the manufacturers of war and their god, the *'Father of Lies'*.

"Whether in the body or out of the body, God knows the American War—as the Vietnamese rightly call it—should be taking place within the body of every man, woman and child in the land of Uncle Sam rather than without the body of every man, woman and child in the land of Vietnam in a maelstrom of his own making and that of the *'Father of Lies', 'a murderer'* (Jn 8:44) and thief whose sole objective is *'to steal and slaughter and destroy'* (Jn 10:10) what belongs to Christ.

"Is that not what war is all about, my son, the crucifixion of others for our sins? We kill who we are for who we are not, and in so doing, become who we are not, the same ego-driven beast that will not rest until the wraith has destroyed the very body he inhabits but does not yet possess, whether it be yours or mine. For the wraith seeks to resurrect from the dead what God has denied all wraiths, an incorruptible body that lives forever."

With that, did I find my self looking into the eyes of my soul as she sat across from me, in front of the fire that burned between us, looking into my eyes to see what I saw in her that she could not see without my eyes, a love for what I knew not that did grip me, from time to time, turning me every which way but loose until I met the body's need for union with the Creator, whether in word or in deed, only God knew for certain.

"How am I to know which path to take if they both use the same body language to express my desire for union with the Creator?" I asked my soul.

"Though you may succumb to the more compelling of the two, I would listen for the silent voice of reason to see what the Speaker of the House had to say before I acted," shed she some light on my conundrum, that I might avoid the improprieties of an unconscious act.

"For the Lord Speaker of the House so loved the body," deferred she to my mentor, "that He sent His only-begotten Son to free man from having to act like an animal, always on the run from the very instinct he fears most, the ability to see as we do, through the all-seeing eyes of the Creator."

"'Amen, I say to you,' my son, many are they who long *'to see what you see but'* do *'not see it, and to hear what you hear but'* do *'not hear it,'* (Mt 13:17) the lone *'sound'* that fulfills the body's desire for union with the Creator, that *'of sheer silence'*." 1 Kgs 19:12.

"For who knows the mind of God any better than the body in its infinite wisdom?" Pondered she over the preponderance of evidence that the body is indeed the source of consciousness.

"Certainly not you," had she fingered me without pretext, "who heed not its warnings, and misinterpret it at every turn, forcing it to do what it was never intended to do. And when it rises up in defiance to thwart your manical departures from the script, you thwart every attempt of the Creator to reunite you with your body, the very roadmap you seek."

"That is why," mentored the Old Indian "you must listen to what your body is trying to tell you, my son. When it is in pain, console it. Stop treating it as if it were a beast of burden. Feel its pain and listen to its entreaties to get your ass out of the Navy before your immunity is compromised and you lose the ability as a CO to resist their every command to partake in the killing of other human beings. Tell the Chief of Naval Personnel how great is the pain you experience as a non-combatant on a man-o'-war in opposition to everything your body stands for. Tell him how you bear the cross of every man, woman and child in the land of Uncle Sam who supports the American War in Vietnam. Tell him how Christ rides your ass through the streets of the New Jerusalem to the acclaim of every ounce of your flesh. Speak to the turmoil in the streets that run through your body like the arteries of a city without spilling blood all over the pages of the book of your life, so unlike those in the book of Christ's life. Speak to the stories of the horrendous crimes against humanity that are spilling out of Vietnam to the jubilation of the serpent who never realized, until it was too late, that it was his skin that hung there on the cross. Speak to the number of bodies pouring out of Vietnam, day after day, as the blood of the body of Christ spills out over the land of the people of Vietnam, to cleanse it of the sins of every man, woman and child of the land of Uncle Sam. And don't forget to address the Chief's resistance to change."

"What do you mean?" I asked the Old Indian.

"So obsessed are he and his kind with the Red sea change in Vietnam, they can't see the rise of red tides of the Permian kind as the far greater threat to the survival of every man, woman and child on Earth. He and his kind fear the climate of change your conscientious objection to the war on nature engenders. They will deny you your sacred right, refusing to change the climate around the Department of the Navy to embrace your kind with open arms," warned my mentor, much to my chagrin.

"Why should I even apply for a discharge as a conscientious objector, if all they're going to do is turn me down?" Protested the CO at the very heart of the matter of the United States versus FR Drury.

"To buy time, my son, and prevent them from shipping you back over to Vietnam, for they will fight you tooth and nail till you yield to the sword. To withstand their onslaughts and sore buffets to the head, you must become their worst bureaucratic nightmare, such a nuisance to them that they'll wish they had never messed with you and had discharged you back when you started to unravel."

"What I don't get is why they would want to hold on to me, knowing how I feel about the military and war in general," questioned I the unraveling of their case against me.

"They want to make it as difficult as possible for you to get discharged as a conscientious objector," replied my mentor, "to punish you for obeying *'God rather than men'*, and to discourage others who might share your beliefs from pursuing the same course of action. They are, after all, in the business of creating combatants, not noncombatants."

With that, was I bumped from the scene around the fire to embrace yet another, a fog so thick, I could not see what bound my outstretched arms and tied my feet to the mood that I was in, for I could not feel my hands or my feet, so close was I to death. And as Death's icy cold breath swirled about the fire that raged within me, I agonized over the mood, I couldn't let go of, to save my life.

"*My God, my God, why have You forsaken me?*" (Mt 27:47) I cried out with a loud voice as the desire for union with the Creator consumed me ere I was given up for dead and laid to rest in a cell block from which not even I could escape without a hand from God.

"In one form or the other, must you contend with the beast that you are and the body's need to recreate itself in body and in spirit," had my soul reminded me ere I arose that Sunday, bright and early, to complete this passage from hell.

"See what happens when you listen instead of imposing your will or what you want to see happen," did she remind me, once the words began flowing freely from my pen again.

So too, was I graced with a visit from Lord Jim, who was forced to pose as my spiritual adviser in order to gain access to me.

"Boy, are you a sight for sore eyes!" I cried out with a loud voice as my body filled to overflowing with the joy that comes with the realization that one has not been given up for dead.

"How are you?" Had he asked with the signature smile of a much humbler man than his unsolicited title suggested.

"As you can see, I'm bursting with joy that I have been '*considered worthy to suffer*' (Acts 5:41) for Christ's sake," I replied to the raucous laughter of two like-minded souls who suffered the cross that each one bore.

"And—you will be happy to know—I have finally answered all of the questions in Article **C–5210** of the **BUPERS Manual**. Now, I have only to type a final copy when I get back to the ship, to forward to the Chief of Naval Personnel for his stamp of approval."

Little did I know, at the time, that the Chief of Naval Personnel deferred all requests for reclassification as a conscientious objector to the requestee's draft board, leaving it up to the members of that board to decide whether to grant or deny an individual's request, a decision the Chief generally rubber-stamped.

"Why, I'm even supposed to send a copy to my draft board, which doesn't surprise me," I complained. "What does surprise me though, given the current climate, is that no one has set his draft board on fire in lieu of his draft card."

That's when Jim brought up the Berrigan brothers, both Jesuit priests, Phil and Dan, and informed me that they and seven other clergy and lay, who would later become known as the Catonsville 9, had taken the 1–A files from a draft board in Catonsville, Maryland, and burned them out back with homemade napalm, igniting a firestorm of controversy amongst the proponents of nonviolence as to whether this was indeed an act of nonviolence in the eyes of God.

For my part, all I could see was more fog, so thick, that the right hand could not comprehend what bound the left hand, much less itself, to the cross as each

The Gauntlet

suffered at the hand of the other. Blinded as such, neither could see what either had seen in the eyes of the other prior to the events that occurred in Catonsville on May 17th to clear the fog of war from our minds, that we might see, with the all-seeing eyes of the Creator, what the might of the right had inflicted upon us. For the left had seen a great light, a beacon that beckoned the few to inflame the rest of us with the fervor of Paul Revere as the Spirit of a revolution in values road roughshod over the Wraiths of State to warn us of our impending doom if we did nothing to deter business-as-usual from plundering Her physique, a body that hung on the cross awaiting the death it must endure to give birth to a new world where the few can napalm draft files, rather than children, with impunity.

As the fog of war lifted from my mind, I could see the light hanging in the bell tower of the Old North Church, warning me that the red tides were coming far sooner than anyone had anticipated.

"O where art thou, Jonah, when most thy people have need of thee?" I questioned the absence of the prophet.

"O where art thou, my son, when most thy people have need of thee?" Had the Old Indian questioned my absence without leave.

"Betty and the members of the Resistance send their love," responded Jim to the *'sound of sheer silence'*.

"Do thank them all for the boost to my morale," rejoined the once and future prophet who did long for his release from the belly of the whale.

"What's a prophet to do when a people reject what he has seen with the all-seeing eyes of God, but disobey orders and burn draft files to dramatize the error of their ways," posed my mentor. "For they must remove the wrongdoing, they heap upon your shoulders, and place it upon their own where it belongs."

"Unlike Jonah," pointed Jim to the meaning of my cross, "you responded favorably to God's call, to which your disobedience fully attests but nonetheless results in your suffering for their wrongdoing."

"So, do I suffer in vain if no minds are changed?" I asked for clarity's sake.

"Not at all," stressed Jim, "you suffer for righteousness' sake, that those who witness the earth-shaking, rock-splitting, tomb-opening events of your death to self will confess, in the words of the Centurion who witnessed these awesome portents as Christ breathed his last breath, *'Truly this was a son of God'*." Mt 27:54.

"O how insufferable is the pain I experience when the person I AM is denied," anguished I over the man in the mood.

"So great was the pain I bore *as My captors 'led Me away'*," proclaimed the Lord in Jim, "*they seized a man, Simon of Cyrene, and they laid the cross on him, and made him carry it behind Me*, (Lk 23:26) until *they came to a place called Golgotha (which means Place of a Skull)*." Mt 27:33.

I Am Who I Am

"While Christ did yet bear the brunt of your pain, and that of everyone else," explained my mentor in keeping with that kept, "Simon of Cyrene bore only the *'lasting, unforgettable confusion'* (Jer 20:11) of getting pressed into carrying a burden that did not belong to him, for the most part, like your impressment into service in the navy, a cross that is not yours to bear any longer than you have."

"Yet, you're the only one who sees the man in the mood," I complained...

"...and the frustration you experience when they fail to recognize you as I AM, a CO and a writer, to keep you from fulfilling your desire for union with the Creator," spoke the Old Indian to the mood in the man Jim struggled to extrapolate from the mood.

"My new book, 'The Non-violent Cross, A Theology of Revolution and Peace,' is due to come out later in the fall," broached Jim the *'sound of sheer silence'*.

"Sounds heavy," waded I into deep waters with Christ on my back.

"That's what Simon of Cyrene thought too, when he picked up where Christ had left off," had Jim pricked my conscience. "For we bear the same burden Christ bore that day, a death to all evil that, in the end, forced another man to carry what Christ could not, the very instrument of His own death. That, my friend, which Christ did bear that day, is the nonviolent's cross."

"And that is the cross you bear, my son," reiterated my otherworldly mentor, the Old Indian.

"I have a couple of letters for you," announced the normally soft-spoken Jim in a louder than usual voice, as he pulled me from my mentor's side with the letters he withdrew from his briefcase and handed to me to read.

"I am writing you," wrote Jim, *"concerning the application of Fireman Recruit E.J. Drury II for a conscientious objector's discharge from the Navy. Since I became acquainted with Mr. Drury more than a month ago, I have discussed with him several times and at length his conscientious objection to military service. I have also observed at close hand Mr. Drury's personal response to the imprisonment resulting from his beliefs in conscience.*

"On the basis of our discussions and of my close observation of Mr. Drury's character, I wish to testify to the profound depth and sincerity of his convictions against participation in war. I would like to make this point clear: Although I have known other conscientious objectors, and in the course of my teaching career as a professor of religion have met many men of deep belief, I can truthfully say that I have never encountered a man with a greater reverence for human life than Mr. Drury. This reverence for life, and resistance to killing, is based firmly on Mr. Drury's Catholic Faith. It is a belief in conscience which has been realized gradually, and with much suffering, over a period of years through his honest response to the question of killing viewed in the light of his faith in Jesus Christ. The sincer-

ity of those convictions can be measured by the suffering and imprisonment Mr. Drury has repeatedly undergone during the past year for the sake of his beliefs.

"As a Catholic theologian and former theological consultant to British and American bishops at the Second Vatican Council, I would like to say also that Mr. Drury's conscientious objection to military service has a solid religious foundation in Catholic doctrine. The right of conscientious objection was explicitly stated by the Second Vatican Council in its 'Pastoral Constitution on the Church in the Modern World' (Part II, Chapter V, No. 79), and was upheld prior to that by Pope John XXIII's statements on conscience in his Papel Encyclical 'Pacem in Terris' (Part II, 'Relations Between Individuals and the Public Authorities Within a Single State').

"I believe therefore that E.J. Drury is fully qualified by faith and conviction, as well as by the teaching of his Church, for a conscientious objector's discharge from military service. For the sake of this man's integrity of conscience, for which he has already suffered amply, I ask that every consideration be given to his application for discharge."

> Sincerely yours,
> *James W. Douglass*
> Assistant Professor of Religion
> University of Hawaii

So touched was I by Jim's letter that I choked up trying to hold back the tears and the gratitude that welled up from my being.

"My God, Jim, you don't know how long I've ached to see such words written in my behalf. So eloquent are they, that I am at a complete loss for the words to express my gratitude. You are indeed an angel, come to my rescue, to whom I shall be forever indebted. Thank you, my dear friend, from the bottom of my heart."

"Unless you know something about me that I don't," laughed Jim, "I am quite the human being that you are."

"No doubt," I chuckled, "but an angel nonetheless, doing God's work."

With that, did Lord Jim depart the brig, knowing that I was in God's hands.

Back in my cell where I belonged, did Sir Knight read the other letter from His Excellency, The Very Reverend Daniel J. Dever.

"This letter is in reference to Fireman Recruit, E.J. Drury II," wrote Father Dever. "Over the past fourteen years as Superintendent of Catholic Schools in Hawaii and Chaplain to the Catholic Students at the University of Hawaii, I have developed some skill in appraising conscientious thought and action. In dramatic instances, at least, I feel competent to distinguish the sincere from the fake.

"Personally, I do not doubt Mr. Drury's sincerity. The total investment of himself in this issue is shown by the months of weighing the problem, the serious study he has made, the persons he has contacted, the inconvenience and embarrassment he has been willing to undergo.

"Mr. Drury has taken a stand for peace at any price to himself. Consistent with this stand he is nonviolent in his approach to others and in defense of himself. Because there are ambiguities in Catholic teaching and practice on the subject of war and peace, there will be those espousing the same faith who understandably take opposing positions in practice. However, in as much as we justify the one, we must be ready to justify the other. It would falsify Christianity at its roots if we were to deny the legitimacy of the conclusions Mr. Drury has drawn from his pondering the problems of war and peace in a Christian perspective."

Sincerely,
Father Dever
The Very Reverend Daniel J. Dever
Superintendent of Catholic Schools

How I wished His Excellency were here, to thank in person, so grateful was Sir Knight for a letter from a tried-and-true stalwart of the community.

"O where, O where can my lady be," wondered I through evening's twilight as the minutes missed passed me by, one after the other, without a sign of soul. If only I could get the great gray whale to cough up this undigested tidbit, I should find her seated round the fire that yearned to speak to my desire.

"O where, O where can my lady be," wondered I through a thicket of thoughts as those that had detained me passed me by, one after the other, with not a word from her. If only I could get this babbling brook to cease its incessant babble, I should find her seated aside the stream that yearned to speak to my desire.

"O where, O where can my lady be," wondered I through a fen of feelings as those that had deterred me passed me by, one after the other, with not a hint of soul. If only I could pull my self from the Great Grimpen Mire, I should find her seated beside the fen that yearned to speak to my desire.

"O where, O where can my lady be," wondered I through sights unseen as those that had enticed me passed me by, one after the other, with not a soul in sight. If only I could get to the bottom of this ill-conceived rhyme, surely I would find her seated inside the scene that yearned to speak to my desire.

"Here I am," satiated she my desire.

"Did you really not see me in the poetry of your prose?" Had she asked as I sat down beside her and watched the last flame flee from me, leaving behind the glowing embers of what was once a burning desire.

With that, did she steal a kiss from me, putting to rest any lingering desire the wolf might have to seek the affections of another, for her hugs and his kisses left little room between them for the shadowy side of the beast to squeeze its way into the life of the wolf, the man and his muse.

In this way, did 'I' bemuse me whene'er the desire for union with the Creator roused me from my slumber to wrestle with what 'I' sought to reveal to me.

"O where art thou, my lady, when most I have need of thee?" Cried out Sir Bored as he paced his cell like a wolf on the prowl for anything that would break the monotony of having nothing to do but stoke the fire that burned with desire for union with the Creator.

But first, Sir Bored would have to break the spell of repeating o'er 'n' o'er in his head what had led to the latest breakdown in the line of communication tween him and his Creator, for the repetitious rabble rousted not the desired conclusion from its seclusion from inclusion. For Sir Bored had so filled the void with repetend that he had left little room for the Creator to get a word in edgewise.

"Listen!" Commanded the Creator, stopping so short Sir Bored's horse that he was thrown overboard to sink or swim with the buoyancy of a salient conclusion at his fingertips.

Thus did Sir Bored learn to tread water while wearing a full suit of armor to protect him from the denizens of the deep should they try again to invade his space with repetend, all he had unless he turned from them to joust in jest with the windmills of his own making, so bored was he, and tired of wrestling with the object of his lust, the Creator of none so noble as he, save one, the White Knight who bears the colors of Thy Kingdom Come. But Sir Bored had seen neither hide nor hair of Sir Michael or his steed since Sir Brook took off with Sir Bored's libido—whether in the body or out of the body is a projection left entirely to the discretion of the producer of such images, She Who Must Be Obeyed, one way or the other.

As the plot thickened, Sir Bored wondered whether he'd been brought here for another excercise in futility or a more than likely lesson in humility.

"Speak, for your servant is listening," (1 Sam 3:10) beseeched Sir Bored of nothing to do but listen to the sound of his own voice emerge from the bloomin' author in 'm.

"See here, my son," spoke the emerging voice of the author in me, "I AM about to transform you into a real author, one who has finally found his own voice, if only you will listen to it instead of all that hardscrabble dribble-drabble, the denizens of the deep dig up to drown Me out."

"No longer shall your *'words fall to the ground',* (1 Sam 3:19) without eye having seen nor ear having heard every word," declared the Speaker of the House where He presided over me and my soul.

With that, did Sir Bored witness the incarnation of the Holy Trinity within the frame of this ill-tempered wit that now shone bright with the White Knight's light.

"Still bored?" Inquired the Author of the House of one dazed knight who stood on the verge of realizing a dream come true, the reunification of the once disparate members of his body which had been so torn apart by war, they had been rendered dysfunctional.

"Nay," said he whom they had kept at bay with all manner of delusions, none of which really spoke to him quite like his own.

"See what you and 'I' can accomplish when we work together," had the Author of the House led me to conclude but not seclude from inclusion.

That I could indeed work that closely with the Creator and not feel the least bit intimidated amazed the hell out of me, which was a good thing, seeing how I cast a shadow, He bore not, for with Christ at my back, I could do no wrong.

With that in mind, did I receive the following letter from a student at the University of Hawaii, I had met at Betty's place:

Dear Butch,

I was not exactly happy to hear that your military career is continuing in the same unfortunate manner that you related to me that nite of Betty Johnson's party—when I met you as we rode up to her house.

It is ironic that when I finally do get in touch with you to express my appreciation to you for sharing some of your background with me, it is in this situation. Many thanks however, for personalizing something to me that otherwise would not be of such significant concern to me now. I can only express my admiration for your perseverance.

Anyway, perhaps—just perhaps—your singular action of solid commitment will encourage others in the military to question their purpose in the military or their personal values. Regardless however of others, don't give up the fight. The many of us on this side of the military line salute you. Keep it up!

With warmest regards,
Sophie Ann Aoki

Boy, did my morale shoot way up, enough to even overcome my boredom for a day or two, as I had a little more than a week yet to serve behind bars.

During this time too, had Jim accompanied Brook back to the brig to see how I was doing.

"What a surprise!" Exclaimed that ebullient persona of mine, which did so mask the pain of the clown who bore the real cross of Christ with a joy that did touch even the most hardened of hearts.

A brief visit though it was, as the two had business elsewhere, it did my heart good to see them both standing there in my corner of the ring.

While Jim preoccupied me, Brook visited yet another client from my cellblock, a recent convert to Buddhism and its attendant pacificism named Steve Guy who was awaiting court-martial for refusing to ever wear his uniform again.

"In one of those rare moments when Steve isn't meditating while standing or sitting on his head in a Lotus position," reveled I in a bit of gossip for Jim's sake, "he mentioned that he had converted to Buddhism under the auspices of Priest Nichijo Shaka, the infamous WWII vet, known then as David Provoo, who had been found guilty and subsequently acquitted of treason for his role in aiding the Japanese as a prisoner on Corregidor."

By the time I had finished my rant, Sir Brook had returned to pick up where Lord Jim and I had left him on the verge of insanity, that fine line between his world and mine, the rule of law and the lawless world of neverending war that has ripped this country apart and left us far more vulnerable to the red tides of an apolitical, more permanent nature—to the once and future tides of the Permian kind.

With their departure from the brig, did I depart for parts unknown, the vast sea of knowledge that surrounded the isle of consciousness upon which I had sought refuge from the rising tides of a self-inflicted wound that threatens to engulf the better part of mankind in a conflagration to cleanse the world of the filth of another faithless generation of Ninevites, so caught up in their own destruction, they can't see it coming. For this generation and those that survive it, though they be few in number, did I weep with the Spirit as Her tears trickled down my face with a sigh *'too deep for words'*. Rom 8:26.

Filled with the Spirit, did I retreat to my cell to await further word from the Author of my being, lest He catch me with anything else in my hand but a pen.

Little did I know, at the time, that I was being investigated by the NIS (Naval Investigative Service) as a possible defector, until a Mr. Barrows showed up at the brig, one day, with an alternate story, to investigate my activities with the Resistance, my distribution of the Kailua Road leaflets about the ship, and my suitability for further service in the Navy, he claimed with some disdain.

Did I know—had he started off on the wrong foot with no basis in fact whatsoever—that the Knights of the Resistance, especially those he mentioned by name, were Reds, and if that wasn't bad enough, freethinking radicals as well?

Whoa, pulled back I on the reins ere my horse trampled the cherished beliefs of a system of greed so hell-bent on plundering the planet for its own profit, it gave rise to a sea of red, a Red Scare that threatened to inundate the world with communists, anarchists and leftists after they had raised a red flag, warning of Cain's treachery, his intention to kill his shadow, come hell or high water.

"To set the records straight," had I torn into the McCarthyistic rant that he had pulled verbatim from the playbook by which he lived, "not all radicals are Red.

Some, like those of us who have risen up, in response to the Spirit's call, to free this country from its tyranny, are as red, white and blue, I daresay, as you or any other true-blooded American who has ever fought for this country.

"You got that, Mr. Barrows?" Trashed I the lie he had sworn to uphold till death did depart with the better part of him, leaving the lie behind to cast its malignant shadow no more.

Having failed to win me over by due process, did he resort to the old standby of comparing the American War in Vietnam to police action taken after Ho Chi Minh and his ragtag band of commies violated a restraining order, that then acting and self-appointed judge, Uncle Sam, had issued, barring him from any further contact with little ole defenseless Miss Saigon.

In violation of the restraining order, per Mr. Barrows' playbook, had Uncle Ho and his ilk taken the bitch hostage, raping her repeatedly, making a ho out of her and giving Uncle Sam the excuse, he needed, to call up the troops.

"Whoa! Hold your horses right there, Mr. Barrows," reined in I another unchallenged whore story. "You've got it all backwards—it's Uncle Sam who, in repeatedly raping the lady-in-waiting, has made a whore out of her and given Ho Chi Minh and his Hanoi Irregulars the excuse, they needed, to free her from the tentacles of the last colonial power to have such a stranglehold on her."

"Tell me then, fair knight," lashed out the Dark Knight of the Barrows, "how would a self-proclaimed conscientious objector, such as yourself, rescue a damsel in distress?"

Having sustained a sore buffet to the head that sent this fair knight reeling, did I stumble into Sir Michael as the Archangel was responding to the distress call that had gone out from the once fair knight before he'd fallen into a swoon.

With sword drawn as I looked on, did Sir Michael pierce the dark cloud that overshadowed the Knight of the Barrows, and after rescuing a soul in distress, did hand the once Dark Knight the damsel no longer in distress.

"And that's how you rescue a damsel in distress, Mr. Barrows," beamed I with great delight.

"I see," mumbled Barrows on a barely audible wavelength.

What he had seen I have no way of knowing. That he had seen something was quite evident as he mumbled and fumbled around with his playbook, trying to pull himself together.

"Well," bumbled Barrows, "that about concludes my interview with you."

"However, I may want to get back with you and your attorney, Mr. Hart, you say, for further questioning," had he left behind this trail of words as he exited.

"He has been given a great gift," tossed Michael this gem my way. "Whether he will use it wisely, only time will tell."

"My gosh!" I exclaimed as we hugged each other in spirit. "How good it is to see you again. I was beginning to wonder if you, too, had abandoned me."

"Naw," he replied. "I've just been busy elsewhere. The work of an angel is neverending. And you seemed quite content without my overarching presence."

"You are my legal guardian, you know," I begged to differ with him.

"Don't remind me," he laughed.

"I'll try to pop in on you more often, to let you know that I haven't abandoned you. If, in the meantime, you need me, call me, and I'll be there for you," left he this parting gift as he disappeared *'in the twinkling of an eye'*. I Cor 15:52.

On the morning of the 29th, did I rendezvous with Sir Brook and the dark side of Herr Barrows at an undisclosed location to sign a declaration of intent, Brook had drafted with Barrows' unwilling approval, that read in part as follows:

...I (the undersigned) *am most willing to relinquish the activities under investigation until I am discharged, if my claim is expeditiously and carefully considered by the Department of the Navy and if I am placed in a noncombatant status not conflicting with my religious beliefs in conscience while awaiting action on this claim.*

Agent Barrows then left us with the understanding that he would inform the Captain of the Davidson of my intent with the hope that the Captain would, in turn, place me in a noncombatant status in compliance with **Department of Defense Directive 1300.6** (Procedures for Processing Requests for Discharge Based on Conscientious Objection, Section B, No. 4) which specifically states:

Upon first referring of the case, pending its decision, the individual should be retained at his command and employed in noncombatant duties.

As I would learn, the double agent had made no effort to contact the Captain of the Davidson, for Barrows had gotten what he wanted, a signed statement that I would not engage in anymore antiwar activities on board the Davidson as long as I was afforded due process. Basically, the double-crossing son of the Great Sea Bitch had made a gentleman's agreement with me that he had no intention of honoring. Like Pilate, he wanted nothing more than to be able to wash his hands of this investigation and be done with it. He just couldn't deal with the fact that a guardian of the Kingdom had freed his soul from the pall that'd hung over his head, keeping him in the dark, up to now, concerning matters of the soul.

It was on the way back to my cell after I had made a head call, the evening of July 3rd, I believe, when I heard a commotion at the front gate that begged for an eye witness.

Staring at the bars in front of him while that rednecked, Marine Sergeant Hamilton harangued him, stood a new prisoner in irons, a marine boot named Laruso, who had told the Sergeant that he had refused orders to go to Vietnam.

"I love Jesus Christ...I will not kill," had Laruso hesitated to say when he was asked why he had refused to go to Nam.

"Whataya gonna do if I start beatin' the shit outta you, you yellow–bellied maggot," bellowed the beast of Hamilton's past as he got right up in Laruso's face.

"It doesn't matter what you or the Marine Corps does to me. God will avenge me," had Laruso sworn in the face of one helluva, pissed–off beast of a sergeant.

With that, did the enraged bull start pounding Laruso, still cuffed and in leg irons, in the trunk with punches that resounded throughout the brig as Laruso slumped to the floor crying.

"Now, are you gonna shut up?" Demanded the rednecked beast. "Ya gonna shut up, huh? Are ya? Huh, huh?"

All this the beast of Hamilton did in the company of two other upstanding, card–carrying members of the Corps, Sergeant Barber and Corporal McClure, who did nothing to stop him. Nor had the beast heard a peep from me who didn't know what, if anything, I could have done, so overwhelmed had I been by the flagrant brutality of the red–haired, rednecked Marine Sergeant from the once confederated, now refederated state of Arkansas.

Upon seeing me out of the corner of his eye, did the beast named Hamilton stop haranguing Laruso, long enough to order me back to my cell.

While Corporal McClure proceeded to lock me down, the other two hauled Laruso's sorry ass back to solitary confinement, where they worked him over for another hour or so before they brought him back, sobbing wet and filled with remorse, repeating over and over, "for Christ's sake I will kill; I will kill, for Christ's sake let me be..." as they unchained Cain and escorted him from the brig.

As for Laruso, I never saw him again, or learned of his fate. Nor, many years later, would I find his name on the Vietnam Veterans Memorial in Washington, D.C. With tears in my eyes, did I thank God that he had made it out alive.

Nor did the guards ever tamper with this witness.

How quickly did I get down on my knees and thank God for Jim, Brook and all the others who had entered my life to protect me from the vicissitudes of the military and such vicious attacks on my inborn being, I Am Who I Am, a conscientious objector, as Laruso had sustained. For him also, did I pray, but with a sigh *'too deep for words'*. Rom 8:26.

So too, did I pen a stark reminder—a crumpled piece of paper, I hold to this day—of the details surrounding the beating of one Prisoner Laruso, to turn over to the authorities once I was freed from the brig.

The Gauntlet

Stuck inside the brig, on Independence Day, did I stave off yet another bout of the returning–to–the–Davidson blues with the help of that heavenly Trio under whose reign I did now abide while I waited to file a claim with the High Priest of the Great Sea Bitch that would absolve me of the charge of pretending to be a conscientious objector as a way to get out of the Navy. Having shed this lie, early on, I so yearned to hand the Captain my declaration of independence, that I could taste the sweetness of the fruit of my labor. And to think, I had only to look into the face in the mirror to see Who I Am, all the solace I needed and more, the comfort of knowing that as a conscientious objector, I Am Who I Am.

Only, my superiors appeared none too eager to get me back, as the master–at–arms didn't come for me until 8:30 in the evening, the day of the completion of my sentence. Nor was I in any hurry to get back to the ship instead of jail.

5

Shadow of the White Kind

Back onboard my old nemesis, did I proceed, with all due haste, to type up my claim on a portable Olivetti–Underwood I had purchased, awhile back, from the ship's store. Though the task proved to be a bit taxing, I did manage, in the wee hours of the morning, to put into print, ten pages worth to be exact, my one claim to fame and first treatment of the subject, A Request for Discharge Based on Conscientious Objection.

As a prelude, I submitted a request at quarters, later that morning, to see the Captain to discuss my status aboard the ship so as to prevent any further conflict. Shortly thereafter, however, I got it back for having requested "to see the Captain" instead of a "captain's mast", an unwitting error on my part. Once I made the change, I resubmitted the request, this time, stapled to a copy of my claim, only to have that too, handed back to me because I hadn't submitted it at quarters, which apparently is the only time one can submit a request chit to see the Captain. Left, for a brief period, to the wiles of my imagination, I resubmitted the request after having informed my PO that our Division Officer had approved my doing so, even though he really hadn't, as long as I went through the chain of command, thus forcing him to accept my submittal.

Twenty minutes later, when the call went out for all hands to appear on the quarterdeck to load ammunition, I continued, as I had in the past without repercussion, to clean the compartment space to which I had been assigned, that morning. Twice did I step aside to let Chief Master–at–Arms Cormack slip by without saying a word to me, as he made his rounds to see that all hands, not on duty, had reported to the quarterdeck for the working party.

"Mr. Drury, you are wanted up on the quarterdeck," had the Chief informed me on his third and final sweep of the ship.

With great reluctance, did I follow the Chief up to the quarterdeck where he turned on me with an order to assist in the handling of ammunition.

"I have to refuse that," made I a profession of faith in keeping with that kept on earth as it is in heaven.

The instant I agreed to let it be done to me on earth as it is in heaven, the earth stood as still as the men loading ammunition stood when they heard me refuse to handle ammunition.

All eyes were upon me as the Chief once again ordered me to handle ammunition, only this time, in the presence of the Officer of the Deck and the duty watch as witnesses.

While heaven rejoiced and a tiny bit of earth proclaimed, "I have to refuse that," so filled was I with the peace that comes with the union of heaven and earth, that I barely noticed the Captain coming up the gangplank as I headed below with the resumption of the loading of ammunition. Out of earshot by this time, I could only guess at what he swore in anger as he glared at me after learning of my refusal. Like any good sailor, in those days, did I tip my hat to the Missus as I disappeared below with his soul in tow, so distraught was he with her attachment to me.

I was later informed that I'd been placed on report for having refused the order of a superior petty officer to abide by his conception of heaven on earth rather than my own. With heaven at my back, had I stood against the might of earth, and garnered the respect of many a mate for the courage I displayed that day. No longer was I seen as the ship's fuckup who had beleaguered the crew, for so long, with the misdeeds of but a shadow of the truth.

At a captain's mast, the following morning, I was taken aback when the Captain informed me, after I'd asked if he had read my CO claim, that he had not seen it. So, I handed him another copy to peruse at his discretion.

"Why didn't you wait until this came up through the chain of command?" Barked the Old Weasel. "You're being a little too pushy, if you ask me."

"You have to be pushy around here to get any help," jumped I into the fray, armed to the hilt with the sharpest criticism yet.

"Drury," he struck back, "I've had just about enough of you, in fact, about all that I can take. Ever since I came on board this ship, you have been a thorn in my side. You never do anything right. Maybe if you could do something right for once, things would go your way.

"Now, get out of here," had the beleaguered knight in khaki ordered the rebellious knight in white.

"Well done, my son," had the *'Ancient One'* (Dn 7:13) assured me as I disappeared below to embrace my soul, as never before, in her entirety.

Like wildfire, had the news of my refusal spread through the ranks of the lowly and lordly alike, as the ship took off for the mainland with eyes set on fighting fire with live fire—more war games and pussy.

"You shoulda seen their faces, when Dury refused to load ammunition," had Marty delighted a fallow group of shipmates with the glory details of my trial by fire. "You'd've thought they were facin' a mutiny, the way they looked when everyone stopped, the moment Dury recused himself from handling ammunition.

"It was a sight to behold," beamed Marty as he basked in the glory of an extraordinarily ordinary event.

On the way back to my compartment space, the following day, I ran into a PO whom I had never encountered before.

"Ain't none of us likes this war any more than you do, Dury," he confessed. "Me, I'm just bidin' my time, doin' what they tell me to do. All power to ya, man. I could never do what you're doin'."

I wanted so badly to tell him that he too could do what I was doing, but stopped short of saying anything but "thanks," as he headed down the passageway, never to cross my path again.

Just as the others had stopped loading ammunition, the moment I recused myself, had he, in his own way, shared in their show of support for me.

And whether he knew it or not, I stood for many a sailor on the ship.

Boy was I ever blindsided though, when the XO threw a mast for me, once we hit Long Beach, to refer the charge against me, for refusing the order of a superior petty officer, to a summary court-martial, set to convene in five days. Before I could even pull myself together, enough to respond, I was dismissed and sent below without having had the chance to utter a single word on my behalf.

"Take heart, my son," had the Old Indian consoled me. "You have taken the moral high ground right out from underneath their feet, a drubbing they will not take lying down. No matter what happens, you must stand firm and waver not in the least. And please rest assured that we have your back."

As soon as I could, I fired a letter off to Brook, special D, apprising him of their treachery, and waited and waited for a response that never came in time. By the fourth day, I was in panic mode. So I made a long distance call at which time he gave me the name of a local attorney to contact.

"If William Smith is not available," he went on to say, "don't panic. Although you have no right to challenge the officer who is to preside in your case, you may challenge him for cause at the time of the convening of the summary court-martial. You must support your challenge for cause by reference to the facts that you believe indicate that he is prejudiced in your case. If you refuse a summary court-martial, you can be awarded a special court-martial, which carries with it, as you know, a maximum of six months confinement as well as the right to have a lawyer assigned. Since it will take time to convene a special court-martial, you will have returned to Hawaii by then, so that I might represent you at the court-martial."

With that, did the operator break in to inform me that I would have to insert more change into the pay phone if I wanted to continue the conversation.

"Do as I have suggested, and everything will be alright. And good luck!" Had Brook managed to squeak by the operator before she cut him off.

Right away, I called William Smith, who was unavailable for the day but did give me the name of another attorney, who was also not available, the day of my court-martial. In the end, I had no one to turn to but the Holy Spirit, who would not forsake me if I held tight Her hand as She forded yet another stream of consciousness with my child likeness.

"Hold fast to your childlikeness," had She warned me, "lest the Evil One come and steal it away from you. For it is written that you must *'become like'* a child to *'enter the Kingdom'*." Mt 18:3.

As a child, did I come and go from the Kingdom of Heaven on earth, for 'twas She to whom I owed my allegiance, and no other, much less this can of nitwits.

Why the Captain would have appointed the same officer who had witnessed my recusal, to preside over this sham, was beyond belief, so much so, that I questioned the officer's ability to render a fair and impartial verdict as he tried to convene the court-martial.

"That's why," I concluded, "I refuse to cooperate with this travesty of justice in any way," whereupon I sat down on the floor, at the invitation of my heavenly Mother, the Holy Spirit, crossed my legs and closed my eyes, put my fingers in my ears and bowed my head as She filled my soul with the courage to hold fast.

"Your body will let you know when it is safe to come out," gave way She to the tapping on my shoulder.

"Yes," I said as I let down my guard and opened my eyes to the outside world.

To my amazement, all had left but the master-at-arms, who informed me that Lt. Smyth had referred the charge against me to a special court-martial just as Brook had predicated, whereupon I was dismissed and sent below.

"How'd it go?" Asked an eagerly awaiting audience when they saw the big grin on my face.

"Beyond all expectations," had I enticed others to gather round.

"Once I had recused myself from their latest attempt to railroad me, I staged a sit-in, closed my eyes and plugged my ears until all had left the room save the master-at-arms. For my recusal, I was awarded a special court-martial, a venue that provides me with a far better chance of beating the charge on the basis that as a noncombatant-in-waiting, I'd been given an illegal order."

"I'd've loved to have seen the look on Smyth's face when you sat down and shut him out," quipped Marty as the others dispersed with thoughts of their own on a sit-in taking place in the Navy—at a court-martial—by the defendant.

"Unheard-of!" Screamed every ounce of their flesh as they struggled to reconcile this picture of the Navy, at war with one of its own, with the view that obligated them to serve their country, right or wrong.

Only this time we were dead wrong. For we had no business interceding in the civil war that broke out between North and South Vietnam after the South refused to abide by the Geneva Accords of 1954, to hold nationwide elections to choose a new government to reunify a country that'd been torn asunder under the terms of the peace agreement—that ended 100 years of French colonial rule—as both Hanoi and Saigon jockeyed for control. Because the North had gone over to the communists, we saw the war not as a struggle for national unity—as had been our own Civil War—but as a push for Communist domination of Southeast Asia, with Vietnam being the first domino to fall if we didn't intervene on behalf of the South after it seceded from the union and established a new republic, though in name only—an unfortunate oversight which blindsided us to the true nature of the war, that of a people determining for themselves how they want to be ruled.

In the end, I wanted no more than what Ho Chi Minh sought, the reunification of the body and soul of what heads of state had ripped apart, leaving the world fragmented and ripe for war, the only rite left when right is forsaken and the ego prevails over the uncertainties that abound like red flags, warning of the dangers ahead if we continue down the road of greater loss of life to our own undoing and that of the world as we know it.

In the same way that Uncle Sam held on to Miss Saigon, did I cling to Mary, for Miss Saigon had no more love for Uncle Sam than Mary seemed to have for her sugar daddy. Still, I could not let go of the ever-fading possibility of Mary reciprocating, any more than the body of Uncle Sam could free its projection of soul from an ever-fleeting image of Miss Saigon as Commander of the USS Vietnam.

Before these images came crashing down around me, I received a letter from her ladyship that broached the subject of love or lack thereof on her part.

"I don't know how to thank you enough for the beautiful lei," she wrote. "It was out of this world. I received it Memorial Day and wore it to work the next day. I got so many compliments on it, Butch, thank you so much. Receiving it put me clear up on cloud nine. I wish I could have gotten the kiss that went with it. Believe me, I intend to cash in on it when you get home. Thank you dearly.

"In your last letter, you said that I loved you. Butch, I don't think I do. I believe love is something you recognize right off. I have my doubts, as you know, so I don't see how I can love you and still be doubting it. If I did love you, I would *know it, and I wouldn't have all these questions. I would like this whole subject to be a closed book until I see you again, and we can discuss it in person, not in a letter. I can't put on paper what I really think and feel, so I think it would be better if we let this drop. I know how important it is to you, and its just as important to me, but I can't seem to write what I really want to say. You keep telling me I do love you and I keep saying I don't. I care about you very much, Butch. I want to know how you are, what you're doing, and where you are. But that isn't the kind of love you're looking for. I've got to be fair to you, and that's why I'm saying this. I'm not going to write any more on the subject, cause I've said all that I can now.*

"*Thank you for sending me the pictures. They really turned out beautiful. You can take some of the best pictures I've seen.*

"*Lunch hour is just about over, so I'd better sign off. Thank you again for the flowers, Butch. They really made me feel great. Take good care of yourself and write whenever you have time. I look for your letters. Take care.*"

Love,

Mary

With more or less than six months of active duty yet to serve, depending upon the type of discharge that I received, like Mary, I was too busy courting a new life to know how I really felt about her. And now that I no longer clung to her for dear life, I knew, for the first time, that if I had to choose between the two, I'd pick my newfound love over Mary hands down.

Did that necessarily mean the two were mutually exclusive? No, it simply meant that for the time being, my soul was focused on my life as a conscientious objector and all that entailed. The question now was whether Mary would have anything to do with a conscientious objector. If not, then our relationship was doomed, and my fear of losing her if I shared my newfound love with her—which I hadn't yet—was all for naught.

As such then, did I win the heart of my soul, in a pact sealed with a kiss that was out of this world as we locked lips over my having finally found something outside my self and Mary into which I could pour my heart and soul.

Because so much of my relationship to Mary had been spent apart, leaving us little time to lock lips, maybe I no longer bore the projection of her soul any more than she bore mine.

"I'm not so sure she's the one," intimated my soul as she searched my heart for clues to the true nature of my relationship to Mary.

Stunned, I asked my soul, "Why do you say that?"

"I don't feel at home in her when you are with her," had she stirred up the need to take a closer look at what she was feeling.

"Does she not reflect you?" Inquired I of but a mere image of her.

"You shower too little affection on her for me to feel at home in her," dropped she this bomb on me, "for you fear that any affection at all will entice you to enter her abode, not as I have, but as you will."

"Is that not what I seek, to become one with her in whom you feel at home?" I begged to know beyond the sliver of a doubt.

"You are hooked on a feeling for a person whose dwelling you have yet to enter in any meaningful way," had she responded to the shadow of a doubt. "You have no inkling of what lies at the heart of her dwelling any more than she does.

"Has the Spirit given you any sign that she's the one? If not, how will you know when the right person comes along? Is that not what Mary means when she says she should know? Obviously, the Spirit hasn't given her any indication either.

"Why is that? Could it be that neither one of you is ready for what you seek in the other? For in the eyes of the Spirit, you are too young yet in the ways of the world to be pondering marriage.

"Don't you think then, that it's about time you leveled with her?" Asked she no more of me than I would ask of her, a letter signed, sealed and delivered to the one I <u>thought</u> I loved, explaining the last year and a half of my life as if that person really did matter, enough to at least tell her the truth.

Truth is, I had outgrown Mary and <u>thought</u> that I no longer needed her after I'd given birth to a life that had taken shape without her womb. For I was developing so fast that I wasn't sure she could ever catch up with me, or would even want to get caught up in the hell I was experiencing, given the ever-widening gap between her understanding of the world and mine. Besides, I was already having enough trouble trying to convince my superiors that I am a conscientious objector without having to explain myself to a girlfriend who had not the empathy to feel the pain of a noncombatant's tortured conscience when he is forced, against everything in his nature, to participate in the killing of other human beings in any manner whatsoever.

Out of loneliness, had I sought Mary's affections, for I had watched all my friends scatter to the four winds like leaves whose time had come for them. Left behind to grapple with the darkness that overshadows the ways of the Spirit, in Mary, I encountered a spirit willing to help me find my way. In my desperation for anything, remotely satisfying, did I cling to her for dear life, so lost was this soul of mine in the other.

All the while did my passion rage within me like one beast of a wildfire after another. Even in the Navy, where I had found safety in numbers, had the beast jumped the fireline betwixt its world and mine whenever it flew into a rage to satisfy its unquenchable thirst for life.

"O noble beast, in whom I dwell, how can I break free of my shell without having to go through hell?" Did I beseech what I eschewed, but must outreach to end this feud.

"Lend me thy ear that ye might hear what's near and dear," did the beast engage the root of its rage, Sir Knight's lonely page, the ego backstage.

"No sin ask of me, I do implore thee or in fear must flee," did I confront the noblest beast upon which my eyes did e'er feast.

"For love ye lack, turn not thy back on thine own pack," whispered the walls of my dwelling in a manner most compelling, reigniting fires dispelling the loved ones I'd been repelling.

"When you withdraw from the world," had the Old Indian signaled, "you lock your self up within your body to the exclusion of everyone else, including friends and loved ones, the pack to which you belong, until your body rouses you from your one-sidedness with sensations that it is time to come out and embrace the other side of nature. Only, you refuse to listen to the walls of your earthly abode until you are blazing with desire for union with the other, more outgoing side of your nature as seen in every skirt that catches your eye with the promise of fulfilling your wanton desires to express your soul in the way you see fit."

"Heaven forbid that you should muzzle me for your own pleasure," exclaimed my soul.

"Indeed," had I asserted that the word might become flesh.

With that, did I embrace my soul in the ecstasy, I had sought elsewhere.

Only, my outer relationships were changing as I grew tired of Marty always bitching about the Navy but never doing anything about it, and sought instead the company of those more willing to give flesh to their words like Lady Betty and the other knights and damsels of the Round Table, known in these quarters as the Hawaii Resistance. But alas, I was in California and they were in Hawaii, so I'd have to make do with the friends I had, no matter how annoying Marty could be.

Unable to find anyone to go ashore with me in Long Beach, did I step from the twilight zone to the steady beat of a drum that grew louder and louder as it lured me into a march against the very war, the Spirit had encouraged me to protest in the shadow of the white kind, that is, while wearing my service dress whites in keeping with that kept on earth as it is in heaven.

"I can't believe what I'm seeing," caught a middle-aged man my attention as he approached me from the starboard side of life, "a sailor in uniform marching against the very war he's supposed to be fighting."

"I can't either," I replied with the discomforting laugh of a madman who's been extricated from the loony bin with a hand from the Spirit. "For I am finally fighting the very war I'm supposed to be fighting, the battle against the Dark Lord with whom I had made a pact when I sold my soul to Uncle Sam and joined the lunatic fringe waging this war for naught but their own demise."

"O, you're sick, I mean real sick," expurgated he who had been ripped from the sidelines to engage the embodiment of a shadow of the white kind.

"Yep, I'm sick, damned sick—and tired—of trying to persuade the Navy to yield to the conscientious objector stuck inside this sailor's suit," reflected I but a shadow of the white kind, much to the chagrin of the man, I'd left standing in the middle of the street, dumbstruck.

So beside my self was I when my soul approached from the port side of life, that I froze as she hugged me for having given her flesh.

"What's the matter?" She asked.

"When you draw me into your world," I complained, "I lose contact with mine, for I can't be conscious in real time and dreamtime at the same time. If I'm awake in one, I'm asleep to the other, and I don't like losing consciousness in public for fear of making a fool of my self, living dreamtime in real time."

"Is not our goal to express dreamtime in real time, to give word to the flesh?" Had the one inquired of the other in her quest for the unity I sought in another. "And do not the words, I inspire in thee, satisfy the flesh and put to rest the fantasies that do vex thee so?"

With that, did I find my self running scared because I didn't know if I was fleeing her world or mine as I could no longer tell them apart—a dream come true, I was told, to differentiate it from a psychotic episode and alleviate my fear of having lost touch with reality.

The instant I decided to go back to ship instead of jail, I left heaven behind and stopped dreaming in real time as I boarded the ship with an imponderable ache in my heart. O, how I wanted to reconnect with my soul and dream in real time again, an experience that'd been so sensual, I could still taste it's sweet scent. But alas, I had chosen an alien band and no longer courted heaven on earth as I went below in search of soul in real time though.

"I'm over here," intimated my soul from where she stood beside my bunk as I started dreaming in real time that I am Who I Am regardless of where I make an effort to be I Am Who I Am, whether that be on or off the cross, the ship posed.

In an experience that was out of this world, on the one hand, and yet very much in the body, on the other hand, did I meld with the Creator and my soul in such a way as to leave behind a trail of breadcrumbs in case I lost my self again.

There, lying on my bunk, as my soul had indicated, did I find a letter from a CO counselor at the Central Committee for Conscientious Objectors (CCCO) in Philadelphia, PA, named Mike Wittels, to whom I had written in June, asking for advice, so lost for words had I been with regard to filling out my CO claim.

As good fortune would have her way, according to Mike's letter, I could now be legally represented at my exit interview with the Captain, the basis upon which he is required to make a determination as to my sincerity and forward to the Chief of Naval Personnel his recommendation as to whether or not I should be retained or discharged from the Navy as a conscientious objector.

Unfortunately, in answering the question which asks *"how, when, and from whom or from what source you received the training and acquired the belief which is the basis of your claim,"* I hadn't been quite as graphic as Mike had stressed in his letter, for fear of coming across as a lunatic. However, in light of the Captain's failure to interview me, I did have the option, according to Mike, to reapply should my current application for discharge be denied. At that point, I could get as graphic as I have been, thus far, with you, the reader of this madcap escapade through the mind of one really crazy knight.

The other letter lying on my bunk was from a journalist at the Honolulu Star-Bulletin, named Tomi Knaefler, who had interviewed me in the chaotic days leading up to the ship's departure from Pearl Harbor to take part in war games off the coast of California.

"I trust you're still seeing the sky without bars in between," had she written.

"I've written your story, but it's being held up so that a comparable article on a nonobjector with similar background can be worked out. Theoretically, the two run side by side will provide a balanced view. So, hopefully, that'll be achieved soon.

"Meanwhile, I would still like to have a picture of you to run with the article. As I didn't get one yet, I assume that time was too short for you Saturday morning.

"The picture should be sharp and in black and white, not color. Best get a smiling, informal shot with ship in background or such—in uniform would be fine.

"Be hearing from you, then."

Keep the faith,
Tomi Knaefler

Apparently, I had become quite the cause célèbre, much to the chagrin of the Navy, who was taking a beating on my behalf, for a change.

"See what can happen when you conduct yourself on earth as you would in heaven," popped in my soul who, for the most part, remained out of sight though she be ever at my side.

"When you lost your self for my sake, and became part of a cause, much larger than your self, you left behind the self-centeredness of your youth to embrace the world of other-centeredness. As such, did you regain the self-control that had so eluded the young man who wants for nothing now that he has freed his soul from her bondage to the flesh of another human being.

"O, how I have longed to celebrate this moment with you," expressed my soul as she embraced *'something greater than Solomon here'*. Mt 12:42.

In one of those rare moments when the three below—body, soul and spirit—become one with the Three Above—Father, Son and Holy Spirit—did I lose my self to the incarnation of the Word. Thus did I learn to write from the perspective of three persons in one as the First gave the Second the Third, the aha moment that let me know, the word flowing from my pen was indeed *'the Beloved with whom'* I Am Who I Am, the real Author here, was *'well pleased'*. Mt 3:17.

As the celebration began, I found my self mixing with the likes of my soul, one of whom introduced me to my Self, an old wise man, I was told, who looked so much like my mentor, that I mistook him for the latter.

Shocked, I asked my Self, "How can this be?"

"For mortals it is impossible, but for God all things are possible," (Mt 19:26) had I Am Who I Am, the real Sage here, intervened.

No sooner had God taken the old man from me, than I wondered why the only real father, I ever had, had been yanked from my side at such a crucial time in my life.

"I am your real Father," had the real Sage here reassured me, "always have been and always will be."

"However, knowing that You are also God changes how I relate to You from hereon out," bemoaned I the loss of the human scale of our relationship.

"I only hope that you treat Old Yahweh with a little more respect than you showed My servant, Hewhay," asserted I Am Who I Am.

"Heaven forbid that I should ever treat I Am Who I Am as badly as I have, Old Hewhay," declared a much humbler self, this time around.

"Will I still be able to talk to You as if You were my father?" Begged the child in me with the penchant to be an old wise man.

"I would have it no other way," had the one Old Man promised the other in his youth.

"I love You," had the child embraced his penchant for the Old Man.

"I love you too, My son," had the *'Ancient One'* endorsed the youth's penchant to grow up to be an old wise man.

Turning to my soul, at that point, I asked her, "if I am one with you, how can I be your father?"

"While you are not my father, by any stretch of the imagination, Hewhay is about as close to God as you may ever get to becoming one with the Father as I am one with the Father and you are, occasionally, one with me," had my soul reminded me of my infidelity. "For the closer you get to mirroring the real Author and Sage here, the more the Father will immerse Himself in you and your work, that you might become one with Him Whom you mistook for Hewhay. On that day, you shall look upon the face of God as you do your own."

Until then, I would have to face off with yet another gung ho Naval chaplain, to ascertain whether I was as true a conscientious objector as I claimed to be.

"You're no conscientious objector," barked the Chaplain as I was about to inform him, before I was so rudely interrupted, that I am one of the many incarnations of Who I Am, fleeing Egypt, these days, for the Promised Land.

"And you're no chaplain," I Am Who I Am struck back in righteous indignation, "for if you were a real chaplain, you would know *'there is something greater than Solomon here'*. You would see Who I Am." Mt 12:42.

"Come now, Peter," snarled the pirate in khaki, "don't you think it's about time you let go of these childish fantasies, face reality and quit using conscientious objection as a ruse to get out of fulfilling your military obligations?"

"Now see here, Hook," pushed back I AM, "don't you think it's about time you embrace your fantasies, and quit using your chaplaincy as a ruse to get out of fulfilling your real obligations to God and country? For you do them both a great disservice, denying Who I Am."

"How do you come off telling me what to do?" Demanded the cocky pirate in khaki, my unconditional surrender to his abuse of power.

"The words are heaven sent, Hook," had Peter rattled the old pirate's cage.

"You're unreal," had Hook lashed back ere accusing the lad of his own sin of having lost touch with reality.

"In your dreams, Hook!" Shouted Peter across the bow. "In mine, you are so out of touch with the Old Man upstairs—the only reality I know—that you can't even see Who I Am when I AM standing right here in front of you. And you call yourself a chaplain!"

With that, did all manner of civility fall from grace as the chaplain in khaki did thrice deny me in a shouting match that ended with the crow of a cock (Mt 26:75) and my ouster from Graceland without His Grace's blessing.

"Get out of here," yelled Hook as Peter fled lest he fall prey to Hook's sinister rejectionism of his conscientious objection as pure fantasy which, in reality, is none other than a command from God at its core, though it appear otherwise.

Back in Pearl, a few days later, I phoned Brook, as soon as I could, to let him know how smoothly the court-martial had gone before telling him about my disastrous interview with the Chaplain.

"With interviews like that, accompanying my CO claim," I complained, "I'll never receive recognition as a conscientious objector."

"Let's not worry about that for now," had Brook tried to console me, "and instead concentrate on the special court-martial, looming large on the horizon.

"Once you receive notification, confirming the date and time of your court-martial, it's important that you let me know, right away, to give me enough time to prepare your case for trial.

"Pending its outcome, I don't believe the authorities will cause you any more trouble for now. So please, don't rile them up any more than your conscience compels you, should you be given another illegal order prior to the resolution of your CO claim," had Brook advised me.

After Brook had finished talking with me on the phone, I called Betty to let her know that I had made it back to Hawaii in one piece.

"From what Brook has told us, sounds like the authorities were trying to ship-wreck you on the coast of California," gathered Betty.

"Damn straight, they were when they ordered me to perform an act, I was sure to refuse, and then hauled ass for the West Coast where they could try and sentence me to the brig, with no outside interference, and be done with me, or so they thought," maintained the better part of me, His Innocence.

With much glee then, did I proceed to give her a full account of my response to their attempt to ram through the court-martial before I could access an attorney.

"Ha, ha, ha," laughed Betty as I completed my narration of yet another close encounter with a world I *'do not belong to...any more than'* Christ belonged *'to the world'*. Jn 17:16.

"I would love to have seen the look on the presiding officer's face when you sat down on the floor and slammed the door to you in his face. It's such a marvelous story, sweetheart, that I can't wait to tell Walter," took Betty such great delight in Peter's response to yet another *'ravenous'* Hook *'in sheep's clothing'*. Mt 7:15.

A thieving pirate I am not, for never have I taken, nor ever shall I take the life of another human being. For me to do otherwise would be tantamount to high treason of the Lucifer kind, a betrayal of Who I Am—the very treasure the murderous thieves do ever seek but never find, all the while it's been staring them in the face.

"Listen, sweetheart, if you get into another bind with the authorities, call us, and we'll do everything we can to help you," had Betty brought tears to my eyes.

"After what I've been through, you don't know how much that means to me," had I struggled to give her the emotional equivalent of a hug over the phone.

"You're welcome, dear," had she returned the hug.

Before I would see her again, though, I was given a chance to work in the ship's office, and the weekend to think about it.

"Having invested as little of myself as possible in the war," had I caught Betty's attention, that weekend, at a party to which she had invited me, "I am so tired of doing nothing right, for as long as I have, that I could die for want of something constructive to do. And now I'm finding that even too little is too much to reconcile with my conscience, no matter how tempting or benign the XO's offer of too little, too late, seems to be.

"I'm just plain sick and tired of resisting Who I Am, to appease the devil riding my back like some cruel taskmaster with a whip, who beats me, at every turn, into submission to a greater will than my own, that of the Devil or of the Lord God.

"Do you see my quandry?" Had I sought refuge in the First Lady of the Resistance to recognize I Am Who I Am.

"Nonetheless," said she, "you must perservere, lest they poke out your eyes and steal you blind."

"Heaven forbid such foul play," had young Peter a say in the matter before it got out of hand as it has in Vietnam, where one man's blindness blinds another, eye by eye, until nigh a one can see Who I Am in the other, and be healed.

"*'But blessed are your eyes,'* dear, *'because they see'* (Mt 13:16) what so many upon *'seeing...do not see,'* (Mt 13:13) the truth behind the lies upon which they have based their entire lives," had she spoken in keeping with that kept *'on earth as it is in heaven'*. Mt 6:10.

So ethereal is the truth, and clouded, our vision with the unconscious projections of the beastly side of our nature onto all that commands the beast's attention, we can't even see the truth when it's staring us in the face. Living, as we do, with eyes clouded with lies in a world dominated by the beast, we accept an eye for an eye as the norm rather than the exception to which loving our enemies instead has been relegated. In a crushing blow to the Spirit, for whom the other is everything, we extol the egocentrism and self–aggrandizement of the beast, for whom the self is everything, as the ultimate goal of individuation.

Where the spirit seeks union with soul, doing *'to others as you would have them do to you,'* (Lk 6:31) the beast seeks its own gratification, come hell or high water. For the beast cannot see past the materiality of a world, oozing with soul, so evident to the spirit striving to let go of its projection of soul onto the world.

Wrapped in the silence of my own soul as we walked hand in hand down the beach behind Betty's place, I shuddered at the thought of having to go back inside to intermingle with the more socially adept, so inept was I at socializing with any degree of comfort. At the first rumblings of adulthood in my body, I had become a wolf that feared every human with whom it could not communicate on any other level than that of an animal. As my communication skills waned, I grew more and more isolated from my fellow human beings, less able to communicate with them when I was around them, and ever more fearful of gatherings of two or more, whether family or friends, and even more so if I didn't know them.

With nowhere to turn but the Navy, to whom I owed two years before the mast, needless to say, I was none too happy when I was pressed into serving time on a frickin' frigate, doing *'to others'* what I would never *'have them do to'* me as we shelled the hell out of the NVA (North Vietnamese Army), an act that allowed hell to invade our souls and take control of them for the duration of the hostilities.

"It's been a long time since we've been to a party, together," gathered my soul as she gave hell the boot for the time being.

"Indeed it has," agonized I over the loss of hell from my repertoire.

"You seem reluctant to go back inside," pointed she to the hellishness of the struggle to get out from underneath the skin of the blackest wolf that ever lived, that I might overcome my fear of humans, lest they come for me, armed to the hilt to slay the black beast and set my tongue free.

"Damn straight I am! With you at the helm and the beast on the wane, how else am I to act?" Came back the Comeback Kid.

"Well, you could start acting more like me than a wolf," exalted she in her ascendance to the throne, a reign—she had been warned—that would only last until midnight before it reverted back to me.

Under her tutelage then, did I go back inside, for I'd been given a great gift, the opportunity to experience other human beings from a woman's point of view.

While I felt a bit awkward at first, she felt right at home, weaving in and out of conversations with the nimbleness of a true master of the art.

My task was to observe as I'd been instructed before she turned me onto multiple personality mode with the snap of a finger that broke off all means of communicating with her until the clock struck twelve. Now I knew how she felt, having had no say in the affairs of the cad who had just been deprived of a say in hers for a mere fraction of the many years she had spent in solitary without hearing so much as a peep from me. Hoping like hell that I would not get stuck inside my own body, should she decide to retain the throne after her brief fling with freedom, I could only watch and wait in anticipation of what lie ahead.

So touched was I by how much she was enjoying herself, that I abandoned any thought of treachery on her part as she stimulated the hell out of me, filled me with laughter or brought me to tears with her enactment of **Who I Am**. Why I'd gotten so engrossed in her, by evening's end, that I wished I could be just like her.

"O, but you are, my dear," she insisted as the clock rang in a new day, free of the tyranny of the previous age, one fraught with the dissonance of separate personalities, so often out of step with **Who I Am**.

"All you have to do is let go of your self, and let it be who I am, as you did last night," exalted she in her liberation from the shackles of the antisocial personality disorder that'd hijacked my soul and subjected her to a fate worse than hell, a life of solitary confinement behind the very bars, that demon of a sociopath in me had erected to get her out of the way so that it could have me all to itself.

With its exposure, did the last demon in residence let out a shriek as it fled in anguish over the loss of the very body it had once possessed.

"Whoa!" Whispered that madcap ego of mine as it pulled itself from a dream gone terribly wrong yet justifiably so, in the eyes of the newly dispossessed.

"Well dear, I must say, you sure were the life of the party," had Betty informed me over breakfast at her place, where I had spent the night at her insistence. "You touched many a soul, last night, with the retelling of your naval escapades and other strange goings-on. You're a real hero to them, every bit as deserving, in their eyes, of a Commendation Medal as any other combatant, fighting the war."

"You mean antihero," declared the terribly flawed hero to the boisterous laughter of two like-minded souls.

O, how I wished that she were my mother.

"O, but she is," insisted my soul. "Do you not feel the First Lady's love for the new son, the Lord hath bequeathed her?"

"I do," admitted the teary-eyed young hero to yet another flaw in his personality, an insatiable desire for Our Heavenly Mother's acceptance of the beastly side of his nature.

"And do you not remember how Our Heavenly Mother welcomed the wolf back into Her arms, like a long lost pet?" Had my soul reminded me.

"Now the grey longs for your acceptance," had she directed my attention to the great grey that stood at the edge of the wood, awaiting my response.

"With the grey, you get a mixed bag of light and dark traits, for you can't have one without the other, though the side you nourish is the one that'll flourish," drove she home the last spike in the casket of my old friend, the White Wolf who had sired the grey ere he passed away.

The moment the great grey sensed the intensity of the desire in my heart to be reunited, it came running, like a long lost pet, back into my arms, where I stopped short of letting it lick me in the face as I clung, for dear life, to but a shadow of what once was.

'Twas indeed a sight to see the other wolves back onboard the ship cower as the great grey strutted passed them incognito, for the sons of bitches held no sway over the shadow of the white kind of wolf, now that it was free to be Who I Am.

Since the great grey wasn't too keen on my working in the ship's office, come Monday morning, I declined the offer as a cheap shot across the bow to force me into surrendering to a higher power that had no legitimate reason for keeping an avowed conscientious objector tied to a man-o'-war against the Sovereign Will of my animal nature.

"You must make choices that leave them with no other choice but to let you go," spoke the *'Ancient One'* I AM to Who I Am incognito.

"What choices are those?" Had Who I Am asked I AM.

"You will know when the time comes," confided I AM in the image of Who I Am. "Until then, you must prepare yourself."

As atuned as my senses were to the inevitability of the reunification of my body with its true intent, I needed no stretch of the imagination to convince me that I was getting closer to Who I Am, for no greater desire filled my frame with such anticipation than I AM becoming one with Who I Am.

Then, came the realization that Mary is not a part of who I am, never was, nor ever shall be, which surprised me no more than did the tone of her latest post:

"I don't know why you haven't answered any of my letters, but an explanation would be welcomed. I thought that after I received the beautiful lei everything between us was straightened out. Believe me, Butch, I was right up on cloud nine. I would just like to know the reason you haven't answered my letters. If you don't answer this one, I won't bother you any more."

Love,

Mary

"I wish you wouldn't," snickered I to my self with the satisfaction that the pain, she had caused me, was now hers and hers alone to bother me no more.

With her in mind, did I search my heart for the words to convey the self-defeat that allowed Who I Am to rise up and take control of my life. Via pen and paper alone, did I paint her a portrait of the author as a young man struggling to get out of the Navy, not by subterfuge, but as the bona fide conscientious objector, the Author of my being had summoned from my mother's womb. Freed, at last, from my long imprisonment in nature, I now wrote with the abandonment of an author who no longer feared rejection. As a slave no longer to the flesh but to the word, did I pour my heart out to her until there was nothing left to say.

"Speak, for your servant is listening," (1 Sm 3:10) sought I divine intervention whene'er the well went dry or the Captain wanted to see me.

"Mr. Drury," barked the Cap'n on this particular occasion, "your application for discharge as a conscientious objector has come back to haunt me with new stipulations that require an officer, grade O-3 or higher, to interview you and submit his findings to the Chief of Naval Personnel."

"I knew that was going to happen," spat I into his face.

"That's the problem with you, Drury, you know too goddamn much," sank the lanky Old Weasel his teeth into my ass. "Never in my entire career as an officer in the Navy have I seen anyone factionalize the crew of a ship to the extent that you have, and leave it so divided as to be almost unmanageable. You have been a thorn in my side from the day I stepped onto this ship."

By this time, he was spitting mad.

"Dammit, Drury, for once in your life I wish you would do something right."

"I am," said Who I Am.

"The hell you are," he screamed. "If you were, you'd quit hounding me with this ridiculous business that serving eighteen months onboard this ship, without hearing so much as a peep from you, has somehow turned you into a conscientious objector. Well, I hate to be the one to break the news to you, Mister, but the Squadron Chaplain who interviewed you last spring told me that you're no more a conscientious objector than I am. Now who do you think I'm going to believe?"

"Whether the Chaplain believes in Who I Am is immaterial," came back the Comeback Kid. "When I announced my conscientious objection to you and those present at the captain's mast in March, you didn't place me in a noncombatant status as required by law. Nor did you inform me of my rights as a claimant or of the process I must undergo to pursue such a claim. When you did finally decide to place me in a noncombatant status, four months later at my insistence, you then turned around and ordered me to load ammunition. And now you have the nerve to stand here and tell me that I should do something right for a change.

"I beg your pardon, Sir," pled the Comeback Kid, "but I pledge allegiance to Who I Am and no other god that either you or the Navy may impose upon me."

"Get out of here, you imposter," pointed the Cap'n to the demon in our midst.

"You're right! I'm not a seaman, never was nor ever shall be," stood I my ground in the shadow of the white kind, "for I am Who I Am and the sooner you get that, the better off we'll all be."

"Get out of my sight," cast the Cap'n his eyes askance, lest he see Who I Am.

"As you wish," said I with a sigh to the man at war with Who I Am. "But I will continue to haunt you until you set my spirit free."

Whether he had seen Who I Am, I don't know, as he never gave me any indication that he had. Nor was I ever given the opportunity to find out, as I never laid eyes on him again.

"How'd it go?" Asked Marty as those who recognized my voice gathered round to hear my latest treatise on the mount.

Having satiated their appetite for more of what they knew not, I was left standing there with the only person who had stood at my side when everyone else had abandoned me out of fear.

"Ya know, Dury," confided Marty, "it's been a real honor to have served with you, fighting the forces of evil that could easily have overtaken me without you and the light you ignite to dispel the darkness from our eyes."

"I have known no truer a friend than you have been to me," came back the Comeback Kid. "How often have I seen you go out of your way to defend Who I

Am from the dark forces that overshadow the minds of men with the death–defying trickery of thoughtless deeds of gallantry, glorifying God in country with brutal bouts of savagery, and ritualized butchery in mockery of Calvary, the soul's only sanctuary from idolatry's deviltry."

"Should you ever come to Baltimore after you get outta the Navy, and need a place to stay, it goes without saying that you are more than welcome to stay at my house," attested Marty to the viability of our friendship, that I not forget him.

"Likewise, Marty, my place is your place if you ever come to St. Louis," had I tried to reassure Marty of what is now but a fading memory of the day I left him standing there, frozen in time, unable to yield to its demands to lay his life on the line for any other cause than the machinery of war.

For I had seen the Promised Land, my soul laid bare, enticing me to come hither, again and again, as I inched ever closer to understanding the sensual nature of my desires for that promise in the flesh. O how I longed for the union of my body with its true intent, that promise in the flesh Nature held at bay until I stake my life on the cross I'd been carrying since I left the Academy. Out of desperation, had I sparked a revolution within my being to retake the heartland and restore the gift of life to that promise in the flesh I AM.

Amid trumpet blasts, heralding an event that had yet to unfold, did I let Brook know that my Special Court–Martial had been set to convene at the Headquarters of the Fourteenth Naval District, U.S. Naval Base, Pearl Harbor, Hawaii at 0800 on 6 September 1968.

On my way to quarters, the following morning, I was rendered speechless when a first class petty officer, named Wulff, came out of nowhere to shove me off the fantail from which he then barred my ass until I had removed the whiskers from my face and the peace symbol from the chain around my neck.

By the time I caught up with my body, I found it up in the head, standing in front of the looking glass that mirrored my soul.

"Should I take off the peace symbol?" Sought I what lie beyond the shadow of a doubt.

"You will deny the lordling three times ere he crows like a cock to his superiors, spelling out in great detail how you have torn *'the veil of the sanctuary...in two from top to bottom'*," (Mt 27:51) stated milady in keeping with that kept *'on earth as it is in heaven'*.

With a clean shaven face, had I abandoned my prognosticator to go below to begin cleaning the compartment space to which I had been assigned.

"Dury, ya gonna take off that peace symbol?" Growled Big Bad Wulff as I moseyed on over to the drinking fountain instead, to quench my thirst for the life–giving water that could set my parched tongue free.

Having spun me around after he had seized me by the arm, did Herr Wulff catch hold of the peace symbol with his other paw, to rein me in. As the dire wolf got right up into my face, he growled again, "Are ya gonna take off the peace symbol, like I asked ya?"

"Please take your hands off me and my God-given right?" Came back Kid Comeback as the Water of Life went to his head, to loosen his tongue, that he might speak with authority.

"Take off the peace symbol, Dury," commanded the big bad wolf who broke out into a sweat when he noticed that a crowd had gathered round to bear witness to the crucifixion of the one who bore their sins.

"Please take your hands off me," demanded the Authority invested in me.

"I order you to take off the peace symbol now, Dury," growled he who had no authority to handle a subordinate in the way he was manhandling me.

"Get your clammy paws off me, ya big bad wolf," came back the Sovereign Will of the kid come back from the brink of acridity with a clear conscience.

As His Impotence, Herr Dire Wulff, stormed off to betray me, I sat down with those whom he had left behind, to shed light on the unapparent, that they might see the Word made flesh in the execution of a simple act of civil disobedience.

Accused of appearing at morning muster with a beard, three days old, of wearing a *"nonreligious"* medallion outside my uniform shirt, of disobeying a lawful order to remove the medallion, and of being disrespectful in language toward a superior petty officer, was I rushed off to another hastily held executive officer's mast, where the charges against me were referred to the special court-martial, looming ever larger on the horizon.

Only, Brook was none too happy when I told him about the added charges.

"Where we would have beat the order to load ammunition hands down, with these added charges, we now have a much bigger battle on our hands than I had anticipated," lamented Brook over the unlikely odds of getting me off scot-free.

"I Am Who I Am, Brook, which rankles guys like Wulff, once they realize, they have no authority over the Authority invested in me. To act as I must, in keeping with that kept *'on earth as it is in heaven'*, puts me in the crosshairs of every lifer on the ship gunning for the shadow I bear for them who deny its existence, that they might rid themselves of this last vestige of Who I Am. In my obedience to a higher law than the Uniform Code of Military Justice, have I ripped the veil of blind obedience in two, from the top of the chain of command to the bottom, that all might see the Word made flesh in the breaking of man-made laws in response to the higher calling of the Lord.

"When one is faced with the overriding truth, in the end, what choice does one have but to live it out, so compelling is the truth," had I concluded ere Brook assured me that despite the added charges, he would do his utmost to defend Who I Am, no matter how compelling was the Navy's case against I AM.

Shortly thereafter, was I invited to a conclave of die-hard do-gooders, every bit as willing as the members of The Committee of Responsibility in attendance, to assume responsibility for the high cost of removing and rearranging the cutaneous and subcutaneous tissues of a growing number of Vietnamese children, with jellied gasoline that burned so hot, the lower features of one child's face had melted, fusing an expanded version of his lower lip and chin to his chest.

As Betty introduced me to her guests, I was forced to endure a bit of a hero's welcome before I slunk from the aura of the white knight to match wits with a young pip from Vietnam, seeking to regain use of the arm and leg, flying shrapnel had paralyzed when the same bomb that'd killed his parents, exploded outside their hut. Little did I know that Jacques, as he was called, would litter my evening with the wreckage of one ill-fated attempt after another to beat him at checkers. Having grown weary of fighting him at every turn, with no win in sight, was not I compelled by evening's end to concede to the sovereign will of the young pip I could vanquish in neither war nor checkers.

Although, he sure melted my heart when he stretched out his good arm to give me a hug as I prepared to leave.

"Anh yêu em," reveled he in the Son's love for the Father.

"I love you, too, Jacques," clung I to an image of the Father made flesh, a child made whole as long as I held onto the reality of this dream, that the two might become one ere I opened my eyes to see if the dream had come true—enough of a doubt on my part to dash the hope of ever seeing him made whole again, neither in dreamtime nor real time.

A healer I am not, though the possibility still is. If only I knew for certain, 'twould be to my delight. Where doubt runs rampant, there shall you find me, wrestling with the real healer I AM, in the aura of a white knight.

6

Trial of a Special Kind

As the white knight angled his way across the board, past pawns, courtiers and high–ranking clergy, to greet his attorney, why the outpouring of their support for him and his court challenge so imbued him with the Holy Spirit, that some say he shined brighter that day than he ever had.

And so did the court open, in accordance with the collective will of the Navy, at 0843 hours, 6 September 1968, in direct conflict, however, with the Sovereign Will of Who I Am.

"The court will come to order," commanded the Judge Advocate and Lieutenant Commander presiding over the formalities of the day and a board that consisted of three additional officers—a lieutenant and two ensigns.

"The prosecution is now ready to proceed with the trial in the case of United States vs Fireman Recruit E. J. Drury USNR, *who is present in court,"* had Trial Counsel, LT K. Norgaard JAGC, the presence of mind to say on cue.

"As President of the board, I am required to 'inquire whether counsel for either side elects to conduct a voir dire examination to determine if there is possible ground for challenge for cause?'"

"The prosecution does not," had Trial Counsel recited from rote.

"I have several questions I'd like to ask the members of the court," had Brook spoken from the heart like a true attorney.

VOIR DIRE EXAMINATION

Questions by the defense:

Q. Mr. MacDougal, are you acquainted with the Navy Regulations for the processing of conscientious objectors?

A. No, sir.

Q. What is your duty in the Navy?

A. I am an electronics officer on the USS O'Bannon.

Q. On your ship, do you have any knowledge of any man in your crew who has ever applied as a conscientious objector?

A. No, sir.

Q. So you really have no knowledge at all?

A. I would say so.

Q. If an enlisted man came to you and said, "I'm a conscientious objector," what would you understand your obligation to be under Navy Regulations?

A. I would look to the Naval Regulations before I were to know my obligation.

Q. How about you, Lieutenant Rapson? Are you familiar with the regulations concerning conscientious objectors in the Navy?

A. No, sir.

Q. Ever have any reason to look into the matter of conscientious objectors on the part of any individual associated with the Navy?

A. No, sir.

Q. What is your duty in the service?

A. I am attached to staff duty here at CONSUBRON 7.

Q. And what ship, if any, have you served on?

A. I have served on the USS Forrester.

Q. And during that service did you have any occasion where an individual applied as a conscientious objector?

A. No, sir.

Q. If an individual approached you as an officer, and said, "I am a conscientious objector," and you had authority over that individual, what would you do?

A. I would have to do the same as the other court member said.

Q. Lieutenant Commander Drew, what would you do if an enlisted man came to you and said, "I don't know what I'm supposed to do, but I wish to apply as a conscientious objector?"

A. Well, this would be the usual test case, because I doubt that he would know specifically what he should do.

Q. Would you understand your duty as his commanding officer to inform that man of the steps that he must take to process his claim?

A. If he asks me for assistance, I certainly would, and I would start out by perusing the Bureau of Naval Personnel Manual.

Q. Now, Ensign Beal, have you had any contact with any member of the Naval Service who has claimed to be a conscientious objector?

A. No, sir, I haven't.

Q. Do you have any knowledge as to what a conscientious objector is?

Trial of a Special Kind

A. A conscientious objector would be a person who, because of certain beliefs, religious or otherwise, feels that particular duties are against the particular beliefs of a particular religion.

Q. And Ensign MacDougal, do you have any understanding or knowledge or opinion of what a conscientious objector is?

A. My opinion would be very similar to Ensign Beal's.

Q. Lieutenant Rapson, have you ever seen this symbol? (Defense Counsel draws symbol on blackboard.)

A. Yes, I have.

Q. And what does that symbol signify to you, if anything?

A. I've seen it in relation to the International Peace Movement.

Q. Commander Drew, do you have an opinion of the significance or meaning of the symbol?

A. That's the symbol for the Committee on Nuclear Disarmament.

Q. And do you have an opinion as to whether that symbol has any broader implication than its initial adoption?

A. Well, you see it being displayed by groups who don't necessarily have nuclear disarmament as their primary goal. And most recently at the Chicago convention, I think, the sign was demonstrated. Only, I don't think there was much said about nuclear disarmament at the Chicago convention.

Q. Ensign Beal, are you familiar with that symbol?

A. I've seen it displayed at various places.

Q. When you see it, what do you feel?

A. I've always had the impression that it means peace.

Q. How do you feel about peace?

A. I think it's a great thing, if we can only manage to get it.

DEFENSE COUNSEL: *I have no further questions at this time.*

PRESIDENT: *Prosecution?*

TRIAL COUNSEL: *I have no questions.*

The court noted that there were no challenges for cause from either side.

PRESIDENT: *Before we proceed, court members are instructed that any facts, opinions and circumstances revealed by the members in the voir dire proceedings on challenges may not be considered by members of the court for any other purpose, and you should totally disregard any such matters during your deliberations in the case. Are members of the court satisfied that they can continue to sit and decide this case solely on the basis of the evidence yet to be presented?*

Very well. The record will show that all members responded correctly to the question. Please proceed.

TRIAL COUNSEL: *Fireman Recruit Drury, how do you plead?*

DEFENSE COUNSEL: *To all the charges and specifications, FR Drury pleads not guilty.*

PRESIDENT: *Mr. Hart, would you care to make an opening statement before the presentation of evidence?*

DEFENSE COUNSEL: *Yes, I would, Mr. President.*

Gentleman, in this case, the charges and specifications look somewhat like the garden variety, disobeying–an–order case, failure to wear one's uniform in the proper manner, and some insubordination to a superior. Underneath the charges, we will show there is much more here. This is the case of a young man who, after entering the Navy due to a matter of confusion with respect to his military obligations, grew more and more to the position of a conscientious objector. That is, he became one who, because of religious training and belief, is conscientiously opposed to participation in war in any form. More specifically, he found that he could no longer take part in activities which directly contributed to a war effort.

Due to what must be a failure of communications, not only in the Navy but in the armed services, this young man was not made aware upon inquiry that he had the right to apply administratively for a discharge as a conscientious objector. We will show that all of Mr. Drury's troubles, and the charges specifically today, arose out of the frustrating attempt to make his position known. We will show, for example that last March, after a captain's mast with Captain Whitaker, attended by other members of the crew, Drury requested Captain Whitaker to furnish him the necessary form to apprise him of the procedure for applying as a conscientious objector. We will show that the Navy regulations require that when a man makes his request there is a duty on the officer to whom that request is made to aid the individual in filing his application, and specifically to assign the individual duty not inconsistent with his religious beliefs. We will show that Captain Whitaker specifically disregarded Mr. Drury's request and failed to do anything about his claim.

Later, Mr. Drury was forced to seek outside help. He did so by going to a group of young men in our community who are working for the cause of peace, and we will have some evidence of what the nature of their activities have been. He was put in touch with ministers who were able to inform him that in fact he did have a right to make his claim as a conscientious objector. He was eventually introduced to an attorney, that is myself, who helped him make the claim which he has made to the Navy. We are not going to offer the defense to any of those charges that the man was religiously opposed to doing his duty, because I'm sure you all know, the military knows, and if the military knows, the civilian courts recognize such a defense. But we will show that the order to load ammunition on July 6, was an illegal order, in that such an order came after Drury had made a request of his Captain to be processed as a CO, and after that request was rebuffed. Fur-

thermore, with respect to the other charges, we will show that the symbol which Mr. Drury was wearing is one that is worn by several members of the crew and has been for a number of weeks; that members of the crew of the Davidson have worn not only peace symbols, but beads, rings, other nonreligious symbols around their necks for sometime without complaint.

We will show that the words which Drury is accused of saying to Wulff were words that were spoken in a respectful manner, even after significant provocation by Wulff, after the Wulff manhandled Drury, spun him around and grabbed him by the arm and by the medallion around his neck. We will show that Mr. Drury has engaged in a number of activities which might reflect upon immaturity, but in no way indicates willful disregard for military regulations. We will show that Drury has made an effort, and did make an effort, to bring his claim to the attention of the military, and was rebuffed at every count. We will show that in fact the very week before the incident involving the refusal to load ammunition occurred, Drury had an interview with a member of the Office of Naval Investigation, who came all the way from Washington to investigate the group with which Drury has allied himself, and in the course of that interview reached an understanding that if Drury could only be permitted to file his application as a conscientious objector, he would do all he could to refrain from any activity which would be disruptive of military procedure. Such interview occurred while Mr. Drury was at the Brig in Pearl Harbor for an unrelated matter. And on the very day that Drury got out of the Brig and he made an attempt to bring his claim to the attention of the Command, he was given an order to load ammunition, that is, an order inconsistent with his religious beliefs. And it is out of that incident, and out of the incidents involving his search for peace—and I use that word in two ways: internal peace and peace for our country—that this young man is being charged.

PRESIDENT: *Call your first witness.*

TRIAL COUNSEL: *The Government stipulates that the accused, Drury, received on 1 February 1967, active duty orders from the Commandant, Ninth Naval District, dated 9 January 1967, ordering him to return to active duty.*

DEFENSE COUNSEL: *Yes, we stipulate to that.*

PRESIDENT: *Very well. FR Drury, do you consent to that stipulation?*

ACCUSED: *Yes, I do.*

PRESIDENT: *Very well, the stipulation will be accepted.*

TRIAL COUNSEL: *Additionally, Trial Counsel would like to offer as a stipulation that if Sonar Chief John Cormack were in court he would testify as follows:*

That on 6 July 1968, he was in duty status as Chief Master–at–Arms; that he was wearing a tropical khaki uniform, a gold badge of office on his khaki shirt; that on the morning of the same day the USS Davidson was engaged in an all-hands evolution involving the loading of ammunition, and as the Chief Master-at-Arms he was charged with the responsibility of insuring that all hands participated; that while carrying out his responsibilities, Chief Cormack found Drury below decks, working in one of the compartments; that upon determining that he had not been excused from the all-hands working party, he took him to the fantail of the ship and there ordered Drury to pick up individual five-inch rounds of ammunition from the pallet as they came on board, and hand them to another enlisted man; that Drury refused to carry out this order.

Additionally, it is stipulated by Chief Cormack that, as far as he knows, Drury has never been known to be in any kind of trouble before, and has never refused to obey the order of the Chief prior to this incident.

Does defense consent to the stipulation?

DEFENSE COUNSEL: I stipulate to that.

PRESIDENT: Drury, do you consent to that stipulation?

ACCUSED: Yes, I do.

PRESIDENT: Very well, the stipulation as offered is accepted. And at this point, I instruct the court members that with respect to the stipulation which has been accepted, stipulation as to testimony does not indicate the truth of the indicated testimony, nor does it add anything to the weight of the evidentiary nature of the testimony, but stipulated testimony may be attacked, contradicted, or explained the same as testimony given by a witness in person before the Court.

Now, with that understanding, we will proceed.

Kenneth Wulff, Electrician's Mate First Class, USN, USS Davidson, was called as a witness for the prosecution, was sworn and testified as follows:

DIRECT EXAMINATION

Questions by the prosecution:

Q. Are you acquainted with the accused in this case?

A. Yes, sir, I am.

Q. Will you point to him and state his name, please.

A. That's Drury, fireman recruit (indicating the accused).

Q. I would like to call your attention to the 16th of August 1968. Did you have occasion to see Drury on that date?

A. Yes, I did.

Q. When did you first see him?

A. In the morning at quarters on the fantail.

Q. What was Drury wearing at the time?

A. As we fell in for morning quarters, Drury came down the fantail wearing his working uniform with a medallion around his neck outside his dungaree shirt.

Q. Would you describe this medallion?
A. It was a chain link with a peace symbol on the bottom.
Q. Was there anything else unusual about Drury's appearance?
A. Yes, he was unshaven at the time.
Q. Did you have an occasion to see Drury later on that same day?
A. Yes, sir, at approximately 12:30 that afternoon.
Q. Would you describe that incident, please.

A. I seen him as he was going down in the berthing compartment, and he still had his medallion around his neck, which early in the morning, I had told him to remove, being that he was out of uniform with it on. And again I told him to take it off, and he wouldn't take it off.

Q. Did Drury say anything during this incident?

A. Yes. I told him to take it off, and then I asked him if he was going to take it off, and at this time, while I was holding on to the medallion, the chain of it, he told me to take my slimy hands off of his personal property.

Q. Did Drury take the medallion off at the time?
A. No, sir, he did not.
TRIAL COUNSEL: I have no further questions.

CROSS EXAMINATION

Questions by the defense:
Q. Wulff, how long have you served on the Davidson.
A. Five months.
Q. During that time, other than the matters that you just testified to, have you had any contact with Drury?
A. Just living on board the same ship with him.
Q. Did you ever see any other members of the crew wearing anything around their necks, that you can describe as a medallion, or nonreligious?
A. Yes, sir.
Q. In fact, a number of members of your crew wear...
A. That's negative, sir. I wouldn't say many of them.
Q. Would you say more than one?
A. No, sir, just one other.
Q. And how was your knowledge of that one other gained?
A. I seen him wearing a string of beads around his neck, inside his shirt.
Q. Did you see anything hanging from the string of beads?
A. No, sir.
Q. Did you tell him to take his beads off?
A. Yes, sir.

Q. What did he do?
A. He took them off.
Q. Did you see anybody else wearing beads or medallions after that time?
A. No, sir.
Q. Now, Wulff, do you understand your obligations as far as dealing with the individuals who are inferior to you in rank, when they are conducting themselves in ways in which you believe violate naval regulations?
A. Yes, sir.
Q. Do you believe that you have the right to physically touch any individual whom you believe is violating naval regulations?
A. No, sir.
Q. Isn't it true, that on at least three occasions you have touched Mr. Drury?
A. Once I touched him. Twice. Twice I've touched him.
Q. Now, isn't it true that on the date in question, August 16, you had occasion to touch him after you observed the medallion around his neck?
A. Yes, sir.
Q. And that touching was in the form of a shove?
A. I took him over to the side to inform him to remove his medallion.
Q. And you used a manner of moving him to the side which involved your making physical contact with him deliberately, isn't that true?
A. Yes, sir.
Q. And then later that day, around noon, down in the compartment, you again had physical contact with him?
A. Yes, sir.
Q. In fact, you grabbed him by the arm.
A. I turned him around so he would talk to me, because he wasn't paying any attention to me.
Q. And you also grabbed the thing he had around his neck, didn't you?
A. Yes, sir.
Q. You recall, don't you, that when you turned him, he asked you to remove your hand?
A. Yes, sir.
Q. In fact, he asked you two or three times, do you recall that?
A. Yes, sir, he did.
Q. And you recall that he asked you in a way that was not disrespectful, the first two or three times?
A. No, sir, it was not.
Q. Now, do you recall an incident in July, before the August 16th incident, when you put your hands on Mr. Drury?

A. *I don't recall what incident you're talking about.*

Q. *Wasn't it an occasion when you observed Drury shuffling some papers?*

A. *Yes, sir, now I remember.*

Q. *And you commanded that he stop shuffling those papers, didn't you?*

A. *Yes, sir.*

Q. *And in fact at the time, you put your hands on him to, shall I say, convince him that he ought to stop shuffling the papers. Isn't that right?*

A. *Yes, sir.*

TRIAL COUNSEL: *Mr. President, we are going to pose an objection to that question. We fail to see the relevancy of this prior incident.*

DEFENSE COUNSEL: *If you please, Your Honor, this goes directly to the heart of the predisposition of the witness to abuse Mr. Drury, and it is absolutely relevant on the matter of his disrespect to the witness.*

PRESIDENT: *Let me make sure, for a ruling on relevancy, the time frame which you're establishing. You're talking about July, the month preceding this event?*

DEFENSE COUNSEL: *That's correct.*

PRESIDENT: *Very well. Subject to the objection of any member of the court, the objection is overruled. Continue with your examination, Mr. Hart.*

Q. *Do you recall the question?*

A. *Yes, sir.*

Q. *You did shove him, didn't you, at that time?*

A. *Yes, sir, I did.*

Q. *What were the exact words which Drury used with respect to the removal of your hands from his person as he requested that that be done?*

A. *Take your slimy hands off of my personal property.*

Q. *Do you recall that it was "clammy" rather than "slimy"?*

A. *No, sir, I remember it as "slimy".*

Q. *Weren't you kind of heated up by that time?*

A. *Yes, sir, I sure was.*

Q. *And you felt that you could not conduct yourself according to the regulations? You found it necessary to put your hands on him, didn't you?*

A. *I felt that I conducted myself accordingly, sir.*

Q. *Do you know of any regulation that permits you to manhandle an enlisted man?*

A. *I don't feel it was manhandling, sir, not in the least.*

Q. *Do you know of a regulation that permits you to put your hand on an enlisted man if he's doing something other than physically abusing you?*

A. *No, sir, I do not.*

Q. *There is no such regulation, is there?*

A. *I told you, I don't know right off hand.*

Q. *What is your rate?*

A. *Electrician's Mate First Class, sir.*

Q. *It means that there are a number of people on board who are below you?*

A. *Yes, sir.*

Q. *You have the power, or duty to order them to do certain things, don't you?*

A. *Yes, sir.*

Q. *And you are not familiar with any regulation which permits you or does not permit you to put your hands on another person?*

A. *I don't know very much about regulations, sir, if there is or there isn't one.*

Q. *Do you recall whether other people witnessed this attack?*

A. *Yes, there were.*

Q. *Did you know at the time of the incident whether Drury had made an attempt to file an application as a conscientious objector?*

A. *No, sir.*

Q. *Did you ever hear anything on the ship about that?*

A. *Since the incident I have. Before the incident, no.*

Q. *How did you determine that Drury had not shaved for three days?*

A. *Just a guess, sir.*

Q. *It might have been that he had not shaved that morning, rather than three days, am I not right?*

A. *Not for the length of the beard that he had.*

Q. *Oh, well, what was the length of that beard?*

A. *Well, I would say about 3/16 of an inch.*

Q. *Did you measure it?*

A. *No, sir. But I could look.*

Q. *You took a quick look?*

A. *Yes. Over a period of about three minutes.*

Q. *Other than that symbol that Drury was wearing, he was in all respects dressed correctly, wasn't he?*

A. *Yes, sir.*

Q. *Did you take a look at Drury when you saw him at quarters in the morning?*

A. *Yes, sir.*

Q. *Did you say anything to him about that beard at that time?*

A. *Yes, sir, I told him to shave it.*

Q. *Did you say anything to him about it at noon?*

A. *Not concerning the beard because he was shaven at the time.*

Q. *Have you told individuals who are not clean shaven in the past to shave?*

A. *Yes, sir, I have.*

Q. And have you observed whether or not such individuals have complied with your instructions?

A. Yes, sir, I did.

Q. Did you have any case where that individual complied with that instruction and later was charged with not having shaved?

A. No, sir, I've never run up against this.

Q. And you had no intention of charging him with not shaving until the second incident? Isn't that true?

A. If he was shaved, I wouldn't have.

Q. But he wasn't shaved?

A. Yes, sir, he was.

Q. Didn't you put him on report for failing to shave?

A. For quarters, yes, sir.

Q. When did you make that report?

A. At noon.

Q. Yes, after you had observed his clean shaven face, right?

A. Yes, sir.

Q. Right.

DEFENSE COUNSEL: I have no further questions.

REDIRECT EXAMINATION

Questions by the prosecution:

Q. How close were you to Drury when you made the estimate of the length of his beard?

A. I was standing right next to him, about eight or nine inches, a foot apart.

Q. During the incident with Drury below decks, did you at any time strike him?

A. No, sir.

Q. Did you manhandle him in any way?

A. I turned him around. I don't consider that manhandling.

TRIAL COUNSEL: I have no further questions.

RECROSS EXAMINATION

Questions by the defense:

Q. You grabbed him by the arm, did you not, and spun him around bodily? And turned him around, you did that, didn't you?

A. Yes, sir, I did.

Q. It was very obvious at 12:00 noon, when you came over to him, that he was clean shaven?

A. Yes, sir.

Q. And you had no intention of putting him on report for failing to shave in the morning, did you? Not until the incident below decks at noon?

A. (The witness did not reply to the question.)

Q. Well, did you?

A. No, because he complied with my order.

Q. What do you think about people who wear peace symbols?

A. Not too awfully much.

Q. You don't go too much for that peacenik stuff, do you?

A. No, sir.

Q. Why?

A. I just don't agree with all their opinions.

Q. You have any discussion with the accused as to what his opinion was with regards to peace?

A. No, sir, I've never talked to him.

Q. Something bad about that thing, isn't there?

A. What thing?

Q. That peace symbol. I mean that indicates to you something subversive, doesn't it? Something really not in keeping with the American tradition?

A. That's right.

Q. In fact, when you see that thing you bristle, isn't that right?

A. Yes, sir.

Q. In fact, when you saw that thing around Drury's neck, you bristled?

A. Yes, sir.

Q. That doesn't belong in the Navy, does it?

A. No, sir. It doesn't.

Q. That does not belong in our country, does it?

A. I don't believe so.

Q. In fact, that indicates to you a whole realm of views and ideas to which you disagree totally.

A. Yes, sir.

Q. And you'd think less of me if I wore a peace symbol, wouldn't you?

A. Yes, sir, I would.

DEFENSE COUNSEL: *No further questions.*

PRESIDENT: *Is there anything further of the witness, prosecution?*

TRIAL COUNSEL: *Prosecution has no further questions.*

PRESIDENT: *Very well.*

The witness was warned, was excused subject to recall, and withdrew from the courtroom.

PRESIDENT: *The court will be in recess for approximately ten minutes.*

The court recessed at 1010 hours, 6 September 1968.

PRESIDENT: *The court will come to order.*

TRIAL COUNSEL: *All parties who were present when the court recessed are again present.*

At this time, the prosecution asks the court to take notice of naval regulations dated 20 March 1959, particularly sections 1161.1a which requires enlisted men to be clean shaven, and 1161.1c which says:

> "No articles, such as pencils, watch chains, fobs, pins, jewelry...or similar items shall be worn or carried exposed upon the uniform...No eccentricities of dress, such as earrings, shall be permitted."

DEFENSE COUNSEL: *Yes, we stipulate to the existence of the regulations, and I understand the request that the court take judicial notice of the same.*

PRESIDENT: *Is there any objection to the court taking judicial notice of these specific provisions of the naval regulations?*

DEFENSE COUNSEL: *No objection.*

PRESIDENT: *Very well, subject to the objection of any member of the Court, the Court will take judicial notice of the existence and the effectiveness of Article 1161, subsection 1a and subsection 1c.*

TRIAL COUNSEL: *The prosecution rests.*

PRESIDENT: *Very well. FR Drury, the Government has concluded its case against you. Now you have the right, if you wish, to present evidence in your own behalf, and you are under no legal obligation to present any evidence at all. The burden is always upon the Government to prove your guilt beyond a reasonable doubt. However, if you elect to present evidence, that evidence will be considered by the court for all purposes, either for you or against you, as the case may be.*

Now, as the accused you have certain rights as a witness. First, you may be sworn and you may take the stand as a witness in your own behalf, but if you do that, whatever you say will be considered and weighed as evidence against you by the court as is the testimony of any other witness, and you may be cross-examined on your testimony by the trial counsel and even by the court. If your testimony is to be restricted to less than all the offenses charged against you, and if you do not testify concerning others, then you may be questioned about the whole subject of those offenses concerning which you do testify. But you may not be questioned about any offense about which you do not testify.

Secondly, you may remain silent, and say nothing at all. You have the right to give no testimony if you wish, and if you do not testify, the fact that you do not take the stand yourself will not count against you in any way with the Court. It will not be considered as an admission that you are guilty, nor can it be commented on by counsel in addressing the court.

Do you understand your right to present evidence, including the right to testify?
ACCUSED: *Yes, I do.*
PRESIDENT: *Very well, defense may proceed.*
DEFENSE COUNSEL: *If such is in order, Mr. President, at this time, based on the evidence produced by the prosecution, I would move for a finding of not guilty as to Charge II, Specification 1, three-day growth of beard, based on an allegation, number one, that at the time of the observation and the decision to put the accused on report, the accused was clean shaven; number two, that such an order was given merely to increase punishment.*
PRESIDENT: *Would you care to reply, Trial Counsel?*
TRIAL COUNSEL: *As to Charge II, Specification 1, I think that the time the accused was placed on report is really of no importance. The mere fact that at the time charged the accused was in violation of the general regulation is enough.*
PRESIDENT: *Trial Counsel, I notice that paragraph 1161.1a is the regulation that says you've got to shave except when a beard is being worn. Isn't that exactly what the accused was doing? The exception which is authorized says: "...the beard shall be kept short..." In this case, it was very short, 3/16 of an inch.*
TRIAL COUNSEL: *Mr. President, this perhaps raises an exception, which I believe is an affirmative defense, but it also states that it shall be "neatly trimmed". There is no evidence that this was a "neatly trimmed" beard, or a failure to shave. Mr. President, it is my understanding that if a man can wear a beard, he must be authorized to do so.*
PRESIDENT: *I don't detect anything in the Article that says anything about authority being given. That authority is implied except when a moustache or beard is being worn. In other words, the regulation implied that you can wear a moustache or beard for those people who are so inclined. Just because he is clean shaven today does not mean that he has decided not to wear a beard continuously.*
   Mr. Hart, do you have any comment on this?
DEFENSE COUNSEL: *Other than to bring the obvious fact to the court, that no man could exercise what is apparently his freedom to grow a short beard without growing a short beard. One can't trim his beard until he grows a beard. All we have is evidence by the prosecution, that the witness observed a 3/16th inch growth, which we have to, I think, take as having been uniform, and that nothing indicates a violation of any regulation.*
PRESIDENT: *Subject to objection of any member of the court, the motion for a finding of not guilty with regard to Charge II, Specification 1, alleging violation of a lawful general regulation—the motion for a finding of not guilty is granted.*
   There is no objection. Consequently, the court members are instructed as to Charge II, Specification 1, the accused stands, in effect not guilty. Accordingly,

you are instructed not to consider Specification 1 of Charge II as being before this court for any purpose hereafter.

Proceed if you will.

DEFENSE COUNSEL: *Now, if the Court please, I would like to call Mr. Drury to the witness stand.*

PRESIDENT: *Very well. I caution you again about your rights to testify, comprehensively or with regard to a specific specification.*

ACCUSED: *Yes, sir.*

The accused, FR E. J. Drury, USNR, USS Davidson, took the stand in his own behalf, was sworn and testified as follows:

DIRECT EXAMINATION

Questions by the defense:

Q. You are being charged, are you not, with appearing at morning muster on August 16, 1968, with a medallion around your neck, and worn, as charged, outside of your uniform shirt?

A. Yes, I am.

Q. Were you wearing a medallion that day?

A. Yes, sir, I was.

Q. And do you have that medallion in your presence now?

A. Yes, I do.

Q. Would you take that medallion out and show it to the board?

A. (The witness displayed the medallion to the court.)

Q. Now is this the medallion that you were wearing on the day in question?

A. Yes, it is.

REPORTER: *This will be marked Defense Exhibit C for indentification.*

Q. And how long had you been wearing this medallion before August 16?

A. I bought it the evening before.

Q. Had you worn any other symbol or medallion before August 16?

A. Yes, I had.

Q. And what does that other symbol or medallion look like?

A. It's a rosary I use to pray to Our Blessed Mother for enlightenment.

Q. Now would you describe the medallion for the court?

A. Well, it kind of looks like a man who has been crucified upside down within the construct of a teardrop rather than on a cross.

Q. And what is the meaning of that medallion for you?

A. It signifies peace and love, the fragility of the former and the real power of the latter.

Q. Does it have any significance, you would ascribe to it as being religious?

A. Very much so, I would say.

Q. And what is the nature of that religious significance?

A. It is the very cross upon which the Navy hath hung a son of God, and turned him every which way but loose, a state of affairs which doth bring a tear to the eye of him beholden to the sanctity of life and the nonviolent cross he bears for all to see what true peace entails.

Q. So your opinion as to this thing is that in your scheme of values it is a religious symbol, is that correct?

A. Let's put it this way, the only thing the medallion lacks is the blessing of Holy Mother the Church, a sprinkling of holy water, in other words, and a blessing that any priest could perform upon request, making it no less holier than any other medal, cross or rosary worn by millions of Catholics around the world.

Q. Do you know of any other members of the crew who wear symbols or medallions similar to the one that you have identified as Defense Exhibit C?

A. Seaman Rick Little wears a peace symbol around his neck.

Q. And do you know whether he was wearing that peace symbol on the morning of August 16, or some time before that?

A. Yes, sir, he was.

Q. Would you agree that the difference between jewelry and the symbol you are holding in your hand, or a rosary, is that jewelry has no significance other than that it's decorative?

A. Yes, I would.

Q. You ever wear this peace symbol as an earring?

A. No, I haven't.

Q. Now on the morning in question, August 16, would you tell the court exactly what happened to you from the moment that you woke up?

A. Well, I got up late, cause I'd been out late the night before, dressed and hurried up to quarters with the medallion safely tucked between my T–shirt and dungaree shirt which, unfortunately, I am in the habit of wearing with the top button unfastened. I assume the medallion slipped out of the dungaree shirt when I stooped over to relieve the discomfort in my shoe that was hobbling my effort to get to quarters on time. But I was completely taken aback, when the Wulff grabbed me by the shoulders, spun me around and shoved me down the port side of the ship, all the while I struggled in vain to free myself from the devil's iron grip. Having been brought to a standstill, I went below, as the Wulff had ordered, to remove the medallion and shave.

Q. And so what did you do down below?

A. I removed the medallion and shaved as ordered, and once I was done shaving, put it back on, at the insistence of the other Authority invested in me.

Trial of a Special Kind

Q. Now where did you get this peace symbol?

A. I bought it at the Navy Exchange on the submarine base in Pearl Harbor?

Q. When you put this peace symbol back on, what did you proceed to do, if anything?

A. I went about my daily routine.

Q. What did that include?

A. Cleaning our berthing compartment. That is my job on the ship.

Q. And when you had the initial contact, on the quarterdeck, with the man who asked you to remove it, how would you describe the way in which he put his hands on you?

A. No matter how hard I tried, I couldn't turn around to find out what was going on. Nor could I stop him from shoving me across the quarterdeck, he's that much bigger and stronger than I am.

Q. How tall are you?

A. Five feet, ten.

Q. In fact, he's approximately three or four inches taller than you, is he not?

A. Yes, sir.

Q. And how would you estimate the weight difference?

A. Quite a bit, I'd say, about 50 pounds. He might weigh around 200.

Q. How much do you weigh?

A. About 150.

Q. So you went down below, you took off the peace symbol, and you shaved. Now what was the reason why you put it back on?

A. I put it back on at the insistence of the other Authority invested in me, that all might see me as I AM.

Q. All right, then what happened?

A. Well, I wore it all morning, mostly outside my T–shirt while I worked, and later on, inside the dungaree shirt I had donned ere Wulff caught up with me around noon, and asked me if I was going to take it off. Caught off guard, I walked over to the water fountain to get a drink, which allowed him to sneak up behind me and grab my arm, ere turning me around and grabbing hold of the chain as he got up in my face, demanding I take it off. Ignoring all the bluster, I politely requested that he please take his hands off me. When ordered again to remove the medallion, I politely requested, as before, that he please take his hands off me. The last time the Wulff asked me, I requested, with all the respect due his rank, that he remove his sweaty hands from me and my personal belongings. And as those who'd gathered round drew closer and closer to see that his abuse didn't get out of hand, I felt emboldened when he let go his evil grip on me and fled like a dog with his tail between his legs to report my insubordination.

At one point, I did take off the medallion, but put it back on after we got into a discussion down in the compartment, and decided that I had the right to wear it since other crew members were wearing beads, chains, and all, hassle-free.

Q. Who's "we"?

A. Third Class PO Bardon, Third Class PO Crosby and First Class PO Martucci.

Q. And when you put it back on again, where did you put it?

A. I put it inside my dungaree shirt.

Q. And after you put it back on, did anyone ask you to remove it?

A. No.

Q. How long did you wear it after that?

A. Well, shortly thereafter, I was taken up to see the Executive Officer, who asked me if he could see the medallion. So I took it out and showed it to him. When he asked me what it meant, I told him "peace", whereupon he told me that I would be going up to mast shortly. Up at the mast, and all through the mast, I wore the peace symbol, and was never ordered to take it off. And after the mast, I continued to wear it as long as I could.

Q. Now, did not a general order come down from the command of the ship with respect to wearing beads, peace symbols, or anything shortly after the incident involving your peace symbol?

A. Yes, it did. They passed word at quarters—I don't remember the date—that we could wear beads or peace symbols around our necks as long as they were kept inside our dungaree shirts.

Q. And it's your testimony that at the time when you appeared at muster, you assumed your peace symbol was inside your dungaree shirt, but because you had bent over, it had come out inadvertently, is that correct?

A. Yes.

Q. Now, I direct your attention to the period of time just preceding your entry into active duty in the Navy. And I ask you where you were?

A. I was in St. Louis, working as a lab technician for National Lead.

PRESIDENT: *What time frame are you talking about Mr. Hart?*

DEFENSE COUNSEL: *February of 1967.*

PRESIDENT: *Anything happen early in 1967 relevant to the charge we have?*

DEFENSE COUNSEL: *The history of this man's involvement with the military specifically bears to Charge I, the fact that he willfully disobeyed an order.*

PRESIDENT: *Trial Counsel?*

TRIAL COUNSEL: *I'm assuming that we are now delving into personal beliefs?*

DEFENSE COUNSEL: *Indirectly, yes. I also want to show the development of the accused's beliefs causing him to reach a position that he is a conscientious objector, and the incidents leading up to the failure on the part of the Navy to recognize the process and his claim that he is a conscientious objector, which was followed by what, we will attempt to show, was an illegal order.*

TRIAL COUNSEL: *It is the Government's position that whether or not the accused is a conscientious objector is not material or relevant to Charge I. I believe that a person's belief, religious or otherwise, is no defense for disobeying orders.*

DEFENSE COUNSEL: *It is not a defense of the accused for religious reasons per se, that he refused the order from a military point of view. He does not contend that. But he does contend that the order given was an illegal order in that he had made efforts to bring his claim as a conscientious objector to the attention of his command, and had they recognized that claim and begun processing, they were under statutory obligation to assign him duties not inconsistent with his religious beliefs, and that the order to load ammunition being one clearly opposed in terms of religious beliefs to those beliefs, such order was illegal.*

For our authority, we rely on a Board of Review case from the Army, entitled United States vs Sigmund, CM416356, U.S. Army, 2 January 1968, and I give a copy of this case as reported in Lawyer's Service to the prosecution and also offer one up to the court for its examination. In this case the accused was on orders requiring him to be transferred to Vietnam. He disobeyed an order of his superior officer to board an airplane to go to Vietnam. The defense in that case, as we are doing here, challenged the legality of that order and requested permission to introduce evidence, as we are doing now, in open court on this question.

The Law Officer in that case permitted an out–of–court hearing for the defense to put on this evidence. I think that the case speaks for itself. I'll be happy to wait a few minutes while the court reads this case.

PRESIDENT: *I have not seen this case. Bear with me. The record will show that the President is referring to a 3–page document which has been presented by defense counsel and will be made a part of the record.*

Well, I've read the summary of U.S. vs Sigmund as reported in the 3–page document I referred to, and are you arguing that it stands with the proposition that the order to join the working party was illegal?

DEFENSE COUNSEL: *Yes, sir, that's what we're arguing here, that the accused made efforts, beginning about March of 1968, to bring to the attention of his command his position as a conscientious objector. He was either ignored or rebuffed or sent in some other direction. In fact, on the day in question, and this will be our offer of proof, after he got out of the Brig, and after he had had a conversation with a man from the Office of Naval Investigation, and apprised the investigator of his claim, entered a request chit and made an effort to see the Captain on this claim, even though, earlier in March, he had declared to the Captain that he is a conscientious objector. This is our offer of proof, failure to process this claim. The* rebuff that he received vitiated the legality of the order, because had the claim been processed, he would never have been ordered to load ammunition. He might have been ordered to continue to clean the compartment which, I think, he would argue to the court, is not inconsistent with his religious beliefs.

PRESIDENT: *The Sigmund case stands to the proposition that the order to go to Vietnam was illegal because he had submitted his application. For a conscientious objector, you've got to hold him. You can't transfer him to Vietnam. Consequently, the order was patently illegal, only I don't see the analogy.*

DEFENSE COUNSEL: *Well, the analogy of this is that not only was he to be retained in his unit and not transferred to Vietnam, which is not relevant here, but he was to be assigned duties that were analogous to his position.*

PRESIDENT: *I'd have to see the navy regulation. This is an Army case.*

DEFENSE COUNSEL: *Well, I have this and I will show it to the court. The Navy regulations, in all respects, are the same. With respect to this command that he be retained in his unit and assigned duties in minimum conflict with his professed beliefs, the regulations are identical.*

PRESIDENT: *All right, in view of DoD Directive 1300.6 of 10 May 1968, there is an analogy, and this discussion was precipitated because of my comment not because there is any specific objection. So there's no ruling to make. I understand your theory, and you may proceed.*

DEFENSE COUNSEL: *Thank you, Your Honor.*

Q. Now, going back to your initial entry into active duty in February of 1967, would you outline for the court, rather briefly with respect to your position as a conscientious objector, the events leading up to that day in March when you made the statement with respect to your position to Captain Whitaker.

A. "You do not belong here," whispered the formless intuition that had left me with little reason to board the Davidson, other than the fact that I had consigned two years of my life to the Navy, to be used as a weapon of war. Once I overcame my hesitation, and boarded the ship, I lost my way, for I no longer knew where I belonged, or to whom I owed my allegiance—whether that be to the voices in my head or to the devil in the deep blue sea, only God knew for certain.

To make room for the truth to come into its own, and to take ownership of my body, like the mendicants of old, had I refused to take anything by mouth but water until rapid heart palpitations, on day twenty, betrayed me to the Corpsman who, in turn, betrayed me to my division officer when I continued to refuse to eat. "Man does not live on bread alone, but on every word that comes from the mouth of God," (Mt 4:4) had I informed my Division Officer, in response to a much higher calling than a mere officer's command to eat—circumstances which left him with little recourse but to betray me to the XO. When the XO threatened to charge me with the destruction of government property, should I damage "my body" fasting, I refused his order to eat as well, forcing him to yield to the fleet Chaplain who convinced me to break my fast before it broke me or permanently damaged any of my organs as my body began to cannibalize itself to stay alive.

PRESIDENT: *When was this?*

A. This was in April of '67.... That evening, as I made my way up topside to contemplate the day's events, a voice rang out from somewhere deep within me. "You must find out why you want out of the Navy," commanded the One Voice.

As I sat down on my usual perch, laughing and crying at the same time, I felt as if my pursuit of a discharge from the Navy had just been endorsed by the Highest Authority invested in me, the very source of truth itself. And so did I embark on the single most important quest of my life for I was not to be handed the answer on a silver paten but was made to search for it like any other mendicant in those days, by turning inward in line with the Scriptures.

Several days later, I was summoned to the XO's office to sign a paper which stated that I was being considered for discharge, and that any further irregular behavior on my part may be cause for discharge from the Navy for reasons of unsuitability.

Well, I was about as unsuited for the Navy as I had been for the Naval Academy once I realized I could never order a subordinate to kill another human being, a crime against humanity that not even I could commit according to the Lord God. "And if anyone asks," said the Lord God, "you tell him I made you that way."

Q. *Now Drury, did you not have quite a bit of difficulty with your stepfather with regard to your appointment to the Naval Academy?*

A. Yes, I did. You see, my stepdad suffers an unnamed trauma that he experienced as a corpsman in the Navy during World War II, and as a result, has become a paranoid alcoholic who carries a gun, going so far as to sleep with it under his mattress. And if you know anything about an alcoholic, you can't argue with him, especially when you know he has a gun, and have seen him threaten other people, even the members of his own family. You don't argue with him, period. You do what he says, for in his eyes, might makes right, and he is always right, even when he is wrong. And he was dead wrong when he decided, without checking with me, that the Naval Academy would be a good fit for me.

But I could never tell him that until I had been up there for four miserable months, wrestling with the likes of Jekyll and Hyde, the cold–blooded, state–sanctioned killer hiding behind the facade of a lily–white, military uniform, for that is what we are, gentlemen, "c o l d – b l o o d e d k i l l e r s"—a truth with which I failed to come to terms in the yearlong hiatus that followed my release from the Academy but not from the Navy in November of '65.

By November of '66, I had been reclassified 1–A and ordered to report for induction into the Army after the folks at my Reserve Center had reported me as delinquent due to some foul-up in paperwork on their part. To rectify the situation in the only way they could, I was called up for two years of active duty in the Navy, and ordered to report to Treasure Island, California, on 5 February 1967.

Q. All right. As a result of that confusion between the Reserve Center and your draft board and yourself, you then entered the Naval Service?

A. That's right.

Q. At that time, you did not consider yourself a conscientious objector, right?

A. No. In fact, I didn't even know what a conscientious objector was. Nor had I ever heard of the term before.

Q. But you had a feeling, did you not, with respect to your religious beliefs and your growing uneasiness with the Navy?

A. Yes, sir.

Q. Now, would you continue to tell the court about the development of those beliefs?

A. To get my body to do what it was not made to do, to serve the god of war rather than the God of Love, took all the energy I had, and then some, so great was the demand from within for my misplaced attention. I can't tell you how many times my attention was pulled inward for extended periods of time in which I might find my self painting an image of my soul, for example, when in actuality I was flinging paint at some pipes along the starboard side of the ship. Unaware of the mess I'd made until the Boatswain's Mate ordered me to go below, I turned and walked past the crowd that'd gathered round to see me paint my way out of the Navy, leaving behind but a fleeting glimpse of what I could not grasp.

Having lost control of my body after I'd turned it over to the Navy, in the weeks and months that followed, I fouled up everything I touched or was assigned to do, unintentionally at first, until I realized that I had no other choice if I wanted to remain true to Who I Am, the huge unknown that sabotaged every attempt I made to satisfy my obligation to the Navy. Like a mouse in a maze, did I learn to obey the Authority within to shirk any false sense of responsibility the Navy had imposed upon me, for I am answerable to the one God only, and no other god before me, neither the Navy nor anyone else dressed to kill.

Assigned to a gun mount for general quarters, had my body, in its infinite wisdom, taken extreme measures to remove me from a situation I found so morally repugnant that I blacked out with the deafening sound and the sickening smell of sulfur that accompanied the first round from its chamber. Recalling nothing more until I find my self staring into a mirror, later on down below, had my body, in the meantime, gotten reassigned to the mess decks for GQ, an option that appeased *neither my conscience nor a body, tired of doing as little work as possible to assuage my conscience without having to refuse to have anything at all to do with the Navy. Like a stubborn mule then, did my body continue to resist doing what was incompatible with its truest instincts.*

Q. Now, why did you determine that that course should be followed?

A. Since I didn't know I was a conscientious objector, my body had no other way of showing me that I was unsuitable for military service. And because I was counseled again, in early July, that my command was still considering discharging me for reasons of unsuitability, why wouldn't my body continue to resist doing what is evil if such a tactic could free it from its indenture to a sinful way of life.

Q. This is July of '67?

A. Yes, July of '67. But when I talked with my Division Officer, later that month, I learned that my command had reconsidered, choosing instead to transfer me to R Division to work as a shipfitter. Still, I could never shake the feeling that I didn't belong there either, for I found no kindred spirit amongst the shipfitters.

Swept away with the rest of the crew to the gunline off the coast of Vietnam, to kill our fellow man, I was abhorred when we, excluding myself, jumped up to give ourselves the wildest standing ovation I had ever seen after scoring a direct hit, according to our spotter, on the 152nd round fired. And when the High Chaplain called upon the God of Abraham and Moses, over the intercom of all places, to help us tear the VC to shreds with our shells, I was blown away as his words ripped into me like the shrapnel on the tips of the whips that tore into Christ's flesh before we murdered Him.

Yes, gentlemen, we murdered Him, and have never stopped murdering Him, we gentlemen in uniform. When we kill, we operate from the beastly side of our nature, Dr. Jekyll's nightmare, Mr. Hyde. Whereas beasts can kill with impunity, we cannot, because we were made that way. Only we have the free will to choose between the two, to live as Dr. Jekyll or to die as Mr. Hyde.

When my shipmates would turn to the Old Testament to justify their actions, I turned, instead, to the New Testament which they view as implausible and imagined. "Not so," I'd say as I turned my cheek to their eye for an eye and a tooth for a tooth, that they might see Christ as the quintessential human aspect of our beings, and quit killing each other for Christ's sake or any other ill-conceived notion.

We project so many of our internal conflicts onto other unsuspecting souls rather than reclaim them as our own, and save ourselves from a multitude of sins. When we turn the other cheek, we provide our antagonist with a mirror image of his humanity, which he can either accept or reject and, in that case, continue pounding, and pounding, and pounding to the nth degree, the nails into the hands and feet of his humanity until he has crucified the Christ therein, once again.

Shortly thereafter, I was put on report for having failed to appear at my appointed place of duty after I went below to get some soap to clean the head to which I had been assigned. For such a grievous offense, I was restricted to the ship for fourteen days and given forty–five days of extra duty.

Before the ship departed from the gunline and headed home, I would fall asleep, one night, on the 4–8 a.m. shift of the Sounding and Security Watch, and as a result, would be banned from ever standing watch on the Davidson again, the only repercussion I incurred besides the ass–chewing I got from my boss, the First Class PO in charge of the shipfitters, for such a minor infraction.

A month or so after returning to Pearl Harbor, I managed somehow to get into trouble again, although to this day, I do not recall what I had or had not done, so caught up with my own soul had I been when a petty officer, on his way up the ladder from our compartment space, growled that I was on report. Charged with dereliction of duty, leaving my appointed place of duty, and failing to shave that morning, I was blessed with thirty of the most glorious days of correctional custody I have ever experienced in the Naval Station Brig at Pearl Harbor. At one with my soul, I was in heaven, for I had finally found where I belonged, and of all places, in the one I had feared the most, the brig.

Q. When did you go to the brig? Is this the first time you went to the brig?

A. Yes, in November of '67.

Q. What incident led up to this?

A. To this day, I have no idea of what transpired outside my body, I was that engrossed with my soul at the time. For all I know, I may have been charged for having done nothing, or so it would seem in view of the charges filed against me.

Q. So you were charged with doing nothing when you should have been doing something.

A. Yes, that's right.

Q. Now, at this time, would you please recall the nature of your religious beliefs for the court?

A. Dying to the beast is what Christ did on the cross; and He expects no less from us than that we lay down our lives for each other rather than the beast.

When "his disciples realized that" Jesus "was about" to be betrayed, "they asked, 'Lord, shall we strike with a sword?' And one of them," Simon Peter, "struck the high priest's servant and cut off his right ear. But Jesus said in reply, 'Stop, no more of this!' Then He touched the servant's ear and healed him." Lk 22:49-51

Thereupon Jesus asked Peter the same question I've been asking my self, here of late, "Shall I not drink the cup that the Father gave me?" Jn 18:11

"I most surely would," said I, "if only I could find the couplet that described my condition, the two words I had never heard before but longed to hear."

Q. *So this was your developing religious belief sometime in November of '67?*
A. *(The witness nods his head.)*
Q. *And then what happened to you?*
A. With my anniversary date fast approaching, I was granted thirty days of leave effective 5 January 1968. Although my leave was pretty uneventful, on the morning of the day I was expected back on board the Davidson, I stumbled across the reason why I wanted out of the Navy while reading an article in the February issue of The Atlantic Monthly, entitled "Leo Tolstoy's Advice to a Draftee". As I honed in on the question of "what should a man do who has been called upon for military service—that is, called upon to kill or to prepare himself to kill?"—I was completely blown away with Tolstoy's response. "For he who understands the true meaning of military service," I read with great relish, "and wants to be moral, there is only one clear and incontrovertible answer: such a person must refuse to take part in military service no matter the consequences." Needless to say, I was in heaven until my soul reminded me that heaven came at a great price, the consequences I would suffer should I outright refuse to take part in the Navy as I knew I must if I wished to maintain my moral integrity. Instead, I printed copies of Tolstoy's letter and circulated them about the ship to let everyone know, in a roundabout way, Who I Am.

Q. *What was the approximate date on which you printed this letter?*
A. I would say around the second week of February.
Q. *Now this is 1968?*
A. Yes.
Q. *All right, what happened as a result of this?*
A. There were two things really, the first being a very contentious confrontation with the Captain that ended with him yelling at me to "get out" of his stateroom, and me shouting back over my shoulder, "God is my Captain, not you," as I high-tailed it out the door after he had threatened to charge me with sedition, and had gone so far as to ban me from passing out pamphlets on the Davidson, in a futile attempt to silence me. The second confrontation, this time with a psychiatrist the Captain had sent me to see, several days later, was a bit less contentious but had a much more profound outcome when the psychiatrist asked me why I hadn't applied for discharge from the Navy as a conscientious objector if I felt so strongly that military service, or the killing of other human beings, is wrong for me.

"What's a conscientious objector?" Had I asked the psychiatrist who deemed it necessary at that point, to hand me a dictionary in reply.

As the Holy Spirit opened my eyes to the two words I AM, I knew beyond the shadow of a doubt that I AM a conscientious objector, always have been and always will be one who refuses to serve in the armed forces or bear arms on the grounds of moral or religious principles, according to Mr. Webster.

Q. When did you first learn the existence of the term "conscientious objector?"

A. About the 20th of February of '68.

Q. Had you ever heard the term "conscientious objector" used at any other time during your first year of active duty?

A. No, I had not.

Q. Did you know that such a classification existed for those in the military?

A. No, I did not.

Q. Before this incident, had you ever been informed there was a way in which you could have claimed status as a CO?

A. No, I had not.

Q. OK. Then in March, what transpired?

A. After spending a week or two in the scullery, where I'd been banished from the rest of the crew for pamphleteering, I fell into a deep depression from which I could find no way out until I exploded, one night, pitching pots and pans in every direction before I fizzled out on my rack down below and refused to go back up there to clean up the mess I'd left behind. To the acclamation of my soul, and guardian, Michael the Archangel, I had finally told the Navy what my spirit guides had been trying for weeks to get me to say, "No, 'no more of this!'" Lk 22:50

"I want to declare myself as a conscientious objector," I told Captain Whitaker at the captain's mast to which I'd been summoned the following morning.

Q. What happened after that?

A. The Captain looked at me with an evil eye, closed his little black book and walked out without saying a word.

Q. What was the date of this captain's mast?

A. It was about 12 March of '68.

Q. And you were charged for having pitched some pots and pans about the mess decks?

A. Well, not exactly. I was charged with two counts of disobeying the lawful order of a superior officer when I refused to go back up and clean up my mess, and one count of willfully destroying government property, for having damaged a pot or two, I presume.

Q. And when you went to this captain's mast, who was there with you?

A. There were about a half dozen members of the crew like my buddy Marty Cisna, my division officer, Ensign McClintic and the XO, Lieutenant Kihune. The rest I don't remember.

Q. What happened after that?

A. I spoke to the XO, before I was led away, who assured me that he would look into the matter of my conscientious objection as soon as we pulled into port, as we were still out at sea at the time of the mast.

Q. Now let me ask you this. After you made your statement to the Captain, and after you had this consultation with Kihune, did the Captain or Kihune make any statement to you that you were to be assigned any special duties?

A. No.

Q. Did they indicate to you that they were going to treat you as one who had claimed conscientious objector status?

A. No. I was sent to the brig for 20 days of correctional custody as soon as the ship pulled into Pearl Harbor, and was told nothing more.

Q. Now when you were in the brig did you meet with anyone in particular?

A. Yes, the Squadron Chaplain.

Q. What was his name?

A. I don't recall his name, although he was sent by my command.

Q. Did you tell him that you wished to apply as a conscientious objector?

A. I did.

Q. What did he say when you told him that?

A. He said, "Well, you only have about six or seven more months to go before your enlistment is up. You can hack it for that long."

Q. When did you come out of the brig?

A. About the 1st of April.

Q. And then what happened?

A. So deep in thought had I been as I made my way to the exchange, one afternoon shortly thereafter, that I literally bumped into the very ticket that threatened to send me back to the brig where I belonged if I refused to salute His Ensignship as he insisted I do.

"Why should I salute what is not of God's doing?" I asked of him who held no sway over me.

"You're on report," he barked as I left him feeling out of place.

For disrespecting a superior officer, I was given a summary court-martial at which I pled guilty with the stipulation that I be given the opportunity to introduce mitigating circumstances regarding the frustration I'd experienced trying to get anyone to help me apply as a conscientious objector.

Q. This was sometime in April?

A. Yes, around the 16th. When I told the presiding officer, Lieutenant Smyth, that I refuse, from hereon, to handle ammunition or to take part in general quarters, I was asked to leave the room for about twenty minutes before I was recalled and sentenced to 30 days of hard labor in the Naval Station Brig at Pearl Harbor.

Back where I belonged in segregated confinement, I started to write down some of what I was feeling but ended up writing a manifesto entitled, "I Object", which is over there on the desk. Can I read that?

Q. *I hand you a statement signed by you on May 13, 1968, which you claim to have composed while you were a prisoner in the brig. Is that correct?*
A. Yes. This statement reads as follows:

> "As a morally responsible individual, I conscientiously object to war—legalized killing under the pretense of God and country—to the killing of men like yourself bound under the pain of sin to obey the laws of God; to the devastation of the land and natural resources bestowed upon us by God to fulfill our needs; to men being trained to kill a man, the likeness of God, and to destroy life; to the waste of using God–given talents and resources in committing the hideous crimes of war; to coercing individuals into being accomplices to these crimes and supporters of their perpetraters; to forcing individuals into the position of choosing to obey either the laws of their country or the laws of God; to obligating one to offend God and endanger his soul.
>
> "And I base these moral objections of mine on the fact that I choose to obey the laws of God in which I am commanded to serve God with all my heart, with all my being...and with all my mind, to love my neighbor as myself, and to NOT KILL, rather than sin and endanger my soul.
>
> "In view of the moral imperative ensuing from my preceding statement, I am obligated to utilize every form of protest and means of civil disobedience at my disposal to end the American War in Vietnam and the military draft that feeds it, to win support for the cause of peace which mankind will not find unless it turns with confidence to the mercy of God."
>
> Signed on this 13th day of May, 1968
> E. J. Drury II

One afternoon while I was still in the brig, I received a suggestion from the Holy Spirit to thumb through a section of the Honolulu Star–Bulletin, lying nearby, until I found an article about a person, She wanted very much for me to meet. When I feasted my eyes on the article, I couldn't believe that I had finally found someone, and a professor at that, who felt the same way that I did about war.
Q. *In fact, isn't he a professor of religion at the University of Hawaii?*
A. Actually, he's associate professor of religion at the U of H.
And while I was still in the brig, I received a visitation from a truly holy man, named Chaplain Carroll, who was kind enough to give me a summary of the process spelled out in Article C–5210 of the BUPERS Manual *for those seeking discharge from the Navy as a conscientious objector.*

"You should pursue your conscientious objection with all due haste," warned the Chaplain before he vanished from my purview, never to be seen again.

Q. *So, when did you go back to the ship?*

A. *I got back to the ship around the 15th of May, went straight to the personnel office to wade through the pages of the BUPERS Manual until I found the article concerning conscientious objectors, as Chaplain Carroll had said I would.*

Later, I ran into my Division Officer, Ensign McClintic, who informed me that I would have to answer the questions in C–5210 and submit them to the Captain before I would even be considered for discharge as a CO. Until then, I made clear to him, that I would refuse to handle ammunition or participate in general quarters, terms he reluctantly agreed to after he had consulted the BUPERS Manual.

Q. *When you say he agreed to that, what do you mean?*

A. *I felt as if I had been granted permission to not participate in either activity as I was told to report to the mess deck for GQ from thereon.*

Q. *Mess deck?*

A. *Yes, that's right, until I was accused of filling the heads of those, also assigned to the mess deck for GQ, with seditious ideas, and was ordered thenceforth to report to sick bay instead.*

Q. *Go ahead.*

A. *Sometime around the last week of May, we loaded ammunition...*

Q. *You had a drill?*

A. *No, 'twas an actual loading of ammunition. And even though an all-hands working party had been called, I stayed below and continued cleaning our quarters while the master-at-arms came and went without saying a word to me.*

Q. *And you did not load ammunition at that loading ammunition session?*

A. *I did not.*

Q. *Nor did anyone request you to do so?*

A. *That's right.*

Q. *Nor was there any action taken against you later because you had not done it, right?*

A. *Right, there wasn't.*

PRESIDENT: *Was this prior to 6 July?*

DEFENSE COUNSEL: *Yes. This is an ammunition loading prior to the one in question in this case.*

Q. *So there were a total of two: the one in question and the other one that took place at the end of May, in which you did not participate, right?*

A. *Right, I did not participate in May, because of the understanding I had with McClintic.*

PRESIDENT: *Excuse me. I am going to interrupt at this time, to declare a recess.*

Court recessed at 1150 hours, and reconvened at 1340 hours, 6 September 1968, with all parties who were present when court recessed again present.

PRESIDENT: *You may proceed, Mr. Hart.*

DIRECT EXAMINATION (continued)

Questions by the defense:

Q. *After that meeting and discussion with McClintic, what did you do?*

A. I went back up to personnel to copy the questions from Article C–5210 but ran into a brick wall when I tried to answer them, they are that tough.

Q. *Do you recall what some of those questions are?*

A. Yes, I do.

Q. *And do you want to familiarize the court with what those questions are?*

A. Well, what is the nature of your basis for claiming yourself as a conscientious objector? What is the nature of your religious beliefs for claiming status as a conscientious objector? What are some of the creeds or statements from your church concerning conscientious objection? Under what circumstances would you resort to the use of force?—tough questions for one not used to putting his thoughts down on paper, and reason enough for turning to a professor for help.

Q. *When did you go down to see him?*

A. About the 20th of May.

Q. *And what happened at that meeting?*

A. I had given him a copy of my manifesto to read before I shared with him any of the details of the events of the past year that led to my declaration of conscientious objection to military service, back in March. Somehow, I wound up with a copy of CCCO's Handbook for Conscientious Objectors to help me answer the questions in C–5210 as thoroughly and honestly as possible, in anticipation of the inquisition a CO must undergo to determine his sincerity or lack thereof on the part of his interrogators.

Q. *All right, then tell the court what happened.*

A. Well, Professor Douglass proceeded to introduce me to three persons who would prove to be as key as he to my survival as a CO: The Reverend Father Daniel J. Dever for spiritual counsel, yourself for legal counsel, and First Lady of the Resistance Betty Johnson for tactical support. And over the course of the next two weeks, I would spend as much time as I could with my newfound friends whose love and encouragement was the nourishment I needed to complete my CO claim.

Then, one night in early June, I received word from the Holy Spirit to grab a handful of leaflets from the table just inside the door to Betty's beachfront lair as I was leaving. For what reason I knew not until the following morning when I was urged to plunk one down onto a table to entice the First Class Petty Officer, who

Trial of a Special Kind

had tried but failed to entice anyone to take my life, into reading such "shit" as he would say. With that, I disappeared to the head from which I was startled when he showed up, pulled out his lighter and lit the leaflet on fire...

Q. *You mean he took the piece of paper and started to burn it?*

A. *Yes, and then threw it down to stamp out the conflagration I had started.*

Q. *This pamphlet was just a piece of paper with some writing on it?*

A. *Yes, and for having obeyed the Captain of my soul, I was banished to the brig for thirty days of correctional custody, and fined half of my allowance for two months. But before the Captain of the ship could leave the room, I made it clear that I would be back again...and again...and again.*

PRESIDENT: *Excuse me. Let's go back to this pamphlet again. I'm sorry, Mr. Hart, but I don't understand the relevancy of this testimony.*

DEFENSE COUNSEL: *Are you asking as to the sequence of the events, the relevancy to the charges here?*

PRESIDENT: *Yes.*

DEFENSE COUNSEL: *This is another incident of Mr. Drury's efforts to bring to the attention of the Naval personnel what his beliefs are.*

PRESIDENT: *This document with a paragraph on it expressed his beliefs?*

DEFENSE COUNSEL: *Yes. And I have a copy of it, reconstructed, I believe, and I will show it to the witness and he will read it to the court.*

A. *This statement is entitled "Don't". And it states:*

> "We appeal to your conscience. You are being asked to kill Vietnamese on their own soil. You will kill so that America can force her will on the people of Vietnam. Some of you will be killed in the process. Will you be dying for a just cause? Will you be dying to protect freedom of choice for Vietnam or denying them freedom? Are you the least bit unsure? They tell you that you don't have a choice if you gotta go, you gotta go. Not really. But the alternatives are rough. It might mean jail. We can offer a little help, like lawyers and counselors and community support. But the final choice is yours. For information, contact the Resistance at 262–9236. Whatever you decide, good luck. We will work for peace, and try to bring you back home as soon as possible."

Q. *What did this pamphlet mean to you at the time?*

A. *Look! This is* Who I Am *and no other god before me. I mean I was in heaven, living as* I AM, *expressing* Who I Am, *passing out leaflets and speaking out against the war or sitting in jail for having done so, writing out my CO claim. What more could I have asked for, other than my freedom from this life of sin.*

Q. *What happened as a result of bringing those on the ship?*

A. *I was sent to the brig.*

Q. *What happened in the brig?*

A. *As I was being admitted to the brig, the guards on duty confiscated the materials I had brought with me to help me fill out my CO claim, then refused to give them back to me, denying me access to you, Professor Douglass, and even the Brig Warden when I asked to see any one of you. Left with no other option, I staged a sit–in, the following morning, and refused to budge or go out on a work detail, when ordered to do so, until they let me see the Brig Warden.*

Q. *Why did you want to see him?*

A. *I wanted to tell him that I was not being provided a means of communicating with him, or with my attorney or my spiritual advisers, and that I was not being given access to the materials I needed to assist me in filling out my CO claim.*

Q. *Even though you had been advised to fill it out, and wanted to fill it out, you were prevented from doing so, is that what you're telling me?*

A. *That's right, until you showed up and brokered a deal with the Brig Warden that returned the materials to me and gave me full access to him, my attorney and spiritual advisers, with the understanding that I was to perform seven days of extra duty for having refused a direct order, the Holy Spirit had directed me to refuse if I wished to stay in Her good graces.*

Q. *Now, did there come a time when you had an interview with a man named Barrows?*

A. *Yes, sir. He's the official from NIS, who told me that he was investigating my involvement with the Resistance and the Kailua Road leaflet, and my suitability for further service, when in reality, he was investigating me as a possible defector. But the guy was a walking pack of lies that labeled my friends as commies, and our intercession in Vietnam as the war to stop the commies from taking over the world, when in reality we are the belligerents interfering in Vietnam's struggle to purge itself of the last vestige of colonial rule, and keep the South from seceding from the Union. And after I refuted his comparison of Vietnam to a woman being raped, by identifying Uncle Sam as the rapist, I think he realized that I wasn't some misguided eight ball, he could bowl over with his lies.*

"Tell me then, how a CO would rescue a damsel in distress," had the Dark Knight of the Barrows asked me.

"Why, the same way you would, Barrows, if you were in God's hands, with a hand from God, and a little help from your friends, the other members of the resistance, rising up all over this land to force Uncle Sam's hand to withdraw," I replied.

Q. *All right, now, did you have a conversation with him and me in an office in this building during this investigation?*

A. *Yes, I did.*

Q. And did you discuss with him and with me how you would conduct yourself after you got out of the brig?

A. Yes, I did.

Q. I show you a copy of a statement dated June 29, 1968, that has a signature on the top line, and ask you if you recognize that signature?

A. Yes, that's my signature.

Q. Now would you please read that part of the statement which indicates what your understanding was?

A. It reads as follows:

> "I am, however, most willing to relinquish the activities under investigation until I am discharged, if my claim is expeditiously and carefully considered by the Department of the Navy, and if I am placed in a noncombatant status not conflicting with my religious beliefs in conscience while awaiting action on this claim."

Q. What did you understand the meaning of Barrows' signature was on that statement?

A. I took it to mean that I would be given limited duty consistent with my religious beliefs, and would not be ordered to perform such duties as loading ammunition, that are clearly inconsistent with those beliefs.

Q. What did you do when you got out of the brig on July 5?

A. That night, I typed up my CO claim, and in the morning submitted a request to see the Captain, only to have it handed back to me because I had requested "to see the Captain" instead of a "captain's mast" to discuss my status on board the ship and hand him a copy of my CO claim.

Q. You had put "I wish to see the Captain" and they said, "That's no good, you have to put down captain's mast"?

A. Right. And then I resubmitted it, this time, stapled to a copy of my CO claim, only to have it, too, handed back to me because I hadn't submitted it, according to protocol, at quarters. Having been thrown into a real dither, I mulled over the matter as I putzed around, cleaning our berthing quarters. When word went out, calling all hands to report aft to load ammunition, I stayed put as the master-at-arms came and went, on two different occasions, but reappeared a third time, to tell me that I was wanted up on the quarterdeck.

Q. Did you know at the time what you were wanted for?

A. No, I didn't. So I naively walk onto the quarterdeck, where he turns and, out of the blue, orders me to start handling five-inch shells which, of course, I refuse to do. When asked a second time in the presence of the Officer of the Deck and the duty watch, I tell him again that "I can't do that", whereupon he tells me to go below.

Q. Did he put you on report?

A. Well, later he told me he had put me on report.

Q. And did you ever get to see the Captain?

A. After I had submitted my request/CO claim a third time, I did get to see the Captain about a day or so later, and hand him a copy of my CO claim when he said he hadn't seen it after I asked him if he'd had a chance to read it.

Q. Now this was another copy?

A. Yes, it was.

Q. And this stapled request came in after you were given the order?

A. Right.

Q. But the first request came in before you were given the order?

A. That's correct.

Q. Go ahead.

A. After I'd handed him another copy, he accused me of being a bit too pushy because I hadn't waited for it to come up through the chain of command. When I told him that I had to be pushy because no one around there seemed to want to help me, he blew up, right in my face. "I've had it with you, Drury. You've been a thorn in my side ever since I stepped foot on this ship. You never do anything right," to which I responded, "O, but I AM now, Sir". And without making any attempt to discuss my claim with me, he ordered me to "get out" of his stateroom.

Q. He kept your papers at that time?

A. Yes, he did.

Q. Do you know whether those papers are being processed now?

A. My dossier was sent to Washington about a month ago, but has since been returned pending an interview with an officer, grade O-3 or higher, as required by Article C-5210 and DoD Directive 1300.6 before the officer can write the letter of recommendation required to accompany my claim when it is sent back to Washington for consideration.

Q. Now, at the time in March when you were at a captain's mast, saying to Whitaker that you wished to claim status as a conscientious objector, did Whitaker make any effort to tell you what to do?

A. He did not.

Q. Did he advise you of any rights pertaining to Veteran's benefits?

A. No, he didn't.

Q. In April, when you indicated to Smyth that you are a conscientious objector, did he advise you of any rights under C-5210 of the BUPERS Manual, or 1300.6 of the Department of Defense regulation?

A. No, he didn't.

Q. *Did he indicate to you anything having to do with the loss of Veteran's benefits?*

A. *He did not.*

Q. *With respect to your conversation with McClintic in May, I believe it was, did he indicate anything to you with respect to your rights under 5210?*

A. *No. He did come back, after he had read the Article, to tell me that I would have to fill out the questionaire in 5210, which I already knew.*

Q. *Now he did indicate to you, did he not, that you were to perform duties down in the compartment and in the infirmary?*

A. *Actually, I told him that as a conscientious objector, I would refuse to load ammunition or participate in general quarters, and would limit my duties to compartment cleaning only.*

Q. *And he agreed with that?*

A. *He agreed.*

Q. *Now, directing your attention to the date of August 16, 1968 at approximately 1230 hours, I ask you where you were wearing the peace symbol when the First Class Wulff asked you to take it off?*

A. *Inside my blue shirt, outside my T-shirt.*

Q. *All right. Was any part of the symbol or chain visible?*

A. *You could see the chain.*

Q. *But you could not see the symbol?*

A. *No.*

Q. *Had you worn the peace symbol on board the ship before the date in question?*

A. *Yes. The night before I had worn the peace symbol all around the ship, even while leaving and reboarding the ship on two or three different occasions, in full view of the officer of the deck. And no one said a word to me about wearing it outside my blue shirt.*

Q. *Did you draw any conclusion about this lack of comment about the peace symbol?*

A. *Not really. I wasn't doing anything that other members of the crew, who wear things around their necks, aren't doing.*

DEFENSE COUNSEL: *You may examine.*

CROSS EXAMINATION

Questions by the prosecution:

Q. *I believe you stated at the very beginning of your testimony that you considered this peace symbol has a religious significance?*

A. *Yes, I did.*

Q. *Is it recognized as a religious symbol?*

A. While it lacks a priest's blessing and the sprinkling of holy water that makes any medal holy, I'm sure that either priest who will be testifying here today on my behalf would be more than happy to perform this miracle for you.

Q. You appeared at quarters on the morning of the 16th, accidentally or otherwise, this symbol was outside of your dungaree shirt, is that correct?

A. I assume it was outside my dungaree shirt, otherwise the Wulff would never have attacked me in the manner in which he had.

Q. When you initially came into the Navy, you volunteered, is that correct, or were you drafted?

A. Sir, I was shoved into the Naval Academy, kicking and screaming on the inside, by a stepfather who had decided that was where I belonged. And even though I refused to take the oath, I couldn't keep my self, no matter how hard I tried—and believe me, the struggle was great—from signing my name on the line that gave the Navy the authority to use my body for an indefinite period of time that almost cost me my soul.

Q. When, after you entered the service, did you first have serious questions regarding the religious beliefs that related to your duties?

A. When I realized, while I was still at the Naval Academy, that I could not order a subordinate to do what I myself, in good conscience could never do, that is, to kill another human being on command, I knew I didn't belong there any more than I do now as that subordinate, sitting here before you.

Q. Isn't it true that you didn't really consider killing until you knew you were going to Vietnam?

A. Listen! I knew, before I even stepped foot on that ship, that I did not belong there, for I was not about to live the rest of my life, with the nightmare that I had killed Who I Am—a belief that'd taken root in me long before the American War in Vietnam.

Q. I believe you stated, while you were in Vietnam, you were upset with the Chaplain when he called upon God to assist us in tearing the enemy to shreds with our shells?

A. I was so upset, I almost threw up, to rid my body of this abominable petition before it poisoned my mind with murderous thoughts and rose up as a wraith to slay my soul and deprive me of everlasting life.

Q. Do you consider these firing exercises wrong or evil?

A. Yes, Sir, I do.

Q. Why are they wrong or evil?

A. The sole purpose of these exercises is to kill, maim and destroy—there's no place for that in the kingdom of God, for our task is not to subject others to the raw power of the beast, but to die to it as Christ died on the cross.

Trial of a Special Kind

Q. *Do you consider Moses acting in an evil way when he called upon God to kill his enemies?*

A. Moses also sacrificed animals to God, a horrid practice by today's standards, but commonly accepted before Christ died to the beast that still slaughters its enemies, much less for God and country than for those in power.

Q. *Moses was a very holy man, was he not?*

A. Moses also killed a man in his youth. Christ, on the other hand, never took another man's life, yet had His taken at the hands of men like Moses in his youth, that we might live not as beasts, killing one another, but as Christ, the full human being whose end the beast seeks.

Q. *When did you have this conversation with the Chaplain in the brig?*

A. Early in March of this year.

Q. *Was that with Chaplain Barr?*

A. I remember only that he was the Division Chaplain.

Q. *How did the Chaplain happen to come to see you?*

A. He had been asked to see me by my command.

Q. *And you discussed your CO beliefs at that time?*

A. Yes, I did.

Q. *When were you first informed about the proper steps to take to claim CO standing?*

A. It wasn't until May, when Chaplain Carroll came to see me.

Q. *Is your position a religious or moral one?*

A. My position is steeped in some of the oldest and newest traditions of the Catholic Church, and is based upon the sole fact that God made me this way.

Q. *Do you subscribe to the philosophy of love thine enemies?*

A. I do.

Q. *Would that apply to the North Vietnamese?*

A. Very much so, I would say.

Q. *To the South Vietnamese?*

A. Even more so.

Q. *And yet, you are opposed to helping South Vietnam?*

A. I am opposed to killing other human beings to prop up one puppet dictator after another, each more corrupt than his predecessor, just to keep a colonial foothold in Vietnam, under the guise of fighting Communist hegemony, and to help a small minority in the South secede from the Union against the wishes of the majority of the people in both the North and the South of Vietnam.

Q. *What is the proper procedure for seeing the commanding officer of the Davidson?*

A. One must fill out a formal chit, requesting a captain's mast.

Q. And to whom do you give this request?
A. To one's immediate superior.
Q. Did you include a copy of your CO claim with your initial submittal?
A. I did not.
Q. It was after this first request that Chief Cormack told you to handle ammunition, wasn't it?
A. Actually, it was after my second attempt to which I had stapled a copy of my CO claim.
Q. On any request did you state why you wanted to see the Captain?
A. Yes, for reasons of conscientious objection and to discuss my status on board the ship in order to prevent any conflict.
Q. And this was on the first request?
A. It was on all the requests.
Q. When did you first read the provisions of the BUPERS Manual?
A. The latter part of May.
Q. And you state that you got out of the brig on 5 July?
A. That's correct.
Q. Were you in the brig in May?
A. I was were I belonged until May 15.
Q. After May 15, you went back to the ship?
A. Yes, I went back to where I didn't belong.
Q. When did you again get sent over to the brig?
A. I got back to where I belonged about the 5th or 6th of June.
Q. When did you complete your conscientious objector statement?
A. I'd say about the 29th of June.
Q. What date did you first inform someone in authority within the Navy organization that you are a conscientious objector?
A. I told my commanding officer at a captain's mast on the 12th of March.
Q. It was after you informed the Captain in March that you saw this Chaplain in the brig whose name you can't remember.
A. Yes.
Q. When Chief Cormack gave you the order to handle ammunition and you refused, did you tell him why you refused.
A. No, I just said, "I have to refuse that."
TRIAL COUNSEL: I have no further questions.

REDIRECT EXAMINATION

Questions by the defense:
Q. Why didn't you tell him why you would not handle ammunition?

A. One, Cormack didn't ask me why, and two, I didn't feel like I had to explain myself to the OOD, Lieutenant Smyth, who has known why ever since I told him, back in April at the summary court-martial over which he presided, that as a CO, I would refuse to handle ammunition or participate in general quarters from thereon out. And that is why I believe, to this day, Smyth was the chief instigator of this whole affair.

Q. Now, this claim for conscientious objector status that you filed is approximately seven pages long, is that right?

A. Yes, it is.

Q. I show you a copy of that claim, dated 29 June 1968, and ask you if you recognize it as the claim which you filed?

A. Yes, I do.

Q. I will show you a copy of BUPERS Manual Part C, Section 5210, and beginning at part 2, will you just read the questions so that the court may know what you had to respond to?

A. Yes. Do you believe in a Supreme Being? Describe the nature of your belief which is the basis of your claim and state whether or not your belief in a Supreme Being involves a duty which to you is superior to those arising from any human relation? Explain how, when and from whom or from what source you received the training and acquired the belief which is the basis of your claim? Give the name and present address of the individual upon whom you rely most for religious guidance in matters of conviction relating to your claim? Under what circumstances, if any, do you believe in the use of force? Describe the action and behavior in your life which, in your opinion, most affected your religious conviction which gave rise to your claim? Have you ever given public expression, written or oral, to the views herein expressed as the basis for your claim? If so, specify when and where.

Q. To answer these questions, what kind of preparation did you do?

A. A lot of reading and soul searching, to help pull my thoughts together.

Q. Did you make any contact with any of those on whom you rely for religious guidance.

A. I met with Professor Douglass on several occasions, even while I was in the brig, to discuss the role of suffering in my life, and to get copies of Church documents that support conscientious objection and the right of an individual to seek such status.

Q. What about Father Dever?

A. Yes. I met with Father Dever as well as Father Graff and Captain Cloonan, who is the Chaplain here at Pearl Harbor, and with countless others whenever I had questions or sought clarification of matters having to do with my CO claim.

Q. Did you prepare the answers to these questions while you were in the brig at Pearl Harbor.

A. Yes, I did.

Q. Before the date of the request that you be permitted to see the Captain, had you made other requests to see the Captain on your ship?

A. Yes. I put in a request, in June of '67, upon which I had written "I wished to see the Captain" rather than requesting a "captain's mast," and was allowed to see CAPT Stanfield without having to change the wording of the request.

Q. Do you today stand by the position which you took in your claim for conscientious objector status?

A. Yes, I do.

Q. And briefly stated, what is that position?

A. My postion is that I can no longer, in good conscience, participate in an organization which uses violence as a means to accomplish its ends, and which makes me an accessory to its crimes and forces me to support such criminal activity.

Q. And you are willing, are you not, pending decision on this claim to be assigned duties not inconsistent with your beliefs?

A. That's correct.

DEFENSE COUNSEL: *You may examine.*

TRIAL COUNSEL: *I have no further questions.*

EXAMINATION BY THE COURT

Questions by the President:

Q. How many times have you spoken with Mr. Douglass?

A. At least once or twice a week, when I'm not out at sea or in the brig.

Q. Have you adopted an evangelical approach to your personal views in the sense that you are actively trying to convince others to adopt your views?

A. Having found Who I Am has filled me with so much joy that it is hard not to share that joy with others who may not know where they belong. Sir, you don't know how wonderful that is, until you have gone astray for as long as I have, and like a lost sheep, have been found again. For I Am Who I Am and no other god before thee, and must therefore act accordingly, more like Jonah, if you wish, than St. Paul the Evangelist, and for that reason alone, must be about the business of getting the beast to cough up Who I Am.

Q. What purpose were you attempting to serve by taking aboard the ship the statement from the Fort de Russy sit-in?

A. I wanted so badly to get off that ship, that I would have done anything illegal in the eyes of the Navy but not God's, to give me the peace and quiet I needed, to fill out my CO claim. So I challenged the authority of Captain Whitaker to keep me from passing out leaflets on board a ship owned and operated by a government that espouses freedom of the press. And I accepted the challenge of my Captain and personal Savior to live out Who I Am, rather than some facsimile of the truth dressed to kill.

Q. Let's assume we didn't have a war, but have the potential for war any time. In the absence of an armed conflict, would you be able to express yourself with regard to your philosophical and religious views?

A. While I was in boot camp at the Naval Academy, being trained to kill, I realized, one day, that I could never kill another human being on command, but knew not what to do with such feelings since I had never heard of a conscientious objector. As these feelings intensified over time, I withdrew, at their insistence, to embrace a kingdom yet to come that inhibited my ability to function in a world so out of kilter with Who I Am that I could hardly move much less concentrate on my duties to either one as they were in constant conflict with each other. Dependent upon what the psychiatrists would unearth in their struggle to determine the cause of my inability to function as the Navy saw fit, I would eventually have been discharged as the CO I AM or have been booted out of the Navy for reasons of unsuitability.

Looking back, I realize now that the firing exercises alone would probably have been enough to push me over the line, psychologically speaking, to embrace 'thy kingdom come, thy will be done on earth as it is in heaven'. Mt 6:10.

Q. In your direct examination you described an episode involving an encounter with an officer on board your vessel you did not salute and you quoted yourself as saying "I don't respect your being an officer not of God's doing". Can you elaborate on that at all?

A. I was charged with saying those exact words by an inner spirit, neither foul nor fiend, who knew what would lead me back to the place where I belonged to put pen to paper, a CO claim in waiting, before the sixth day of the seventh month when hell would try to take me down should I attempt to stand up for Who I Am without the necessary paperwork—cryptic words indeed to one not of God's doing.

Q. How is it that you considered the agreement you reached with Mr. Barrows as being effective with the commanding officer of the Davidson?

A. Barrows told me that he'd had a previous discussion with the Captain, and after I had signed the paper, that he was taking it over to the ship to discuss it with the Captain.

Q. Did you ever receive any confirmation that the Commanding Officer of the Davidson had concurred with the agreement you had with Mr. Barrows?

A. *I did not.*

Q. *With respect to Specification 2 under Charge III, alleging disrespectful language and quoting you as saying "Get your slimy hands off my personal belongings," did you realize at the time these words were uttered, their exact meaning or the critical nature of that language?*

A. *I was merely expressing my disgust with him, first and foremost, because he wouldn't let go of me after I had asked him twice to please take his hands off me and my personal belongings, and secondly, because his hands were drenched in sweat and felt cold and clammy or slimy and downright disgusting to me.*

Q. *You made reference to the fact that you had distributed on board the vessel a document, and that this matter was brought to the attention of the Commanding Officer who then instructed you not to do that any more. What time are we speaking of?*

A. *February of '68.*

Q. *And would you describe again the nature of that document?*

A. *It was a letter written by Leo Tolstoy, advising a young draftee...*

Q. *Yes, that's all right. I have identified the document now. At that time, had you considered applying for conscientious objector status?*

A. *As a result of this matter, I was sent by my command to see a psychiatrist who asked me why I didn't apply for discharge as a conscientious objector.*

Q. *Who was this?*

A. *The psychiatrist.*

Q. *Suggested that you claim yourself to be a conscientious objector?*

A. *Yes.*

Q. *But before that you had distributed the letter from Tolstoy to a draftee?*

A. *Yes.*

Q. *Did that letter make any reference to conscience, or opposing war?*

A. *The whole letter was about conscience and opposing war and military service as well.*

PRESIDENT: *I think that concludes the questions by the court. In view of the questions asked by the court, is there any further examination by counsel for either side?*

TRIAL COUNSEL: *I have no further questions.*

REDIRECT EXAMINATION

Questions by the defense:

Q. *In February, this psychiatrist you saw, was that Dr. Lazaroff?*

A. *Yes, it was.*

Q. *And was it not soon after your meeting with Dr. Lazeroff that you informed the Commanding Officer of the Davidson of your desire to claim status as a conscientious objector?*

A. Yes, in fact two weeks later at a captain's mast on the 12th of March.

DEFENSE COUNSEL: *I have no further questions.*

I was excused and resumed my seat as the accused at counsel table.

The court recessed at 1450 hours, and reconvened at 1455 hours on 6 September 1968.

James Douglass, Assistant Professor of Religion, University of Hawaii, was called as a witness for the defense, was sworn and testified as follows:

DIRECT EXAMINATION

Questions by the defense:

Q. *Mr. Douglass, how long have you been at the University of Hawaii?*

A. I began teaching at the University on the first of February of this year.

Q. *And would you tell the court what your background is with respect to your religious training?*

A. I received a MA in theology from the University of Notre Dame, after which I spent two and a half years in Rome on further graduate studies in theology and as an assistant to several British and American bishops at the Second Vatican Council. Then I taught theology for one year at Bellarmine University in Louisville, Kentucky, spent the next two years in Canada with my family, writing a book on the theology of war and peace, and have written articles on this particular moral question for a number of Catholic and Protestant periodicals.

Q. *What is the title of that book?*

A. It is "The Non-violent Cross, A Theology of Revolution and Peace", which will be published on October 15 of this year by the Macmillan Company.

Q. *Now, Professor Douglass, are you acquainted with the accused?*

A. Yes, I met him in the latter part of May of this year.

Q. *Under what circumstances?*

A. He telephoned me one morning from the library at the University of Hawaii, and said that he had read an article about me in the newspaper and wanted to talk to me about conscientious objection in the military service. I told him to come right over to my office, that I would be glad to talk to him.

Q. *And you eventually had a discussion with him with respect to that subject?*

A. Yes. We talked for about an hour and a half, and then went down to discuss it further with Father Dever, head of the Catholic school system in Hawaii.

Q. *Now, I show you Defense Exhibit C which has been received in evidence, and I ask you whether you recognize the symbol?*

A. It's known as a peace symbol.

Q. What do you understand the meaning of this symbol to be?

A. Well, its original meaning had to do with the campaign for nuclear disarmament. Since then, the meaning has morphed in such a way that when I asked yesterday the eight or ten people of religious background precisely what the meaning was, they identified it in general without identifying it specifically with the Committee for Nuclear Disarmament. I personally regard it as a kind of sign of contradiction, much like the cross in our present day.

Q. Could you elaborate a bit on that as a sign of contradiction?

A. For a number of people, the pursuit of peace, that is identified with the peace symbol and recognized in God's peace coming into history, is much like the cross, in that a number of priests, disregarding the cross, are uniting it with this symbol so that this contradiction can be known in a more vital way today.

I brought along a newspaper clipping which illustrates one priest, though it's not isolated to any one priest, who was wearing the cross in that manner. I attended a mass, a month ago in New York State, in which about a hundred people participated, where the celebrating priest wore the peace symbol around his neck so that the liturgy centered around peace in many people's minds.

This is also true in a lot of matters in theology, emphasizing the realization of God's purpose in history, that the pursuit of peace is very much identified with the pursuit of love and of the Church.

Q. Your opinion is there's really no distinction between the pursuit of peace and the pursuit of love?

A. No, I think they are to be identified. I think you could make distinctions, but as a practical fact the formal pursuit of peace today is where the forward part of the Church is moving in history. This I believe very deeply.

Q. Now you conclude, do you not, that the peace symbol may be for many people a religious symbol, similar to the cross or any other religious symbol?

A. Yes.

Q. Directing your attention to that first meeting with Drury, tell the court briefly what took place.

A. While Mr. Drury described his experiences with the Navy, he did so with an exuberance and a joy which, in terms of what happened to him, was to me deeply impressive. I don't want to exaggerate his character, but I thought of people like Thomas More and Franz Jägerstätter, an Austrian peasant who exuded a similar kind of joy and commitment when he refused to serve in Hitler's Army. And he told me of his refusal to participate in an exercise which he felt was immoral. When I asked him what the source of his decision was, since he had voluntarily entered the military, he said simply "by reading the Bible," which to me was *deeply impressive when I found out that he had had no counsel or contact with any other group. Simply through his religion, he had reached these convictions which involved him in very real suffering, and he had reached this state from conscientious objection. He did not have any background in Biblical theology, but he read, simply read what was said, and he reached the conclusion that he would not participate, and that he had communicated this to other people on the ship.*

Q. Did you make any suggestions to him at that first meeting with respect to what he should do?

A. I made two suggestions, first of all that he immediately talk to Father Daniel Dever so that he could have the counsel of a Catholic priest, and also have a person who could serve as a witness in his defense should he get involved in further conscientious refusal with the military, because I knew, after some discussion, Father Dever could reach a conclusion whether he considered Mr. Drury to be a conscientious objector. And I also recommended that he immediately contact a lawyer so that he could have legal counsel should the need arise.

Q. Did he indicate to you at that time any effort on his part to make a claim as a conscientious objector?

A. He said that he had on several occasions stated the basis for his refusal to cooperate, but that he had been rebuffed.

Q. Did you have occasion to have other meeings with him?

A. I saw him frequently during the next two weeks, before he was put in the brig for a month. And during the period that he was in the brig, I visited him on two occasions, once with yourself and then with mutual friends at a later date.

Q. What took place at the meeting where I was present?

A. Well, by then my primary impression of Mr. Drury is always that he had not displayed discouragement, which I know had been profoundly distressing to other men in the same kind of situation. His joy seemed to grow as his commitment in conscientious objection was expressed.

Q. Was it as the result of being in the military?

A. No, it was some kind of joy that comes out of any person who is expressing something which they believe in, and of any person who is fulfilling himself in terms of standing up for what he believes and in doing so in a nonviolent way, in a loving way, and a truthful way, all of which are characteristics of Mr. Drury.

Q. Now, you've had occasion to meet with Drury over the past few months, have you not?

A. That's correct.

Q. What has been the nature of those meetings?

A. He has been working to obtain data for his CO application. He has been obtaining letters from various people. He has been actively expressing his posi-

tion with a number of different Catholics, acquiring along the way a deeper and deeper familiarity with his position, which was solidified before he ever met me—perhaps I understand him better, what Mr. Drury stands for.

Q. From your contacts with him and your observations of him, do you have an opinion as to his character?

A. Well, I have already described my opinion of his character. I regard him as one of the most courageous persons I've ever met.

Q. With respect to his trait of honesty...

A. He is deeply honest. I have never seen him say anything which I didn't think he didn't believe. If he has ever been dishonest, I have no evidence of it at all.

DEFENSE COUNSEL: You may examine.

CROSS EXAMINATION

Questions by the prosecution:

Q. Professor, bear with me here. If you take the cross from the Tower of David as an acceptable religious symbol, would you classify this symbol along with the other symbols as a religious symbol?

A. Yes. As I said, I think the peace symbol is a contemporary part of the Cross.

Q. It is the same, has the same meaning as the Cross?

A. Yes, because...well, there are very few people like Mr. Drury who understand the meaning of the Cross.

Q. How many meetings have you had with him?

A. Dozens. It would be hard to estimate. There was a period of one month when he was in the Bay Area and out of Los Angeles on a ship. But during the past four months, I have seen him frequently, at least every week.

Q. Do you subscribe to Drury's belief as a proof of Christ's claim against war and violence?

A. Yes, I do. I am convinced that the direction of Christian faith must be deeply against war and violence, regardless of where it comes from.

Q. How do you reconcile this message of peace and love that comes from the New Testament with all the violence in the Old?

A. Because the New Testament is a development of the Old, I don't think the message of violence is as emphatic as you suggest. The concept of revelation which I believe is a developing revelation, which is not only completed with the conclusion of the New Testament, but is a continuing revelation by God in history coming forward from the New Testament so that there are many prophets of peace today, like Martin Luther King, or Mohandas K. Ghandi, who reveal even more profoundly that which we have found within the New Testament, and who are developing these concepts.

TRIAL COUNSEL: *I have no further questions.*
DEFENSE COUNSEL: *Does the court have any questions?*

EXAMINATION BY THE COURT

Questions by the President:

Q. *Did you recommend to the accused that he speak with a priest so that he might develop a witness for his belief?*

A. *I think he should have spoken to a priest so that he would have a way of developing, in a more institutional form, his ideas which are rooted in the Catholic faith, but which were developed in a purely personal fashion. I think in order to have support for that belief that he would need counsel for understanding what he would receive from someone like Father Dever so that he might not be as isolated as he had been over the last year.*

Q. *You testified the accused's motives were born of a reading of the Scriptures without any formal theological training.*

A. *That's correct.*

Q. *Is your testimony then that he attests to that fact?*

A. *That's what he told me, and that's what I understood, and that was why he believed that he should not participate in this war, not because he believed that this war is unjust, but because Christ preached nonviolence.*

Q. *Would you consider that elementary schooling in a Catholic school would have, of necessity, contributed to this feeling?*

A. *Yes, he stated that one of his primary influences was a Sister that he had in elementary school. I did ask him if he had had any further contacts with her, and he said he hadn't seen her or heard from her for some time. Nonetheless, there had been an indelible impression made on his mind by the goodness or the love manifested in his Catholic primary school education.*

Q. *With regard to Defense Exhibit C, this so called peace symbol, how do you account for it considering its origin and its present nebulous use, which you contribute to uncontrolled evolution?*

A. *I think this is highly possible in the history of the Church, that a symbol will come into being when it expresses something very much in the minds of a man who believes. It's not a matter of choosing a symbol in a logical fashion. It's a natural expression of what men believe in, and I think in this particular instance, especially after the Second Vatican Council, there's a new consciousness among Catholics of the extent to which peace is involved in the work of the Church in this world. In fact, the document at the Vatican Council which supports conscientious objection is called "The Church in the Modern World", so that there is a new modern understanding of the significance of Christ's presence in history, not of some-*

one beyond history, or of someone returning at the end of history, but of someone being present in all men, moving through history and making history sacred.

Q. Your contact with the accused has been that you can express positive opinion concerning his conscience?

A. Yes, sir.

Q. Now would you repeat that again for us?

A. Well, I think I said that his honesty is deeply impressive, the depth of his commitment, the extent to which he had suffered as a result of this commitment, has been tested, and proved to be rock solid. I think the only way a person realizes whether he is deeply committed in conscience is by passing through some kind of suffering. This is what occurred to Mr. Drury, and that is the reason why that causes some kind of contradiction. Because if you love, simply because of that love, men will resist that love to some extent. If you try to love unequivocally and indiscriminately without dividing mankind into parties, into places or into groups, then the likelihood is that something will happen like it did to Jesus. And this is what happened to Mr. Drury, to my understanding.

Q. You're defining a martyr.

A. Not Mr. Drury. He's still very much alive.

PRESIDENT: Martyr tendencies. The court has no further questions. In view of the questions asked by the court, are there any questions by either counsel?

TRIAL COUNSEL: *Prosecution has no questions.*

DEFENSE COUNSEL: *Defense has none.*

The witness was excused and withdrew from the stand.

Father Daniel J. Dever, Roman Catholic priest, St. Pius Church, Manoa, Hawaii, was called as a witness by the defense, was sworn and testified as follows:

DIRECT EXAMINATION

Questions by the defense:

Q. Father, when did you make your first contact with the accused?

A. Sometime in May, I believe.

Q. What were the circumstances leading up to that?

A. As I recall, Professor Douglass suggested that we meet in our office on Bishop Street, the Department of Catholic Schools.

Q. And, briefly, what took place at that first meeting?

A. Just to get acquainted with Mr. Drury, and also to discuss his views regarding conscientious objection and the relationship of his views with his professed beliefs in the Catholic Church.

Q. Now I show you Defense Exhibit C and ask you to examine it, absent the chain from which it hangs. Do you recognize that medallion?

A. Yes, I recognize it to be a peace symbol.

Q. Do you attach any significance to it today in connection with religion?

A. The significance that I attach to it would be that which men who use it give to it, and I would imagine that, from what I know of symbolism, that it could be taken to be a religious symbol by some and properly so.

Q. And do you have personal knowledge of religious persons, clergymen specifically, who take it as a religious symbol?

A. I have seen clergymen wearing it and I have seen pictures of other clergymen wearing it.

Q. How, if at all, does it differ from the symbol of the cross that some clergymen wear?

A. In terms of its religious significance, the cross itself was a symbol that was despised in the beginning, and it was only later on recognized as having a significance of victory and hope. But in its origins, it was so despised that the true Cross was lost, so that meaning attached to a symbol from time to time, by different people, convey the symbol of the Cross as a symbol still to be despised.

Q. So do you believe that the peace symbol may mean or have meaning to those concerned with their religion similar to the meaning the Cross has for other religious people?

A. I prefer to put it this way. I think that those who think of peace as being a symbol in terms of its religious significance, that is, the peace of Christ, any symbol that is acceptable, or communicated this to others, would serve that purpose. And this serves the purpose for some. For those, who think of peace in a Christian context as a religious idea, could use this symbol to convey that to other men.

Q. Now, would you explain to the court the extent of your contact with the accused, and the nature of it?

A. The extent of the contact was over three or four months. But in that time, I met Mr. Drury four or five times, and spoke to him over a period of an hour or two on several occasions.

Q. And during those periods did you discuss with him his position as a conscientious objector?

A. I did.

Q. Did you form any conclusion with respect to the position he has taken?

A. Yes, I did. I have had occasions to discuss this with a number of people, and I have concluded, this represented to me a very sincere instance of a man who had based his objection on his religious belief in Roman Catholicism. Let me add to that if I may. I was kind of sensitive to the possibility, because I think as you gentlemen know too, within Roman Catholicism, it hasn't been traditionally accepted. That there is a strain of pacifism running through Christian traditions has not been an acceptable thing for Roman Catholics in our times, in that we could be easily discredited or looked upon with suspicion if we try to base this objection on Roman Catholic beliefs. And I was fairly sensitive to this in this case, but I am convinced that this is a general, sincere expression of conscientious objection, consistent with Catholic beliefs.

DEFENSE COUNSEL: *You may examine.*

CROSS EXAMINATION

Questions by the prosecution:

Q. *Father Dever, is this peace symbol as widely accepted as the Cross is in the Roman Catholic Church?*

A. No. I think, I would be very truthful to admit that this has religious significance for some and for others it is not tied in necessarily with religion. The Cross is loved as a symbol and hated for the same reason that it is a symbol of a very significant religious event. I think the peace symbol could be quite neutral, aside from its religious connotations.

TRIAL COUNSEL: *I have no further questions.*

EXAMINATION BY THE COURT

Questions by the President:

Q. *Could it also be a political symbol?*

A. I would be open to that possibility, because a symbol has an expression that has to be agreed upon by a community of people for its meaning. If I may, I would like to present a symbol that could have no other significance than a very practical or pragmatic symbol. It's an old mud hen with an olive branch, and there's an anchor. Now that of itself doesn't tie in with political or religious symbolism. And yet it has become a great symbol of hope. Now, hope can be a very neutral word. It could be a short-term expectation of it. But it has taken on, for those who have religious beliefs, an ultimate value, hope in Christ as the final symbol of peace and the realization of that. So that is why a symbol like this would not have any more meaning than that which a community of believers communicate to each other. And I admit that it could have political significance for others.

Q. *I note that it also has a dove and an olive leaf.*

A. This is hope for peace.

Q. *Have you specifically discussed the meaning of the so-called peace symbol with Drury?*

A. I have not.

PRESIDENT: *In view of the questions by the court, are there any questions by either counsel?*

Trial of a Special Kind

Neither counsel had any further questions.

The witness was excused and withdrew from the witness stand.

Father Donald J. Graff, Roman Catholic priest, Associate Superintendent of Catholic Schools, Director of Religious Education, Diocese of Hawaii, was called as a witness for the defense, was sworn and testified as follows:

DIRECT EXAMINATION

Questions by the defense:

Q. Father Graff, how long have you known the accused in this case?

A. For about two and a half weeks.

Q. What were the circumstances under which you met him?

A. One night around 8:00 o'clock in the evening, Butch came to see me at the Cathedral, he wanted to talk. So I brought him up to my room where we talked about his past, his situation in the military, and his concern about the future, till three in the morning.

Q. Did you discuss with him his claim as a conscientious objector?

A. I did.

Q. And what do you understand his present position to be?

A. I think he's very much involved with the position of the Church today. He came to me with knowledge of the Church Fathers, and with the content of the Vatican Council. He always showed a great deal of sincerity in his knowledge and in the dialogue we shared. I thought it was a very sincere, very knowledgeable position. Certainly, I don't think it could be questioned.

Q. I now show you what has been marked as Defense Exhibit C, and I ask you if you recognize it?

A. That's a peace symbol.

Q. Do you have any knowledge as to its meaning today in religious circles?

A. The first time I came across this symbol was when I had seen a report of a Jesuit priest with this symbol worn by him. So I looked into it and found out what it means. And to me it seems to embody the concept of peace, in a very Christian context, especially in relation to my first encounter with it.

Q. Do you consider it to be religious, a symbol that may be taken by those who are sincere in their religious beliefs as indicative of those beliefs?

A. I think so. New symbols come, they develop and they're given meaning. I would definitely look upon this as a Christian symbol of peace.

Q. What are the values and traditions that you call to mind when you see this symbol?

A. Christ's message is His great concern for His fellowman, and the concern He had for nonviolence when He said to Peter, "Put away your sword", the position of the Church Fathers as evidenced by the great goodness of Pope John's "Pacem in Terris" of the Vatican Council, the paragraph concerned with peace and the involvement of Christians in teaching the Christian way.

Q. And that's the symbol which calls those values to mind for you?

A. Yes. It certainly does.

DEFENSE COUNSEL: *You may examine.*

CROSS EXAMINATION

Questions by the prosecution:

Q. Father, do you know whether or not this symbol has a meaning other than its religious meaning?

A. That I don't know.

Q. Do you know whether or not it has been adopted by political groups as a peace symbol?

A. Not to my knowledge.

TRIAL COUNSEL: *I have no further questions.*

DEFENSE COUNSEL: *I have nothing.*

The witness was excused and withdrew from the witness stand.

Fireman Martin Cisna, USN, USS Davidson, was called as a witness by the defense, was sworn and testified as follows:

DIRECT EXAMINATION

Questions by the defense:

Q. What is the nature of your contact with the accused?

A. I'm one of his friends on the ship. I talk to him. We're pretty good friends.

Q. Directing your attention to a date sometime in the early part of March 1968, do you recall being in attendance at a captain's mast at which the accused was again the accused?

A. Yes, I do.

Q. Do you recall an event with respect to a claim that was made by the accused at that captain's mast?

A. Yes, I do.

Q. Would you relate to the court exactly what took place?

A. After mast had been held, Drury asked the Captain that he be claimed as a conscientious objector.

Q. Did you observe the Captain do anything?

A. He closed his book and walked away.

Q. Did he say anything?

A. Not to my knowledge.

Q. Now Fireman Cisna, were you aboard the Davidson on August 16, 1968, the date on which it is alleged that Drury had contact with a First Class Wulff?

A. Yes, I was.

Q. Directing your attention to the time, approximately 7:30 in the morning, did you observe any contact between Drury and First Class Wulff?

A. Yes, I did.

Q. Would you relate to the court what you observed?

A. I was already at quarters, Wulff was in the first class stand. When Drury came around the corner of the ship, Wulff took off, went and got him, turned him around and pushed him around the corner where I couldn't see them any more.

Q. He did what?

A. He grabbed him, turned him around and pushed him around the corner where I couldn't see them.

Q. Did you hear the Wulff say anything to Drury at the time?

A. No, I didn't.

Q. Did you hear Drury say anything?

A. No, I didn't. I was too far away.

DEFENSE COUNSEL: *You may examine.*

CROSS EXAMINATION

Questions by the prosecution:

Q. Do you go on the beach with Drury?

A. Occasionally.

Q. Do you consider yourself a good friend of his?

A. I'm a pretty good friend of Drury, yes I am.

Q. At the time at quarters which you just described, did you notice Drury's appearance?

A. Just his uniform, I noticed.

Q. Was he wearing anything around his neck that you noticed?

A. I believe he was wearing his peace symbol.

Q. I show you the peace symbol which is marked Defense Exhibit C. Is this what he was wearing?

A. I don't know, I didn't see it. I could only see the chain.

Q. You couldn't see the medallion?

A. No, sir.

Q. Was this chain outside of his uniform?

A. He has a habit of wearing his uniform with the top button open, and I could see the chain.

Q. When you saw Drury, were you looking at him full on or from an angle?

A. *Maybe a slight angle, but pretty much straight on.*
TRIAL COUNSEL: *I have no further questions.*
The witness was excused and withdrew from the courtroom.

BT3 Rufus Crosby, USN, USS Davidson, was called as a witness for the defense, was sworn and testified as follows:

DIRECT EXAMINATION

Questions by the defense:

Q. *How long have you known the accused in this case?*

A. *About a year and a half I believe.*

Q. *Under what capacity do you have contact with him?*

A. *As a shipmate.*

Q. *Now, directing your attention to August 16, 1968, at approximately 12:30 hours, I ask you if you observed the accused?*

A. *Yes, sir.*

Q. *Would you tell the court under what circumstances you observed the accused?*

A. *Well, I was going up the ladder to the head as he was coming down. He had his religious medallion on. I got hold of it, but didn't take it out of his shirt, and said to him, "What have you got here, Drury?" I don't remember what he said in reply. By the time I got back, I seen Drury, standing down there by the drinking fountain, and the Wulff, EM1, had hold of his arm and this medallion. Drury was kind of leaning back, and the Wulff was talking down to him. At that point, the Wulff said, "Are you going to take that medallion off?" And Drury said, "Get your clammy paws off me." That's when the Wulff said, "You're on report."*

Q. *Do you know whether there has been a practice on the ship, at least up to and including August 16, 1968, with respect to the wearing of medallions, medals, religious symbols, etc., around the necks of some crew members?*

A. *There hadn't been anything said at all either way, as far as I know.*

Q. *But other crewman have worn such symbols?*

A. *Yes, that's true.*

Q. *Do you yourself wear a kind of article around your neck?*

A. *Yes, sir, I do.*

Q. *Will you show that to the court?*

A. *(The witness complies.) It's a ring from my fiancee, and I've worn it for a year and a half.*

Q. *Has there been any occasion where you have been asked to remove that?*

A. *Never.*

DEFENSE COUNSEL: *You may examine.*

CROSS EXAMINATION

Questions by the prosecution:

Q. How was Drury dressed when you saw him?

A. He was in his blue dungarees, with the top button of his shirt open.

Q. Was this medallion visible through the opening in his shirt?

A. No, you could only see the chain.

TRIAL COUNSEL: I have no further questions.

The witness was excused and withdrew from the courtroom.

MM3 Michael Bardon, USN, USS Davidson, was called as a witness for the defense, was sworn and testified as follows:

DIRECT EXAMINATION

Questions by the defense:

Q. What is the nature of your contact with the accused?

A. Well, he's been on the same ship as I was for the past year and a half.

Q. And over that period of time have you had personal contact with him?

A. Yes, I have. On numerous occasions we've worked together as mess cooks, or compartment cleaners.

Q. In your observations of him, during these periods of working together, do you have an opinion as to his ability to carry out the functions of his assignment?

A. Yes, the duties that he's assigned, he carries them out, so far as I am concerned, satisfactorily.

Q. Now directing your attention to August 16, 1968, on board the Davidson, at about 7:30 in the morning, I ask you if you saw the accused at that time?

A. Yes, I did. I was at quarters when I first observed Drury.

Q. Would you tell to the court what happened after you first observed Drury?

A. Well, I saw Drury coming on my left to go to quarters, which was directly in front of me and his division head's quarters on the opposite side of the ship. He got about midway between us when I saw the Wulff, EM1, grab hold of him, turn him around, and walk him back down the side of the ship about ten or fifteen yards. I think they had a talk, but I couldn't really hear what they were saying?

Q. Did you have occasion to see Drury later on in the day?

A. Yes. I was down in the compartment, over by my rack which is near the scuttlebutt, when I realized there was some disturbance going on. I came around and the Wulff had Drury by the arm. He had the chain in his right hand, and he was talking about this peace symbol.

Q. Did you hear the Wulff say anything?

A. Yes, he asked Drury, "Are you going to take this off?" And Drury said, "When are you going to take your hands off me?" He asked Drury again, "When are you going to take this off?" And Drury said, "Are you going to get your clammy hands off me?" The Wulff said, "You're on report," turned and walked off.

Q. Now Mr. Bardon, do you have any knowledge of symbols or medallions or beads or any other articles worn by members of the crew of the Davidson?

A. I know that they're worn.

Q. Have you ever observed any members of the crew wearing symbols such as the peace symbol, which is Defendant's Exhibit C, other than Drury?

A. Yes, I have noticed other people wearing them.

Q. Do you have an opinion as to whether Drury was polite when you observed him with the First Class Wulff?

A. Yes, he handled it better than I would have myself. I think he handled it exceptionally well.

DEFENSE COUNSEL: *You may examine.*

CROSS EXAMINATION

Questions by the prosecution:

Q. When you saw Drury at quarters on the morning of the 16th, what was Drury wearing?

A. Dungarees. I did notice that he had his medallion on.

Q. You saw the medallion?

A. Yes. I don't know whether I saw the medallion before he was turned around or after, or whether I saw the medallion in the process of this. I didn't know what was going on, so I can't say for certain.

Q. You have testified that other members of the crew wear beads or whatever. Do they wear them outside of their uniform shirts?

A. I can't really say. I've seen some on the outside and some on the inside. The only other person I've seen wearing a medallion, was wearing it on the outside.

Q. Do you wear one?

A. No, I don't.

TRIAL COUNSEL: *I have no further questions.*

The witness was excused and withdrew from the courtroom.

BT3 Michael Martucci, USN, USS Davidson, was called as a witness for the defense, was sworn and testified as follows:

DIRECT EXAMINATION

Questions by the defense:

Q. How long have you known the accused in this case?

A. Since he came aboard the Davidson.

Q. And what's the nature of your contact with him on the ship?

A. *I don't work with Drury, but I see him daily.*

Q. *Would you describe yourself as a good friend of his?*

A. *An acquaintance.*

Q. *Now, directing your attention to August 16, 1968, at about 12:30 in the afternoon, did you have occasion to observe Drury with one First Class Wulff?*

A. *Yes.*

Q. *And would you tell the court what the circumstances of that meeting were between Drury and the Wulff?*

A. *The Wulff was talking to Drury. He had Drury by his arm and he had Drury's medallion in his hand. He said to Drury, "Are you going to take this off?" And Drury said in reply, "Are you going to let go of my arm?" Again, the Wulff asked Drury, "Are you going to take this off?" And Drury said, "Are you going to let go of my arm?" With that, the Wulff asked him again, "Are you going to take this off?" Then Drury told him, "Get your clammy paws off my arm."*

Q. *Now Martucci, did you observe the point where the Wulff actually grabbed the medallion?*

A. *Yes.*

Q. *Where was the medallion when he grabbed it?*

A. *Between his dungaree shirt and his T-shirt.*

Q. *So it was inside of his outside shirt?*

A. *Yes.*

Q. *Was the outside shirt buttoned?*

A. *Yes, except for the top button.*

Q. *So you observed the Wulff grab the entire chain and medal and pull it out of the outside shirt, is that correct?*

A. *Yes.*

Q. *Would you describe the extent of the touching and pushing of Drury for the members of the court and the record?*

A. *He had a firm grip on Drury's arm and then he had the medallion—you could see he had some force on the medallion, that he was pulling on it and that Drury showed no physical restraint. He didn't try to break away. And then finally, when the Wulff said, "You're on report," he let go of Drury.*

Q. *Do you have any knowledge of the men aboard the ship, other than Drury, wearing peace symbols, medallions other than traditional crosses?*

A. *I seen Little wearing the medallion.*

Q. *Have you ever worn a medallion or any kind of symbol around your neck?*

A. *I have a chain, I wear a religious medal, but the religious medal is broken off. It was given to me by my aunt, who has since passed away. I sort of keep this* (indicating chain) *as a remembrance.*

Q. *No one has asked you to take it off, have they?*
A. *No sir.*
Q. *When you observed the Wulff and Drury, you heard Drury make the statement, "Are you going to get your hands off me," would you describe Drury's conduct at that part?*
A. *I would say he was polite.*
Q. *There was no violence in his actions?*
A. *There was no forcing in his actions.*
DEFENSE COUNSEL: *You may examine.*

CROSS EXAMINATION

Questions by the prosecution:
Q. *You mentioned that Little wears a medallion?*
A. *Yes, sir.*
Q. *Where does he wear it? Does he wear it outside of his uniform, too?*
A. *No, sir. When I seen Little with a medallion, I think it was inside his T-shirt. All I seen was the chain.*
Q. *This religious symbol that you are wearing, where do you keep that?*
A. *Inside my T-shirt.*
TRIAL COUNSEL: *I have no further questions.*
The witness was excused and withdrew from the courtroom.
Seaman Ricky Little, USN, USS Davidson, was called as a witness by the defense, was sworn and testified as follows:

DIRECT EXAMINATION

Questions by the defense:
Q. *How long have you known the accused in this case?*
A. *A little over a year.*
Q. *What has been the nature of your contact with the accused?*
A. *Friendship.*
Q. *You work on the ship together?*
A. *No, we're on separate details.*
Q. *Do you have any knowledge of the regulations recently issued aboard the ship with regard to wearing peace symbols, medallions?*
A. *Yeah. They brought this out yesterday morning, I think it was. They came out at quarters stating that we can wear anything around our necks, peace symbols, beads or medallions as long as it is inside our shirts.*
Q. *Shirts, meaning your outside shirts?*
A. *They stated T-shirts.*

Q. *Do you wear a medal?*
A. *Yes, I do.*
Q. *How long have you worn that?*
A. *I've worn it on two separate occasions, once about three or four months ago before I misplaced it and then another one about a month ago, which I've worn ever since. I have two of them that I wear.*
Q. *Has there ever been an order given you to take off your medal?*
A. *Yes, two days ago.*
Q. *Not before two days ago?*
A. *No, never.*
Q. *And then yesterday there was an order that one could wear medals provided they were kept inside the T-shirt?*
A. *Yes.*
Q. *Would you show the court what your medal looks like?*
A. *(Witness displays peace symbol medallion to the court.)*
DEFENSE COUNSEL: *Let the record show that the witness is displaying a medallion signifying the peace symbol such as we have described throughout the proceedings today.*
PRESIDENT: *The record will show the description as stated by defense counsel.*
DEFENSE COUNSEL: *You may examine.*

CROSS EXAMINATION

Questions by the prosecution:
Q. *What type medallion is the one that you have?*
A. *It's the same thing; it's just smaller.*
Q. *How much smaller?*
A. *Quite a bit. The other one I wear is the same as Mr. Drury's. We bought them at the same time.*
Q. *Have you ever worn those medallions on the outside of your uniform shirt?*
A. *No.*
TRIAL COUNSEL: *No further questions.*

REDIRECT EXAMINATION

Questions by the defense:
Q. *You say you have a medallion which was purchased at the same time as Drury's Defense Exhibit C?*
A. *Yes.*
Q. *Where did you purchase it?*
A. *At the Navy Exchange on the Sub Base.*

RECROSS EXAMINATION

Questions by the prosecution:

Q. For those of us who may be interested, how much did it cost?

A. It's a dollar ten.

REDIRECT EXAMINATION

Questions by the defense:

Q. You stated that to your recollection you did not wear your peace symbol at any time outside your shirt?

A. Not while in uniform.

Q. Would it refresh your recollection that at one time when you were working back in the torpedo room, you wore it outside of your uniform?

A. Yeah. When there was no one else around, Butch might have been there. Yeah, I guess he was; we were talking at that time.

DEFENSE COUNSEL: *I have no further questions.*

TRIAL COUNSEL: *No further questions.*

The witness was excused and withdrew from the witness stand.

DEFENSE COUNSEL: *The defense rests.*

PRESIDENT: *Any further evidence by the prosecution?*

TRIAL COUNSEL: *Prosecution will request a five-minute recess.*

The court recessed at 1630 hours, and reconvened at 1635 hours on 6 September 1968.

EM1 Kenneth Wulff was recalled as a witness by the prosecution, was reminded that the oath previously taken was still binding, and testified as follows:

DIRECT EXAMINATION

Questions by the prosecution:

Q. I'd like to call your attention to an episode involving the accused in the early afternoon of 16 August. Do you recall that episode?

A. Yes, sir.

Q. Would you describe Drury's appearance at that time?

A. His appearance at that time was that of having his dungaree shirt open.

Q. Completely open?

A. No, sir. I believe that was the top two buttons. It could have been just the top button, but it was in an open position where the medallion he was wearing while he was walking along was flopping outside of his shirt.

Q. I show you what has been identified as Defense Exhibit C. Is this the medallion?

A. It looks a lot like it, sir.

Trial of a Special Kind

TRIAL COUNSEL: *I have no further questions.*

CROSS EXAMINATION

Questions by the defense:

Q. *Describe the flop.*

A. Well, the bottom part of the medallion itself was alternating between inside the shirt and flopping outside the shirt while he was walking along.

Q. *You say you're not sure whether the top two buttons were unbuttoned?*

A. No, I'm not sure. But it was open and the medallion was flopping out.

Q. *But you saw the chain, didn't you?*

A. Yes, I saw the whole thing.

Q. *Would you put this (Defense Exhibit C) on just for a second?*

A. (Witness complies.)

Q. *What size neck do you have?*

A. Sixteen.

Q. *Would you say that was average or above average?*

A. I would say for my size average.

Q. *How big are you?*

A. Six feet two inches.

Q. *And how much do you weigh?*

A. Two hundred and fifteen pounds.

Q. *That medallion comes down to the third button on your shirt, does it not?*

A. Yes, sir, it does.

Q. *You can take it off.*

A. (The witness complies.)

DEFENSE COUNSEL: *I have no further questions.*

The witness was excused and withdrew from the courtroom after being reminded that the warning previously given was still binding.

TRIAL COUNSEL: *The prosecution has no further rebuttal.*

DEFENSE COUNSEL: *In rebuttal, we will call FR Drury to the stand.*

I took the witness stand, was reminded that the oath previously taken was still binding, and testified as follows:

DIRECT EXAMINATION

Questions by the defense:

Q. *Is this the symbol that you were wearing on the day in question?*

A. Yes, it is.

Q. *What size neck do you have?*

A. Fourteen and a half.

Q. *That's about average for your size?*
A. *Yes, it is.*
Q. *How big are you?*
A. *Five ten.*
Q. *How much do you weigh?*
A. *Just about 150 pounds.*
Q. *Will you try this on?*
A. *(The witness complied.)*
Q. *And where does it come down to on you?*
PRESIDENT: *Can you stand up?*
A. *(The witness complied.)*
Q. *How many buttons did you have unbuttoned on your dungaree shirt?*
A. *I had them all buttoned except for the top button.*
Q. *The chain probably was visible, was it not?*
A. *Yes, it was.*
Q. *But the medallion part was where?*
A. *The medallion was under my blue shirt.*
DEFENSE COUNSEL: *I have no further questions.*

CROSS EXAMINATION

Questions by the prosecution:
Q. *Drury, you testified earlier that this friend of yours who passed you on the ladder had pulled it out of your shirt, is that correct?*
A. *Yes, it is.*

REDIRECT EXAMINATION

Questions by the defense:
Q. *And after he pulled it out of your shirt, did you replace it?*
A. *Yes, I put it back between my T-shirt and my dungaree shirt.*
Q. *And the buttons to your dungaree shirt were...*
A. *All buttoned except for the top button.*

RECROSS EXAMINATION

Questions by the prosecution:
Q. *Why didn't you have the top button of your dungaree shirt buttoned?*
A. *I got into the habit of leaving the top button of my shirts open as a kid, and never stopped—the habit is so ingrained in me.*
Q. *And the medallion is usually between your dungaree shirt and your T-shirt. Are you able to feel it?*

A. *I really don't pay that much attention to it as it rarely falls out of my dungaree shirt, even when I stoop over to do something. Most of the time, it just shifts around under my dungaree shirt. So yes, I feel it from time to time.*

Q. *Did you feel it when it was outside your dungaree shirt on the morning of 16 August?*

A. *I did not.*

TRIAL COUNSEL: *I have no further questions.*

DEFENSE COUNSEL: *No further questions.*

PRESIDENT: *No questions.*

I was excused from the witness stand and resumed my seat at counsel table as the accused.

PRESIDENT: *Any further evidence by counsel for either side?*

Neither counsel had any further evidence to present.

Following closing arguments by both the defense and the prosecution, the court recessed at 1720 hours, 6 September 1968, to allow the President to put his instructions in order, and reconvened at 1800 hours, 6 September 1968.

The President then proceeded to instruct the members of the court as follows:

PRESIDENT: *Gentlemen of the Court, when the court closes to vote on the findings, each of us must resolve the ultimate issue of guilt or innocence of the accused in accordance with the law, the evidence admitted in court and our own conscience. Unless the guilt of the accused as to any offense charged has not been established beyond a reasonable doubt, it is our duty to find the accused not guilty of the offense.*

In the Specification *of* Charge I, *the accused is charged with willfully disobeying a lawful order of a superior petty officer to handle ammunition, in violation of Article 91 of the Uniform Code of Military Justice. Now, where a serviceman has made application for classification as a conscientious objector, his Commanding Officer is, at that time, required, pending decision of the application, to see that the serviceman will be employed in duties which involve minimum conflict with his asserted beliefs. If you find that proper application was made in this case, then a subsequent order to that serviceman to handle ammunition is illegal. Proper initial application does not require specific accompanying documentation.*

With regard to Specification 2 of Charge II, the accused is charged with violating a lawful general regulation in violation of Article 92 of the UCMJ. To find the accused guilty of this offense, the court must be satisfied by legal and competent evidence beyond a reasonable doubt that the accused violated such general regulation, which provides that "No articles, such as pencils, watch chains, fobs, pins, jewelry...or similar items shall be worn or carried exposed upon the uniform," by appearing at morning muster with a medallion around his neck and outside his uniform shirt.

In Specification 1 of Charge III, the accused is charged with willfully disobeying the order of a superior petty officer in violation of Article 91 of the UCMJ. To find the accused guilty of this offense, the court must be satisfied by legal and competent evidence beyond a reasonable doubt that at the time and place alleged, the accused willfully disobeyed a lawful order from EM1 Kenneth Wulff, USN, to remove the medallion from around his neck.

In Specification 2 of Charge III, the accused is charged with being disrespectful in language towards a superior petty officer in violation of Article 91 of the UCMJ. To find the accused guilty of this offense, the court must be satisfied by legal and competent evidence beyond a reasonable doubt that at the time and place alleged, the accused used the language as alleged, to wit: "Take your slimy hands off my personal belongings," or words to that effect; and that that language was directed toward and within sight and hearing of said EM1 Wulff.

You are advised that my ruling on the defense motion for a finding of not guilty as to Specification 1 of Charge II should not influence you in any way when you consider the guilt or innocence of the accused.

Voting on the findings is by secret written ballot, and is mandatory. The junior member of the court shall, in each case, count the votes. The count shall be checked by the President, who shall forthwith announce the result of the ballots to the members. As there are four members present, unless at least three members concur in a finding of guilty, then a finding of not guilty automatically results.

During the course of the accused's direct examination, he recited to the court previous instances where he had appeared before captain's mast and in one instance, court-martial. I specifically instruct the court members that this evidence apparently offered by the accused as necessary in his recitation before this court, is not to be considered by the court as an indication that he is guilty of any of the offenses charged today.

There being no objections to the instructions from either counsel, the President instructed trial counsel to remove all Manuals for Courts-Martial and any other legal references from the courtroom.

At 1633 hours, 6 September 1968, the court closed for deliberation, and reconvened at 2007 hours, 6 September 1968.

PRESIDENT: *The record will show that during the closed session of the court, no member of the court had access to any Manual for Courts-Martial, trial guide or any other legal authorities whatsoever.*

FR E. J. Drury, it is my duty as President of this court to inform you that the court in closed session and upon secret written ballot, two-thirds of the members present at the time the vote was taken concurring, finds you: Of Charge I and the Specification thereunder, not guilty; of Charge II and Specification 2 thereunder, guilty;

of Charge III and Specification 1 thereunder, guilty; of Charge III and Specification 2 thereunder, not guilty.

Prosecution then presented evidence of one prior conviction, and defense counsel, with my consent, entered into a stipulation with the prosecution that on 16 April 1968, I had a summary court–martial for violation of Article 89, disrespect towards a superior officer; that the sentence as approved by the supervisory authority on 6 May 1968 amounted to confinement at hard labor for one month and forfeiture of $90 per month for one month. Prosecution had no further matters in aggravation.

After I was advised by the President of my right to present evidence in extenuation or mitigation, including the right to remain silent or to make a sworn or unsworn statement, Brook requested the court to take those matters presented in the case into consideration as extenuation and mitigation, especially as they refer to my claim as a conscientious objector. Brook read to the court certain statements I had made in answer to questions concerning my conscientious objection to military service, that I am a member of the Roman Catholic Church, and also quoted pertinent remarks of Pope John XXIII as found in his encyclical, "Pacem in Terris".

The President instructed the court on the maximum punishment that could be adjudged for the offenses of which I had been found guilty, and instructed the court on the procedure to be followed when voting on the sentence to be adjudged.

With neither counsel having anything further to offer, the court closed at 2032 hours, 6 September 1968, and reconvened at 2131 hours, 6 September 1968.

The President announced that the court in closed session and upon secret written ballot, two–thirds of the members present at the time the vote was taken concurring, sentenced me to be restricted for a period of 60 days, to perform hard labor without confinement for a period of 45 days, and to forfeit $96 per month for a period of six months.

Having trumped the Jack and the Ace with a deuce and a trey, the court adjourned at 2133 hours, 6 September 1968, leaving behind the White Knight and Sir Brook of Hart to pick up the pieces of a shattered dream, a high stakes game that after having been dealt a winning hand, ended in a draw when the White Knight drew a wild card from the deck that greatly diminished his odds of beating them at their own game.

"Thanks for the valiant effort," had the Jack dealt this card from the bottom of his heart.

"You were the valiant one today," had the Ace of Hearts thrown down more truth than either he or the Jack of Hearts realized at the time.

# 7

A Testament to Who I Am

  While I would much rather have preferred sixty days of impoundment to the brig than to the ship, I couldn't imagine going back to not being **Who I Am**, so imbued was I with the Holy Spirit. Whether or not the world agreed with Her assessment of my actions, in Her eyes, I could do no wrong as long as I lived in Her as She lived in me—a daunting task for one who has lost touch with the feminine side of the Trinity as I had when I joined forces to fight against Her rather than with Her at the helm as Queen of all that reflects what She embodies.
  With Her approval, had I offered, in the days leading up to my trial, to collect signatures from the other members of the crew, on a petition calling on Congress to repeal the draft and to replace all draftees, currently serving time in the armed forces, with volunteers who had no qualms with killing other people on command. As the petition wound its way about the ship at Her discretion, in the days since my trial, I had acquired a fair number of signatures before it fell into the hands of the ship's captain, who was none too happy when he found the latest issue of an underground paper called ACT, attached to the same clipboard as the petition. Stuck on the ship with the threat of a general court–martial now hanging over my head, and with no way to contact anyone, other than by mail, I sat down to write a letter to my other mother, Betty, to let her know, I was in trouble again, for having unwittingly disseminated, about the ship, information on the best places to go if one chose to desert one's assertion of the American War in Vietnam.
  But before I could even post the letter, one of the most courageous knights I'd ever met, Sir Jay of Wallrabenstein, did miraculously appear on board the ship to dissuade me from desertion of my assertion to stay and fight as he had since he turned down the IV–D deferment, to which he was legally entitled as a divinity student, and refused induction instead.

"Boy, are you a sight for sore eyes!" Cried out he who had been stripped of the freedom to conspire with those in possession of their right minds, the real makers of peace, and their better angels, not caught up in the insanity of war.

For try as it may, the war machine could not isolate me from the One Big Soul whose members, though many, looked out for each other just as She looked out for them and they looked out for Her.

And as I struggled to find the right words to pin me down to a cross, not of my own choosing, I saw the spirit of Sir Jay rise up from the dead weight he carried each day as he ascended Calvary to hang from his own cross as a model for all to see.

"Are you as willing as I AM to die for what you believe?" Had he asked of me as his spirit rejoined a body willing to die for the sins of others.

"To live or not to live in exile, that's the question," responded the war weary waif in me. "Lord knows how much I have already suffered for the sins of this nation, serving time for crimes I never committed. Asking me to endure a sentence of another two or more years of imprisonment, handed down by a general court-martial, would be enough, I'm afraid, to push me over the edge of a black hole from which not even I could escape dissolution."

"In exile, would you be as effective a witness to Christianity, to its becoming a fuller reality?" Had Sir Jay gone right to the heart of the matter. "Is your aim witness or escape? Don't think me harsh; for I think you must be sure in order to live with your final decision.

"As I understand the incident, your possession of ACT was not an act of civil disobedience, but a slipup. If so, I'd say there might be difficulty in getting you convicted. That's an important possibility to keep in mind.

"Whether you choose exile or prison, you will suffer, and in your suffering, you will be united with Christ. For you are very much a Redeemer of mankind," had he pointed to the truth of my being ere he disembarked from hell's grip on me, to let Brook know that I was in a real pickle again.

"O, where art Thou when most I have need of Thee?" Cried out the one spirit to the other Most Holy, She who must be obeyed in such matters as these, where one false step could imperil the soul and delay Her ascension to the throne as Queen of body and soul.

Having come and gone in the guise of a cleric, had not Sir Jay acted as Her emissary while She did seek a diplomatic solution that reflected the will of the Father of this incident?

And am I not just a pawn in their game, who must sit tight until moved to take another leap in faith, come what may? Why should I concern my self then, with what is going on behind the seen, if I am in such good hands? Should I not be more concerned with discerning the next move I am willing to take, with or without a hand from them, when the time comes, and I must choose?

"O, where art thou when most I have need of thee?" Cried out a body in need of an angel with whom to collude on a more intimate level than I could with the Holiest of spirits, She who must be enfleshed if I am to remain faithful to Who I Am.

"You have yet to meet the young lady intended for you," responded She who must be obeyed both in flesh and in spirit. "When you do, you will know that she *'is bone of'* your *'bone and flesh of'* your *'flesh',"* (Gn 2:23) for I am to marry Who I Am on that day.

"O, where art thou when most I have need of thee?" Cried out the detainee in me, in need of counsel of the legal kind.

"O, where can I find Who I Am filled with the desire to seek?" Had my old girlfriend, Mary, addressed in a letter she had just sent me.

Dear Butch,
Well, I guess another chapter has been added to my book. About two weeks ago, I had firmly resolved never to write to you again. I felt that the gap between us was too wide, that it wouldn't be worth your time or mine to continue writing. I could understand your present position in the peace movement, but I couldn't accept it. I waged a total war against myself on this, Butch. I weighed both sides as fairly as I could. Finally, I decided that this was too big an issue. Needless to say, I've done more thinking on the matter, and have talked to more people. I'm more sympathetic towards the peace movement now. There's this girl at the office whose brother is facing a prison sentence for refusing induction. I let her read your paper on conscientious objection. That's what started me thinking about my own brothers. Anyway, I guess you might say that was the turning point. I still have quite a bit of reading and discerning to do on the matter. At least, my mind is more open and receptive to new ideas, hence the very big delay in writing this letter. Butch, I had to straighten all this out with myself first, before I could write you.

Butch, I hate to end this letter now, but I have to go back to work. Will probably write more tomorrow night.

Take care and write soon!
Love,
Mary

Well, I did write soon, only to let her know that she would not hear from me again, for she had finally convinced me that she did not love me. Nor did I see her, any longer, as the one meant for me, confirmation of which I had not received from the Holy Spirit until recently.

As I agonized in the garden of my own soul, I sat down on my usual perch, late that night, to contemplate my deliverance from the evil that had befallen me.

"*'If it is possible, let this cup pass from me',*" had I prayed to the Father in Jesus' own words, "*'yet, not as I will, but as you will'.*" Mt 26:39.

Sometime after midnight, I retired to my bunk, where I broke out in a cold sweat as I walked off the end of a gangplank, and fell into a restless sea of dreams which tormented the hell out of me by daybreak, leaving me none the wiser yet free of all that had weighed me down.

"Trust in Me," had the Spirit asked of me in return for the peace of mind She had bestowed upon me.

"I do, but I don't know what to do, whether to flee for my life or stay and fight the good fight," so moved was I to submit my plight to Her tender loving care.

"Trust me, you will be so moved, when the time comes, that you shall know, beyond the shadow of a doubt, the Father's will for you," had She confided in me.

"As my other Mother, and Queen as well, how shall I address thee from hereon?" Bowed I before Her on bended knee.

"As you are moved, my son," had She been so moved to say.

"I love you, Mother," I blurted out as the image of a Lady in Blue faded from my memory.

"I love you, too, dear," warmed She my heart to no end.

"You are to tell no one what has transpired here, between you and the Lady, until you are of an age to do so responsibly," had another voice from out of the blue warned me.

Stepping from one dream to another, did I encounter Sir Brook as he rode up on my gallant white steed to challenge the Captain of the salt sea ship Davidson, Sir Robert of Whitaker, to release me from my indentured servitude to a way of life unbefitting of **Who I Am**.

"I'll talk to you after I have finished cooling the Captain down, enough for him to make a more levelheaded decision about what is to be done with you, given the circumstances in which you continually find your Self at odds with the Navy," strategized Sir Brook in a manner of speaking.

"Godspeed," breathed I with a sigh too deep for words, that he might be filled with the Holy Spirit.

The hours dragged on, or so it did seem, before Brook could broker a deal to which the Captain would agree to recommend me for an administrative discharge rather than a court–martial, but only if it were by reason of unfitness instead of unsuitability as had been previously recommended.

"That could mean a discharge under other than honorable conditions," had Brook tweaked my elation before it swelled my head and filled my heart to overflowing with gratitude to the Lady in Blue for having set in motion my eventual liberation, at any cost but my soul, from Uncle Sam's hold on me.

Within days, was I officially notified that:

In accordance with the BUPERS Manual, Article C–10311, thou art being considered for an administrative discharge which couldst be under conditions other than honourable because of frequent involvement of a discreditable nature with military authorities, and that thou art subject to and mayst be separated with an undesirable discharge which mayst depriveth thee of all veteran's benefits based upon thy current period of active service, and mayst subject thee to substantial prejudice in civilian life in situations wherein the type of service rendered in any branch of the armed forces or the character of discharge received therefrom hath a bearing.

Thou hath the right to a hearing before an Administrative Discharge Board, consisting of at least three officers.

Thou mayst appear in person, with or without counsel of thine own choice, at all open proceedings of this administrative discharge board. Furthermore, thou mayst employeth civilian counsel at thine own expense.

Thou mayst challengeth any voting member of the board for cause only. This challenge is madeth only on the grounds which plainly discloseth that the member canst not rendereth a fair and impartial decision. The challenged member mayst be examined by thee, thy counsel and other members of the board. The commanding officer, upon being informed of the circumstances of the challenge and the recommendations of the other members, mayst appointeth a substitute for the challenged member if he deemeth such action appropriate.

Thou mayst at any time before the board conveneth or during the proceedings submit any answer, deposition, oral or written sworn or unsworn statement, affidavit, certificate or stipulation in thy behalf.

Thou mayst request, in writing, the appearance before the board of any witness whose testimony ye believeth wilt be pertinent to the case. Ye musth specify in thy request the type of information the witness canst provideth.

Thou mayst or mayst not submit to examination by the board. Thy failure to submit to examination before the board mayst not be considered prejudicial.

Ye or thy counsel mayst question any witnesses appearing before the board.

Failure to invoketh any of these rights, after thou hath been apprised of same, canst not be considered as a bar to the board proceedings, findings, or recommendations.

If ye elect to a hearing by the Administrative Discharge Board, the time and date wilt be announced by the Senior Member of the board.

His Lordship,

Cap'n Robert Whitaker

A Testament to Who I Am

On Friday the 13th, exactly one week from the date of my court-martial, did I find my self confronting yet another board with Sir Brook of Hart at my side to see that I received a fair and impartial hearing, the reality of which did slip through my fingers and out the door like a vapor as I watched that pompous little kahuna, Kihune, and the other members of the board take their seats with the predetermined dispositions that did drape their bodies and cast a pall over the proceedings.

As the preliminaries fell by the wayside, Sir Brook did hold the little kahuna responsible, during show and tell, for pooh-poohing last year's recommendation to discharge me for the less egregious reason of unsuitability, an accusation the XO would neither confirm nor deny even though his face did smack of guilt.

Yet, the XO continued to insist that he was perfectly capable of letting go of the conviction, he has held since he shared it with me over a year ago, that he would personally see that I paid dearly for my disobedience in obedience to Who I Am, thus dashing any hopes we'd had of having him removed from the board for cause.

"Gentlemen, today I am being considered for an administrative discharge based solely upon my judicial record since my first misstep onto the Davidson," I testified under oath when called to take the stand, I had lacked the power to see what had not been evident to me at the time. "While it is true that I have defied every aspect of military life, I only did so in response to an inner urge, calling for my complete nonparticipation in a way of life so abhorent to my being, that my body would burn with desire until I sparked a conflagration with the Navy, to satisfy Who I Am.

"Do you know what that's like, gentlemen, to have your body hijacked from both within and without—so that it is no longer at your command—by forces so diametrically opposed that you don't even know which way to turn until the one gains the upper hand? Well, I'll tell you what it's like, pure hell.

"At first, I nonparticipated unwillingly, as I feared the consequences, and lacked a reason for doing so, the two words God had commissioned me to find after I had fasted from all food for twenty days, an action or lack thereof that brought my plight to the attention of the command, even though I could only explain it in terms of my bodily urges, the only manner in which my plight did express itself in those days. As my courage increased over time, I grew less fearful of the punishment meted out to me, and over time, began to participate more fully in a kingdom that was not of this world, and that often pulled me from the murderous realm—I had entered when I went on active duty—at the most inopportune times, making it look as if I had abandoned the Navy, which in deed I had.

"Having failed to report, on 13 May '67, the approach of an oncoming torpedo after hitting Captain Stanfield in the head with orange peelings I had thrown over the side while standing watch during a fleet exercise, I was charged with dereliction of duty, with abandoning my post, not in body but in spirit, to indulge a fantasy that had demanded my immediate attention. For my efforts or lack thereof, was I awarded thirty days of extra duty at the first of six captain's masts, I would face while I remained in Egypt under the tutelage of the Father in heaven, for the Pharoah would not let go his grip on me until this Moses had proved, once and for all, that he should be released for his adherence to a Higher Authority than any man-made law, or transgression thereof in obedience to the One, being held hostage here, against His Will.

"Again, on 29 June 1967, was I charged with participating in the affairs of this world according to the New Testament rather than the Uniform Code of Military Justice, when I made an urgent head-call, on two different occasions, without first getting permission from the petty officer in charge—who was never anywhere to be found—as I had been ordered, whether I had to defecate or not. For having twice failed to go, at the time prescribed, to my appointed place of duty, and for having failed to obey an order that took not the needs of my body into consideration, I was awarded twenty days of extra duty and was busted to the rank of a seaman recruit.

"On 10 October, I would again be charged with having failed to go, at the time prescribed, to my appointed place of duty, when I left the head, to which I'd been assigned, without the approval of whom I knew not, to fetch what I did lack, the scouring powder to clean the head. For my awful crime, was I restricted to the ship for fourteen days, and ordered to perform 45 days of extra duty, neither of which could impede the work that consumed me, the incarnation of Who I Am.

"By 18 November '67, I was back before the Captain for what I knew not until I was informed of the charges against me, that I had been derelict in the performance of my duties, in that I had failed to shave that morning, and had left my appointed place of duty to experience at-one-ment with my soul. For my transgressions on the physical plane, I forfeited a half month's pay, and was confined to the Naval Station Brig at Pearl Harbor for thirty days of correctional custody.

"Well, I have to tell you, gentlemen, I was in heaven while I was in the brig, for I had finally found where I belonged. And despite my fear of confinement, I fell so in love with the space it provided me, that when the time came, I did not want to leave. So wonderful had been my sojourn there, why in the world would I ever want to go back to where I didn't belong. But back to hell was I dragged, kicking and screaming on the inside, and making such a commotion within, that I barely made it up the gangplank before I blacked out, so distraught was I over my loss.

"As Christmas came and went without incident, I went on leave for thirty days on 6 January 1968, which turned out to be a real eye-opener when I ran across an article in the Atlantic Monthly, in which Leo Tolstoy advises *'he who has been called upon for military service—that is, called upon to kill or to prepare himself to kill—and who wants to be moral,* that *such a person,'* as I AM, *'must refuse to take part in military service no matter the consequences.'*

"With that, did I return to free Who I Am from the shackles of an ironclad lie by circulating copies of Tolstoy's letter about the ship, a tactical maneuver for which I was taken to task and was sent, on 20 February, to see the first psychiatrist to ever ask why I had never applied for discharge as a conscientious objector, words I had never heard before I consulted the dictionary the good doctor handed me. The instant their meaning greeted my eyes, I started crying and laughing at the same time, so overjoyed was I with having found Who I Am.

"I Am Who I Am, a conscientious objector, had I foisted upon Captain Whitaker at my next mast, on 11 March 1968, for having disobeyed an order, disrespected a superior petty officer, and destroyed government property in a fit of rage to gain recognition for Who I Am, so help me God, crimes of passion for which I was fined half a month's pay and confined to heaven for another twenty days of correctional custody under the direction of the spirit guides who do dwell in such high places.

"My command, however, turned a cold shoulder toward me, but no more so than did the fleet chaplain who reported to the Captain, after a brief debate with the person I AM, that I am no more a conscientious objector than he or the Captain, neither of whom was any better a judge of character, in God's eyes, than the other.

"In my bid to get back to where I belonged after having been released from the brig for time served, did I refuse to salute a god whom I did not serve, out of deference to the God I do serve, which resulted in a summary court–martial, on 16 April, that found me guilty of failing to salute a false god, and sentenced me to forfeit $90 of pay for one month, and to thirty days at hard labor, this time, under lock and key rather than as a trustee out front. At that point, I informed the officer, presiding over the court–martial, to expect more of the same until I was placed in a noncombatant status while the Navy considers me for discharge as a conscientious objector.

"Having had my eyes opened to the existence of guidelines for processing requests for discharge as a conscientious objector, I found Article C–5210 in the BUPERS Manual, once I returned to the ship, and wrote down the questions I would have to answer, to even be considered for discharge as a CO.

"In the interim, did I defy a direct order from the Captain, in deference to the will of the Father, when I let slip from my hand a single leaflet that did ignite a firestorm, a slight of hand for which I was convicted at a captain's mast, fined half a month's pay for two months, and confined, on 6 June, to a cell at the back of the brig for 30 days of correctional custody, enough time for me to complete my application for discharge as a CO in the peace and quiet of my own womb.

"After having made several attempts to submit my claim, following my release from the brig, a superior petty officer ordered me to load ammunition, contrary to the Sovereign Will of my being, leaving me with no other choice than to recuse my Self from this prelude to violence, a charge for which I received a rather hastily concocted summary court–martial that was referred to a special court–martial when I refused to cooperate with the proceedings without my attorney at my side.

"Later that month, was I charged with disobeying an order to remove a peace symbol hanging from a chain around my neck, a charge for which I would later be found guilty, and at the same special court–martial, not guilty of having disobeyed an order that, according to the BUPERS Manual, I should never have been given once I had expressed the desire to be processed out of the Navy as a conscientious objector.

"So you see, gentlemen, that all my actions were the mere manifestations of a body that wanted nothing to do with what it perceived as evil but lacked the awareness to convey that message in any other manner than having as little to do with this occasion for sin as possible. Once I woke up to my true calling in life, my actions were all directed toward getting me back to where I belonged, whether that be the temporary haven, the brig provided, or noncombatant status while I sought discharge from the Navy as a conscientious objector."

With that, did Brook hand a copy of my CO claim to the board and dismiss me from the stand without further ado.

After closing remarks from both sides, the Board adjourned.

So hastily had the proceedings been conducted, I felt as if it all had been a dream from which I had just awakened. Now, I had only to await word as to whether Washington concurred with whatever the members of this nightmare of a board decided in the secret machinations of their own minds.

Outside, I ran into Chief Neely who had this to say in passing: "Today, I heard words I would never have expected to come from the mouth of a recruit. I only wish that I had known."

"Me too," I fired back ere he disappeared. "Life would've been a lot simpler."

Back to hell was I dragged, and nailed to the cross where birds of prey swirled about my head, and the days dragged on and on, with no end in sight.

Then one day, came word that all reserves, who had served eighteen months or more of active duty as of 1 October 1968, were eligible for early discharge.

Clearly, I fell under the spell of that mandate until I was told that I didn't qualify because I was on administrative hold, pending the completion of my sentence and word from Washington as to the nature of my discharge. At first, I felt as if God had let me down, but soon realized that my path aimed at expelling me as a misfit rather than a killer under honorable conditions.

Before the reserve cut, only one other member of the crew, a signalman named Rick Little, would apply for discharge as a conscientious objector, a pronouncement that came out of nowhere and about knocked me off my feet.

"In the past, when I would sit and listen to you talk," had Rick confessed to me that day, "what you had to say seemed so foreign to me, that your words, even your actions, roared past me as if I were untouchable. Little did I know that like water they were slowly percolating down close to my heart to awaken the seeds of truth lying dormant there. Then, one morning I woke up and there it was, right in front of me, the next step in my life. I knew exactly what I had to do, but shuddered at the thought, considering what you have gone through. I didn't say anything to you, at the time, because I was afraid you would question my motives before I'd had a chance to look into them."

"I sure would've, even as I do now," confessed the doubting Thomas in me.

"As did I," had Rick assured me.

"And I, my own motives," I acknowledged, "only because I had judged myself as unworthy of such a calling."

"Yeah, I felt the same way," added Rick.

"Huh, I wonder if other COs are plagued with the same doubts?" Puzzled I over a matter for which not even he had an answer before we had to part ways and embrace our temporal duties.

So inane was the two hours of extra duty I was being asked to perform each day, that I ruffled a Chief's feathers when I only shined a spot, the size of a fifty-cent piece, on a ladder from which he had ordered me to remove all the tarnish.

"Why you little prick, I oughta ring your neck," cast the Chief such shadowy aspersions upon me as he grabbed me by the arm and got up in my face upon his return to see what I had accomplished in two hours.

"You best be taking your hands off me if you don't want to lose your rank as a Chief for having manhandled a subordinate," had I reminded the Chief of the consequences for his actions.

With nothing more to be said, did he let go his grip on me and stalk off down the passageway, turning just enough, at one point, to give me the finger.

After thanking God for my deliverance from evil, I shook my head in disbelief and went below to recover from the glancing blow of the cocky knight in khaki.

To ash did September leave no more to remember than a dying ember.

By that time, I had twenty-one more days of extra duty and another five weeks of restriction to wade through before I could resume my role as a knight around the Resistance Round Table, for all else was meaningless drudgery that was not of God's doing. With Sirs Jay and Brook checking up on me at least once a week, I didn't feel so forlorn, which seemed to make the time go by a little faster as I yearned for more freedom to exercise my right to protest the American War in Vietnam.

On 17 October, the day before the ship deployed for Vietnam, those who qualified for the reserve cut were rounded up and hustled off ere I could tell a single one good-bye.

And since the ship could not take an avowed CO into a combat zone, I was transferred to the USS Goldsborough DDG-20, while I awaited word from Washington on the status of my claim.

As I prepared to leave the ship, I asked the XO, who was standing nearby, if he would have held on to me as long as he had, knowing what he knew now.

"Well, we tried to make life for you as miserable as possible, hoping you would go AWOL or commit some other grievous offense," he confessed. "But you proved to be much stronger and smarter than we had anticipated. You would only commit little piddly offenses, just enough to get under our skin, and keep us from sentencing you to Portsmouth, and sticking you with a bad conduct discharge. In hindsight, we should have gotten rid of you a long time ago."

"It was all God's doing," I assured him with a smile before I disembarked, never to see his sorry ass again.

With only three more days of extra duty, and another nineteen days of restriction to suffer through, did I walk up the gangplank to board the last place any sane person would expect to find an avowed CO and war resister awaiting expulsion from the Navy.

"What the hell am I doing here?" I asked my Self as I handed my evil orders to the officer of the deck who summoned another inmate serving time to show me to my quarters below, where I was impounded for the remainder of my sentence.

"Patience, my son," had the Self I AM counseled the self I am not. "'I' have seen to it that you will be asked to do no more than the law allows."

Upon my arrival, I was immediately placed in a noncombatant status by the XO who, in turn, asked me what duties I was or was not willing to perform.

"I refuse to handle a weapon or load ammunition, to participate in general quarters or stand watches as I am under strict orders from the Spirit to perform only the duties of a compartment cleaner if I wish to stay in Her good graces, and compromise my position as a CO any further than do these lethal weapons upon which the Navy insists on sticking me, against Her wishes, presumably to make an example out of me. If I am asked to do anything that offends the Spirit, I am under orders from Her to sit down on the deck, as I have in the past, with legs crossed, and take no food by mouth until She lets me know that I am no longer under duress," I informed him with all due respect and the calmness of the Spirit, Who was putting words into my mouth faster than I could regurgitate them.

"I give you my word," he assured me at the direction of the Spirit, "that you will not be asked to do anything that conflicts with your beliefs. However, I do expect you to observe the rules of life aboard the ship, such as attending quarters in the morning, reporting to your duty station on time, and performing your duties as a compartment cleaner in a seamanlike manner. And since you are still restricted to the ship, I also expect you to report to the quarterdeck when asked to do so, to let the officer of the deck know that you are still onboard and haven't left the ship at any time between calls."

"In addition, I am placing you with the shipfitters since that is where you served while you were onboard the Davidson," had he concluded.

"I think I can handle that," had the Spirit nudged me into saying with a smile. "And I appreciate your candor."

"As do I, yours," had the Spirit put words into his mouth, that he would never have expressed otherwise.

"You may go now," he then told me.

"Thank you, Sir," I replied as I departed, thinking that I may have blown his mind with matters he had never encountered before nor may ever encounter again—close encounters of the fourth kind.

With no one to talk to, in the days ahead, I moved about the ship as if I were wearing the cloak of the Spirit which made me invisible to everyone who could not see what we saw in them, souls enslaved to a lost cause, a battle of men's making rather than of God's for which many would pay with their lives. Except for visits from Jay and calls from Brook, I suffered through the last days of my restriction as Christ had, the final hours of His restriction to a dead way of life, but without all the bloodletting that preceded His death at the hands of those willing to kill, on command, anyone deemed to be an enemy of the state.

During that first week on the Goldsborough, I finally received news that Washington had rejected the admin board's recommendation on the grounds that the sitting members, consisting of officers on the Davidson with whom I had had run-ins at one time or another, were not capable of rendering a fair and impartial decision as to whether I should be discharged, and if so, with what type of discharge.

As a followup, did I receive another notice, on 23 October, from the Commanding Officer of the Goldsborough, that I was again being considered for an undesirable discharge, and that if I desired to have my case heard before an administrative board, I could do so at a hearing scheduled to convene at 0900 hours on 7 November 1968, in the General Court–Martial Room of the Commandant, Fourteenth Naval District, U.S. Naval Station, Pearl Harbor, Hawaii.

Right away, did I notify Sir Brook, who was no more surprised than I had been when I heard that I'd been spared the wrath of the Davidson, only to face yet another board packed with men for whom the letter of the law would prevent them from recognizing Who I Am in the breaking of the law in choosing to *"obey God rather than men"*. Acts 5:29.

In the days ahead, would I be subjected to the vagaries of naval gunfire as the gunner's mates in the forward and aft gun mounts took turns ad nauseam, taking potshots at a stripped-down, decommissioned, World War II era tin can. At some point in a long lull, I happen to step out onto the main deck as an antiship missile took its first step, and then another before the misguided projectile honed in on the doomed vessel and dispatched it to its watery grave to lie in state, for the rest of eternity, with a gaping hole in its side.

"What a waste!" Had I declared to those who have misconstrued the meaning of military service as service to God and one's fellow countrymen, for nothing could be any farther from the truth than this lie, the greatest deception ever perpetrated by mankind to convince young men to kill each other to advance or protect a way of life not of God's doing, by twisting and turning God's gifts to us into an abomination of weaponry to which we pay homage with our son's and daughter's lives and all the talent we can steal from God and our fellow countrymen.

But alas, my fellow shipmates have never experienced what I have heard coming forth from the mouths of those inner mediators through whom the Father had toiled, day and night, to mold and shape me into His own image and likeness, the conscientious objector I AM.

"For *'one does not live by bread alone, but by every word that comes forth from the mouth of God'*," (Mt 4:4) had I reminded the members of the board as I summed up my testimony on the seventh of the second ember of '68.

"It is my sincerest hope that my testimony has enabled you to see the obedience to Who I Am in the disobedience of who I am not—the love in the perceived sin of choosing to live in the Father as He lives in me, in contradistinction to everything for which the Navy stands. For it was He Who made me this way, and when the time came, pulled me from the depths of the Big Sleep to mentor me in the ways of a conscientious objector until I was able to live in Him as He lives in me with the unyielding determination of the one true God I AM. I am a conscientious objector, not a killer, and I want no part in the killing of other human beings as manifested in my behavior toward the Navy over the past year and a half, that all might see what it's like to live in Him as He lives in those who have chosen to live in Him, often under the most adverse conditions imaginable."

Before I was excused from the witness stand, Brook asked me to clarify a matter I had touched upon in my CO claim but had never mentioned in court or at a hearing, regarding my sixth grade teacher, Sister Mary Paulus, and the tremendous influence she'd had on me.

"Ah, yes, Sister Mary Paulus," I recalled with a sigh too deep for words.

"If only she were here today, she would be proud of the diamond she saw in the rough, and tried to polish ere the time came for him to stand out from the body of mankind as a beacon for all to see their way through the storm that would engulf them in the vicissitudes of a war not of God's doing. And she did this by instilling in me a love for my fellow man that relied not on guns but on Christ to win the hearts of those who had been indoctrinated in the ways of the Old Testament, of taking an eye for an eye, and a tooth for a tooth instead of turning the other cheek, to be slapped and spat upon as if love were the ugliness the sinful see in the sinless rather than in themselves.

"She taught me how to pray from the heart, and how to wait for it to open itself up to receiving any word from God in whatever form it might come, whether that be through an active imagination or something as dramatic as a burning bush, for God only speaks frankly to those who have an open mind.

"'So don't be afraid if you hear voices or see visions, for they are all perfectly normal,' she once told me. 'Just ask them what they want, and they will tell you.'

"'For the day will come when you will remember me in your need to know how to proceed with your soul under seige,' had she prophesied. 'May you have the fortitude to cling to God when that day sets upon you like a thief in the night to rob you of your soul and the great mental capacity you possess for doing good.'

"'Take care, my child,' blubbered she with the Spirit at her side to console her as I moved on with a heavy heart, never to see her again in the flesh.

"Sister Mary was the first person to have introduced me to Gandhi through a little blurb in the monthly messenger we received while I was still in grade school at St. Michael the Archangel—a memory that has only recently come to the surface to serve me well."

MR. HART: *Now you stated that within a month upon your entry upon active duty, you engaged in activities outside of naval regulations, including I think the first activity which you state was a hunger strike. At that time, did you have any knowledge that you could have claimed status as a conscientious objector?*

RESPONDENT: *I did not.*

MR. HART: *Then your statement was that the first time you had such knowledge was when you spoke with the psychiatrist in February of '68.*

RESPONDENT: *That's correct.*

MR. HART: *Before you came into the service did you know whether or not a deferment for conscientious objection could be granted to one as a civilian?*

RESPONDENT: *I did not for the simple reason that I didn't even know there was such a thing as a conscientious objector.*

MR. HART: *I have no further questions.*

Only, I had yet to assure the Senior Member of the Board I understood that the statement I had made as testimony on my behalf would be given fair weight in the proceedings of the Board, and that I had elected to make the statement to submit for further appending to the forwarding letter with whatever recommendation, the Board came up with, to the Chief of Naval Personnel.

With that, did Brook submit one further piece of evidence he felt might be of help to the Board during their deliberations—a copy of my CO claim.

At that point, was I finally excused from the witness stand so that I might recall the testimonies of Father Dever and Professor Douglass who had actually testified before I had.

Looking back, Brook asked Father Dever, after having established his credibility with a few preliminary questions, if he had formed an opinion as to my sincerity.

FR. DEVER: *Yes, I have taken him to be perfectly sincere right from the beginning, and since then I have felt my judgment is correct. Although I've had several persons come in, this was the first one I had that meant a lot to me because it is so difficult to be sincere when taking a position on conscientious objection within the Roman Catholic Church where there is an ambiguity in theory, a just war theory that was created at the time of St. Augustine, to allow Christians to participate in the defense of their country and in warfare. Previously, the Church had taken a very hard line position against the participation of Christians in war. This other position of a just war then went on for another thousand years before they started to reevaluate that, to consider whether the principles to justify war still hold up, such as whether noncombatants would not be injured, that a greater good would come from war, that it was a matter of lasting good, and so forth.*

Also coming out again in new force is the earlier Christian position of pacifism that has run consistently through theology but now and then sort of underground. And I think this is what I mean by the ambiguity. Both are vying for a principal position in theology today, and I think—although I am not a pacifist—I've been very interested in this case to see whether we could come to a conclusion that a man who has thought deeply about it today would be able to be accepted as a sincere conscientious objector. And I have drawn that conclusion in the case of Mr. Drury.

MR. HART: *Now did you know that Mr. Drury has been involved in numerous actions which were in violation of the Uniform Code of Military Justice?*

FR. DEVER: *I took it to be, as far as he expressed himself, consistent, that is, this is how I call attention to my case. For the reason that I mentioned earlier, particularly with the Roman Catholics, there's a feeling—not here, gentlemen, but in the community and in the Church, that a Roman Catholic is not always sincere when he talks about conscientious objection. And so the hearing, the ready access, the receptivity of such a person is not great, and sometimes all you can do is create a fuss, or a commotion, and I took it to be that.*

MR. HART: *Would you characterize these things as basic immaturity, or do you think it might reflect upon Drury's credibility?*

FR. DEVER: *It didn't for me reflect upon his credibility. Whether I would, if I were in that position, choose that way of acting, I think, is not pertinent. I don't know whether it was a matter of immaturity either, but if I were in the same position, it may be the only option, and so it may look like immaturity—certainly it would not reflect on credibility. And it may be a very courageous and mature way of acting even though under some other standards, it could be looked upon negatively.*

MR. HART: *Now, through your knowledge of Drury, could you express to the Board what your opinion would be with respect to Drury's adjustment in civilian life after he is discharged from the service, no matter what kind of discharge he gets?*

FR. DEVER: *Well, if I had a job opening, I would hire him. I have perfect confidence in him. In fact, as I understand, he would not have to be here now, he would already have been discharged if he had not chosen to take this course of action which therefore is of a great inconvenience to him as he continues to remain within the system, and make a contribution in terms of going along with the democratic processes involved. I have been very impressed with the number of hearings, the very elaborate process the military has evolved to handle cases like this. So that his being here, even going through this process is serving the cause and the country, and is a benefit to all of us in a democratic society. I think we could be proud of what I have seen here, considering what we have heard from courts in a totalitarian society, the kind of justice meted out. So I think it has been a very mature action on his part and one that shows courage and sacrifice. I would recommend him for a job or hire him myself if I had one for him.*

Having no further questions, Brook then turned the interrogation of Father Dever over to the Recorder, Lieutenant Gleason, who asked Father Dever how he felt about someone not obeying the law.

FR. DEVER: *Well, as I look at it in this context there is something far more important, even to me, and that is the man, the opportunity to express himself, to be himself and be heard. And if that expression, or the acceptability to a hearing, and if their judgment is limited, and if perhaps that's the only way a person feels in a situation he can express himself, through minor misdemeaners, such an expression would be acceptable to me in the light of the total good that was attained by it.*

RECORDER: *You know that a person who disobeys the law will have to answer for it.*

FR. DEVER: *Well, I wouldn't want to answer that in general, sir. Again restricting it to this case and to the very important realization that there is a great delay in justice in a matter of conscientious objection, that when a man finds himself in a situation where he maybe shouldn't be accepted, I believe the system is inadequate. In that case—and I'm not speaking of Mr. Drury having been subject to the draft—but I mean in the total context of our boys being brought in and then only later on beginning to have a chance to reflect, and yet within the system not being given enough opportunity to express themselves, I can see the importance of the curbing of this. I mean where would we be in the organization if everybody can say "I opt out now".*

But because of this need for order in an organization, and obedience and so forth, there is a tendency not to give a person as quick a hearing, or be receptive and responsive to his expression of conscience, and so in a case like this there are misdemeanors which force the issue. They are relatively minor in light of the total issue before us. And I would think they are quite acceptable in the long run.

With that, did the Recorder stand down to allow Brook a final question.

MR. HART: *So that there is no confusion on this, I want to ask you whether this is your position, that while you don't condone activist behavior, your testimony here is that you find that such acts may be the only way that a man in Drury's circumstances is able to bring his CO claim to the attention of his superior officers. Is that your testimony?*

FR. DEVER: *Yes, and in fact I do not want to deny that they do not violate the Code. I'm saying "I", and I'm outside of this thing looking in, would still justify them in terms of the larger context and the greater good, even though I admit that they are misdemeanors and they violate the Code.*

There being no further questions by any member of the Board, the Recorder or Counsel, Father Dever was excused and withdrew from the courtroom.

Professor Douglass then took the stand, and after answering a series of questions to establish his credibility, testified as follows:

MR. HART: *Did you have any knowledge at that time in May when you made the decision that Mr. Drury was a conscientious objector, as to what it takes to make a case that one is in fact a conscientious objector?*

PROF. DOUGLASS: *Well, he would be a conscientious objector in quite the traditional sense. He had based his belief that he was a conscientious objector on his faith in Jesus Christ, because of the teachings of the Catholic Church with regard to warfare, and in particular with regard to the teaching of the Gospel. He believed from his understanding in conscience of Jesus' words in the Gospel that one should not kill, and this is quite a traditional position for a conscientious objector, and he believed in no killing whatsoever, so that his position and views were extremely solid, both from a biblical standpoint and also from the teaching of the Church in the Vatican Council which upholds the right of conscientious objection.*

MR. HART: *Now, Professor Douglass, are you familiar with Section 6(j) of the Military Selective Service Act of 1967, as it pertains to conscientious objection?*

PROF. DOUGLASS: *Yes, I am.*

MR. HART: *Will you tell the Board your understanding of that section as it applies to Drury?*

PROF. DOUGLASS: *As far as religious training and belief goes, he explained to me in my office that morning that it was due—I asked him what the background was that led to this conviction. He related it to his teachings and his training in a parochial school, St. Louis I suppose it was. He recalled his teaching with regard to love and charity, Jesus, and a particular Sister in that school. He related it very much to his whole Catholic faith, and he believed from his examination of the Scriptures and from his understanding of Christ which he had been taught in his background that one really should not kill. And he said that he had reexamined this very carefully in the years since he had gone into the Navy because new questions had been raised and many things had returned to him at that time, and that these positions had solidified during that period.*

MR. HART: *Has Drury ever told you that he has been involved in petty offenses against the Uniform Code of Military Justice?*

PROF. DOUGLASS: *Yes, the first one when he was in the brig.*

MR. HART: *And did you form any opinion as to the relationship of these offenses and his claim as a conscientious objector?*

PROF. DOUGLASS: *These offenses, if you want to call them that, were simply statements of his belief to bring his position to the attention of his officers and the other people on board the ship. The protest in the brig, if you want to call it that,* when he put on a T-shirt, the saying "Christ taught nonviolence", is what I understood all of his actions were, statements of what his conscience believed.

MR. HART: *Were you able to form an opinion with respect to Drury's sincerity?*

PROF. DOUGLASS: *From the first moment I met him, I believed that he was absolutely sincere and absolutely truthful. In all the time that I've met with him, I have never had the slightest question that he was not telling the truth. And I've had questions about other people. I think he is one of the most truthful men I have ever met.*

MR. HART: *Through your contacts with Drury, would you be able to express an opinion as to the type of discharge that this Board might award him?*

PROF. DOUGLASS: *Well, I think that the Navy should be honored to have a person who takes such responsibility with regard to the actions which have been carried on in the way that Drury does. I think my understanding of what one should do in any position, whether it would be in the Navy or in civilian life, is to understand the nature of his job, what you're supposed to do, and then to take the responsibility for it. And I would assume that people whom the Navy is proud of, who are going to war, are those people who believe in it. Mr. Drury does not believe in it and I would think from that standpoint that the Navy should release him and not make him go to war, in the same way that a person in a civilian occupation who does not believe in a particular job and says in conscience that he cannot remain part of it, I think this business should honor him by respecting that position and severing the relationship, if there is an honest relationship between the two of them. I would think that this kind of responsibility speaks well for itself in the Navy, whether it's a position for or against the Navy.*

MR. HART: *What would be a good example where a man, who is working for a business, disagrees with the policy of the management, and takes steps to sever the relationship. How would they act with respect to references? In other words, the analogy here being that the Navy is in a position to award a discharge, which could be an excellent reference, an honorable discharge; a general discharge, which would be a very good reference; or an undesirable discharge, which would be a very poor reference that might ruin your life.*

PROF. DOUGLASS: *In a particular instance which makes the analogy quite close, there is a gentleman in Honolulu who had been working for the telephone company as an executive for the last thirty years, and who recently told the phone company that he felt he had to leave the company because he worked in a peace group, and wanted to work for civil rights, but found that he felt less free to do this as an executive where everywhere he carried the telephone company behind him. And in that instance, the relationship was one of respect on both sides, and the man left with the highest recommendations. I see no reason why the Navy can't operate with as much respect for conscience as an institution in civilian life.*

MR. HART: *Even though one of the ways, the Respondent has brought attention to the Navy, was by violating, on numerous occasions, the Uniform Code of Military Justice?*

PROF. DOUGLASS: *If there were a procedure whereby a conscientious objector could be discharged expeditiously from the Navy, this situation would never have arisen; or if there had been a response from the commanding officer to his initial statement, that situation would never have arisen. I think that the primary problem with a conscientious objector in the service today is that it is very well known that very few men are given discharges as conscientious objectors, which leads to a greater increase in desertion and to disobedience of commands in the Navy because either the man will feel that he cannot go through the proper procedure at all, or will not be given a "Yes" to his request—in which case he will desert—or he feels that the only way to bring this to the attention of his officers is by disobeying an order if these procedures are not fulfilled in any other way.*

MR. HART: *Now, some of Drury's offenses predate the first time he made any kind of formal request to any superior officer concerning conscientious objection. Relying on your knowledge, can you shed any light on this problem for the Board? There seems to be some kind of inconsistency here, and Drury's record shows these offenses.*

PROF. DOUGLASS: *Well, I don't think Mr. Drury even knew that there was such a thing as conscientious objection, just as I think many people throughout the United States know that there is such a provision in law for conscientious objectors. I think it is even less well known in the service that there is a provision in military law for a conscientious objector.*

When he came to see me in the office, the concept of conscientious objection was relatively new to him. He was quite excited by the fact that he had learned there was such a thing which gave him a legal basis for his position against killing, so that someone in his position, who doesn't know anything about conscientious objection, is not left thinking that he has only one option, and that is to say "No, I will not participate in any action against my conscience."

MR. HART: *Do you see a problem for someone in Drury's circumstances, where there is a supreme law on the one hand, the law of God, which takes precedence over the law of man, and the law in the Uniform Code of Military Justice?*

PROF. DOUGLASS: *Well, it is a very old problem, how any man responds to a law that is in conflict with his conscience. Perhaps the classic statement of this in our own time, from a dramatic standpoint, is the story of St. Thomas More, how he went as far as he could under the law before he had to say that neither the law nor the authorities recognize what I must in conscience do. At this point, I have to say no.*

There are all kinds of tensions between morality and a man's belief and the overall law. It is a permanent human condition. And if law is not behind the moral character of where a society is moving or should move, it's only by taking such positions in conscience that the law will eventually change to respond to consciences. This is always the tension, that the consciences of individual men will always be out ahead of the law. And for this reason, it's extremely important that there be nonviolent acts of conscience in order to move the law towards such changes. I believe that men such as Mr. Drury will make it more recognized that there must be recognition of the need for discharges for conscientious objectors from military service.

MR. HART: *The fact that discharge is provided for in naval regulations...*

PROF. DOUGLASS: *It is provided for, but in fact, under the current policy with regard to conscientious objectors, very few are granted. I think the policy, the way it is now, is blocked. In fact, I should add that I spoke to Senator Inouye about two months ago, and discussed this problem with him because he is on a committee in Congress to approach the problem of desertion from the armed forces. I suggested to him that the reason why there is such a high level of desertion is that there is, in effect, no provision made for conscientious objectors to be released from the service.*

Into the ring, leapt an eager Recorder when Brook abdicated questioning of the witness to Mr. Gleason.

RECORDER: *Professor, you say that there is no provision in the law for conscientious objectors, or rather, there is a provision in the law for conscientious objectors, but that policies differ in the way it's carried out. Have you made a study of this?*

PROF. DOUGLASS: *No, my knowledge of this is only from knowledge of individual objectors like Mr. Drury who have a general belief that these applications are not expedited, and from reading reports from groups like the Central Committee for Conscientious Objectors who have made studies of this. And if in fact this is not true, then the armed services should make it known, because it is believed by almost everyone that that is not the case today, that these applications for conscientious objection are, as a policy, being denied with very few exceptions.*

RECORDER: *Do you know why Drury was referred to your attention?*

PROF. DOUGLASS: *He was not referred to my attention. He said he had read an article in the newspaper which had included statements of mine against the American War in Vietnam. He said he felt that I might be someone he could speak to about this.*

RECORDER: *Are you associated with any political group?*

PROF. DOUGLASS: *No political group. I'm affiliated with religious groups who are opposed to the war, clergy and laymen who are concerned about the American War in Vietnam, a nationwide group which has a chapter here in Hawaii. I also support a group of men who in conscience do not cooperate with the draft.*

RECORDER: *What is your relationship to the organization?*

PROF. DOUGLASS: *I assume you are referring to the Resistance. It is a relationship of support; and I help them in any way I can to state that this is a moral position of which they can be proud, and that I will stand in solidarity with them on this position. I have engaged in demonstrations with them, and attend their meetings regularly.*

RECORDER: *You say Drury came to you after a study of conscience and the Scriptures, and decided he wanted to be a conscientious objector?*

PROF. DOUGLASS: *He had studied the Scriptures and realized that he could not agree to kill, and it was sometime later that he realized that there was conscientious objection to which he could appeal in law for this position.*

RECORDER: *How did he approach this commitment?*

PROF. DOUGLASS: *His commitment was quite profound before he ever heard about me. If I'm not mistaken, he was in the brig when he read the article about me, for having disobeyed some orders.*

RECORDER: *And this was an outgrowth of these studies, pure and simple?*

PROF. DOUGLASS: *Yes, I would say so. I would say that it takes a significant degree of maturity to reach such a conviction in a situation quite discouraging to it. I mean to reach a position of conscientious objection once one is already in the service is a very hard thing to do. It is much easier to say, "Well, I'll wait until I get out." But he reached these convictions in a process which was working in the opposite direction, and knew, of course, this would be very painful for him.*

Having no further questions, the Recorder stepped aside to allow Brook to ask a few more for clarity's sake.

MR. HART: *Regarding Mr. Drury's maturity, would you distinguish between his maturity with respect to his convictions, at the time he objected, and his maturity with respect to certain petty misdeeds with respect to his military duties?*

PROF. DOUGLASS: *Well, I don't think that once Mr. Drury agreed to take a position of this sort in the Navy with no one really on his side, and without any support from anyone on the outside, prior to coming to me, one could expect that this action, as an individual in conscience, could be considered to be a responsible one from the standpoint of his superiors, because the whole direction of their* notion of responsibility is in a completely opposite direction from his. And without any knowledge that he had a legal way to express these views, it would of course, from that standpoint, be seen as an irresponsible action because it was in the opposite direction. I personally would not describe these actions as immature, but I can certainly understand how they would consider these actions immature.

MR. HART: *Earlier, you gave some testimony about how the Navy and other branches of the armed services have handled conscientious objectors, even though the Military Selective Service Act of 1967 provides for their exemption, and the Naval regulation C–5210 provides an elaborate procedure for the discharge of those who are found to be conscientious objectors. Now, is it your understanding that Mr. Drury was treated other than the way outlined in the applicable Navy regulations?*

PROF. DOUGLASS: *That is correct.*

MR. HART: *Does the Board have any questions?*

SENIOR MEMBER: *Mr. Douglass, during your testimony you used the analogy of a civilian employment where it might interfere with a conscientious and moral conviction of an employee. Without specifically relating to the case at hand, I would like to determine your feelings with regard to an employee who had certain commitments and obligations to that employer which he failed to carry out prior to reaching a relationship with the company which would allow him to honorably sever his relationship with that employer on the grounds of his moral convictions.*

PROF. DOUGLASS: *Well, the only function of such an analogy is if the analogy is completed, and that would mean, in the case of the employer and employee that you're talking about, that the employee had a contract with that company which would not permit him to leave it when the employer asked him to do something which he, in good conscience, could not do. This is the case that we're dealing with. In that case, of course, he would have to refuse, the same way that Sir Thomas More refused to do something which his King asked him to do even though he was profoundly attached and loyal to this King.*

There being no further questions, Professor Douglass was excused and withdrew from the courtroom.

To give the Recorder and Counsel time to prepare their closing arguments, the Board reconvened after a brief recess.

SENIOR MEMBER: *Mr. Hart, are you ready to present your closing statement?*
MR. HART: *Yes I am.*
Gentlemen, I think it is quite correct to say that having before you a man who has had as many infractions of the rules as Drury has had, the inclination would

be "Well, at the very least, the man ought to be discharged". His retention in the Navy under these circumstances would probably not be in the best interests of the Navy, and based on what Drury has offered today, it would hardly be in his best interests. Assuming that would be your conclusion, you would have to go one step further and determine what kind of discharge should he be awarded.

As you can see by his record in the presentation today, Drury is a young man who is really a diamond in the rough with high intelligence and extraordinary moral convictions, who can go into the world and in whatever area he chooses to study, most likely succeed.

I disagree with Mr. Gleason that you are not interested in extenuation and mitigation. I think this is just the kind of thing, gentlemen, which you should consider when you decide what to do with this man, and one of these matters has to do with Drury's repeated attempts to claim status guaranteed to him under the Statutes of the United States. And the Statute says that no person shall serve who, by religious training or belief, is conscientiously opposed to participation in war of any form. Drafted on the Statute is DoD Directive 1300.6 and Article C–5210 of the BUPERS Manual. And those regulations say that when a man makes a claim as a conscientious objector, certain things are to take place. He is to be assigned duty not inconsistent with his professed beliefs; he is to be counseled with respect to the law; and he need not submit any particular documentation immediately for the claim. It is only enough that he make the statement to his commanding officer, and a Board of Review has so held in the case of United States vs Sigmund. And it was on that case that the special court–martial relied in Drury's last court, in ruling that the order to load ammunition was an illegal order.

What Drury is trying to tell the Board is this: During the period of time from February '67 to February '68, I committed many acts, a hunger strike, negligence with respect to being absent from my post—we have one involving failure to get permission to go to the head—many petty acts, somewhat disruptive of the daily routine. This was a young man trying to make a statement in the only way he knew how. Most certainly, had he been more sophisticated, he would have gone to the Captain right away and said, "Listen, I'm a conscientious objector. And now I make my claim." But I think we have established that Drury did not know he had such rights in military law. Now you gentlemen know that these regulations—I don't know if you have them all here—there's a lot to them, and no officer in the service, or even an enlisted man, could know all of them. Certainly, one which applied to such a small percentage of the men in the Navy is unlikely to be known to a man in Drury's circumstances. In fact, he tells you—you may judge as to whether you believe him—he did not know that he had this right. And he did not know until that day in February 1968 when by chance he happened to have a meeting with a psychiatrist, that there was such a legal channel open to him, that there was a possibility without violating any regulations or running afoul of the system, he could have applied for the service to recognize his religious claim. But what happened after he learned that?

After he learned that he could make such application, his Captain, his Executive Officer, a Chaplain, a civilian from the Office of Naval Investigation, all took steps which, in one way or another, ignored or directly rebuffed Drury in his effort to make his claim. So it appears to me that you have to disregard substantially any of the acts of misconduct which occurred prior to February of '68, if you believe that Drury was sincerely trying to do the only thing that he could do to bring these matters to the attention of the Captain. Superior officers are charged under these regulations, under the **Department of Defense Directive 1300.6**, with certain duties which they failed to carry out. You have to look to see whether this course of conduct that preceded his attempts to have himself classified were part of his effort to make his claim known, and get it before those persons in Washington who decide. Now, how does this thing work?

The man makes his claim on a form which we have submitted. After he has made notice that he wants to claim, he is put on noncombatant duty, and counseled with respect to certain rights. He has a meeting with a psychiatrist, a meeting with a Chaplain, and another meeting—by the way, which I think is a recognition that there should be some personal contact between the Navy and the individual claiming this—and that is, that he is to be counseled and interviewed by an officer of the rank of O-3 and above. At that interview his attorney may be present. The officer of rank O-3 or above must have knowledge of the conscientious objector provisions, and must be familiar with claims made by conscientious objectors. In that interview, he is to determine what the sincerity and the nature of the belief of the applicant might be and write a report which is to be submitted to the Department of the Navy. And along with this goes certain recommendations for approval or disapproval of those in the chain of command.

All Drury wanted was that that procedure be afforded him in his case. And had anyone told him back when he came into the service—you recall the unusual conditions under which he came into the service—that this was open to him, you can only use your judgment to decide whether based on what he knew and what he did after he knew about his rights, he would have done that then. And he most likely would have refrained from these petty acts in which he engaged.

In addition, I think it would be relevant to point to this man's background with regard to his upbringing and his psychological training—a young man from a broken home. Now we aren't going to get out the tissue paper and rags at this time. We aren't asking the Board for sympathy of that kind. It's a factor that has been *a part of his life. It's a factor which will place this thing in the context in which you gentlemen can view it. And this broken home was an unusual broken home. It was not a mere divorce situation. It was a situation where his father had been committed at an early age due to shell shock after service in World War II, and his stepfather, apparently with a view towards what kind of education he should have, forced Drury, totally against his will, to go to the military academy at Annapolis. And even though the man is highly intelligent, graduated, as he said, 3 out of 356 in his class—probably could have gone on to any school in the country—in order to satisfy his parents and in order to go anywhere, he went to the Naval Academy. And how did he do there?—3.8 out of 4.0. I don't know whether any of you gentlemen have gone to the Naval Academy, but I know that the standards there are fairly high. So we have someone here who is perfectly capable of doing the job, but who is conscientiously and religiously opposed to what the Navy is doing.*

Now we may disagree with him as to whether what the Navy is doing is proper in our framework. Some of you may feel that what the Navy is doing is totally consistent with your own religious points of view. But one thing I think we would try to do is recognize that we do have good faith differences and agree that some of us would hold the positions that he does, in conscience and with a view towards his religion, and it would go unchallenged. In other words, what I'm saying is Drury's position isn't necessarily right or wrong, but it must be respected because it is conscientiously and sincerely held. Now this is not by way of saying that once one holds a position conscientiously and sincerely held, that he means he should violate the law. You have no more right, because you believe that it's proper to go 90 miles an hour, to go out and drive 90 miles an hour in a 30 mile an hour zone.

Perhaps it is easier to see this situation in his hunger strike, for instance, an act which was destructive to Drury. It was a statement of his sincerity, of his concern, of his feeling that there was something morally and religiously objectionable about the service he was being asked to do. This was not a situation where he tried to sabotage or take action against anyone, but one in which this man attempted to get the military to recognize his sincere religious objections according to its own regulations. Let me out of here, so that I can continue in society in a way which will not violate my beliefs. And this would be of no avail if Congress and our Department of Defense and the Department of the Navy had not known that there are such questions. And from what I can gather from the voir dire, few if any of you have had any contact with a conscientious objector before. I say if this is not one, what is one?

Now the man has certain convictions, he is entitled to make known. Why did he do so in a way which violated military regulations? Perhaps he could have done that under other conditions, where he knew he had such rights. After all, it's hard to inquire about something if you don't know that it exists, and you are put in a position to make it, with this man's particular psycho-social makeup. You have before you reports of doctors who have examined Drury in the course of his military service, and those reports, I think, indicate that the Navy was well aware of what Drury's psychological position was—I believe his first examination was April '67. This would have been a month or two after his initial incident of rebelling. Reading those reports which, I believe, you have had a chance to peruse, though you may want to read them more carefully, you see a situation here where you have a young man who has a certain amount of emotional instability in his makeup. Certain references to abnormal sexual adjustments and relationships are relevant in determining whether it would be reasonable to require this man to be held to a standard of conduct required of some other ethical man.

I call your attention specifically to the comments and recommendations of each of these doctors as they conclude their reports. Drury has been referred to as an emotionally unstable person with a schizoid personality. We need not go into the technical meaning of such terms; but we all know that this is something unusual. We all know that this man suffers under certain kinds of psychological disabilities that perhaps we do not suffer. And yet you gentlemen had a chance to observe this man's demeanor and make judgments about his credibility today with respect to his religious beliefs and his position and opposition to participation in war. Even with this other evidence, I ask you to consider whether those positions and oppositions are not sincerely held. I think you all can conclude that they are.

Now Dr. Lazaroff, a Lieutenant Commander and psychiatrist who saw Drury last February, says this: He has had continued difficulty in the service and it is recommended that he be given a trial of duty, and if there is any further difficulty, administrative discharge be considered for reasons of unsuitability—in other words, a general discharge for reasons of unsuitability due to Drury's inability to adjust. While the Navy was looking at this fellow and his inability to adjust, Drury was saying to the Navy, "Look, yes it's true that I can't adjust, but that's not the key inquiry. The key question here is, you do have regulations, you do have laws which recognize my religious convictions and my opposition to war and my failure to adjust based on my religious convictions. And I ask you not to kick me out because I'm emotionally unstable, which I may be, but because of the sincerity and depth and nature of my religious convictions".

But his commanding officer, and his executive officer, even a Chaplain and certain other individuals who had occasion to be questioned by Drury with respect to his rights, all ignored him. So he engaged in acts of petty violations. Finally, he disobeyed an order.

Taking into consideration Drury's psychological condition, and more importantly, his sincerely and deeply held convictions, I ask you in that framework to consider what type of discharge, if any, he should receive. I suppose you could recommend an honorable discharge. And whether it would be facetious of me to argue such an alternative to the Board, I don't know. But I think in some ways you might agree his way, his grappling with these deep problems of conscience, Drury is highly honorable. On the other hand, Drury has, and we readily admit, committed many minor offenses in the Navy. Would an honorable discharge in these circumstances recognize the fact that whatever we agree upon he has committed these offenses. Or you have the choice where you could give this man an undesirable discharge for reasons of misconduct or unfitness. This discharge would operate substantially to his prejudice for the rest of his life. It might prevent him from making the adjustment that he will seek to make, when and if he gets out of the service. It might prevent him from going to a school of his choice. It might prevent him from contributing in some helpful and constructive way to this country, which I think you all will agree he desires to do. It would certainly act as a continued punishment for his misdeeds in the Navy, all of which I have already pointed out to you. He has had adequate punishment.

And so it seems to me reasonable and equitable that you recommend a general discharge under honorable conditions for reasons of unsuitability as Drury is unsuited for the military. His religious beliefs and convictions do not allow him to contribute in any meaningful way to the military establishment. He might be able to contribute in some constructive way in a civilian capacity; and if he is awarded such a discharge, you gentlemen today will be taking the first step towards helping him in making that adjustment and becoming a loyal and productive citizen.

SENIOR MEMBER: *Thank you very much, Mr. Hart.*

RECORDER: *Gentlemen, perhaps I run the risk of sounding redundant, but I feel I must reiterate the question for your decision today, which is not whether Drury was justified in violating our Code, or whether he is a conscientious objector or not. The Bureau of Personnel is now in the process of deciding Drury's service classification. It is not for this Board to dwell upon. Drury has already been tried and sentenced by due process as to these offenses. That due process must be presumed authorized and correct. Now this case is an exceptional one for boards of this type because Drury committed these offenses deliberately. Counsel wants to shrug off Drury's offenses as those of an immature person. In fact, they have been classed as being petty. Gentlemen, I don't believe the articles violated and listed for you are petty. They in themselves might be, but together they are not. Nor by any stretch of the imagination could you compare Drury with the nonviolent objector, Martin Luther King, who preached civil disobedience.*

When you disobey the law, you will have to pay for this disobedience. King knew he would have to go to jail, pay a fine or post bail, and this he was ready to do. Gandhi preached nonviolence, and he was also ready to pay the price. He knew full well that the law was the law, and it must be obeyed; there wasn't any question in anybody's mind about it. The early Christians practiced nonviolence, and they knew they had to pay if they violated the laws also.

Now Drury has violated the law in much the same manner. I don't intend to put Fireman Recruit Drury on the same scale, but he has broken the law. The decision is not has he been punished enough, but should he be discharged, and if so, what type of discharge should be awarded. Now I ask you to think of all the men in your divisions on the Goldsborough who have never been to mast or even to executive officer's review, who will be getting out of the Navy eventually with an honorable discharge. Maybe they didn't salute correctly once in a while, or didn't get back in time some morning, but at least their service to their country was honorable. They did the best they could and they served well until the time came along when they were released from active duty. Drury had the same military obligation to his country, and on the record he did not fulfill it. With the string of Captain's masts he has and the list of violations he has—he even has trouble remembering all of them—I might ask, does a man like this deserve an honorable discharge? Would you be fair to all the other men in the Navy?

Now if you believe he has performed honorably, I don't want you to rule that out of your minds, then an honorable discharge by all means. But Drury has been an administrative burden to the Navy. The hours and days of time consumed by his offenses, petty officers, division officers, legal officers, executive officers, and captains—the Lord knows that every one of these men have enough to worry about.

Gentlemen, Drury is unfit for Naval service, in spite of his religious beliefs and his convictions. I don't believe that's even a consideration. In a sense he has so outraged the sense of every Navy man in this courtroom who has served his country honorably.

SENIOR MEMBER: *Thank you Mr. Gleason.*

MR. HART: *Gentlemen, perhaps I run the risk of sounding redundant as well, but Mr. Drury is unsuited for military service precisely because of his religious beliefs and extraordinary moral convictions which, along with his psychiatric evaluations, are just the kind of things you should consider when you decide whether to recommend an administrative discharge under honorable conditions for reasons of unsuitability as his doctors have recommended. For I truly believe that every petty officer, division officer, legal officer, executive officer and captain who has dealt with Drury, over the past year and a half, on any other basis than that of his conscientious objection has, in a Tolstoyan sense, so outraged every moral person who, rather than kill on command, has served his God, I Am Who I Am, honorably.*

On that note, the Board adjourned at 1535 hours, 7 November 1968.

"I Am Who I Am," I said to Brook as we walked out the door with another board behind us. "Whether they see me as I AM is at best questionable. And whether they reconcile the passive resistance of a stumbling passive-aggressive with the actions of the conscientious objector, Lazaroff awakened from the dead, remains to be seen. If, on the other hand, they see my conscientious objection as a ruse to whitewash my record in order to get out of the Navy under more honorable conditions, they will most assuredly nail me to the cross with an undesirable discharge hanging over my head, to discourage wholesale conscientious objection to participating in a service which does not serve people but kills them instead. I mean what kind of service is that?

"Anyway, regardless of the outcome, my dear Mr. Hart, you have outdone yourself, defending the way of the Cross as it has manifested itself in my life. You have been my saviour when the Lord could not be there with me to see that I got a fair hearing. You were great—as superb an advocate for Who I Am as I AM.

"And I thank you, from the bottom of my heart, for your service," I finally got around to telling him.

"You're more than welcome, good buddy," replied Brook.

"Don't forget me now, after you get out. Write me occasionally, to let me know how you're doing. We lawyers are a forgotten breed, you know. We get people out of trouble, and then we're forgotten until they need us again."

"I won't forget you," I said as we parted company.

[And even though I never wrote to him after I got out of the service, I never forgot him. When I finished revising the first volume of this duology, I sent him a signed copy, after which we reconnected by phone.]

8

Unshackled

No longer shackled to the ship, I was again free to come and go as much as one could under the circumstances. As I reconnected with those who love Who I Am, I learned that my contact at Catholic Peace Fellowship, Jim Forest, had been to Hawaii to explain why he and thirteen other clergy and lay, known as the Milwaukee 14, had taken ten thousand 1-A draft files from an office of the SS, carried them across the street to a war memorial, and using homemade napalm, set them on fire.

While many in the peace community had grown to accept draft-card burning as a valid means of nonviolent protest, a smaller contingent could never extend the same mantle of acceptance to the burning of draft files which, in the eyes of their defilers, belonged not to the Kingdom of God and therefore had no right to exist.

Having been called *"to set the earth on fire, how"* they wished *"it were already blazing"* (Lk 12:49) with the fervor of the Spirit, that all might live in Her not as Uncle Sam lives in Her, but as She lives in them and they live in Her as one.

In fact, *"they don't belong to the world any more than I belong to the world,"* (Jn 17:14) had it occurred to me as I wound my way up to see the ship's commanding officer, CDR Lautermilch, at his request—two weeks after my last hearing.

"Have a seat Mr. Drury," offered he such little solace. "I've received word from the Chief of Naval Personnel that your request for discharge as a conscientious objector has been denied as *'indefensible by any stretch of the imagination, no matter how well conceived the story line may be'*."

"It is the Son of Man Whom they have rejected, Sir, not me," had the Spirit set my tongue a-wagging with a story line this man-o'-war could not refute as he struggled, momentarily, to regain control of the conversation.

"That may well be, but as your commanding officer..."

"Excuse me, Sir, but you are not my commander, as I choose to *'obey God rather than men'*," (Acts 5:29) had the Spirit seen that I dropped this bomb on his head to obliterate any misconceptions, he might have, of who was in control here.

"While I am commander of this ship, you will do as you are told," bellowed that wraith of a commander. "You will resume your duties as a combatant, and will be expected to deploy with this ship in the morning. Is that clear, Mr. Drury?"

"Yes, Sir, I do whatever the Commander of this ship tells me," pointed I to the sacred vessel in which I did dwell in peace with Who I Am.

"If I chose to, Mr. Drury, I could have you put in irons and confined to the brig until the ship is prepared to get underway," remonstrated the commander as the wraith fizzled out with a little help from the Spirit. "Instead, I have chosen to let you decide how you will leave in the morning, shackled or unshackled."

"Utter not another word," had the Spirit whispered in my ear.

Left with nothing further to say, did the commander dismiss me.

"Thank you, thank you, thank you," prayed I to the Spirit and the other two members of the Trinity as I raced below, at Her suggestion, to grab a few things before I slipped from the ship, and beat feet for the nearest phone booth.

"Hello Betty, this is Butch. Listen, I've just learned that my CO claim has been denied, that the Goldsborough is set to deploy for Vietnam in the morning, and that Lautermilch has threatened to put me in irons if I refuse to go. I've got to get out of here before he carries through with his threat."

"Where are you now, dear?"

"I'm at a phone booth on the base, but I could meet someone in about fifteen minutes, at the bus stop outside the main gate."

"Good. I'll have Colleen meet you there, hopefully before the MPs do."

"Thank you, thank you, thank you," I prayed aloud as I hesitated to let go of the only lifeline I had.

"Well, dear, I better let you go so that you can get out of there while you can," had Betty encouraged me to hang up the phone.

Having fled the base without incident, I arrived at the bus stop to see Colleen pull up, moments later, in their flower-power painted car. As I was getting into the car, I saw two MPs broach the keepers of the gate, and knew, from that moment on, that I was in God's hands.

"Boy, that was close," I said as we got the hell out of there without a tail.

"Would you mind dropping me off at Jim's office?" I asked her.

"Not at all. What are you going to do?"

"To tell ya the truth, I won't know until I've had a chance to speak with Jim, as that seems to be where the Spirit is leading me."

With that, I fell silent, as did she until we arrived in the vicinity of Jim's office.

"Are you sure you don't want me to wait for you?" Had Colleen asked me as I was getting out of the car.

"Naw, I'm in Jim's hands now, but thank you for the offer. When I know more, I'll give you guys a call. See ya. And thanks for the lift."

"Shalom," she wished me as I closed the door on a life that might have been, had I not chosen another.

But Jim wasn't in his office, and wouldn't be until he had finished teaching his last class of the day.

"O where art thou when most I have need of thee," I cried out to the Spirit Who showed not Her face until I saw Jim's, all lit up with Hers as he reached out to me from afar to pull me back into the here and now with the warmest smile the two of them could ever have shared with me.

"Boy, am I glad to see you," had I addressed them both as one.

"The Navy has denied my CO claim, and is shipping me back to Nam in the morning," had I informed the one who did not know what the other already knew.

"Oh no!" He exclaimed. "What are you going to do?"

"If I refuse to go, I'll be placed in irons, I've been told, until the ship's at sea, leaving me with no other choice but to go AWOL and miss ship's movement, knowing full well that for all my efforts to avoid this occasion for sin, I could wind up in Portsmouth for two years, if not more, and get stuck with a bad conduct discharge—not exactly what I had in mind when I started out on this crusade."

"Come on in," he said as I followed the Spirit's lead into his office.

"To seek or not to seek sanctuary to dramatize my plight is a question upon which the Spirit has remained eerily silent whenever I broach the subject," I confessed, "which leads me to believe that the Lord may have something else in mind that you may be instrumental in helping me find."

"For now, why don't you come home with me, so Sally won't be late for her rehearsal, and eat dinner with the kids while I make a few phone calls," offered Jim this little tidbit from the Spirit.

"Amen," I said as if I had just received communion, for *'one does not live by bread alone, but by every word that comes forth from the mouth of God'*. Mt 4:4.

Not a word passed between us on the way to Jim's place, so intent were we on quelling the chatter that keeps one from hearing the *"sound of sheer silence"*.

"Hi!" Came my queue to enter the scene in which the actress, who plays Jim's wife, greets me in the theatrical performance of their lives.

"It is such a pleasure to meet the celebrity about whom I have heard so much, and a pity I must go," had she managed to flush a blush from me in passing.

"Goodbye, darling. Dinner is on the table. The kids were hungry, so I let them start eating. Help yourselves. There's plenty of food. Shalom!"

And out the door she flew, lest she be late for a very important date with a two-bit part in a play.

"Help yourself," had Jim encouraged me to eat while he followed the Spirit's lead.

"Brook would like to speak to you," came back Jim, moments later.

"What's this I hear about your going AWOL?" Had Sir Brook been stirred to ask of his young charge.

"Brook, I'm not going with the Goldsborough when it departs in the morning," hammered I home Who I Am, "lest I be shackled to the ship for all to see."

"Of course not," conceded Sir Brook after a brief pause for solemnity's sake.

"Jim also mentioned that you are awaiting word from the Spirit as to whether or not you should seek sanctuary on Her behalf. Knowing the consequences, as you must, you would do this based upon Her word alone?"

"Damn straight, whether I want to or not, for She's the only defense I have."

"I'm not so sure," countered Sir Brook at the insistence of the Spirit. "There may be one legal maneuver yet to pursue, though it'd be a long shot."

"Well, what is it?" I begged to know.

"There's a remote possibility, very remote," he reiterated, "that I could secure a writ of habeas corpus on your behalf, which would keep the Navy from removing you from the jurisdiction of the Federal District Court of Hawaii until it show cause why you should not be released from the Navy as a conscientious objector."

"You're kidding," questioned I the reality of what I was seeing.

"Let me speak to Jim," beseeched the light that shone so bright at the end of the tunnel between Sir Brook's world and mine.

"Jim," I hollered, "Brook wants to talk to you again. He's got a plan that not only offers me a legal way out but also has the Spirit's approval written all over it."

After Jim hung up the phone, I asked him, "What else did Brook have to say."

"He asked if you could spend the night at his place, in case he has any questions as he works on the petition for the writ of habeas corpus," responded Jim. "But he wanted to talk to Judge Tavares personally, to see if Tavares is open to meeting him in the judge's chamber prior to court, to rule on the petition before your ship departs at 9 a.m. After he has received confirmation from Tavares, he'll call back to let us know whether the judge has agreed to meet him early enough to get you back to Pearl Harbor on time, should the judge grant the petition.

"Brook also warned me not to get your hopes up too high as there is no legal precedent for resorting to a writ of habeas corpus to stop the military from sending a member of a branch of the armed forces into a combat zone because of his religious beliefs," had Jim nonetheless failed to dampen my enthusiasm, for I was about as high on the Spirit as I could get.

In no time, did Brook call back to tell us that he had a 7 a.m. appointment with Tavares in the judge's chamber, preceded by a clandestine meeting with me at his place posthaste.

With all due haste, did Jim and I round up the kids and depart for Brook's place, where we were greeted by his wife at the front door.

"Come on in," she invited us. "Brook's been expecting you."

"I've heard so much about you, that I'm glad to have had the chance to meet you," had she too managed to flush a blush from me in passing.

"If you need me for anything," offered Jim, "don't hesitate to call me."

"Thank you, Jim," replied Brook.

"Shalom," wished Jim, as Brook and I in turn wished him the same.

And with that, did we set about the task at hand. As I stood by to answer an occasional question or two, Brook worked feverishly through the night in the struggle to set self aside, long enough to capture the Spirit's intent before he handed what he had written over to his wife to be typed. In keeping with such a high standard, we didn't complete the brief until 4 a.m., when Brook's wife finished typing the last page, free of typos.

After a bit of a nightcap that included a toast to the success of all our efforts, Brook's wife set me up on the couch with a pillow and a sheet where I fell fast asleep until I awoke, about a quarter to six, to the smell of fresh-brewed coffee.

So immersed were we in our own thoughts and feelings, that we failed to see as the Spirit sees the outcome of an event before it has taken place.

"When I saw how far you were willing to go, I had to do something, anything to keep you out of Portsmouth," confessed Brook as we drove down to the federal court building, riding high on the Spirit.

"God bless you, Mr. Hart, for it is all I have to give you for your service above and beyond the call of duty."

"I'm afraid it's going to take more than a blessing to convince the judge to rule in our favor," bemoaned Brook.

"That's why the Spirit picked you to stand in Her stead, for you are the blessing in disguise," hammered I home Who She Is.

"Now, I want you to wait close by," had Brook instructed me as we stood outside the judge's chamber. "I probably won't need you. But if the judge should want to hear from you personally, I want you to be available."

With that, did Brook disappear as the door to the judge's chamber closed behind him.

As the minutes sped by with reckless disregard, and cast a pall over the hour hand, I couldn't imagine what was taking so long. Yet, I wasn't too concerned until the clock struck half past eight in the face.

"My God, my God, why have you forsaken me?" (Mt 27:46) Succumbed my soul to the same deadly torpor, the judge had, an affliction of the soul neither could have overcome if the sun hadn't flooded the judge's chamber in light of God's presence—which was quite palpable as Brook would later recall—while He (meaning God) and Brook encouraged the judge to set aside his reservations about setting a new legal precedent and grant the writ with a clear conscience.

Another ten nail-biting minutes would pass before Brook arose from the judge's chamber, dressed in white linen.

"We got it!" Held he high the mandate that would *'lead'* me *'not into temptation, but deliver'* me *'from evil'*. Mt 6:13, RSV.

"Yahoo!" Rejoiced I in the sanctity of the moment.

"Come now," had Brook ushered me out the door. "We've less than twenty minutes to get you to Pearl Harbor before your ship leaves."

With minutes to spare, did we pull up to the keep of the keepers of the gate to whom Sir Brook presented his credentials, and showed the Holy Writ.

Having never seen a holy writ, in keeping with that kept, did the keepers of the gate consult with their immediate superior and the Officer of the Day, as they all huddled round the writ before the keepers of the keep agreed to wave us on.

With stern out and bow yet tied to the pier, did we skirt the crowd that had gathered to wish loved ones on board farewell, as those members of the crew, not involved in getting underway, stood at attention down the main and middle decks along the starboard side of the ship.

"I am an attorney," Brook hollered as he waved the Holy Writ in the air to get the attention of the officer standing on the weather deck off the starboard side of the bridge. "And I have a court order restraining the Navy from removing a member of your crew from the jurisdiction of the Federal District Court of Hawaii."

"Just a moment, please," acknowledged the officer.

No sooner had the officer disappeared from the weather deck to the bridge than the ship reversed rudder until the stern line strangled a bollard onshore, so that one of a handful of officers, who had answered the call to report to the fantail, could experience, first hand, the power of the written word while the others stood round to hear Sir Brook expound upon the dictums of the Holy Writ.

How anyone, much less a fireman recruit, could bring the movement of a ship to a standstill left everyone else not involved in the conversation, standing there staring at such strange goings-on.

Not until the Big Brass from headquarters showed up did the command go out from the highest ranking officer among them, to the Commander of the Goldsborough to cut me some orders, transferring me to the Transient Barracks, Naval Station, Pearl Harbor, Hawaii.

Never again would I be forced to man a man-o'-war against the Sovereign Will of the Father with Whom, at least on this particular matter, I was at one.

Prevented from boarding the Goldsborough, I stood by as another member of the crew, who had been dispatched to empty the contents of my locker into my duffel bag, dragged it across the quarterdeck, and instead of handing it to me, threw it down onto the pier, and walked away without saying a word.

As for the yeoman, who had typed my orders and had seen that they were signed, he could've cared less what the Navy thought of his salute to the divinity that radiated from my face and touched him deeply as he handed me my orders.

"Thank you," I said before he fled from an aspect of God he could not accept should it pertain to him as he feared it might.

While Brook dealt with the last of the Big Brass, I watched the Goldsborough get underway minus one opposer out of the lot or so I thought until one sailor raised his hand high in the air and gave me the V sign for peace. As others followed his lead, I raised my hand as high as I could and gave them all the peace sign in return, which prompted a number of lifers to give me the finger instead.

The Spirit just looked at me and winked.

"You see, all was not for naught," said She. "The Goldsborough is just as divided as the Davidson, only not as blatantly as your country—quite a tribute to you and the truth for which you stand, I would say."

"They paid tribute to you, Milady, not me," I replied.

"Well said," had She responded, "for you have found favor with the Father in heaven."

And as the crowd on the pier dispersed, so did She in a breath so to speak.

"It appears as if we, or should I say you have driven the last nail into the coffin of the sailor in whose shadow I have been forced to walk in circles around the person I AM until I got close enough to see Who I Am," spake I in a breath or two or three to fill the vacuum She had left behind.

"No," countered Sir Brook, "you said it right the first time. Without your courage, I would not be standing here, in the shadow of Sir Thomas More, basking in a victory which in the past would have cost you your life, a prospect I saw coming and hoped to avert, though you be denied the reputation the saint enjoys today."

"Didn't JFK say something to that effect?" Inquired Sir Brook.

"Not quite. If I remember correctly, he stated that *'we must face the truth that... war will exist until the distant day when the conscientious objector enjoys the same reputation and prestige the warrior does today',*" had I quoted the late President John F. Kennedy for clarification's sake.

"Promise me now, that you will stay out of trouble," implored Brook as I walked him to his car. "You are finally in a position you have sought for some time. You're off the men-o'-war, awaiting discharge or a hearing in federal court that may, in all likelihood, grant you release from the Navy. I think you could see to it that you lay low in the interim."

"I'll try. But you know me," I haggled, "I go where the Spirit moves me."

"That's what I'm afraid of," bemoaned Brook. "Don't you think that you could contain this Spirit a little."

"She is my Queen, Brook, and spiritual directress who leads me not astray if I but heed Her words, for *'one does not live by bread alone, but by every word that comes forth from the mouth of God'*.

"That is the choice you or I face every day of our lives, to contain the Spirit as She would want to be contained," I concluded.

"In Her hands then, must I leave thee," bade Sir Brook his young charge.

"And may the Spirit be with you too," had I wished him as he sped off to his next appointment, running a tad behind schedule.

"Mother knows best," yielded I to the Third Person of the Trinity as I threw that half-starved duffel bag of mine over my shoulder, and with Her blessing, stepped into my new role as a transient between Her world and mine.

After I had gotten all checked in, assigned a locker and a bunk, I don't remember a thing until I awoke the following morning to an article in the Honolulu Star-Bulletin about which I had dreamt and now found lying in front of me on my bunk.

Ship sails, Objector Stays Here

The USS Goldsborough sailed from Pearl Harbor for Vietnam yesterday morning minus one sailor.

He is E. J. Drury, 21, a fireman recruit aboard the ship who has applied for an administrative discharge from the Navy.

Attorney Brook Hart filed a petition for a writ of habeas corpus on Drury's behalf and Federal Judge C. Nils Tavares held a 7 a.m. court hearing. The early morning hearing was necessary because the Goldsborough was scheduled to leave at 9 a.m. yesterday.

> Tavares scheduled a hearing for 2 p.m. Friday at which the Navy must show cause why Drury should not be released. In the meantime, Tavares ordered the Navy not to remove Drury from the jurisdiction of Hawaii.
>
> Hart said Drury is a conscientious objector whose religious opposition to war had not matured when he was called to active duty in February of 1967.
>
> He said Drury now realizes that his religious principles compel him to be a nonviolent and that participation in any branch of the armed forces would violate his conscience.
>
> Hart said Drury attempted unsuccessfully to obtain a discharge as a conscientious objector while serving at Pearl Harbor earlier this year.
>
> The petition said Drury attempted to bring his claim to the attention of the proper authorities by wearing a peace symbol on his uniform and refusing to obey an order to remove it.
>
> On another occasion, he refused an order to load ammunition.

Although Betty had already seen the article before I called her, in all the excitement, she nonetheless congratulated me, and in the same breath, invited me to a party she was having that evening, following dinner in celebration of our victory over Navy.

While I was certainly the talk of the party, for awhile, I was even the talk of the town, or at least, of the peace community, which didn't hurt my self-esteem any, unlike the Navy's unsuccessful bid to squash *Who I Am*.

When I heard that two MPs had come knocking on Jim's door, looking for me in the middle of the night I stayed with Brook, I couldn't believe the Navy would go to such lengths to bring me back into the fold, to which I no more belonged than did the man in the mood that would overwhelm me with sexual feelings should I veer the least bit from *Who I Am*, so strong is the desire for unity with the body.

Several days later, I received a letter in the mail from a person who goes to the trouble of printing a return address on the front of the envelope, but never once reveals his name.

Dear Mr. Drury,
I have read of your problems in our local newspaper.
There seems to be great unrest in the military these days, especially in regards to Vietnam.
If your actions are of conscience and sincerity, I strongly support them. But if it is because you are afraid to go to Vietnam, that is a different matter. I hope it is the former.
I, myself, am a civilian who has tried to obtain CO status without success. Although I am in little danger of getting drafted, I'm doing it on principle.
Good luck and may God watch over you.
Aloha

Like any concerned war resister in those days, did Jay and I go to the address on the envelope, the day before Thanksgiving, to see if this guy needed help. After introducing myself as the objector to whom he had written, I finally coaxed him into opening the door but only as far as the security chain allowed, for he wanted no part of our group, our help or publicity we were told as he closed the door in our faces, and asked us to go away and leave him alone. Stunned, Jay and I looked at each other, shrugged our shoulders, and left, never to hear so much as a word of thanks from this self-identified Jehovah's Witness for our efforts.

As I worked on assembling a newsletter to circulate about the base, the first week of the last ember of the year, I received a letter from my Stepdad after he had seen a clip regarding the departure of his Stepson's ship minus the stepson.

Dear Butch,
Through a television newscast, we learned you have a slight disagreement with the way our Chief of Naval Operations and the Defense Department are operating. So you stand on your right to object. You know, it is wonderful to live in a country where you are entitled to voice your opinion without being executed. Of course, the only way we attained that right was by fighting oppression over the years. Hitler was merely a reformer in 1936, but had Europe defeated by 1940. Korea was just a police action to stop Red China, even if the job was never completed—and now Southeast Asia. Well, I suppose some people say we are wrong in being there. We could pull out and let the V. C. commies take over and enslave the country with no plans to expand to other countries, right? Sounds a little like

1936, doesn't it? No, this time it is different. They have no conquest in mind other than self–determination on their terms, meaning "my way, or else".

Then on the other hand, why should I write to you regarding a mess over there that should not concern me? I have a comfortable income, a $25,000 home, and a new Plymouth Road Runner Sports Coupe to park next to the Fury and Mercedes Benz, your Chevy and Pat's Ford. My total obligations are less than $10,000, and that is on the house. Why should I care what happens over there? Same question keeps popping up, doesn't it? Why should I care? Well, maybe it is because I studied history, or should I say, history as it was taught when I was in school than it is today at Mehlville, where a few pages on the bombing of Pearl Harbor and the retaking of a few Pacific islands taught you all about oppression and the reasons to oppose it. They failed to explain what would have happened to our country and way of life had we failed to go overseas to stop oppression—troops from Japan and Germany acting as police in New York City, St. Louis, Los Angeles—work in a factory or on a collective farm for the "Party". It can't happen here; we are a free people. Why are we free? By pulling out?

There are subversive groups, with their causes, the same as Hitler, Castro, Kaiser Wilhelm, and Tojo, that are allowed, through freedom of speech and other rights granted them through our form of government, that look to the day when they can undermine our government structure through student exploitation and ignorance of history. Will you be a part of such a movement?

A few questions come to mind. Where did you get the money to file suit against the Government? What is the background of your benefactors?

At this point, you probably have had your laughs, and are thinking, "Old Man, you may have been a WWII hero but this is 1968," or "put down the flag, you're over the hill". You might be right, Butch, but I pray to God that the day I put down the flag, it is put over my grave at Jefferson Barracks National Cemetery.

Get yourself straightened out and come home. I'll send you back to school or whatever you need, but this foolishness has to stop. You're an American, I hope!

Dad

Having rid their homeland of 100 years of French colonial rule, thanks to Uncle Ho, a majority in the North and South are fighting to reunite their country under whatever banner can free them from the tyranny of Uncle Sam's obsession to intervene in another country's affairs, this time, to stop the spread of communism, the only bloc to which the North can turn for the war matériel they need to castrate Uncle Sam for the rape of Miss Saigon, and drive his minions from their land.

So yes, I do *"have a slight disagreement with the way our"* country is conducting its affairs in Vietnam, forcing 4.3 million people off their lands into hamlets to *"work on collective farms for the Party"* of South Vietnam's first president and self-appointed dictator, Ngo Dinh Diem, who has refused to hold national elections in accordance with the Geneva Accords of 1954, because he knows Ho Chi Minh would beat his ass in a fair election.

It is our oppression of Vietnam that I am fighting, *"Old Man"*, our interference in a civil war between various parties in the North and throughout the South seeking reunification, and the secessionists in Saigon struggling to maintain an unpopular dictatorial city-state, masquerading as the Republic of South Vietnam.

I am also fighting the oppression of our celestial body, Earth's subjection to a way of life that eats away at her like a cancer that robs the many of the means to contain the Spirit as She would want to be contained—the next evolutionary step in the advancement of life on Earth, should we defeat this cancerous growth before Earth self-destructs, as she must, to rid herself of what no longer contains the Spirit as She would want to be contained.

In the battle for the supremacy of one ideology over the other, each side demonizes the other with its own demons, by giving them a form that is easier to slay than a demon, which are driven out of the body but never slain, and only then with a hand from God Who partakes not in the killing of other human beings.

So you see, *"Old Man"*, we are the enemy, and that's no laughing matter when precious lives are lost fighting for the wrong cause.

You are, I hope, a member of the body of Christ. If so, may I suggest that you quit your foolishness and start acting like a real human being instead of a beast.

As for my benefactors, they are peacemakers like me, who have turned to the nonviolent ways of the early Christians, Gandhi and Martin Luther King to fight for truth and social justice rather than any misguided ideology, or sack of liers in Washington, doing everything in their power to suppress what Christ saw as He hung from the cross—what is really going on behind the scenes that flare up on our television screens, night after night, like a bad dream gone further awry.

And I'm not laughing, *"Old Man"*, I'm crying over you and what your way of life has done to me, yourself and thousands of other tormented souls. And I don't mean to *"put down the flag"* either. I mean to snatch it from those who have lost sight of 1776, and run with it to the top of God's holy mountain where I intend to plant it, as did the marines on Iwo Jima, only this time, on behalf of the kingdom of God. And *"I pray to God that the day I put down the flag, it is put over"* the grave of your way of life, one, I dare say, that has not given body to the Spirit as She would want to have been embraced.

While I may be an American by birth, I am first and foremost a member of the body of Christ as are you and every other person for whom Jesus died. And just as I would do my body no harm, so must I do no harm to this celestial body of ours or any of its members to whom I am as inextricably bound as they are, to me. So why on earth, or in God's name, would I or anyone else want to harm any part of our celestial body?

To the kingdom of God, and that alone, do I owe my allegiance, for Earth is my sovereign queen, and God, my ruler. As far as America is concerned, I owe her but the clothes on my back which were given to me to fight a temporal war for which I am not suited, for mine is a spiritual war in which I fight demons, and slay dragons, not men.

"At this point, you probably have had your laughs, and are thinking," Son, you need to wake up to what is real, and seek professional help while there is still time to save you from a fate worse than your father's.

"O, but I have been saved," sayeth I, "from the hell that drove my father insane, and which, to this very day, drives you to drink, for I have found the real meaning of peace, and hope that someday you, my father and other PTSDers like you, will also find peace of mind."

"And I have found my own kind as well, those with whom I most identify, the real peacemakers of the world, who rescued me from the jaws of the Military-Industrial Complex just as the beast was fixin' to suck any semblance of a real life from me as it has from you, my father and countless other souls who have been forced to kill on command, or be killed, in opposition to every moral fiber of their bodies, the carnage of which cries out unceasingly, 'but thou shalt not taketh another man's life, lest ye looseth thine as recompense'."

"Now dear," interjected the Spirit, "this is not the time to stir up your stepfather's demons, lest he shoot and kill another in a barroom brawl."

"That is why you must never forget from whence you came, for you are as much a part of the Earth as I AM. However you treat your earthly mother, you treat Me. So, if you must chastise your stepfather, keep in mind Who I Am.

"As the Father gives to Me what is mine, so must you give to the woman, you will one day marry, what is hers, for you are as much a part of her as she is part of you, and I am part of the Father. And as the Father and I give to you what is yours, so must you give to Us what is Ours, for the Father and I are as much a part of you as you are part of Us.

"Nothing mirrors the Trinity more perfectly than family. And no one embodies the Trinity more completely than the Son. For I AM He as Who I Am is He as I Am Who I Am, and We are all one person in the Son, as you, your mother and father are all one person in you," She concluded in keeping with that kept.

Needless to say, I did not reply to his letter, but left him hanging until he realized—after many a shouting match between the two of us—that I had marched to the drumbeat of a very different authority than he had. With his acceptance of

Who I Am, I could accept the sacrifice he had made as a Navy corpsman, during World War II, who saw untold horrors in the South Pacific, freaked out, and later received a medical discharge for injuries to the body, but more importantly to the soul, the life of which the Spirit had spared, that he might savor hers lest he succumb to the precursors of the enemy without to destroy himself from within.

Having finished typing up the newsletter on my trusty ole Olivetti–Underwood, I spent the better part of my time off—the following week—at Betty's place, retyping each page onto stencils while Giff spiffied up the front page with an artsy rendition of the title, and once completed, took it to a printer to have it transferred electronically to a stencil so that we could run off about a hundred or so copies of the newsletter on his Mom's gestetner before the stencils wore out.

To grab my readers' attention, the image seared into the front page depicted four boonierats, so full of themselves, they crouched like great white hunters in a semicircle close to the ground, with M–16s nestled in their arms, and trophies in hand, the heads of the two decapitated VC lying at their feet—all for the want of a case of scotch, the prize that went to the first member of the "Hatchet Battalion" to bring in the head of a Ho Chi Minh Hanoi Irregular to kick around a bit before they laid it to rest far from the prying eyes of an investigative reporter on a mission from God to expose the criminality of war.

"My God!" Screamed a guilty bystander, though neither he nor God had lifted a finger to intervene before the once humane had succumbed to the dark side of human nature, and like Jekyll, had been transformed into beasts instead.

Though rumors abounded, no one from the press had ever stumbled upon a dismembered body until that fateful day when a German photographer happened upon the grisly scene to capture the triumph of the beast over man.

Nor was this the first instance of a beheading by either side, as the practice continued unabated on both sides, minus the "Hatchet Battalion" designation lest we be seen committing the same war crimes as the enemy.

"Where goes this spilt blood?" Inquired the Grand Inquisitor of the thief of life.

"From rags to riches and back with renewed vigor," answered the thief whose thirst for more would eventually *'set the earth on fire'*.

"How I wish it were already blazing!" (Lk 12:49) Anticipated the GI's only Son, ere He shed His blood to quench our thirst for more.

"As others have given to you what is yours, so must you give to others what is theirs, for they are as much a part of you as you are part of them," rippled My Lady's words throughout my being in one orgasmic wave after another, for I had yet to love my neighbor as She loved me.

Like Her Son, had I been asked to sweat blood rather than shed it with a vengeance as doth the Beast and Knight Tempter of all who find it far easier to attack and kill the evil we see in our neighbor but not in ourselves, a rift we have perpetuated by not giving our neighbor what is theirs, saddling them, instead, with debt to increase our net worth, for without debt there would be no money to spill blood over, nor ideology to sweat when they came after us with pitchforks demanding we turn everything over to them that is rightfully theirs.

"O, where art Thou when most I have need of Thee?" Sought I the guiding hand of divine inspiration whene'er darkness descended upon me with nigh a word in sight until She clasped my hand and whispered in my ear words sublime.

So taken aback was I when a jaygee gave my old shipmate, Rick Little, the finger, I asked him, "what was that all about?"

"Well, I gave him the V sign," had Rick replied, "and when he asked me what it meant, I insisted that it stood for peace.

"'No,' had he refuted, insisting that 'Winston Churchill had used the V sign to symbolize Britain's victory over Germany.'

"When I wouldn't back down," continued Rick, "he gave me the finger instead, and asked me what it meant.

"'Fuck you,' I responded, at which point he shook his head and walked away.

"Why is it, when you offer some people peace, they give you the finger?" Posed Rick this deeply perplexing philosophical question.

"Why is that?" Had I asked the Spirit at a later date at which She was privy to my ruminations.

"They fear the feminine side of their personalities will rise up, as she has in you, and conspire to overthrow the masculine ego's suppression of the feminine, to restore order to both sides of the brain where the two rule as one, though each gives credence to the other's realm of expertise rather than lording it over the other as have your shipmates for whom peace means one thing only, giving you the shaft both literally and figuratively speaking," had the Spirit conveyed to me the meaning of this experience in real time.

With regard to the newsletter, my intent was to give voice to the voiceless, like Rick and Marty, Laruso and myself, who had been pushed around and intimidated for expressing our opposition to war in general but more particularly to the American War in Vietnam which so outraged our consciences that we had no other choice but to act upon our feelings if we didn't want to lose our souls in the mad rush to see who orgasmed with Death first, one's self or his soul, the Faustian bargain one is forced to make to stay alive. Simply put, my real interest lie in reconnecting as many guys as I could with their souls, a bond the Navy had broken, using all manner of subterfuge to cut them off from their feelings about killing other human beings, to make killers out of them while they were in boot camp acquiring the skills they would need to function as a well-greased cog in some of the most disceivingly efficient killing machines to arise from the Dark Lord's vast treasure chest of exotic weaponry hidden deep within the imaginations of the manufacturers of war, criminals, everyone of them, who have led many a young man astray.

"O, where are you when most I have need of thee?" Hath many a young soldier, who has been mortally wounded, cried out to his mother ere fleeing the scene of his body's demise after having killed Vietnamese on their soil, using sticks and stones to impose our will on them, the unpardonable sin for which he had forfeited his last attachment to his mother, a mere fifty-eight thousand two hundred and twentieth of the mass of Americans who'd lose their lives by war's end.

"Yet, you persisted in this folly despite your mother's misgivings. Why?" Inquired the Grand Inquisitor of the spirit of the dead soldier.

"I had no choice. I was drafted, Sir, and forced to kill for the living," answered he who now stood at attention before the GI.

"My Son never once raised a hand to strike down those who had abused their power, just because they could, to take His or anyone else's life to protect a dying way of life. Yet, My Son lives and you die fighting for your own extinction. How do you account for this?" Toppled He the young man's defense.

"I'm a soldier, Sir. I do what soldiers must do to stay alive. And now, Sir, I am at your command for the same reason," broached he the breach between them.

"I need no hired gun, who heeds not My commands," fired back the GI.

"I have always followed orders, Sir, from the highest authority down through the chain of command," insisted he who had yet to die to his self.

"I am the Highest Authority, He whose commands you have disobeyed," bellowed the Old Bag of Wind.

"My orders came not from you, Sir..."

"Enough of your impudence, Soldier! To the front do I remand you, this time, to depose demons and to slay dragons rather than men," blew He air into the young man's nostrils.

"Aye, aye, Sir!" Exhaled he lest his buddy CPR the hell out of him.

"I thought we had lost you," had his buddy welcomed him back.

"I died, not once but twice, and have come back to slay dragons," muttered he in his delirium as his buddy helped a medic load him onto a stretcher and into a chopper to evacuate him to the nearest field hospital for further medical attention. Though his recovery would be a long and arduous one, due to the severity of his wounds, he found consolation in knowing that God had spared his life to spar with the beast from the deep to which men have sold their souls for massive sums of black gold, leaving the rest of us to clean up the mess and fight their fires. And he foresaw the day when those who had sacked the planet for her wealth would be hunted down like Nazi war criminals and made to pay for their crimes against

Mother Earth, the gravity of which would do her irreparable harm and drive the rest of us to the brink of extinction as they turned up the heat.

"Remember, Soldier, you always have a choice, My way or the highway to perdition," had the Grand Inquisitor reminded him ere he caved into the effects of the morphine he had been given to ease his pain.

"What will happen to this soldier?" Had I asked the Spirit for foresight.

"He will become part of a movement to see that Mother Nature is declared a person, giving her the opportunity, through her attorneys, to confront her abusers in a court of law for the first time in her life.

"Is not she, the one who must be obeyed?" Had I asked the Spirit for clarity.

"Am I not the Spirit of She Who Must Be Obeyed?" Inquired She Who now stood before me in all Her glory as I bent a knee and bowed my head to the Queen of Heaven and Earth.

"Then, who am I?" Sought I the truth of my being.

"I Am Who I Am," annointed She, this amalgam of Her and the Father that craved the love of God more than anything else on earth, "and I dub thee, Sir Eodor, Knight of the Queen's Realm of Expertise."

As the Spirit of Nature extended Her hand out to me, I took hold of Mother Nature's once badly mangled fingers and with great care kissed them to seal my bond with the other side of my brain and it's Queen forever.

"Don't let them take your life," stressed the Soldier in distress.

"Here, now, don't let them take this away from you," had I advised every sailor to whom I handed a copy of the newsletter.

Pending further investigation of an alleged violation of Article 134—conduct discrediting the service—I was taken into custody, the next day, by two NIS operatives, and posited in the brig after I had invoked my right to remain silent until I had consulted with my attorney who was away on business till the end of the week, leaving me with no other choice but to reach out to Betty for legal assistance.

"There's no need to worry, dear," assured Betty. "I'll have Bill Thompson get in touch with you first thing in the morning."

"Thank you, thank you, thank you," had I acknowledged *'something greater than Jonah here'*, (Mt 12:41) that amalgam of the Father, Son and Holy Spirit in Betty who, in keeping with that kept, had given back to Them what is Theirs.

Only Bill Thompson didn't show up until my interrogators were threatening to produce a witness if I didn't talk, who they claimed had seen a sailor, fitting my description, out sowing the seeds of dissension amongst the faithful.

If in deed this was to be their next move, then I had the right, according to Bill, to appear in a lineup with five or six other individuals resembling the witness's description of the offender in question so that I didn't stand out from the pack.

"Furthermore, my client is not to be intimidated or interrogated by any official from NIS without his attorney present. Is that clear?" Had Bill gotten their attention.

And so did I appear in a lineup, on Friday the 13th, with five other individuals dressed in white linen, and all sporting a mustache in keeping with the witness's description, to ascertain the guilty party amongst us, though he be guileless in the eyes of God.

As the fear of fingering the wrong dude filled his frame, and a wink from the Spirit caught my eye, how sweet it was when their only witness could not identify me, much to their exasperation and to his dismay.

"Thank you, My Lady," whispered I so as not to alarm anyone lest they catch sight of me talking to a presence they could not feel.

"Thanks, Bill," said I as we shook hands before he departed.

"No more newsletters now!" Insisted Bill.

"No more newsletters," I agreed, for I had been granted fifteen days of leave, the icing on the proverbial cake to celebrate my victory over those who had sought to crucify me for doing God's work.

Why, even the Captain of the base went out of his way to wish me a Merry Christmas and a Happy New Year ere I left the base to spend the holidays with the Johnsons at Betty's insistence.

And though it wasn't home, it was a home nonetheless, that unlike mine was filled with love and respect for each other.

That night, as the desire for union with **Who I Am** filled my body to overflowing, I tossed 'n' turned into the wee hours of the morn, awaiting the breakthrough that'd greet me should I free my self from the clutches of the wolf that absconded with my body in an effort to reunite us as in the days of yore when man and beast were one with the Father though separate in nature until man'd been awakened from the Big Sleep, God had induced to rob him of a rib. But I could not see what lie beyond my reach in the hinterlands of my being where the wolf had dragged me in my unwillingness to come to terms with the animal side of my nature.

"As the wolf gives to you what is yours, so must you give to the wolf what is his, for you are as much a part of the wolf as he is part of you," whispered She Who Must Be Obeyed from deep within my being. "So deny not the wolf's need for companionship, lest he gobble up every last stitch of your humanity and spit it out as Hyde had, the last remnants of the good in Dr. Jekyll.

"Go to him, now. You can't refuse what belongs to the Father."

To the next bend, did the wolf lead me, only to leave me laughing and playing with two wolf pups until the Sun had set and the moon did shine with the scarcity of light with which their mother did beam as she lie closeby, fondly watching me play with our kids, for the wolf and I had become one again in the Father.

I Am Who I Am

The Sunday before Christmas, I attended a vigil, outside the gate to Kaneohe Marine Corps Air Station, in support of the two marines, Gary Gray and Tom Met, who had turned themselves in after going AWOL, seeking and receiving sanctuary as a way of recusing themselves from a war that so abhorred every moral fiber of their bodies, they would rather have died fighting against the war than commit themselves to the Great Slaughter.

Confined to the Kaneohe MCAS Brig where they would languish for months while awaiting separate court-martials, the dissident two or "Honolulu Two", as they were called, would wind up spending a year or two each at Portsmouth, the U.S. Navy and Marine Corps prison which is actually in Kittery, Maine, not Portsmouth, New Hampshire, as its name and postal address would suggest.

Knowing full well that I could not relieve them of their pain, did I who had borne their pain weep for them nonetheless as we lifted Gary and Tom up to the Father in a show of solidarity with the birth of *something greater than Jonah here*, a life that bespeaks I Am Who I Am and no other god before thee.

O, the consolation such knowledge doth bring to the neophyte who, in his suffering, hath cried out to the Father in anguish, *"if it is possible, let this cup pass from me"*. Mt 26:39.

Two days later, on Christmas Eve, did Sirs John and Stan, and several other Knights of the Resistance, including myself, a half-dozen women and the founder of the Hawaii Committee to End the War in Vietnam, Dr. Willis Butler, gather outside Our Lady of Peace Cathedral on Fort Street to hand out a bulletin contrasting the death in Vietnam with the birth of Christ, an appalling contradiction that had the potential to stir even the deadest of parishioners from their shallow graves should they heed the babe's call to suckle at Death's withered tit no more.

For I had just been handed a fistful of bulletins when, lo and behold, who should appear in our midst but the Associate Superintendent of Catholic Schools, Father Don Graff, who first shook hands with Dr. Butler, and rightly so, before turning his attention to me.

"How nice it is to have you here. You are welcome to attend mass if you wish," had he reckoned with the force he recognized in me and the company that I kept.

As quickly as he had appeared, did he slip from our midst unaware that we were on a mission from God.

With the Spirit at our backs, did we descend upon the unassuming as we quietly worked our way about the nave, showering the blessed with Pope Paul the Sixth's message to the world, *"No more war, war never again!"* From there, did we retreat to the sidewalk across the street, where rain soon forced us to seek shelter along either side of the steps to the Cathedral, in keeping with that which kept anyone from entering or exiting the church unimpeded.

After a member of the congregation had asked chief usher, Moses Akana, why this kind of material was being distributed at midnight mass, Moses and a fellow rustler took it upon themselves to bar the Catholics amongst us, whom Father Graff had invited to attend mass, from entering the Cathedral on orders from the pastor and celebrant, The Very Reverand Charles A. Kekumano, who in reality was not made aware of our presence until he had finished celebrating the mass.

But the rustlers' hearts had *"grown dull, and their ears, hard of hearing, so they"* understood not *"with their hearts"*, (Mt 12:15) and instead started pushing and shoving us, like cattle, down the steps into the cold, pouring rain.

When, lo and behold, Sergeant Goeas and his two deputies showed up at the OK Corral, they were told that Monsignor Kekumano wanted them to keep the peace rabble out. And so did they commence elbowing and shoving us down the steps, away from the rustlers, in a show of force that prompted Our Lady to remind the lawmen to show more mercy as they went about their business.

As Goeas slammed Sir Jan of Haffner to the ground and slapped some cuffs on him, his wife, Lady LaVerne, who was three months pregnant, rushed to his side, only to be thrown to the ground but never cuffed at the insistence of Our Lady Who continued to intercede as best She could.

In fact, it was at Our Lady's urging that Dr. Butler complained to one of the deputies about the way we were being treated—an effort for which he, too, was cuffed and taken into custody across the street.

Having thrown off their sports coats, did Chief Instigator, Moses Akana, and a fellow rustler jump into the fray with a punch or two from the former that drew blood and blackened Sir Stan's eye while he resisted not the former's blows in keeping with his true calling as a knight of the Resistance Round Table. Before I knew what hit me, Moses had knocked me to the ground with a blow to my jaw. With me out of commission, did Moses turn on Sir Curt of McClain, hitting him repeatedly in the shoulder, to entice him to denounce his calling and fight like a man. Unable to elicit a like response, did he, who was beyond Our Lady's reach, turn and punch me in the jaw again, knocking me to the sidelines before he and his sidekick donned their sports coats and resumed their positions at the top of the steps while Goeas and his deputies rounded up the beleaguered knights, four in all, a page or two and the good Doctor for "disorderly conduct".

Thanks to Our Lady of Peace, neither I nor any of the women were arrested.

Although Our Lady tried, as only the Spirit can, to get the Governor's attention while he was in the sanctuary reading the Epistle, it never dawned on him that the "Fort Street Maul" was taking place on the front steps of the Cathedral, or that six innocent people would be arrested and charged with "disorderly conduct", a charge that'd later be amended to "disturbing a religious service".

As for the Sergeant, he would come under police investigation after Sir John of Witeck, Leader of the Resistance Round Table, filed a complaint against him for his mishandling of the whole affair, for taking the ushers word over ours rather than seeking affirmation from a higher authority as to the accuracy of their claim, and for roughing us up and then accusing us of "disorderly conduct" instead of arresting the ushers for beating up on us when they knew we wouldn't strike back.

Within twenty–four hours of the incident, had Sirs Stan and Curt filed separate complaints with the Honolulu Police Department against Moses Akana, which resulted in his being picked up, booked and released on bond on condition that he appear in District Court at 9:00 a.m. on January 27 to face two counts of third degree assault and battery.

Four knights, a page or two and the good Doctor were booked and released on bond on condition that they appear in court on February 11 at 9:00 a.m.

When an x-ray showed that I had a fractured mandible, after I couldn't even chew a strawberry at breakfast, that morning, I was admitted to Tripler General Hospital where I spent the next thirty days with my jaw wired shut, sucking pureed food through a straw I had to insert into a space between my teeth.

Besides a piece in the Honolulu Star–Bulletin, entitled "Six Are Charged with Disturbing Religious Worship", letters to the editor did soon follow. Noteworthy among them were a letter from a parishioner:

Ironic Beating

> Sir: I was sickened to note the beating of several peace demonstrators in front of Our Lady of Peace Cathedral on Christmas Eve. How ironic that they should be beaten up on the birthday of the most notable protester of them all, Jesus Christ. While the congregation worshiped His divine birth inside, the police and the ushers found great support for their brutality outside. Man is the only animal capable of such incredibly disgusting irony.
>
> This ugly exercise in violence tactics certainly may signal a new joint effort by church and state to further suppress the activities they worship Jesus for performing. Had Jesus Himself been there, He would have found the club of authority just as hard and painful as it was when He made the ultimate sacrifice.
>
> I challenge the members of Our Lady of Peace Cathedral to justify their ac-

tions in relation to those of the "decent" citizens of Christ's era. I am sure that if they are capable of even the slightest self-honesty they will open the floodgates of their pent-up hypocrisy and end the chance of a "God's little police state".

THOMAS PURDY

and another I wrote in response to someone's take on the mauling of the "Fort Street Eight" that really rubbed me the wrong way:

No Disruption

Sir: I was perturbed with the letter from F. Johnson regarding the unfortunate incident outside the Cathedral of Our Lady of Peace on Christmas Eve. As a Catholic serviceman and a Christian witness to the event, may I please endeavor to set Mr. Johnson straight with the truth.

First of all, there was no pushing or shoving by any member of the group which leafleted inside the church, as we were invited to enter the church by Father Graff. Secondly, as all of the leaflets were passed out in the church before 11:45 p.m., 15 minutes before the Mass was to begin, and all the members of our group had left the church before that time also, I don't see how Mr. Johnson can claim that we disrupted the Mass.

I am very pleased Mr. Johnson that you brought up the question of civil liberties because they were most assuredly disregarded by the police as well as the ushers. We were denied entrance to the church to attend the Mass by the ushers and the police on the grounds that we were not members of the parish or the Catholic Church, and that the Monsignor had given the ushers the order to refuse us entrance should we try. What gross untruth! First of all, several of us happened to be members of the Catholic Church as well as the parish of Our Lady of Peace. Secondly, the Monsignor never did give the ushers such an order nor did he even know of our presence until after the mass was over.

I was also appalled by your comment that most of the ushers are well beyond the age of beating anybody up because I happen to be in Tripler Hospital with a fractured right mandible. It seems several of your old and senile ushers couldn't wait to indulge in the extracurricular activity of brute force. They didn't want us to negate the spirit of Christmas or Christianity. True Christians they are? I believe Mr. Johnson that their actions smack of the Red Guard or just plain disservice to Christianity.

E.J. Drury II
Ward 17 USA Tripler Gen. Hosp.
APO San Francisco CA 96438

Shortly after all the finger-pointing had subsided, a bunch of the gang showed up at my bedside, one afternoon, all aglow with smiles that did warm my heart no more than did the card they handed me, upon which were inscribed the words, *"In recognition of heroic action above and beyond the call of duty, the Movement is proud to present to E.J. Drury the coveted Purple Heart"*, the shape of which had been cut out of the front face of the card to reveal its true hue underneath.

"Thank you for such a wonderful gift, one I shall always cherish, for I could not have asked for anything more comforting than this display of love for Who I Am," had I responded with a tear or two to the sound of an infinite symphony of clashing cymbals, a standing ovation that did loose on earth what had been bound in heaven, but was now free to flow.

A day or so later, I received a card from Betty, letting me know that she'd have been up to see me had she too not gone to the hospital and gotten herself admitted to a room, only at Kaiser Permanente instead, while she recovered from an unexpected surgery with an excellent prognosis from her physician, Dr. Willis Butler.

Though I had called her to see how she was doing, I had no idea, to hear her speak, that she had turned her hospital room into a central command post with books, mailing lists and card files, Movement literature and magazines piled everywhere, and walls covered with get-well cards, pictures, news clippings and articles. Why, between watching PBL broadcasts on TV, talking on the phone and seeing visitors, sometimes by the dozens, I heard that she had cranked out as many as thirty letters a day, all the while she was making plans for a four-month tour of Asia, beginning in Fiji on January 28, for a little rest and relaxation with Walter and the kids, and of course, time for her body to heal.

As Betty awakened late one night, she steadfastly insists, to this day, that she had seen a Nightingale, all draped in white linen, shine a little light on one of her wall displays, more out of curiosity than anything else, prompting Betty to comment nonetheless that "resistance even grows in the dark".

Meanwhile, were Sirs John and Jan, and Sir Gene of Parker "scheduled to make their pleas in Federal Court, this week, before Judge Martin Pence", according to Betty, "for having burned their draft cards", charges that would later be dropped after the U.S. Supreme Court ruled, in another case involving a young man who had burned his draft card, that a draft board cannot subject a person to the draft as an instrument of punishment for burning a draft card.

Prior to packing the courtroom in support of the "Hawaii Three", all members of the Resistance and friends thereof were invited to attend "an 8:30 a.m. vigil outside the courthouse", had she drifted ever closer to the disconnect between her world and mine, where she had my back, and I had hers as we stood back to back on the threshold of a dream, where trials do emanate from vigils kept.

"I gather you are stuck in the hospital for awhile," had she inquired within.

"I am," ventured I into the unfamiliar territory of a hospital stay in which the days did drag on in an endless procession bounded by weeks of cruel flirtations with the end no where in sight.

Luckily, I had been blessed with two wardmates, whose mouths had also been wired shut, though for different reasons, and with periodic visitations, both real and surreal, to appease the wolf whilst he did heal with one eye fixated on Betty's world, and the other, on the Spirit's realm and all that that did entail.

Why even Michael showed up, late one night, much to my delight.

"Hey! Where were you the other night, when I was getting punched in the head?" Had I humored him with a slight right cross to no–man's–land, that void between his world and mine.

"As much as I wanted to help you, I could only engage Akana's demons who knew enough, when they saw me, to beat it to the top of the steps where they eventually hunkered down behind your attacker, acting as if nothing had happened. So, count me as having been there, just out of sight," had he reassured me ere I fell back to sleep, all the wiser.

While the killing in Vietnam raged on, Our Lady's pleas to end the violence did fall upon deaf ears as I watched the wreckage of the irreparable that once trickled passed my ward surge in numbers. Knowing full well that I was exhausted and in need of healing, She imposed not Herself upon him who had been so willing to carry Her torch but could now barely speak through his teeth.

When what had been bound on earth had been loosed, why, I was heaven bound until I chomped down on a mushy piece of canned fruit with jaw muscles so weakened from lack of exercise that I felt as if my teeth were floating in my mouth, as if they were no longer anchored to my jaw, a condition that would take care of itself, I was told, as I graduated from soft foods to a regular diet.

Because Betty might have left by the time I was released from the hospital, she called, one afternoon, to wish me the best, and asked that I "please stay in touch", which I did until Walter passed in 1985, and she abandoned their summer home on Bass Lake, Michigan, where I had visited them over many a summer.

And now that I was free to speak again and was no longer dependent upon Tripler Hospital for sustenance, I was just as eager as Sir John to testify at Akana's trial on the 27th, if only the Assistant Prosecutor hadn't been so eager to call Moses to the stand after Sirs Curt and Stan had both testified.

"How is it, Mr. Akana, that you came to be charged with assault against Messrs. Masui and McLain?" Had the judge asked he who had sworn to uphold the Ten Commandments, no more than he had on the Eve of Christ's nineteen hundred and sixty-eighth birthday.

"Well, I was standing outside, facing the church when I felt a blow to the back of my neck, spun around with my arm raised, and struck something," had Moses admitted that he might have "made contact with the person behind him", whom he designated as "Masui".

And even though McClain had assumed "a fighting stance, saying, 'Come on, come on,' he backed away when I took a similar stance," had Akana once again evaded the truth with reckless abandonment.

However, 'twas upon his final denial of ever having struck Sir Curt in the shoulder, that the cock did crow three times.

Seeing how there is "reasonable doubt" of Akana's liability, the judge ruled in the end that the charges were "not substantiated", and therefore found the defendent "not guilty". "If the prosecutor had called other witnesses," admitted the judge in his closing remarks, "perhaps the verdict would have been different."

New charges were immediately filed against Mr. Akana by the third man out and a warrant was sworn out for his arrest.

Having been commandeered to the brig, within days of Akana's acquittal, like Samson was I robbed of what hair remained on my head after the haircut I had gotten at the Navy Exchange failed to deliver a punishing blow to the alter ego of a small-minded, spite-filled petty officer whose life stood in stark contrast to mine, an image of Christ he could never accept, even if his life depended on it.

By weeks end, I found myself standing outside the terminal at Honolulu's International Airport, surrounded by a tight circle of friends, all of whom had turned their backs on me so that I could abandon my uniform with reckless disregard for the lie for which it stood before it slunk to the ground disembodied.

The self-sacrificed who had come out to see me off consisted of no less than Sirs Curt, Gene, John, and Stan, Sir Wayne and his fair Lady, Ladies Claire and Burnetta, and another lass whose name I do not recall. They came bearing gifts not of frankincense and myrrh, but of bread and wine, and a camaraderie that did bind us all to the Three in One Whose blessing we did seek prior to partaking of these precious gifts to remind ourselves that, like our heavenly hosts, we are all for one and one for all, and always will be no matter how far the wind did scatter us in our quest for the Grail and the immortality it imparts to him or her who drinks of it in the spirit of Christ and His disciples.

Only, my hair had been cut so short that, at one point, two of the women in our group had to hold their hands over my head to keep it from getting sunburnt.

After many a hug had been shared, and a tear or two shed, I left Hawaii behind, or so I thought, for unbeknownst to me at the time, I had sustained a wound that would fester below the surface and taint my every step until I expressed it, in a manner of speaking, as Sir Brook had suggested when he proposed that I write a book about my experiences in the twilight zone.

"Who would read it?" Had I asked him on the heels of my last hearing before an administrative board.

"I would!" Voiced he the sentiment of many a seeker of truth.

"And what a great movie it would make!" Had Sir Brook submitted this tantalizing tidbit before I could respond in writing, some twenty years later.

As I waved good-bye with a twinge of heart, I realized just how much I would miss the self-sacrificing folk of the Hawaii Resistance and its Round Table of Knights with whom I had drunk from the cup, Jesus had lifted up long before I left this haven in search of a maven to help me unwind this tale.

As I stepped from one waking dream into another, much ruder awakening by a factor of ten, the height in feet of the wire fence that surrounded the unshackled barracks of '67, it was evident that the ranks of discontent had swelled to the point of forcing the Navy to isolate the growing number of antiwarlike malcontents from the rest of the fold, lest it too succumb to our contagion while the Navy regrouped to thwart the spread of the pandemic that had engulfed the nation.

"Where's your uniform, sailor?" Had my overlord asked when I appeared at quarters, the following morning, dressed in civvies.

"I outgrew my uniform, and had to abandon it," had I quipped before my wings were clipped.

"You better find one, real quicklike," I was told, otherwise I'd find "my cute little ass in the brig" before I knew what hit me.

With a little help from the gentle men who stood by me, was I attired, from head to toe, in the uniform of the day, a tad quicker than lickety-split.

I Am Who I Am

On 20 February, 1969, I was finally discharged from the Navy as undesirable, unfit or incapable of participating in any branch of organized killing under the umbrella of the Armed Forces of the United States of America.

Having been given $50 and an airplane ticket home before I was booted off the base, I had to sign a waiver which read as follows:

   From: Commanding Officer, U.S. Naval Station, Treasure Island, San Francisco, California.
   To: FR E. J. Drury II, USNR
   Subject: Order not to reenter the Department of the Navy Installation at Treasure Island, San Francisco, California.
     1. You are being removed as a trespasser from the Naval Station, Treasure Island, and ordered not to reenter the confines of this installation without the permission of the Commanding Officer or an officer designated by him to issue a permit of reentry.
     2. Whoever enters or is found on any such reservation after having been removed therefrom or ordered not to reenter by any officer or person in command or charge thereof shall be fined not more than $500, or imprisoned not more than six months, or both. Title 18, U.S. Code 1382.
     3. The provisions of Title 18, U.S. Code 1382 also apply to the cases of commission of any unlawful act upon a military reservation.
                       S.I. Kummer
                  S.I. Kummer, LTJG, USN, Separations Officer
                            20 February, 1969
   I signify that I have read and understand the information contained above.
      E. J. Drury II

As I stepped from Treasure Island onto the causeway to Yerba Buena Island, I was overcome by a warm fuzzy feeling for I Am Who I Am, as if the Father had just put His arm around my shoulders to welcome His prodigal son back home.

"You're my voice now, the same voice that has permeated this narrative throughout your ordeal," had I AM annointed Who I Am, after all was said and done.

"I want you to tell everyone whose heart you touch that I Am not an angry old windbag, as you would say, with his head stuck in the clouds, for I Am a guiser of many disguises of which you are but one as is Hewhay but a mirror image of Yahweh, and Jinny, an image of your soul. And as your Father, I would appreciate an occasional hug or two from him in whom I have invested so much," said He as I did embrace another nuance of God with open arms.

The farther we walked, the higher the water in the bay rose until it was lapping at the underside of the bridge, threatening to inundate us in a flood of biblical proportions.

"Surely, this is not happening," had I endeavored to speak above the roar of the waves of death sweeping the planet as in the days of yore, coming to a halt at the foot of the causeway, in the guise of the Four Horsemen and their army of wraiths who feared not Him with Whom I stood, but him down upon whom their red eyes did bare with a crushing stare that shattered their glare into thousands of pieces of unsubstantiated evidence of the holocaust looming on the horizon.

"O, but it is, my son, and at a much faster rate than any previous, organized killing of the imponderable preponderance of life—forms that fail to make Noah's list or meet the criteria for entering the coming age," had Yahweh interceded lest I succumb to the stench of death that clung to every breath I stole from this dream.

"While the method of extermination has not changed, the responsibility for having let all hell break loose in the Age of Man falls squarely upon his shoulders alone," had the Father let loose what man had unloosed on Earth, a mass extinction like no other...

Index

A

abandonment
  write with 138
Able and Cain
  God and the military 105
Abraham 9, 88
  sacrifice
    ego 69
    only-begotten son 70
abuse of power 133, 253
abyss 7, 9, 42, 51
acceptance
  pressing need 73
ACCUSED. *See also* Drury, FR E.J. *See also* special court-martial
  active duty
    initial entry 162
      period preceding 160
    orders 147, 164, 246
  Authority invested 141, 158, 159
    Highest 163
  awful crime 214
  beliefs
    development 160-167
  classified 1-A 164
  conscientious objector
    existence of the term
      first learned 168
  depth of commitment 190
  dereliction of duty 166, 214
  disobeying lawful order 168
  disrespect of superior officer 169
  grievous offense 166
  Kailua Road leaflet
    meaning 173
  minor infraction 166
  misplaced attention 164
  motives 189
  Naval Academy. *See* Naval Academy
  refusal of direct order 174
  refusal to eat 162
active imagination 221

ACT newsletter 208, 209
acts of conscience 228, 229-230
  speak louder than words 87
Adam 82
  able-bodied son 8
  author 59
  fission/split 54, 57
  new 55
Adam and Eve
  great separation 68
  image of God 58, 78
Adam and evil. *See* ego/shadow axis
admin board
  Davidson
    notification 212
    recommendation 219
    show and tell (voir dire) 213
  Goldsborough
    closing arguments 230-237
    notification 219
    testimony
      Father Dever 222-224
      FR Drury 1-222
      Professor Douglass 225-230
    voir dire revelation 233
administrative discharge
  reason of unfitness
    Whitaker 211
  reasons of unsuitability
    Lazaroff 234
    MR. HART 236
administrative hold 216
Adonis 14, 37-39
adversary 56
Adversary, the 39, 80
aha moment 132
aim of desertion 209
Akana, Moses
  charged with assault 258
  chief usher/Chief Instigator 257
  trial 262

Index

allegiance
  She vs can of nitwits 125
  voices in head vs devil 162
alter ego
  obsessive-compulsive 7, 12
    essence 10
    facsimile 38
    vile-looking creature 15
American War in Vietnam 90
  antiwar march in Long Beach 129
  in the body vs out of body 107
  police action 118
  true nature 126
Ancient One. See I AM: Ancient One
animal
  capable of brutality 258
  live or act like 79, 103, 108
animal level 34, 61, 89
  communicate 135
animal nature
  come to terms 255
  descend to depths 21
animus
  Betty J 78
  mother 80
  Nature 77
annihilation of the imaginable 6, 32
antagonist 165
  need 19, 106
antisocial personality disorder 136
antiwar activities
  onboard the Davidson 119
Aoki, Sophie Ann
  letter 116
army of wraiths 265

B

baboon 43-44
back door to interior world 24, 26
bane, Adam's 51
bard 39, 46, 53
Bardon, MM3 Michael 160
  witness for defense. See also special court-martial
    call to testify 197
    examination
      cross 198
      direct 197-198

Article 134
  conduct discrediting Navy
    alleged violation 254
Article C-5210. See also Chaplain Carroll
  conscientious objectors
    claimant's rights 79, 176, 216
    noncombatant duty 72, 79, 231
    procedure for discharge 215, 230
    questions for claimants 80, 171, 172
      read in court 181
  sword in the stone 70
Article C-10311
  admin discharge
    other than honorable 212
at-one-ment 166, 214
authority
  speak with 141
  undermined 99
authority of a different kind 250
author of being 63, 65, 75
  archetype 59, 60
  driven underground 58
  Earnest Hemmingway 51-52
  emerging voice 115
  male member 52
  Old Hemmingway 102, 103
  Old Man in the Sea 55, 70
  resistance 56
  wedding 73
Author of being 138
  failing mark 58
  I Am Who I Am 102, 132
  vague facsimile 7
Author of the House 116
AWOL 240-241

Barrows, Agent 117-119, 174-175
  agreement 119, 183
batter in the box 56
beast 39
  ascent to throne 6
  beauty 54, 78
  bisexual 25
    true significance 46
  Christ died to 179
  die to 166, 178
  noble 129

prisoner 2
shadowy side 115
tame 28
triumph over man 251
true intent 106
worm 74
beast from the deep 253
beastly side of nature 38, 165
  acceptance
    Heavenly Mother's 137
  desire for unity 78
  projections 135
beast of a wildfire. *See* passion
beast vs Spirit 135
Beatitudes redact 28
behavior 45, 181
  activist 224
  god-like 4
  irregular 163
  meaning 61
  perverse 5
  predaceous 73
  toward Navy 220
beheadings
  unabated practice 251
being
  triune nature 18
  true nature 89
beliefs
  personal vs institutional 189
benefactors
  background 248, 249
Berrigan, Phil and Dan 110
Big Bad Wulff 96, 140. *See also* Wulff, EM1 Kenneth
Big Sleep
  awakening
    author 220
    chaplain's soul 5
    Nature 77
  rib robbery 255
birthday
  twenty-first 12
blacked out 164, 214
black hole 30, 80
  cone of emotion 61
  distortion of truth 62
  erogenous zone 50

gravitational pull 78
Kilauea Krater 25
pupil of eye 60
Black Knight 20
black monolith 16-17
black sand beach 31
blind beggar 33
bliss, heavenly 54
blood
  sweat rather than shed 251
blue mood 74, 78
blues
  moody 76
  returning-to-the-Davidson 121
body
  androgynous 23
  beast of burden 108
  bullheaded tendency 4
  Captain/Commander 167, 239
  celestial 249-250
  feminine member 40
  gravitational forces 62
  heavenly 81
  hijacked 213
  incorruptible
    denied all wraiths 108
  lose control 164
  members 56
    dysfunctional 116
  sacred vessel 239
  separation from 24
  stubborn mule 165
  union with true intent 49, 138, 140
body/mind
  split 18
    Adam/Eve 54
    heal 106
    mad marine 66. *See also* mad marine
  union 24
body of Christ
  blood spilt
    cleansing effect 109
  member 249
body's need
  union with the Creator 108, 110
body/soul
  reunion 45, 126
  split 18

Index

bollard 243
bone of your bone 210, 250
boonierats 251
boot camp. See also Naval Academy
   makes killers of men 252
born again 17, 21
brain
   both sides
      art of communicating 77
      restore order 252
      reunite 54
   feminine side
      seal bond 254
brainchild 19, 46
bread alone
   one lives not by 29, 162, 220, 240, 245
brig. See also Naval Station Brig
   departure 11
   protective custody 254
   robbed of hair 262
   where I belonged 166, 180, 183, 214, 216

C

Cain
   unchained 120
   Uncle Sam's shadow 105
Cain and Able 89
call of duty
   service above and beyond 242, 260
Calvary 140, 209
Captain and Savior 183
Captain Cloonan
   Chaplain, Pearl Harbor 40, 181
Captain Hook
   His Grace 133
   LT Smyth 134
captain's masts
   first of six 214
   Kailua Road leaflet 96-97
   request 122, 175
      status on ship as a CO 123, 180
case of scotch
   prize for the head of a VC 251
Catonsville 9 110
causeway to hell 264-265
CCCO
   Central Committee for COs 130
   Handbook for COs 99, 172

brigandage 47
brigation 97
bright shining lie 47, 62
Brig Warden
   access denied 98, 174
   Keeper of the Keep 48-50, 99-100
brute force 260
bull
   enraged 66-67, 120
   rampaging. See eye of storm
bulletin
   Christmas Eve alternative 256
bungling billy. See chaplain: sixth fleet
BUPERS Manual. See Article C-5210; See Article C-10311
   secret scrolls 53
burning ember. See crystal
bush that ever burns 84
butcher knife 105
Butler, Dr. Willis 260
   Fort Street Maul 256-258

Centurion 111
challenge for cause 124, 143-145
Chaplain Carroll
   Article C-5210
      steps to claim CO status 170, 179
   Merlin 52-53, 59
chaplain of sixth fleet
   Chaplain Barr 179
      breaker of fast 163
      bungling billy 4
      debate with I AM 215
      denial of sincerity 139, 169
checkers game 142
Cheshire Cat 96-97
Chief of Naval Personnel 79, 110
   get in touch with God 105, 107
Chief's feathers ruffled 217
childlikeness 125
choice, Soldier's 254
Christ
   final symbol of peace 192
   forsaken 110
   presence in all men 189-190
   quintessential aspect of man 165, 179
Christ at my back 116

Christian faith
  direction 188
Christ's murder 165
Christ's sake 120
  killing for 165
  lose life 5
  worthy to suffer 110
Christ taught nonviolence 46, 189, 226
Cisna, FN Martin. *See also* Marty
  witness for defense. *See also* special court-martial
    call to testify 194
    examination
      cross 195-196
      direct 194-195
civil disobedience. *See* Word made flesh
civil liberties
  disregarded 259
civil war
  North and South Vietnam 126, 249
clammy hands
  Bardon, MM3 198
  Drury, FR 184
clammy paws
  Crosby, BT3 196
  Drury, FR 141
  Martucci, BT3 199
climate change 103
cloak of the Spirit 219
CO claim 183
  attempts to submit 175, 180
  completed 110
  confiscated 98, 174
  denied 239, 240
  returned to sender
    pending interview 138, 176
cold-blooded killers 163
collective farms. *See* hamlets
colonial rule
  French 174, 248
combatant duties
  forced to resume 239
Comeback Kid 136, 139
commandment
  greatest 107
commies 174, 247
  ragtag band 118
Committee of Responsibility 142

communism
  stop the spread 248
communist
  most radical 87
companionship
  desperate for 10
  wolf's need 255
compulsion
  trade one for another 57
conflagration 117, 173, 213
conflicts
  origin 8
conscience 86, 87
  assuage 165
  examination 90
  how to prick 45, 51, 106
  outraged 252
  respect 226
  soul 83
  tortured 128
  violate 246
conscientious objection
  appeal in law 229
  basis 179, 236
    faith in Jesus Christ 112, 225
  claimant's declaration
    March captain's mast 139, 168, 185
    Professor Douglass 172
    summary court-martial 45
  claimant's rights 205, 232
    failure to inform 139, 169
  delay in justice 224
  existence of provisions
    first heard 53
  lack of awareness 164, 222, 227, 231
  ruse 133, 237
  support. *See* Second Vatican Council
conscientious objector 4, 118, 138
  basis
    'I' 104
    Scriptures 186-187
  charge of pretending 121
  Lazaroff awakened 184-185, 215, 237
  only-begotten son 70
  Pearl of Great Price. 53
  primary problem 227
  rebuffed 169, 187, 232
  receptivity 223

Mary's 127
request for discharge
denied 238, 246
returned to sender 79
shadow 73
stuck inside a sailor's suit 130
true calling 216
two words I AM 167, 220
conscientious objectors
current policy 228
handbook. *See* CCCO
consciousness 7, 82, 189
eruptions 22
lose in public 130
source 108
threshold. *See* threshold of consciousness
Consciousness 18, 23
advent 87
consciousness' sake 106
contact of a different kind 106
contradiction 256
suffering of a different kind 190
Cool Hand Luke 66-67
Cormack, Chief John 122-123, 180-181
affidavit 147-148
council
fourth member 21
motto 28
courage 123, 125
creative daimon 39
vile-looking creature 15-16
creative potential 6, 69
Creator 18, 41
all-seeing eyes 111
attempt to reconnect 56
desire for union 38, 110, 112, 115
sound that fulfills 108
meld 63, 130
work together 64, 116
Creator's hand 50
Cretaceous Period 14, 34

D

daily bread 73. *See also* bread alone
daily routine
disruption 50
damsel in distress
how to rescue 118, 174

crime against humanity 163
crimes of passion 215
criminal activity 182
criminality of war 251
Crosby, BT3 Rufus 160
witness for defense. *See also* special court-martial
call to testify 196
examination
cross 197
direct 196
cross 33
author's
horizontal beam 30
meaning 111
ship 130
stake life 140
truth of being 31
wood of 54, 79
impressment into the navy 112
male member's 83
Nature's 111
nonviolent's 71, 112, 158
not of one's choosing 209
one's shadow 69
peace symbol's 46
rich young man's 8
sign of contradiction 186
soul's 76
Cross
meaning 188
true 116. *See also* cross: nonviolent's
loved and hated 191, 192
crucifixion 70
bearer of other's sins 108, 141
cry of a dying soldier 253
crystal
gem of a response 105
spoke in first person 104-105
cup of suffering 211, 256. *See also* suffering

Dapper Dan
refusal to salute 43-44
dark cloud of the unknown 29
Dark Knight of the Barrows 118, 174. *See also* Barrows, Agent

dark matters 78
darkness 128
  no word in sight 252
dark nights of the soul 61
  take the black out 85
  tunnel vision 6
Dear Diary
  womb with a view 78
Dear John letter 11
deception
  greatest 220
declaration of independence 121
declaration of intent 119
defector
  NIS investigation 117, 174
DEFENSE COUNSEL. *See* special court-martial
delirium 102
delusional 105
demon 80
  imposter 139
  last in residence
    expulsion 137
  pattern of thought 65
  stepfather's attempt to kill 105
demon-lie 51
demon lies 65
demons
  Akana's 261
  depose 253
  projections 249
demonstration in brig 46-50
depression 81, 168
  black hole 82
descent into hell 10, 64
  free captive from Instinct 50
desertion 227, 228
desire
  burning 114
  express oneself 80
  union with
    body 61
    Creator 50
    soul 2, 3, 69
desires
  true intent 69
desperation 128
  contact of one's own ilk 90

destruction of gov't property 163
determination, unyielding 220
Dever, Father Daniel
  connubial blessings 73
  Drury's sincerity 222
  spiritual counsel 187
  witness for defense. *See also* special court-martial
    call to testify 190
    examination
      court 192
      cross 192
      direct 190-192
devil
  give soul to 61
  personal 9, 88
  stepfather within 89
devil's advocate 56, 86, 104
  ego 67
Diamond Head 13-14
dick incognito
  author of being 58
  private eye 26, 56
discharge
  misfit rather than killer 217
  reasons of unsuitability
    irregular behavior 163, 183
    nixed 213
    resisting evil 165
discouragement 187
dish and the spoon 55, 56
disobedience in obedience 213, 214, 227
dissociation 103
dissolution 209
dissonant personality disorder 136
divine assistance 101
divine inspiration 252
divine intervention
  inability to write 56
  lost for words 138
divinity
  radiating from face 244
DoD Directive 1300.6
  interview
    officer O-3 or higher 176, 232
  noncombatant duty 119, 162, 231
domino theory 126
double entendre 39

Index

Douglass, Professor James. *See* Lord Jim
- angel to the rescue 113
- author's shadow 76
- Drury's sincerity 226
  - depth of convictions 112
- employer/employee analogy 230
- first meeting with Drury 72-73
- mentor/spiritual advisor 82-83
- MPs come knocking 246
- new book
  - The Non-violent Cross 112
- relationship to Resistance 229
- Star-Bulletin article 70-71, 228
- witness for defense
  - call to testify 185. *See also* special court-martial
    - examination
      - court 189-190
      - cross 188-189
      - direct 185-188

draft as instrument of punishment
- Supreme Court ruling 261

draft-card burning
- first in Hawaii 86

draft-file burning 110, 238

dragons
- slay 250, 253

dream
- bad 249
- come true 130
- gone awry 137
- message from above 17
- waking 263

dreamtime 130, 142
dreamtime's secret 48
dressed to kill 164

Dr. Jekyll 103
- last remnants of good 255
- seen as one's self 107

Dr. Lazaroff. *See also* Lazaroff, LCDR
- psychiatrist 221, 232
  - query 167, 184, 215

Drury, FR E.J.
- administrative burden 236
- attempt to kill
  - father's 105
  - Kraft's 95, 173
- credibility 223

denied access
- Professor Douglass 98, 174
- first misstep 213
- Goldsborough conundrum
  - legal way out 241
- I Am Who I Am 182, 237
- manifesto
  - I Object 52, 169-170
- maturity 229-230
- moral convictions 231, 236
- psycho-social makeup 234
- Purple Heart 260
- quandry 135
- religious training and belief 225
- RESPONDENT. *See* RESPONDENT
- sacred right 109
- seen as I AM 183, 237
- shadow. *See* Douglass, Professor James; *See* Michael; *See* shadow
- sit-ins
  - brig 174
  - summary court-martial 125
- socialization skills 135
- special court-martial. *See also* special court-martial; *See also* ACCUSED
  - call to testify 157
  - examination
    - court 182-184
    - cross 177-180
    - direct 157-177
    - redirect 180-182, 184-185
  - plea 146
  - rebuttal
    - cross 204
    - direct 203-204
    - redirect 204-205
- stepfather within 77, 89
  - let go 71
- transfers
  - Transient Barracks
    - Pearl Harbor, HI 243
  - USS Goldsborough 218
  - Tripler General Hospital 258, 260
- unfit for Naval service 236

dual nature
- secret 25

duties
- God vs Navy 183

E

earth
   inherit 34
Earth
   sovereign queen 250
earth stood still 123
eggman 17, 51
ego
   blow to 80
   confront 35
   lily-white 66
   mad-hatted. *See* mad-hatted ego
   necessary evil 68
   nothingness 65
   old king 69
   prevails 126
   sacrifice 86
   sever ties 74
   tyranny 72
ego backstage 129
ego-centeredness 85
ego of all egos. *See* god of the underworld
ego/shadow axis 67
   ego/Instinct 87, 88
empty imagery 78
empty promises 68
encounter
   most eclectic 81
   orgiastic
      psychological equivalent 52, 79
encounter of the third kind. *See* third heaven
enemy
   precursors 251
   we the people 249
enjoyment
   beast's need 12
epochs
   boundary 14, 95
      KT (Cretaceous-Tertiary) 22
error of ways
   dramatize 111
essence of all emotion 63
essence of feelings 51
eternal return
   myth 40, 55
eunuch
   whole man 3, 21

Eve
   life everlasting 58
   two faces 77
event
   earth-shattering 57
   extraordinarily ordinary 124
   synchronistic 91
every which way but loose 81, 83, 86, 103, 108, 158
Eve's gate
   key 58
evidence
   unsubstantiated
      thousands of pieces 265
evil 165
   Adam's 67
   defined 106
   deliverance 211, 217, 243
   greatest 68
   seen in neighbor 252
Evil Magician. *See* Instinct
Evil One 10, 125
evil orders 218
evolution
   body's 30
   next great step 35, 249
   queen 57
   uncontrolled 189-190
evolution revolution 36
   daughter 78
   sparked 140
evolving revolution 33
executive
   telephone company 226
executive officer's mast
   refusal to load ammunition 124
   refusal to remove peace symbol 141
experiences
   cunning 'n' lingual 85
   out-of-body
      paradox 81
   paired 24, 27
      man in the mood 40
extinction 254
   one's own
      die fighting for 253

extra duty
  7 days
    refused direct order 100, 174
  20 days
    failure to appear 214
  30 days
    dereliction of duty 214
  45 days
    failure to appear 166, 214
    special court-martial 207

F

face of God 69, 81, 133
factionalize
  crew of a ship 138
faculties 86
  development to fullest extent 30
  full possession 21, 27, 29
  last freed 89
  projections
    burden of bearing 35
  transfigured 29
  triumvirate 39
fairy tale
  fracture 83
fall from grace 133
  author's 30, 43
  broken 50
  choice 101
  man's 27
family
  mirror image of Trinity 250
fantasies
  act out 38
  animator of 85
fantasy 133
  give desired reality 61
  real-life 39
farewell party 243
fast. *See* hunger strike
father
  author in midlife 56
  schizophrenic/shell shock 105, 233
Father in heaven
  find favor with 244
  mimic 74
  to live in 220
  tutelage 214

  inane 217
extra mile
  walk in another's shoes 38, 48, 66, 72
eye for an eye
  blindness blinds 135
  endless cycle 73
  turn cheek 165, 221
eye of storm
  rampaging bull 74
eye witness 119

father instinct 57, 60
Father made flesh 142
Father of all insight 63
Father of Lies 107
Father, real 132
fathers
  robbed of 106
Father, Son and Holy Spirit
  amalgam in Betty 254
Father's will 211. *See also* will of the Father
fault line 82, 83
Faustian bargain 252
fear
  darkness' 76
  first line of defense 20
fear of affection 128
fear of confinement 214
fear of humans 136
fear of letting go 10
Federal District Court of Hawaii
  show cause hearing 241, 246
feeling
  hooked on 128
feelings
  give form 82, 101
  true intent 56, 62, 79, 80
feminine pole 3
feminine, the
  masculine ego's suppression
    overthrow 252
fen of iniquity 38
fen that yearned to speak 114
finger-pointing 260
fire of heart's desire 21, 58
fire of inspiration 84
fire that burned within 20

fire that raged within 2, 109
fire that yearned
   to create 101, 108, 115
   to speak 104, 114
firing exercises
   evil 178
   nudge 183
First Lady of the Resistance 135, 137. *See also* Johnson, Betty
fit of rage 215
flag
   put down 248, 249
fleeting glimpse 164
flesh
   words that satisfy 130
   wring knowledge 75
flesh and spirit
   opposition 87
flesh of another
   soul's bondage 131
flight of fantasy 1
   fear of flying 6
flight or fight 211
flood of biblical proportions 265
fog of war 111
food for thought 20, 28, 51, 52, 80
forbidden fruit 70
   orgasm within another. *See* orgasm
forces of nature
   unify 57
force, the 256
foresight 254

Forest, James
   Catholic Peace Fellowship 91
   Milwaukee 14, 238
forges of hell 62
forked tongue 18, 39
formless. *See also* Original Being
   give form 25, 106
   hand writing 103
   Trinity 21
formless intuition 162
Fort de Russy leaflet 182. *See also* Kailua Road leaflet
Fort Street Eight
   disturbing religious service
      six charged 258
      wrongly accused 259
Fort Street Maul
   OK Corral 257
foul play 135
found again 182. *See also* born again
Four Horsemen 265
fox
   ever-elusive 57
freedom
   newfound 91
freedom of the press 183
free speech
   railroaded 97
free will
   Jekyll or Hyde 165
front gate
   commotion 119-120

G

Gates of Eden 12, 24, 57
general discharge
   recommendation 234, 235
Geneva Accords of 1954 126, 249
German photographer 251
give to others
   what is theirs 251
give to wolf
   what is his 255
give word to the flesh 130
God
   evolving image 2
   punished for obeying 109
   ruler 250
   struggling to give birth 6
God of Abraham and Moses 165
god of all gods 16
god of all shadows 67
god of the underworld 52
   ego of all egos 65
god of war vs God of Love 164
God's commission 213
God's doing 218
God's hands 113, 174, 239
God's holy mountain 14, 249
   Diamond Head 15
   Mauna Loa 23, 29
God's presence 243

God's will 61
    out of touch 91
    shadow 6
God's work
    crucified for doing 255
Goeas, Police SGT 257
    investigated for wrongdoing 258
Golgotha 35
    meaning 111
Graff, Father Don 181
    Christmas Eve mass
        invitation to attend 256, 259
    witness for defense. See also special court-martial
        call to testify 193
        examination
            cross 194
            direct 193-194
grail 67, 166
    womb 59
    quest 263
grand freedom 85
Grand Inquisitor (GI) 251, 253
grave mistake 11
Gray, Gary 256
Great Comforter 59
great darkness 95
Great Disruption 34
greater will of mankind 17
    sacrifice serpent 18
great gift 136
    Barrows' 118

H

Hamilton, Marine SGT 47-48, 120
hamlets 248
hand from God 50, 51, 105, 110, 249
happiness
    true 11
    warm gun 7
Hart, Brook
    attorney
        first meeting 73, 172
        legal counsel 141, 187
            long distance 124-125
        brig visitations 116-117
        sent by God 98, 101, 174
    counsel for respondent. See MR. HART

Great Gray Bitch 85
Great Gray Whore 44
    Captain's queen 20
    high priest 70
    Ms. Matte Progress 17
    secret scrolls. See BUPERS Manual
great grey wolf. See shadow of the white kind
great hand 62
great inconvenience 223
Great Liberty 84
great price 167
Great Sea Bitch
    bullheaded son 4, 96
    double-crossing son 119
Great Slaughter 95, 256
great truths
    second of three 52
great void 4, 21
    great separation 3, 16, 31, 38, 71
great wall 24
great white hunters 251
Greeks bearing gifts 27, 38
growth spurt 13
Guenevere. See soul: images
guilty bystander 251
gun
    murderous mesmerization 8
gunline 165, 166
gun mount experience 164
Guy, Steve
    Buddhist pacifist 117

DEFENSE COUNSEL. See special court-martial
    writ of habeas corpus 241-244
Hatchet Battalion 251
Hawaii Resistance 129
    birth 86
    den mother 76, 101
    retained Sir Brook 98
    self-sacrificing folk 263
Hawaii's Volcanoes National Park 22
Hawaii Three 261
heaven and earth
    split 36
    union 123

heaven on earth 12, 123
hell
  emotional 65
  personal
    horror of projecting 52
    pure 213
hemming way
  in earnest 51-53, 69
  in Earnest 55, 57
Hemmingway, Earnest. *See* author of being
Her Ladyship 98. *See also* Holy Spirit
hermit monk
  author 17, 22, 25, 28
  mentor 27
    Old Indian 57
  White Knight 12
Hewhay. *See* mentor
High Chaplain 165
Higher Authority 214
higher calling 141, 162
Highest Authority 253
high stakes game 207
high treason of the Lucifer kind 134
hinterlands 5, 40
  author 1, 255
  Mary O'Daniels 91
His Ensignship. *See also* Dapper Dan
  officer not of God's doing 183
    refusal to salute 169
His Innocence 134
Ho Chi Minh 126, 249
  Uncle Ho 118, 248
holy ghost. *See* mentor: Old Indian
Holy Ghost. *See also* Holy Spirit
  soul 44
holy spirit
  Jesus' appointee 76
  woman of great magnitude 86

Holy Spirit 174. *See also* Spirit
  confirmation 210
  consumed 87
  live as She lives 208
  meld with 98
  only defense 125, 241
  Virgin Mary 21
  womb 18
Holy Trinity 22. *See also* Trinity
  incarnation 115
Holy Writ 243
Honolulu's International Airport
  send-off 262-263
Honolulu Star-Bulletin. *See also* Douglass, Professor James: Star-Bulletin article
  Ship sails/Objector stays 245
  Six Are Charged... 258
Honolulu Two 256
hook 67
hoping against hope 68, 102, 106
house divided 69
  reunited 78
hug
  emotional equivalent 134
human being
  more complete 69
  real 249
humanity
  Christ therein
    crucified 165
  crimes against 109
  Father, Son & Holy Ghost 106
  loss 33
human nature
  dark side 251
Humpty Dumpty 50. *See also* eggman
hunger strike 213, 221
  statement of sincerity 231, 233

I

'I'. *See also* I AM
  collaborate 88, 116
  incarnate 89
  mentor 104
  mystical marriage 90
  Self I AM 218
I AM 35, 83, 244
  acceptance 73

  Ancient One 123, 137
    Old Man 132
      out of touch 133
  denied 111
  genie 32
  living as 173
  one true God 220
  part of Earth 250

Index

promise in the flesh 140
real healer 142
Who I Am 133
I am He... 82, 102
I Am Who I Am 68 . *See* Author of being
   at one with 47
   Authority invested in author 141
   conscientious objector 121, 215
   life that bespeaks 256
   Old Yahweh 132
   on or off the cross 130
   Original Being 67
   served honorably 237
   Sir Eodor 254
   source of subliminal messages 104
   Spirit 250
illusion of consciousness 69
images. *See* language of the body
images that speak 81
immunity
   compromised 108
imprisoned in nature
   author of being 70, 138
   faculties 29
   truth of being 32
imprisoned in Nature
   king 52
impudence
   Soldier's 253
incongruities of the body 64. *See also* body/mind: split
indentured servitude 211
induction
   refused 210
      Sir Jay of Wallrabenstein 208
infidelity 83, 132
infirmity 91

J

Jack of Hearts. *See* White Knight
Jacques
   young pip 142
Jägerstätter, Franz 186
James Dean wanna-be 37
Jehovah's Witness
   letter 247
Jekyll and Hyde 163
jellied gasoline 142

inner spirit
   neither foul nor fiend 183
insight 27
   mind-blowing experience 81
instant gratification 45
instinct
   most feared 108
   play with self 12
   recreate one's self 36
Instinct 21
   banter with mentor 7
   Evil Magician 6
   Frankenstein 35
   mentor's twin 27
   overthrow 24
   way to overcome 59, 89
instinct par excellence 60
intercourse
   reunite self with soul 87
intercourse with impunity 41
intuition 29
   superior faculty 86
I of the Storm 101, 103. *See also* 'I'
ironclad grasp
   Nature's
      free sword 87. *See also* sword in stone
   wean one's self 77, 91
ironclad lie 215
iron grip
   devil's 158
irons
   Lautermilch's threat 239, 240
iron will 62. *See also* will: instinctive
I that cannot see
   self 23, 38
   snake 27
I That Can See 17-18, 23, 27, 33, 35, 104

Jesus
   appoints surrogate mater 76
   betrayal 166
   catches author 50
   most notable protester 258
   Peter's love 42
   prayer to the Father 211
   prototype 21
   seamless garment 9

Jinny 11-12, 101. *See also* soul
   duet 46
Johnson, Betty
   den mother. *See* Hawaii Resistance
   introduction 76, 172
   irons conundrum 239
   legal assistance 254
   overbearing mother 77
   summary sit-in recap 134
   XO's offer 135
Johnson, Colleen
   rebellious daughter 77
   to the rescue 239
Johnson, Gifford 77
   brig alert 96
Johnsons
   Christmas '68 255
Johnson, Walter 262

K

Kahoolawe 22
Kailua Road leaflet 90, 172
   content 173
   ignites firestorm 215
   lit on fire 96, 173
   NIS investigation 117, 174
   trial by fire 95-97
Kaneohe Marine Corps Air Station
   vigil at main gate 256
keeping with that kept 99, 112, 254, 256
   on earth as in heaven 123, 129, 135, 140
Kennedy, President John F.
   prestige of a CO 244
Kennedy, Robert F.
   assassinated 95
Kid Comeback. *See* Comeback Kid; *See* Sovereign Will
Kihune, LT Robert K.
   Victorian cat 96
   XO of Davidson
      hindsight 218
      March captain's mast 168
      offer 135
Kilauea Krater 23
   red glow 25
killer 7
   antithesis 220
   state-sanctioned 163, 217

Jonah
   absence 111
   act like 182
   New Age 18, 38
   something greater than 21, 23
      acknowledged 254
      birth 256
      give berth 89
      subjugation of will 60
joy
   deeply impressive 186
   found in suffering 74, 116
   fulfillment brings 187
Judge C. Nils Tavares 241-243, 245
judge's chamber
   flooded in light 243
Justice winks 100
just war theory 5, 222

kill for the living 253
killing machine
   most efficient/perfect 65, 106
kill on command 219, 237
   innate inability 178, 183, 229
   opposition 179
   or be killed 250
kilt instead of twill 4
king
   appointing male member
      pitfalls 43
kingdom
   not of this world 213
   yet to come
      embrace 183
kingdom of God 8, 17, 178
   on behalf of 249
   owe allegiance 250
King, Martin Luther
   assassinated 32
   Moses 33
King of Hearts 50, 104
Knaefler, Tomi
   letter 131
knife
   Abraham's 71
knight
   red and white 48, 49

Index

knight in shining armor 12, 25, 106
Knight of Queen's Realm of Expertise 254
Knights of the Resistance. *See* Resistance Round Table

L

Lady Betty 101. *See also* Johnson, Betty
   new mother 104
Lady in Blue 211, 212
Lady Liberty
   attachment/engagement 85
   liberation 84
   torch relit 86
lamp of soul
   aura of good will 51
   extinguish 69
lance a lot 55, 59, 78
   soul love 75
language of the body 56, 87-89
   conundrum 59, 108
   images 62, 75
Laruso, Prisoner 120
last attachment
   dying soldier's 253
last temptation 70
Lautermilch, CDR Paul
   CO - USS Goldsborough 238-239
law
   supreme vs man-made 227
law of Nature 52, 86
law of the land
   obey or disobey 107
Lazaroff, LCDR 237. *See also* Dr. Lazaroff
   recommendation 234
leap in faith 209
leave
   fifteen days 255
   thirty days 167, 214
legal precedent 241, 243
Leo Tolstoy's Advice to a Draftee
   circulated about ship 96, 167, 184, 215
lesson in humility 55, 115
letter of the law 99, 220
letters of reference
   Father Dever 113-114
   Professor Douglass 112-113
liberty
   false sense 86

Knight Tempter 251
Kraft, BT1 95-97
   lit leaflet on fire. *See* Kailua Road leaflet
   Mouse 96

liberty or death 52, 89, 106
libido 19, 101
   Sir Bored's 115
life
   port side 130
   starboard side 129
   take into own hands 71
   true purpose
     lost touch 10
   unquenchable thirst 128
   watered-down 19
life of sin
   serving in military 173
light
   hell's 50
   White Knight's 115
lineup 255
lion and the lamb 48
literary device
   role of sexuality 80
little bit of flesh. *See* male member
little objection 49
Little, SN Ricky
   peace sign vs the finger 252
   seeks CO discharge 217
   witness for defense. *See also* special court-martial
     call to testify 200
     examination
       cross 201
       direct 200-201
       recross 202
       redirect 201, 202
load ammunition
   all-hands
     excused 20, 171
     refused 123, 216, 246
       reason 180-181
       show of support 124
   illegal order 125, 231
Long Beach, CA 124-133
   shore leave 129

looking glass 82
  mirror of soul 140
  stained 33
  step back through 87
looking-glass world 2, 61
looming holocaust 265
loose associations 56, 57
loose from the body 10
Lord in Jim 111
Lord Jim 101. *See also* Douglass, Professor James
  brig visitations 110-113, 116-117, 181, 187
  new mentor 104
  unsolicited title 110
Lord of all 43
Lord Speaker of the House 108
lost cause 219
lost for words 130
lot in life 55
love
  hard 90
  incomplete 68
  in perceived sin 220
  newfound vs Mary 127
  true 104
  ultimate act 3
  unequivocal 190
loved ones
  repel 129
love of God
  crave 254
love of my life 58
love thy neighbor
  as Spirit loves thee 251
love triangle
  third person 84
love your enemy
  as yourself 107
lunatic fringe 130
lust
  for truth 23, 54
  intimacy 84
  object 22, 115
  real life 38, 53, 71

M

mad-hatted ego 66. *See also* Uncle Sam
  author 49, 53
    deflate 54
    facsimile 15
mad marine 65-67
  white guard's shadow 66-67
Madonna
  Black 21
  Lady 4
  Milady 2
magic carpet ride 88, 89
magic lamp 54, 57
malcontents
  antiwarlike 263
male bonding
  fear 88
male identity 3
male member 80. *See also* author of being; *See also* creative daimon; *See also* king
  conscientious objector 103
  little bit of flesh 44, 46, 55, 59, 74, 77
  other man in life 39
  overidentification 81
  real power 41
  union with oneself 51
Male Member
  aspect of the deity 78
  'I' 85
  Jesus 42, 44, 80, 84
man
  lesser breed 30
  true nature 68
man and beast
  marriage 80
manhandling
  subordinate 141, 217
manhunt 39
man in the mood 78, 246. *See also* experiences: paired
  anguish 111
  CO and writer 112
  locked up in womb 71
manna 29. *See also* bread alone
man-o'-war
  CDR Lautermilch 238
  noncombatant's plight 108, 137
  USS Davidson 97
  USS Goldsborough 244

Index

marriage
  meaning 3
  unprepared 128
  within a marriage 88
  without Instinct 90
marriage feast at Cana 24
Martucci, BT3 Michael 160
  witness for defense
    call to testify 198
    examination
      cross 200
      direct 198-200
Marty. See also Cisna, FN Martin
  balking horse 17
  old nag 14, 35
  on the beach 12-18
  stalking horse 28
  talking horse 12, 14, 22-23, 33
    transfigured 29
  true friend 139-140
  white horse 13, 30
martyr tendencies 190
Mary. See O'Daniels, Mary
masculine pole 3, 39
  lone monk 34
  union with 88
mass extinction 14
  last species of humans 6
  unloosed 265
master of deceit 6
  one–eyed jack 27
materialism/militarism
  masters of our slavery 33
matter
  final state 62
matters of the heart 99
maturity in immaturity 223
McCarthyistic rant 117
McClintic, ENS D.W.
  agreement 171
  March captain's mast 168
me. See also self
  ego's soul love 67
  figment of the imagination 65
medallion. See peace symbol; See special court-martial
medium security 45
mental anguish 19

mental breakdown 6
mental fog 109, 110
mentor 51, 107
  banter with Instinct 7-8
  greatest faculty 28
  Hewhay 3, 57
    father of soul 1
      genie 54
    mirror image of Yahweh 264
    mistaken identity 133
    private eye. See dick incognito
    Private Eye 27
    Yahweh's servant 132
  old coot 3, 10
  Old Hewhay 124, 129
  Old Indian 104-106, 108-109, 111-112
    holy ghost 101-102
  passing 60
  projections
    Chaplain Carroll 53
    Professor Douglass 71
  specter 89
  subsumption of author 26, 63
Merlin 62. See also Chaplain Carroll
Met, Tom 256
Michael 9. See also Sir Michael the Archangel
  author's shadow 2, 38-40, 42, 75-76
  casts lie into abyss 51
  duet 46
  food for thought 20
  hospital visit 261
Midas touch 6
Middle Earth 4
midnight mass 257
might makes right 163
military-industrial complex
  birth 43
Military-Industrial Complex
  rescue 250
Military Selective Service Act of 1967
  CO exemption 225, 230, 231
military service
  inability to adjust 234
  morally objectionable 233
  refuse to take part 215
  true meaning 5, 167, 220
  unsuitable 165, 236

Milwaukee 14 238
mind of God 41, 108
mirror that never lies 8. *See also* looking glass
misdemeanors
   expression of conscience 224
missing link 28
   author 13, 14, 33
   real 67
mission from God
   investigative reporter 251
   peace demonstrators 256
   soul 55
Miss Saigon
   rape 248
   Uncle Sam's soul 126
   whore story 118
molly 56
   flaming queen 39
   writer of poetic prose 55
molly's place 80, 82
money
   to spill blood over 252
monk. *See also* hermit monk
   imposter 103
   mentor/wolf link 34
   myth 102
   out of touch 91
   Way Magazine 90
mood
   creative 109-110
mood in the man 112
moral character
   societal vs individual 228
moral integrity 167
moral superiority 5
Mordred 55
Moses 214
   killed a man 179
   sacrificed animals 179
      serpent 18

Mother Earth
   crimes against 253-254
Mother Inferior 58
Mother Nature
   crack in physique 23, 51
   declared a person
      legal challenges 254
   liberation of soul 85
   mother of soul 3
   once mangled fingers 254
mother of all insight 63
mother's sin 35
Mother Superior 58-59
movie, 2001: A Space Odyssey 16-18
Mr. Edward Hyde
   beast without a conscience 106
MR. HART. *See also* Hart, Brook
   admin board
      counsel for respondent
         author's manifesto 52
         closing statement 230-235
         examination of witnesses 221-230
         existence of CO provisions 53
         Kailua Road leaflet 90, 96
         questions in Article C-5210 79
         reclosing statement 236-237
Mr. Hyde 103
   Dr. Jekyll's nightmare 165
   enemy within/neighbor without 107
multiple personality mode 136
murderous realm 213
muse 3, 55, 84, 115
mutiny 124
my lady
   Lady Di 78
   soul 74, 114, 115
My Lady 98, 251, 255. *See also* Holy Spirit
myth
   debunk 45
   power 87
mythical world of reality 83

N

narrow gate 68. *See also* back door
narrow slit 82
national unity
   struggle 126
natural man 3

natural selection 73
   true beauty 69
   uniformity 47
Nature
   invisible hand 62

Index

nature of job 226
nature, one's
  union with both sides 88
Naval Academy
  appointment 163
    fiasco 178, 233
  boot camp 183
Naval Investigative Service 117
Naval Station Brig 1-11
  correctional custody
    20 days
      fit of rage 169, 215
    30 days
      leafleting ship 97-121, 173, 216
    30 glorious days
      doing nothing 166, 214
  hard labor
    30 days
      refusal to salute 45-71, 169, 215
Navy
  abandoned 213
  celebration of victory 246
  gall to resist 32
  Self at odds 211
Navy of Uncle Sam
  sole purpose 107
Navy's best kept secret 72
need to write 52
Neely, Chief H.M.
  only wish 216
never-never land 68
newsletter 251
  intent 252
New Testament vs UCMJ 214

O

obedience in disobedience 220. *See also* disobedience in obedience
obey God rather than men 107, 220, 239
objective truth 30
obligation to serve
  right or wrong 126
obsession
  Mother Nature's 58
  Uncle Sam's 248
obsessive-compulsive. *See* alter ego
occasion for sin
  active duty 216, 240

Ngo Dinh Diem
  first president/dictator of Vietnam 249
Nichijo Shaka
  Buddhist Priest 117
nightmare
  killing
    another human being 97
    Who I Am 178
  neverending 102
  shared 42
  worst bureaucratic 109
nightmare of a board 216
Ninevites
  faithless generation 117
NIS. *See* Naval Investigative Service
NIS operatives 254
NIS statement 175
Noah's list 265
no-man's-land 261
noncombatant duty 216, 232. *See* DoD Directive 1300.6; *See* Article C-5210; *See* NIS statement
  failure to implement 79, 139
  Goldsborough implementation 218-219
  summary ultimatum 45, 169, 215
noncombatant-in-waiting 125
noncooperation
  in cooperating with the Spirit 98
nonparticipation in participation 213
"not I"
  give up the ghost 87
  self 47, 86
  transformed 84
nuance of God 264

O'Daniels, Mary 11
  her pain/not mine 138
  letter of remorse 63-64
  quite contrary 90-91
  relationship to author 127-128
  response to lei 126-127
  turning point 210
offenses 218, 231
  inconsistency 227
  statements of belief 225
officer not of God's doing. *See* His Ensignship

Old Bag of Wind 253
Old Fisher King 40, 71
   heal wound 59, 67
   house divided 69
   one wish 68
old guard 65
   caught off guard 98
Old Hemmingway. *See* author of being
Old Hewhay. *See* mentor
Old Indian. *See* mentor
Old King 35, 78
Old Man. *See also* I AM: Ancient One
   stepfather 248, 249
Old Man in the Sea. *See* author of being
Old Mythmaker 83, 86
Old/New Testaments
   violence vs love 188
Old North Church
   light in bell tower 111
Old Testament
   living out 5
      justification 165
Old Weasel. *See* Whitaker, CAPT Robert
old wise man
   youth's penchant 132
oligarchy in America 42
once and future father 102, 103
once and future king 35
once and future prophet 111
one and the same person 81
   I AM 102, 107. *See also* I AM
One Big Soul 209
one in the Father
   wolf and I 255
one person in you
   mother and father 250
one-sidedness 129
One Voice 17-18, 31
   command 38, 163
   singularity 29
one with the Father 132
only-begotten son
   attend to needs 20
   conscientious objectorship 19
   sacrifice 70
only the shadow knows 27, 56, 84
open mind
   God speaks frankly 221

opposites
   irreconcilable 24
   reconciled 48
   union. *See* orgasm, the one
opposition to change 46
oppression 247
   reasons to oppose 248
oppressor
   soul's 71
oral/anal stage 46. *See also* compulsion
oral discourse 78
oral intercourse
   metaphysically speaking
      aspects of personality 58
         soul 74, 81
      holy spirit 76
organized killing 264, 265
orgasm
   acceptance as I AM 73
   psychological equivalent 24, 63, 81
   within another 45, 67, 78
      bottom
         true nature 40
      encounter of the third kind 32
      explosion of mind 56
      meaning 46, 53
orgasm, the one 26, 29
   union of masculine/feminine poles 31
Original Being. *See also* I Am Who I Am; see also formless
   split 36
other-centeredness 131
Our Blessed Mother
   pray for enlightenment 157
Our Father redact 73
Our Lady of Peace
   intercession 257
Our Lady of Peace Cathedral
   chief usher. *See also* Akana, Moses
      denies knights entrance 257, 259
      ironic beating 257-258
   Fort Street vigil 256
Our Lady's pleas 261
overbearing mother
   rebellious daughter within
      Nature's rejection 79
      transference of affections 78

P

Pacem in Terris 113, 194
pacifism
   Roman Catholic Church 191
   versus just war theory 222
pain
   noncombatant's 108
   self-knowledge 75
   writer's 76
pain of separation 7
pamphlets
   Captain's ban 167
Pan
   images 60
      at his best 40
      god of rape 37, 39
      real-life facsimile 38
      St. Paul's problem 41
      the one nymph 30
pandemic
   thwart the spread 263
panic attack 57
Paradise
   peak experience 45
   St. Paul's third heaven 2, 26
parents rift 18
passages from hell 60, 63, 110
passion
   beast of a wildfire 128
passive-aggressive 48, 237
pattern of denial 99
pawn 20, 56, 209
peace
   maligned 48
   real meaning 250
peace creep 50
peacemakers
   real 209, 249, 250
peace of mind 19, 250
   search 147
   Spirit bestows 211
peace sign vs the finger 244, 252
peace symbol. *See also* special court-martial
   refusal to remove 140-141, 216, 246
   sign of reconciliation 49
   sign of the cross 46
   swept in dust 50

peak experiences 31, 61. *See also* Paradise
Pearl of Great Price 3, 53
Percival 59
persona 57, 116
personality
   union of rational & irrational side 88
Peter and the Wolf
   come together 84
Peter Pan 133-135
petition
   abominable 178
   repeal the draft 208
petty tyrant 43, 262
Pharoah's grip 214
philosopher's stone 17
philosophical question
   deeply perplexing 252
pickle 98, 209
pictures worth a thousand words 89
   mirage 27
   quick fix 31
   reflections 53-54
piece of mind 74
piggies 42-43
Pilate 119
pillar of society 25
pirate, thieving 134
Pit of Despair 7, 40
place of duty
   failure to go 214
pledge allegiance. *See* Who I Am
plutarchy 32
poetic prose 35, 57, 114
   beauty and the beast 74
   essence of soul 46
   godawful tree 78
   hocus-pocus 25-26
   idolatry's deviltry 140
   ill-conceived rhyme 114
   noble beast 129
   quantum leap 40
   rascally baboon 43
   St. Paul in ol' Saul 41
poetry in motion 47-48
pole of one's gender
   ego identification 88

Pope Paul VI
    message to the world 42, 256
Portsmouth
    U.S. Navy/Marine Corps prison 218, 240, 242, 256
possessed 137
potshots
    heady onslaughts 75
    naval gunfire 220
power
    made perfect in weakness 2, 41, 69, 70
pray from the heart 221
predator 37
prelude to violence 216
PRESIDENT. *See also* special court-martial
    LCDR K. Drew
        Judge Advocate 143, 144, 145
price tag
    author's head 95
prince and the frog 9-10
Prince and the pauper 95
private eye. *See* dick incognito

Q

Queen of body and soul
    she who must be obeyed 209
queen of hearts 56, 103, 106

R

ranks of discontent 263
R Division
    transfer 165
real information superhighway 52, 59
    inner course 56, 57
    network of neurotransmissions 53
    road to Douglass 71
    stream of consciousness 55, 64, 65
    twixt right/left lobes of brain 48, 82
    yellow brick road 46
        Kamehameha Highway 85
real time 130, 142, 252
rebellious daughter. *See also* Johnson, Colleen
    freed 84
    overbearing mother within 85
    rose up 79
rebellious disease 95, 97
recompense 250

profession of faith 123
projections 78. *See also* pictures worth a thousand words
    chess pieces 20
    clouded vision 135
    freedom of expression 84
    internal conflicts 165
    negative 5
    price we pay 31
    reflections of the truth 60
Promethean Voice 19. *See also* One Voice
Promised Land 22, 33, 133
    soul laid bare 140
prophets of peace 188
protest in brig 46-48, 225
prudence 1
psychiatrist. *See* Dr. Lazaroff
PTSDers 250
Purdy, Thomas
    letter to editor 258-259
Purple Heart. *See* Drury, FR E.J.
pushy 123, 176

Queen of Heaven & Earth 106, 208, 254
quid pro quo 51, 60, 83, 103

RECORDER
    admin board
        LT David Gleason 223, 224, 228
            closing statement 235-236
            objection 49
Redeemer of mankind 209
red flags 126
red fox 28-31, 49
Red Guard 260
Red Menace 85
Reds. *See* Resistance Round Table: Knights
Red Scare 117
Red sea change 109
Red the fox 28
red tides. *See* tides of the Permian kind
reign of God
    reinstate 70
reluctant revolutionaries 35
remove for cause 213

repetend 115
Republic of South Vietnam
   charade 249
request chit
   seeking CO status 180
Request for Discharge
   Based on Conscientious Objection 122
reserve cut 216
Resistance. See also Hawaii Resistance
   author's involvement
      investigated 117, 174
Resistance Round Table
   Knights 95, 129
      Christmas Eve vigil 256
      first encounter 86
      leader of the pack 258
      seen as Reds 117
      shared cup 263
resisters in psyche 5
RESPONDENT
   FR Drury
      conscientious objection
         lack of awareness 221-222
      disavowal of military service 52
   leaflet. See Kailua Road leaflet
responsibility
   false sense 164
restraining order 243, 246
   Ho Chi Minh 118

S

sacred grounds 22, 25
sanctity of life 158
sanctity of the moment 243
sanctuary
   Honolulu Two 256
   to seek or not to seek 240
      on Spirit's behalf 241
sanctuary of God 24
Satan 10
   Eve's 67
   lust for Wisdom 6
Saul in me 69
Saul's demon 41
   David within 47
scene that yearned to speak 114
script
   manical departures 108

restricted
   14 days 166, 214
   60 days 207
restriction
   Christ's 219
Resurrection of the Dead 101
return of the King 44
   death implied 35
revelation by God
   continuing 188
rhyme versus mime 58
rich young man 8-9
righteousness' sake 111
right forsaken 126
rights
   prisoner 100
right to appear in a lineup 254
right to object 247
right to remain silent 254
rigid thinking 5, 34
rise from the dead 9, 48
   one's Self 107
River Styx 65
road less traveled 9, 39, 40
roadmap
   one's body 108
Rulli, ol'
   words of 67, 69
rustlers 257

scullery incident 168
seamless gown 8
sea of dreams 211
seas of the Permian kind 33. See also tides of the Permian kind
Second Vatican Council
   right of conscientious objection 113, 189
seer 63, 104
segregated confinement 50, 97, 169
   soul 77
self
   Adam and Eve created 82
   crucify 104
   die to 10, 111, 253
   give to other/let go 54, 136
   mirror image 43
   one-way street 68

play with 49, 60, 89
recalcitrant 34, 35
set aside 242
unseated from throne 44
Self
old wise man 132
self-control
regain 10, 131
self-defeat 138
self-defense 5
stepfather's claim 105
self-destruction 52
self-destructs
Earth 249
self-honesty 259
self-image 19, 23
self-restraint
true meaning 84
selves
drive extinct 65
Senator Inouye
committee on desertion 228
SENIOR MEMBER
admin board
LCDR G.P. Fitzgibbons 49, 230, 235
sensuality of soul
overidentification 85
serpent on the cross 109
meaning 107
service
Uncle Sam's brand 33, 237
sex
Adam's take 58
goal 21, 71, 84
willy-nilly 103
sexual feelings
inability to accept 20
shadow
author of being 57, 63
author's. *See* Michael
Cain's treachery 117
malignant 118
monk 102
sailor's 244
stepfather's 89
what was once you 106
wolf's 56
womb's 46

shadow bearer 141
shadow in the flesh
author's. *See* Douglass, Professor James
shadow of a doubt 128
beyond 140, 167, 211
shadow of the ego/self 67, 69. *See also* ego/shadow axis
shadow of the truth 123
shadow of the white kind 129
embodiment 130
great grey wolf 137
seaman 139
shadow you see 73
she who deflates egos 54, 67
She who must be enfleshed 210
She Who Must Be Obeyed
aspect of Original Being 21
genius in the bottle 82
Mistress of All Imagery 8, 91, 115
one way or the other
man or beast 80, 86
Nature or Third Person of Trinity 63
SHE 39, 83, 84, 87
Soul of mankind 6
Spirit 254
whore vs virgin 79
ship instead of jail 40, 78, 90, 121
real time vs dreamtime 130
where I didn't belong 180, 214
Ship Sails/Objector Stays 245
show of force vs more mercy 257
sigh too deep for words 117, 120, 211
sign from the Spirit 128
sign of the cross. *See* peace symbol
Simon of Cyrene 111-112
sincere ignorance
no greater danger 40
single thread of truth 57
singularity 62. *See also* One Voice
true nature 68
sinking feeling 3
sins of others
willing to die for 209
Sir Bored 115
Sir Brook of Hart. *See also* Hart, Brook
suggestion to write 263
to the rescue 98, 174, 211
writ of habeas corpus. *See* Hart, Brook

Index

Sir Bully 99-100. *See also* Brig Warden
Sir Curt of McClain 263
   Fort Street Maul
      assaulted and arrested 257
      complaint against Akana 258
Sir Eodor, Knight Exemplar 100
   Fort Street Maul
      assaulted 257
      fractured jaw 258
   letter to editor 259-260
Sir Gene of Parker 263
   burned draft card
      charges dropped 261
Sir Jan of Haffner
   burned draft card
      charges dropped 261
   Fort Street Maul
      arrested and charged 257
Sir Jay of Wallrabenstein 208
   Holy Spirit's emissary 209
   Jehovah's Witness rebuff 247
Sir John of Witeck 86-88, 263
   burned draft card
      charges dropped 261
   Fort Street Maul
      arrested and charged 256-257
      complaint against Goeas 258
Sir Michael the Archangel. *See also* Michael
   archetype of White Knight 29
   guardian 1, 168
      extraordinaire 3, 101
      legal 119
      of truth 21
   to the rescue 118
Sir Stan of Masui 86-88, 263
   Fort Street Maul
      assaulted and arrested 257
      complaint against Akana 258
Sir Thomas More. *See* St. Thomas More
Sir Wayne of Hyashi 86-90, 263
Sister Mary Paulus 225
   indelible impression 189
   prophetess 221
sit-ins. *See* Drury, FR E.J.
Smyth, LT G.S. 126, 176
   chief instigator 181
   presiding officer
      summary court-martial 125, 169

snake 18, 26-27
   Adam's 56
   alter ego 35
   illusions 5
   impalement 44
sociopath
   demon 136
solitary confinement 47
   soul 136
Solomon
   something greater than 132, 133
something far more important 224
Son
   embodiment of Trinity 250
   only-begotten 108, 251
   soul's allegiance 104
son of God 111, 158
Son of Man
   rejected 238
soul
   ascendance to the throne 136
   damned 20
   essence 69
   freed from Old King's side 35-36
   give body to 105
      great need 4, 6
   how to get back in touch 86-90
   images. *See also* my lady; *See also* queen of hearts
      all-tinkering belle 83
      Betty Johnson 76
      Guenevere 75
         white phantom 55, 56
      Holy Ghost 44
      Mary O'Daniels 102
      mirror 81
      prudence 1
      temptress 45
      White Rabbit 53
   muzzle 129
   projection 128, 135
   resurrection from womb 79, 85
   separation 66
   sold to Uncle Sam 5, 130
   strip of all pretense 2, 47
   true beauty 68
   Waikiki Beach 12-13
soul in distress 118

sound of sheer silence 59, 108, 240
  state of author 111, 112
  the Word 58
South's secession 174, 179
Sovereign Will 137, 216
  Kid Comeback 141
  the Father 244
  Who I Am 143
Speaker of the House 108, 115
special court-martial 143-207
  Army Board of Review case
    United States vs Sigmund
      entered into record 161
  captain's mast
    seek noncombatant status 180
  charges added 141
  CO claim
    attempts to submit 175
  DEFENSE COUNSEL
    opening statement 146-147
    voir dire examination 143-145
  Defense Exhibit C
    peace symbol 185-186, 190-191
  DoD Directive 1300.6
    entered into record 162
  Drury, FR 157. See also Drury, FR E.J.; See also ACCUSED
    character 187, 188
    disgust with Wulff 184
    height and weight 159, 204
    retakes the stand 203
    top button issue 158
      explained 204
    failure to shave 152-154
      complied but charged 153, 158
      motion to find not guilty 156
    illegal order 161-162
    judicial notice of Article 1161
      subsections 1-a and 1-c 155
    Kailua Road pamphlet. See also Kailua Road leaflet
      relevancy 173
    load ammunition
      refused 175
        reason 180-181
    McClintic's agreement 177
    medallion. See also peace symbol
      meaning 157, 160
      religious significance 158, 177-178
      tussle over 158-160. See also Wulff, EM1 Kenneth
    peace symbol. See also peace symbol
      place of purchase 159, 201
      religious significance
        nonviolence 193
        peace of Christ 191
        sign of contradiction 186
      wearing of medals
        general order 160
        other crew members 158, 196, 199
        regulations 155, 200
      where accused wore
        berthing 177, 197, 199, 202
        captain's mast 160
        quarters 148, 158, 195
    Wulff bristles 154
  PRESIDENT. See also PRESIDENT
    clarification
      slimy hands issue 184
    instructions
      stipulated testimony 148
    rights of accused 155-156
  sentence 207
  TRIAL COUNSEL
    LT K. Norgaard JAGC 143
  verdict 206-207, 216
  witnesses for defense
    Bardon, MM3 197-198. See also Bardon, MM3 Michael
      Drury's conduct towards Wulff 198
      Drury's work performance 197
      Wulff/Drury quarters/berthing 197
    Cisna, FN 194-196. See also Cisna, FN Martin
      March captain's mast 168, 194
      top button issue 195
      Wulff/Drury quarters 195
    Crosby, BT3 196-197. See also Crosby, BT3 Rufus
      fiancee's ring on chain 196
      top button issue 197
      Wulff/Drury berthing 196
    Dever, Father 190-192. See also Dever, Father Daniel
      Drury's sincerity 191-192
      first meeting 190

Index

Douglass, Professor 185-190. *See also* Douglass, Professor James
    article in Star-Bulletin 185
    first meeting 186-187
    Graff, Father 193-194. *See also* Graff, Father Don
    Drury's sincerity 193
    Little, SN 200-202. *See also* Little, SN Ricky
    peace symbol 201, 202
    Martucci, BT3 198-200. *See also* Martucci, BT3 Michael
    Drury's conduct towards Wulff 200
    top button issue 199
  witness for prosecution
    Wulff, EM1 148. *See also* Wulff, EM1 Kenneth
    height and weight 203
    manhandling of accused 150-152
    modeled peace symbol 203
    right to touch subordinates 150
    slimy hands claim 149, 151
    top button issue 202
spider
  devouring aspect 76
  spinner of tales 52
Spirit 135. *See also* Holy Spirit
  contain 245, 249
  fervor 238
  high on 241, 242
  strict orders 218
  tribute paid 244
  trust 211
  weep with 117
  wink 244, 255
spirit guides 168
spirit of dead soldier 253-254
spirits
  ability to discern 73
Spirit's call 118
Spirit's intent
  capture 242
Spirit's lead 240, 241
spiritual war 250
Spirit Who Is You 18
split from Nature
  Adam's 83
split personality 3, 77

standing ovation
  symphony of cymbals 260
  wildest 165
Stanfield, CAPT Henry
  CO - USS Davidson (Dec '65 - Dec '67)
    orange peeling incident 213
    request to see 182
star of Bethlehem 70
stench of death 95, 265
stepfather 7
  Academy fiasco. *See* Naval Academy
  gun-toting alcoholic 105, 163
  killed a man 250
    served time 106
  letter
    ship sails minus stepson 247
  medical discharge 251
St. Michael the Archangel
  grade school 221
storytelling
  value 88-89
St. Paul 2, 41
  provocation to write 103
  true freedom 87
St. Peter
  banter with Jesus 42
  internalized 101
  put away sword 193
  rob to play Paul 85
  strikes with sword 166
strange goings-on 137, 243
stream of consciousness 1, 3
  ford 125
  life-giving waters 30
stream that yearned to speak 114
strong bond 57
St. Thomas More 186
  shadow 244
  story 227, 230
student exploitation 248
suffering. *See also* contradiction
  real 187
  role 111, 181
Suffering 74, 75
suicide 69
  world on verge 70
suitability for further service
  NIS investigation 117, 174

summary court-martial
  failure to salute false god 44, 215
  refusal to load ammunition 124
    awarded special court-martial 125, 216
    sit-in. See Drury, FR E.J.
suppress
  what Christ saw from the cross 249
survival of the fittest 42
swoon 60, 118

T

talent stolen 220
tea party 54
tension
  conscience vs law 228
thief of life 251
thief, repentant 8-9
third heaven
  author 26
  encounter of the third kind 32
  St. Paul 2, 41
Third Person of the Trinity. See also She Who Must Be Obeyed
  Mother 125, 211, 245
  search 55
  Virgin Mary 22
Thompson, Bill
  attorney of the Brook Hart kind 254-255
thorn in side 45
  Captain Whitaker 123, 138, 176
  stepfather's lust 71
  true nature 70
thorn in the flesh 7
  messenger of Satan 2, 69
    provocation to write 103
thought patterns, rigid 5
thoughts
  reflections of feelings 27
threat
  author posed 95
  general court-martial 208
Three Above/three below 132
Three in One 263
three persons in one 63, 87, 104
  primary goal 82
  three against one 86
  Who I Am 54
Three Persons in One 85

sword
  yield not to 109
sword in the stone 73, 77
  Article C-5210 70
  blade of truth 52
    eluding one's grasp 86-87
symbolic language
  true meaning 17
synchronistic event 41

threshold between worlds 17
threshold of a dream 79, 261
threshold of consciousness 32, 45 83
  Adam's gate 78
  fault line in Eve's body 82
  surface of eye 60
  water's edge 31, 62
tidbit 62
  from the Spirit 240. See also bread alone
  tantalizing 263
  undigested 52, 96, 114
tides of the Permian kind
  once and future 117
  red 109, 111
time warp 22
Title 18 U.S. Code 1382
  trespassing 264
Tolstoyan sense 236
tongue tied 63
torpor 243
to write or not to write 80, 101
trail of breadcrumbs 130
transfiguration
  Marty's 34
transient
  new role 245
transmutation 33
trap 16
travesty of justice 125
tread water 115
treasure chest
  Dark Lord's 253
Treasure Island, CA
  5 February 1967
    reported for duty 164
  20 February 1969
    discharged 264

Index

tree of knowledge 82
trees of Eden 47
trial by fire
    glory details 124
trial of duty 234
Trinity 239. *See also* formless
    aspects 80-82, 88
    feminine side 208
    give flesh to 19
    inner workings 24
Tripler General Hospital. *See* Drury, FR E.J.
true calling 216
    Sir Stan's 257
    unworthy 217

U

ugliness
    sinful see in the sinless 221
un-American 1, 100
uncertainty principle
    one or the other
        imaginal realm/material world 24
        meaning/value 83
        real time/dreamtime 130
Uncle Sam
    aid and abet 105
    mad-hatted ego 14, 15, 37
    mad-hatted militarist 17
    no love lost 126
    rape of Miss Saigon 174, 248
    self-appointed judge 118
    sins 109
undesirable
    further service in military 1
    incapable of killing 264
undesirable discharge
    consideration
        Davidson 212
        Goldsborough 219
uniform
    abandoned 262
    outgrew 263

V

VC (Viet Cong)
    decapitated 251
    prayer to shred 165
veil of blind obedience

truth
    buffer zone 32
    dark intimations 6
    facsimile dressed to kill 183
    glimmer 3
    resurrection 64
truth of being 12, 31
    beastly fear 7
    desire for union 30
    imprisoned in nature 32
turn the other cheek 165
twilight zone 102, 129
twilit zone 26, 101, 263
two persons in one 98, 102

Uniform Code of Military Justice
    petty offenses 223, 225
    versus
        New Testament 214
        supreme law 141, 227
    violations
        Article 89 207
        Article 90 96
        Article 91 205, 206
        Article 92 205
union unheard of in nature 56
union with body
    desire 26, 246
    forbidden fruit 32
union with self
    body's desire 89
United States vs FR Drury 143
    heart of the matter 109
United States vs Sigmund
    Army Board of Review Case 231. *See also* special court-martial
unpardonable sin 253
USS Davidson 96
    all-hands evolution 147-148
USS Goldsborough
    sails without objector 244-246

    ripped in two 141
veil of the sanctuary
    torn in two 140
verdict 125

verge of insanity 117
Veteran's benefits
   CO's loss of rights 176-177
Vietnam
   US oppression 249
Vietnam Veterans Memorial 120
vigils kept 261
vignettes 58
Virgin Mary
   embodiment
      Holy Spirit 21
      Third Person of the Holy Trinity 22

W

walk on water 60, 61
walls of Jericho 25
war
   crucifixion of others 107
   effects on psyche 106
   not of God's doing 221
   only rite left 126
   twixt god and beast 4
   within one's members 8
war crimes 251
war games 20, 124, 131
war on nature 109
war weary waif 209
Water of Life 141
waves of death 265
waves of images 83
Way Magazine 41
   editor
      letter of distress 43
      response 90
way of life
   abhorent 213
   cancerous 249
   dying 253
   not of God's doing 220
   sinful 165
   unbefitting of Who I Am 211
   wife 73
   wrong 2
way of the Cross
   Hart's defense 237
way, the 69, 104
   find 106
   soul shares 105

virgin sought
   glimmer of truth 73
virtual reality 79
   Camelot 75
visitations
   real and surreal 261
voice
   author's 115, 264
   out of the blue 211
voices 221
   dreams 18
   head 4, 162

weak attraction 57
weapon of war
   one's life 162
weasel 96-97. *See also* Whitaker, CAPT Robert
web of intrigue 88
Whitaker, CAPT Robert 20
   CO - USS Davidson (Dec '67 - May '69)
      deal with Brook 211
      March mast
         referenced 162, 168
      Old Weasel 123, 138
      pamphleteering
         authority challenged 183
         captain's mast 96
         confrontation 167
         requests to see 175
white guard 66-67
white knight
   adulterous 55
   aura 142
   keener intellect 20
   Professor Douglass 80
White Knight. *See also* hermit monk
   author 13, 24, 39, 100
   Jack of Hearts 207
   Sir Michael the Archangel 20, 29, 115
white lie 66
white phantom. *See* soul: images
white rabbit 49, 57
   feelings 53, 55
   promise 54
   soul of red fox 31
   unwary 38

Index

White Rabbit 29, 30, 34
   author 37
   emotional fluff 53
   image of soul. *See* soul: images
white steed 12, 24, 101, 211
White Wolf 29
   guise of old mentor 84
   passed away 137
Who I Am 9
   advocate 237
   annointed 264
   desire for union 255
   essence 22
      denying 208
      expressing 167, 173
      resisting 135
      to live out 183
   grand allusion 51
   hammered home 241
   I am 130
      conscientious objector 106
   images
      breaking of the law 220
      Earnest Hemmingway. *See* author of being
      face in the mirror 121
      neighbor 107
      Professor Douglass 70
      saboteur 164
      soul 136
   incarnation 133, 138, 214
   incognito 137
   joy in finding 182, 215
   last vestige 141
   live contrary 105
   long to see 6
   marry 210
   pledge allegiance 139
   rejection 10
   see 244
   squash 246
   stepfather's acceptance 251
   those who love 238
Who She Is 242
Who They Really Are 14
Who We Truly Are 67
wild boar 37-39
wild card 207
will
   greater
      submission 135
   homogeneous 4
   instinctive
      die to 60. *See also* self
      subordination 44
   newly acquired 20
   obtuse 6
   recalcitrant 10
   satanic 16-17. *See also* God's will: shadow
will of the Father 209
   out of touch 91
   versus Captain's order 215
will to survive 65
windbag 264
wings clipped 263
Wisdom 6
   nature's true beauty 74
   object of lust 22
wisdom of Solomon 32
Wisdom's sweet scent 26, 40, 130
withdraw from the world 129
wolf 25, 115
   acceptance
      Our Heavenly Mother's 137
   fear of humans 135-136
   fourth member of council 21
   guise 4
   modus vivendi 28-29
   two worlds 261
wolfman 15
wolf pups
   our kids 255
womb
   enter a second time 21
   hospitable world 82, 85
   morass 71
   Mother Nature's 22
   shallow grave 83, 84
   snake pit 68
womb of imagination 82
   captivated 75
   doomed to 62
   how to access 48
   hymen-like membrane 32
   penetrate 2, 17
   room with a view 81

word become flesh 129
Word made flesh 89
  act of civil disobedience 141
words
  need to ejaculate 46
words vs deeds 88-89
word, the
  slave to 138
Word, the
  God 31
  incarnation 132
  versus Instinct 87
work detail
  refusal to participate 98, 99, 174
wormhole 80
  stretch of imagination 81
worrywart 30
worst enemy 107
worst fear 3, 86
worst nightmare 95
wound 263
  self-inflicted 117
wraith
  ego-driven beast 107
  slayer of soul 178

X

XO of Davidson. *See* Kihune, LT Robert K.
XO of Goldsborough

Y

yellow brick road. *See* real information superhighway

Wraiths of State 111
wreckage of the irreparable 261
writer's block
  solution
    listen
      voice of silence 110, 115
    Nature's 77
    soul's 79
writers of no war 84
writ of habeas corpus. *See* Hart, Brook
written word
  power 243
wrong cause 249
Wulff, EM1 Kenneth 96
  call to testify 148
  examination
    cross 149-153
    direct 148-149
  rebuttal
    cross 203
    direct 202
  recross 153-154
  redirect 153
  tussle over peace symbol 140-141. *See also* special court-martial: medallion

  discussion of duties 218-219

One Final Note

In grateful acknowledgement to the late Dr. Yoav Ben-Dov for permission to use black and white renditions of the eight Tarot-de-Marseille arcana listed below, for the expressed purpose of educating the general public of the deeper meaning of such images in an individual's life.

Chapters:
1 - VIIII L'HERMITE (Hermit)
2 - XIIII TEMPERANCE (Temperance)
3 - XVII LE TOILLE (Star)
4 - XI LA FORCE (Force)
5 - XVIIII LE SOLEIL (Sun)
6 - XII LE PENDU (Hanged Man)
7 - VIII LA JUSTICE (Justice)
8 - CAVALIER DE COUPE (Knight of Cups)

Front cover image: *White Knight* by Sir John Tenniel

Back cover image: *The Damsel of the Sanct Grael* by Dante Gabriel Rossetti

www.ingramcontent.com/pod-product-compliance
Lightning Source LLC
Chambersburg PA
CBHW081209230426
43666CB00015B/2693